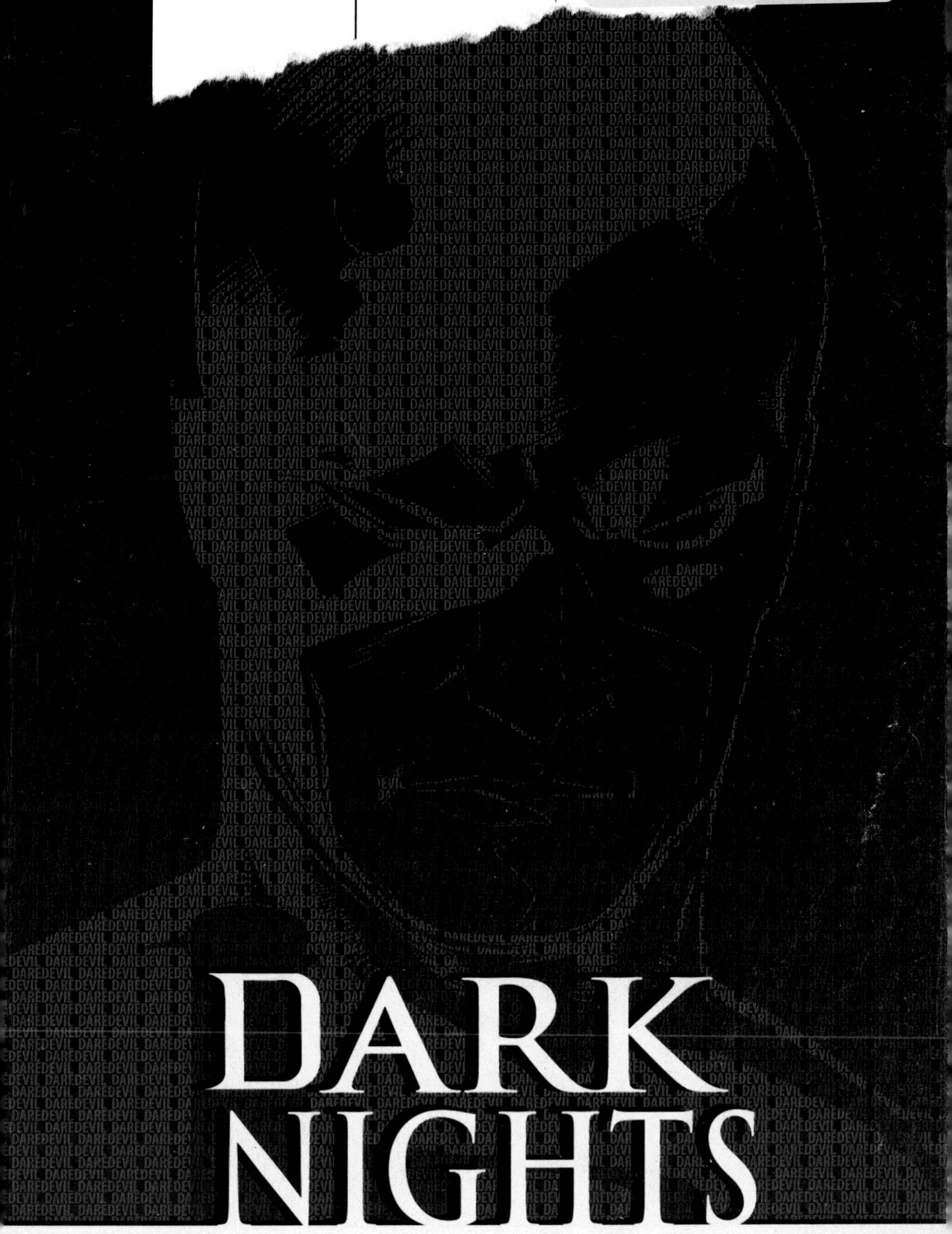

DARK NIGHTS

DAREDEVIL: DARK NIGHTS. Contains material originally published in magazine form as DAREDEVIL: DARK NIGHTS #1-8. First printing 2014. ISBN# 978-0-7851-6799-0. Published by MARVEL WORLDWIDE, INC., a subsidiary of MARVEL ENTERTAINMENT, LLC. OFFICE OF PUBLICATION: 135 West 50th Street, New York, NY 10020.
living or dead person or institution is intended, and any suc
rsons, and/or institutions in this magazine with those of any
Characters B.V.; DAN BUCKLEY, Publisher & President - Pri
e President, Marvel Worldwide, Inc. and EVP & CMO Marvel
Publishing; C.B. CEBULSKI, SVP of Creator & Content Develo
lishing; DAVID BOGART, SVP of Operations & Procurement,
CRESPI, Editorial Operations Manager; ALEX MORALES, Pub
CARR, Executive Director of Publishing Technology; SUSAN
Director of Marvel Partnerships, at ndisla@marvel.com. For
Marvel Comics or on Marvel.com, please contact Niza Disla,
2/24/2014 by SOLISCO PRINTERS, SCOTT, QC, CANADA

10 9 8 7 6 5 4 3 2 1

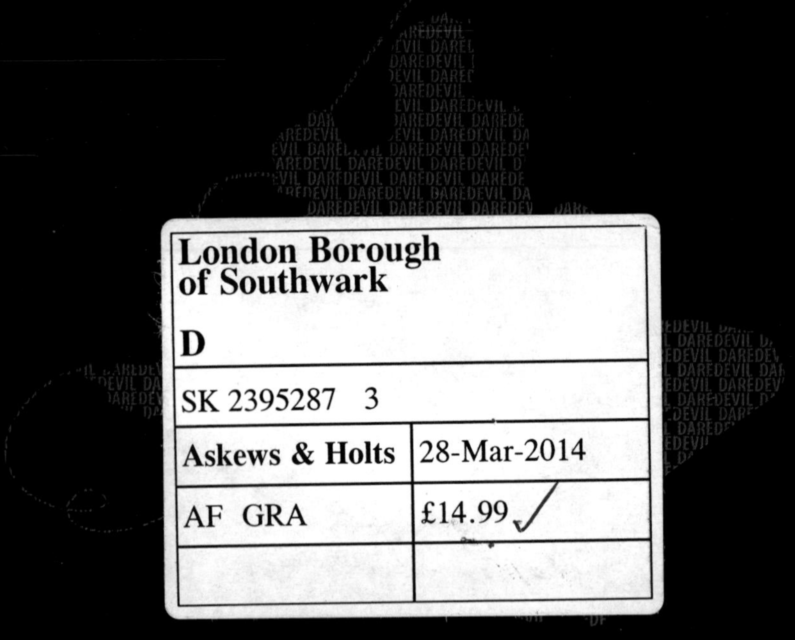

COLLECTION EDITOR: **MARK D. BEAZLEY**
ASSOCIATE MANAGING EDITOR: **ALEX STARBUCK**
EDITOR, SPECIAL PROJECTS: **JENNIFER GRÜNWALD**
SENIOR EDITOR, SPECIAL PROJECTS: **JEFF YOUNGQUIST**
LAYOUT: **JEPH YORK**
BOOK DESIGNER: **NELSON RIBEIRO**
SVP PRINT, SALES & MARKETING: **DAVID GABRIEL**

EDITOR IN CHIEF: **AXEL ALONSO**
CHIEF CREATIVE OFFICER: **JOE QUESADA**
PUBLISHER: **DAN BUCKLEY**
EXECUTIVE PRODUCER: **ALAN FINE**

DAREDEVIL

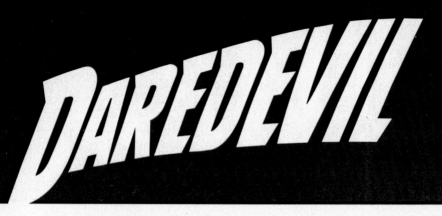

ANGELS UNAWARE

WRITER & ARTIST
LEE WEEKS

WITH *SERGIO CARIELLO* & *TOM PALMER* (FINISHED ART, #3)

A MAN NAMED BUGGIT

WRITER & ARTIST
DAVID LAPHAM

COLORIST
LEE LOUGHRIDGE

IN THE NAME OF THE KING

WRITER
JIMMY PALMIOTTI

PENCILER
THONY SILAS

INKERS
NELSON DECASTRO

WITH *TERRY PALLOT, WESLEY WONG* & *SERGIO CARIELLO* (#8)

COLORISTS
ANTONIO FABELA (#6-7) & ANDRES MOSSA (#8)

COVER ART
LEE WEEKS & LEE LOUGHRIDGE (#1-3), KLAUS JANSON & LEE LOUGHRIDGE (#4-5) and AMANDA CONNER & PAUL MOUNTS (#6-8)

LETTERER
VC'S CLAYTON COWLES

ASSISTANT EDITOR
ELLIE PYLE

EDITOR
TOM BRENNAN

SENIOR EDITOR
STEPHEN WACKER

DARK NIGHTS

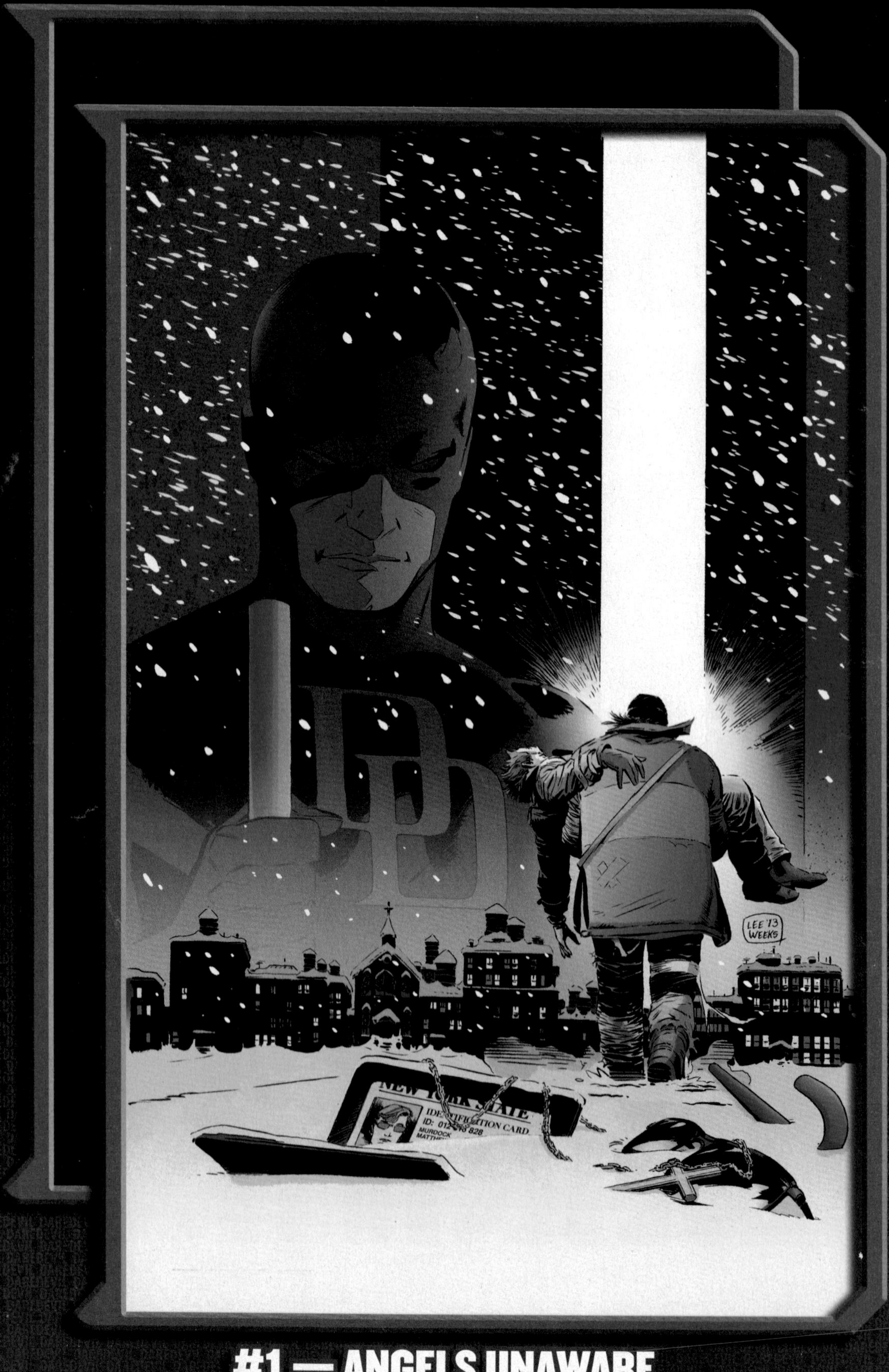
NEW YORK STATE
LEE '13
WEEKS

#1 — ANGELS UNAWARE
PART ONE: WHITEOUT

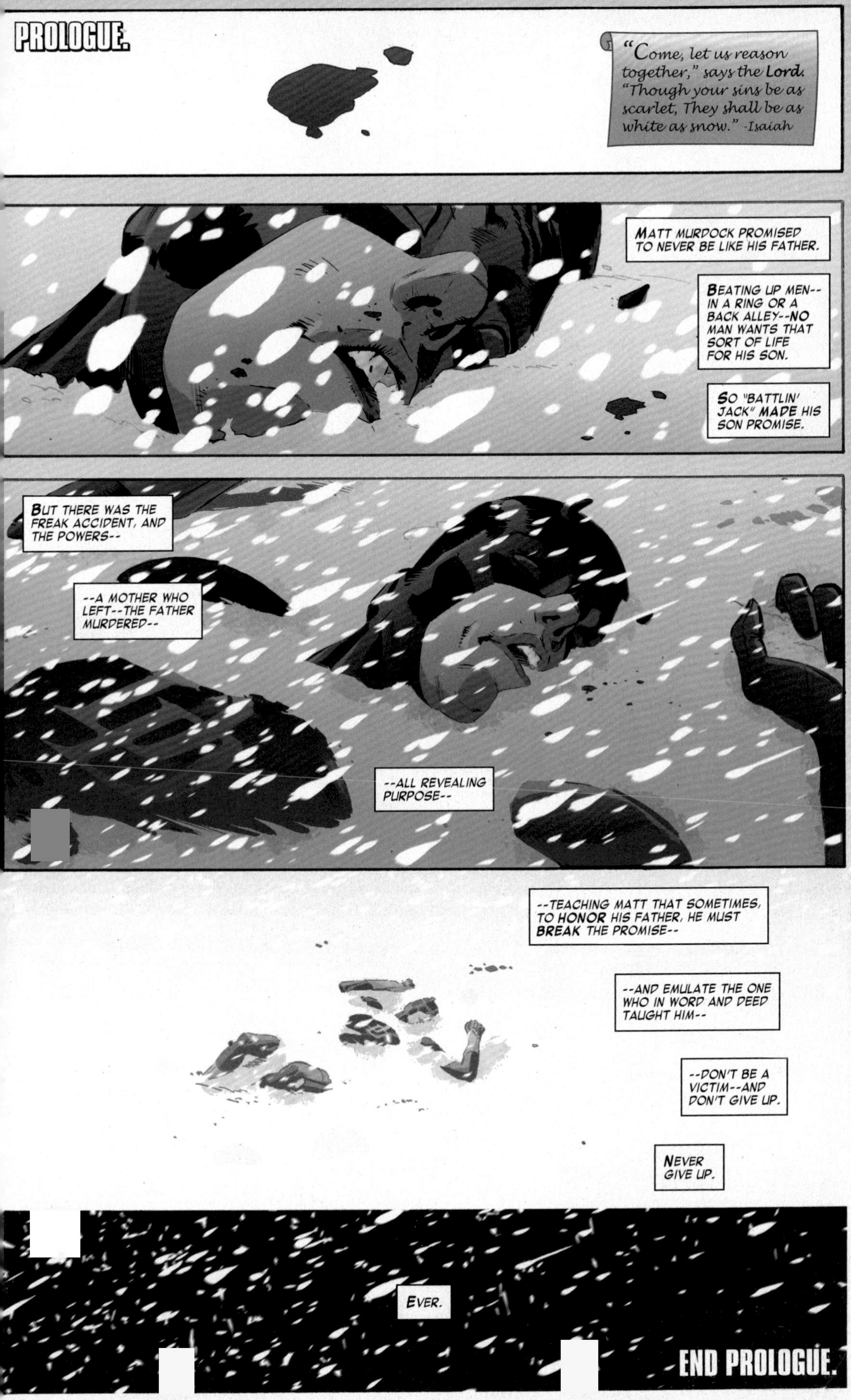
PROLOGUE.
"Come, let us reason together," says the Lord. "Though your sins be as scarlet, They shall be as white as snow." -Isaiah
MATT MURDOCK PROMISED TO NEVER BE LIKE HIS FATHER.
BEATING UP MEN--IN A RING OR A BACK ALLEY--NO MAN WANTS THAT SORT OF LIFE FOR HIS SON.
SO "BATTLIN' JACK" MADE HIS SON PROMISE.
BUT THERE WAS THE FREAK ACCIDENT, AND THE POWERS--
--A MOTHER WHO LEFT--THE FATHER MURDERED--
--ALL REVEALING PURPOSE--
--TEACHING MATT THAT SOMETIMES, TO HONOR HIS FATHER, HE MUST BREAK THE PROMISE--
--AND EMULATE THE ONE WHO IN WORD AND DEED TAUGHT HIM--
--DON'T BE A VICTIM--AND DON'T GIVE UP.
NEVER GIVE UP.
EVER.
END PROLOGUE.

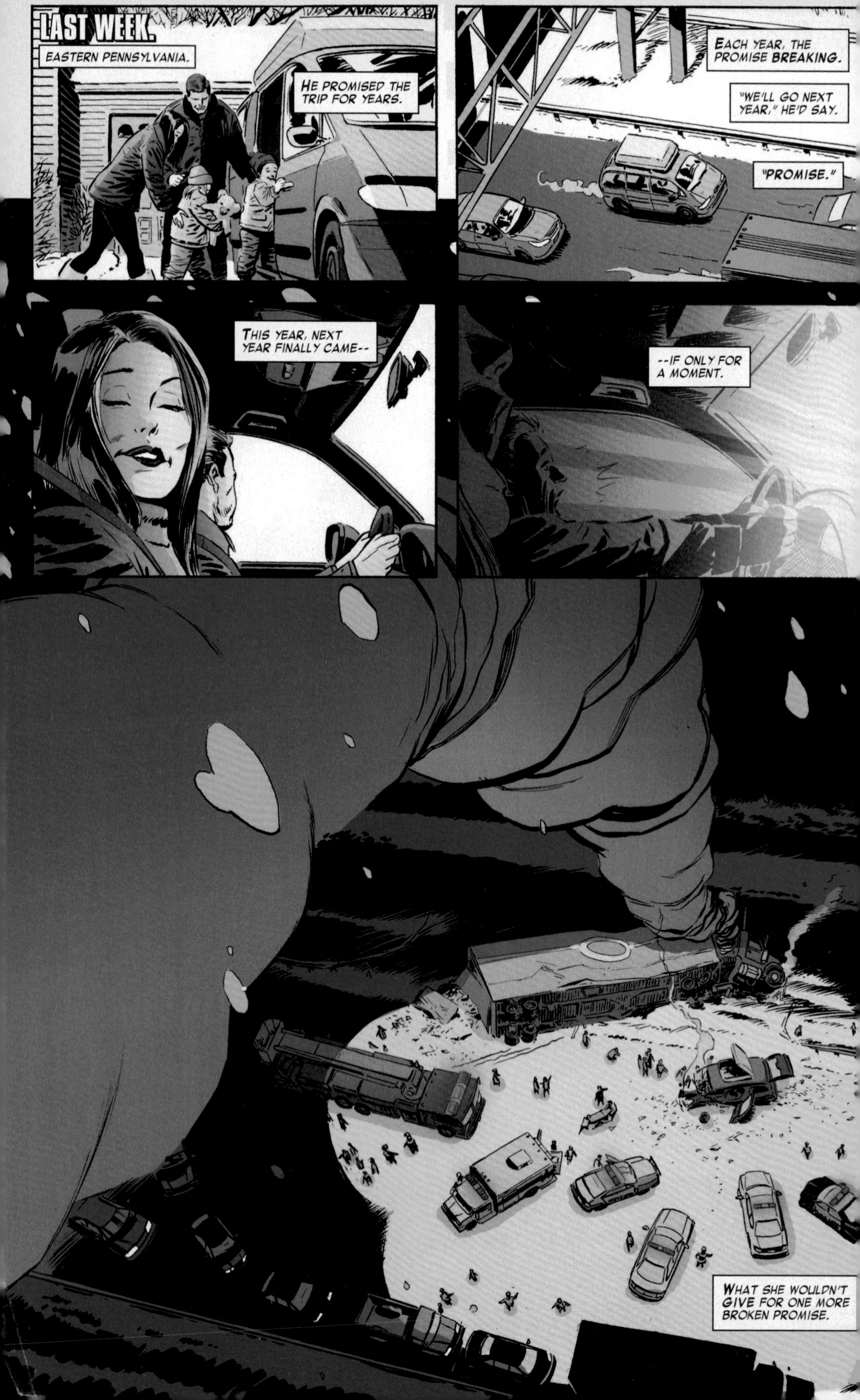
LAST WEEK.
EASTERN PENNSYLVANIA.
HE PROMISED THE TRIP FOR YEARS.
EACH YEAR, THE PROMISE BREAKING.
"WE'LL GO NEXT YEAR," HE'D SAY.
"PROMISE."
THIS YEAR, NEXT YEAR FINALLY CAME--
--IF ONLY FOR A MOMENT.
WHAT SHE WOULDN'T GIVE FOR ONE MORE BROKEN PROMISE.

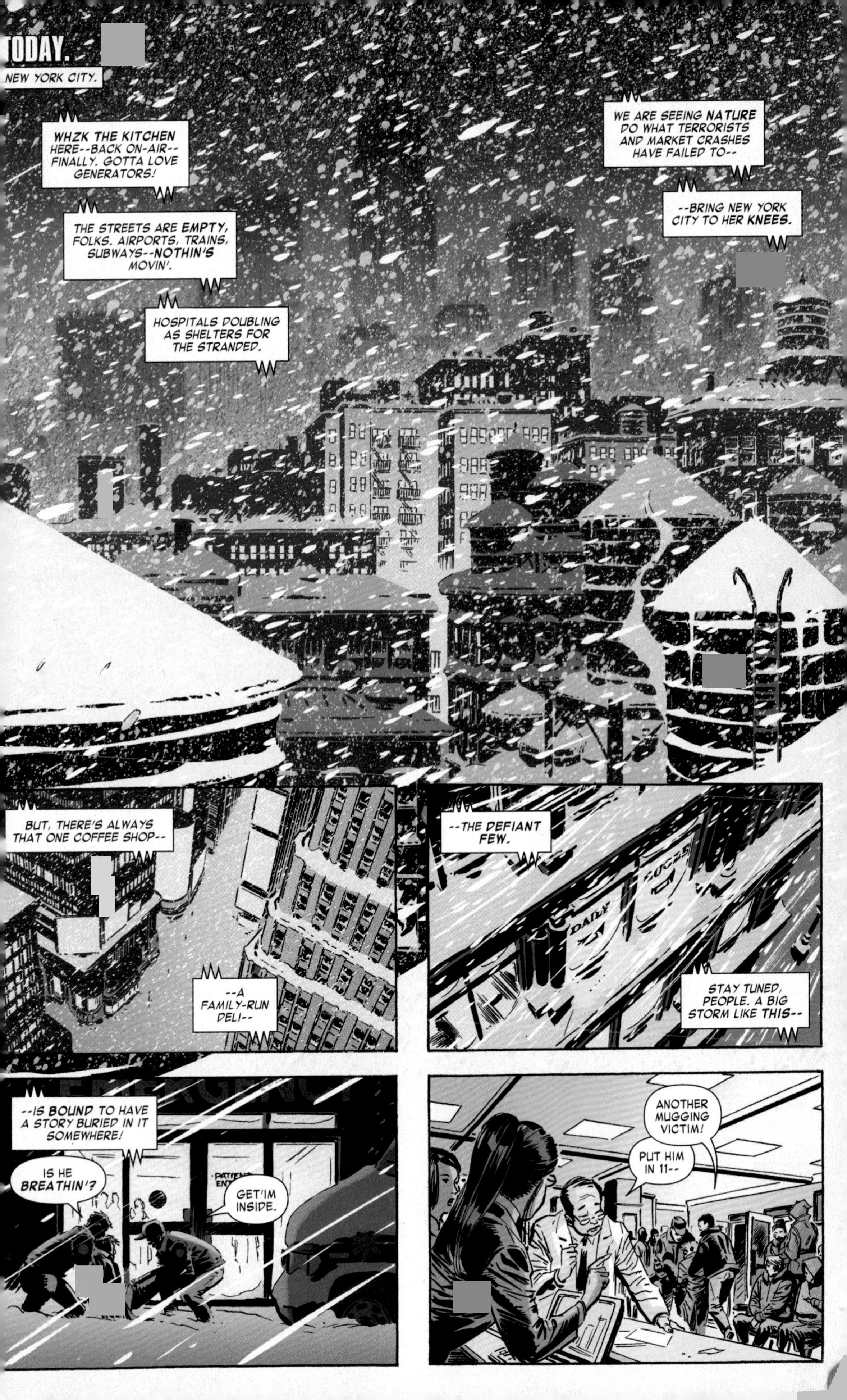
TODAY.
NEW YORK CITY.
WHZK THE KITCHEN HERE--BACK ON-AIR--FINALLY. GOTTA LOVE GENERATORS!
THE STREETS ARE EMPTY, FOLKS. AIRPORTS, TRAINS, SUBWAYS--NOTHIN'S MOVIN'.
HOSPITALS DOUBLING AS SHELTERS FOR THE STRANDED.
WE ARE SEEING NATURE DO WHAT TERRORISTS AND MARKET CRASHES HAVE FAILED TO--
--BRING NEW YORK CITY TO HER KNEES.
BUT, THERE'S ALWAYS THAT ONE COFFEE SHOP--
--A FAMILY-RUN DELI--
--THE DEFIANT FEW.
DAILY
STAY TUNED, PEOPLE. A BIG STORM LIKE THIS--
--IS BOUND TO HAVE A STORY BURIED IN IT SOMEWHERE!
IS HE BREATHIN'?
GET'IM INSIDE.
ANOTHER MUGGING VICTIM!
PUT HIM IN 11--

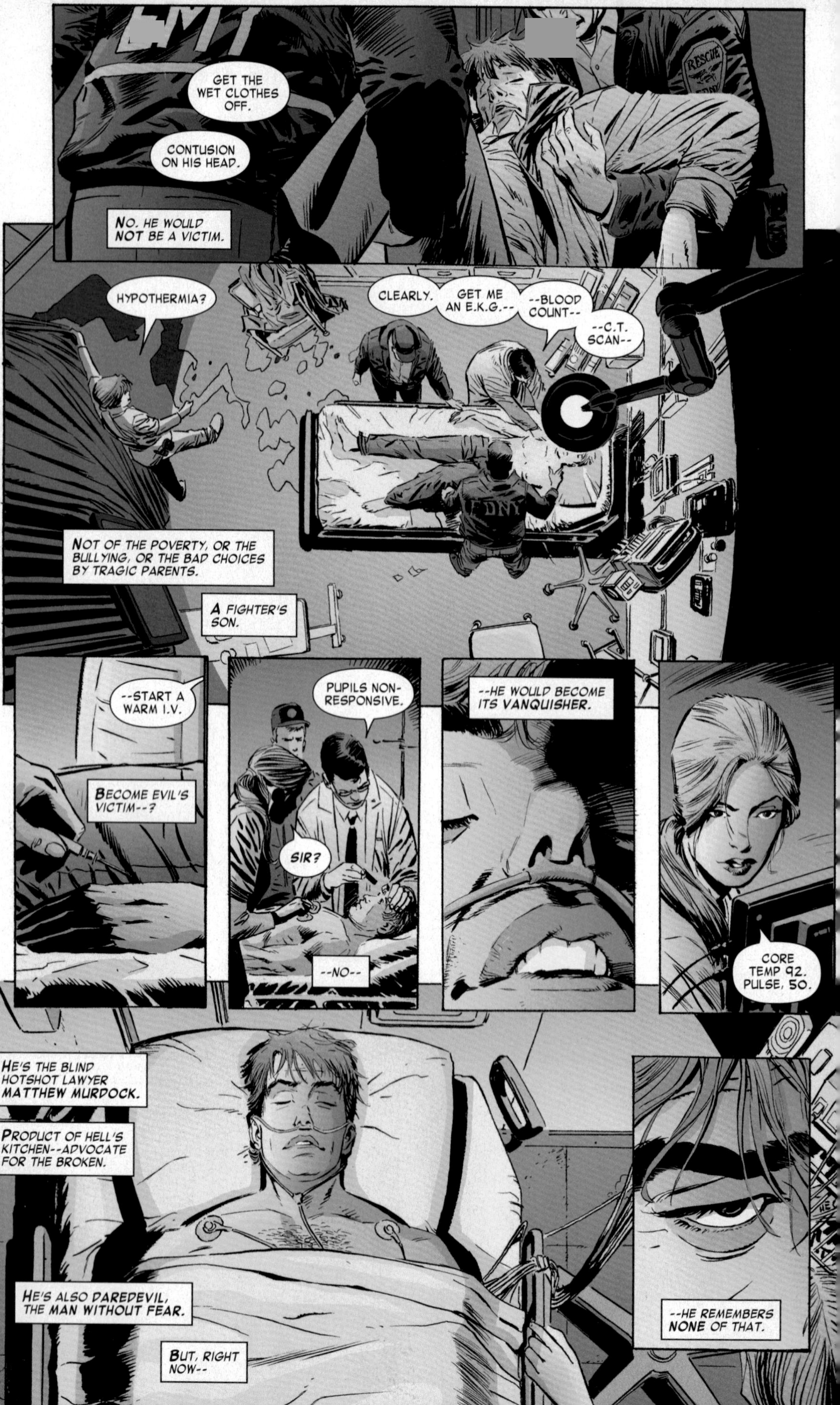
GET THE WET CLOTHES OFF.
CONTUSION ON HIS HEAD.
NO. HE WOULD NOT BE A VICTIM.
HYPOTHERMIA?
CLEARLY.
GET ME AN E.K.G.--
--BLOOD COUNT--
--C.T. SCAN--
FDNY
NOT OF THE POVERTY, OR THE BULLYING, OR THE BAD CHOICES BY TRAGIC PARENTS.
A FIGHTER'S SON.
--START A WARM I.V.
BECOME EVIL'S VICTIM--?
PUPILS NON-RESPONSIVE.
SIR?
--NO--
--HE WOULD BECOME ITS VANQUISHER.
CORE TEMP 92. PULSE, 50.
HE'S THE BLIND HOTSHOT LAWYER MATTHEW MURDOCK.
PRODUCT OF HELL'S KITCHEN--ADVOCATE FOR THE BROKEN.
HE'S ALSO DAREDEVIL, THE MAN WITHOUT FEAR.
BUT, RIGHT NOW--
--HE REMEMBERS NONE OF THAT.

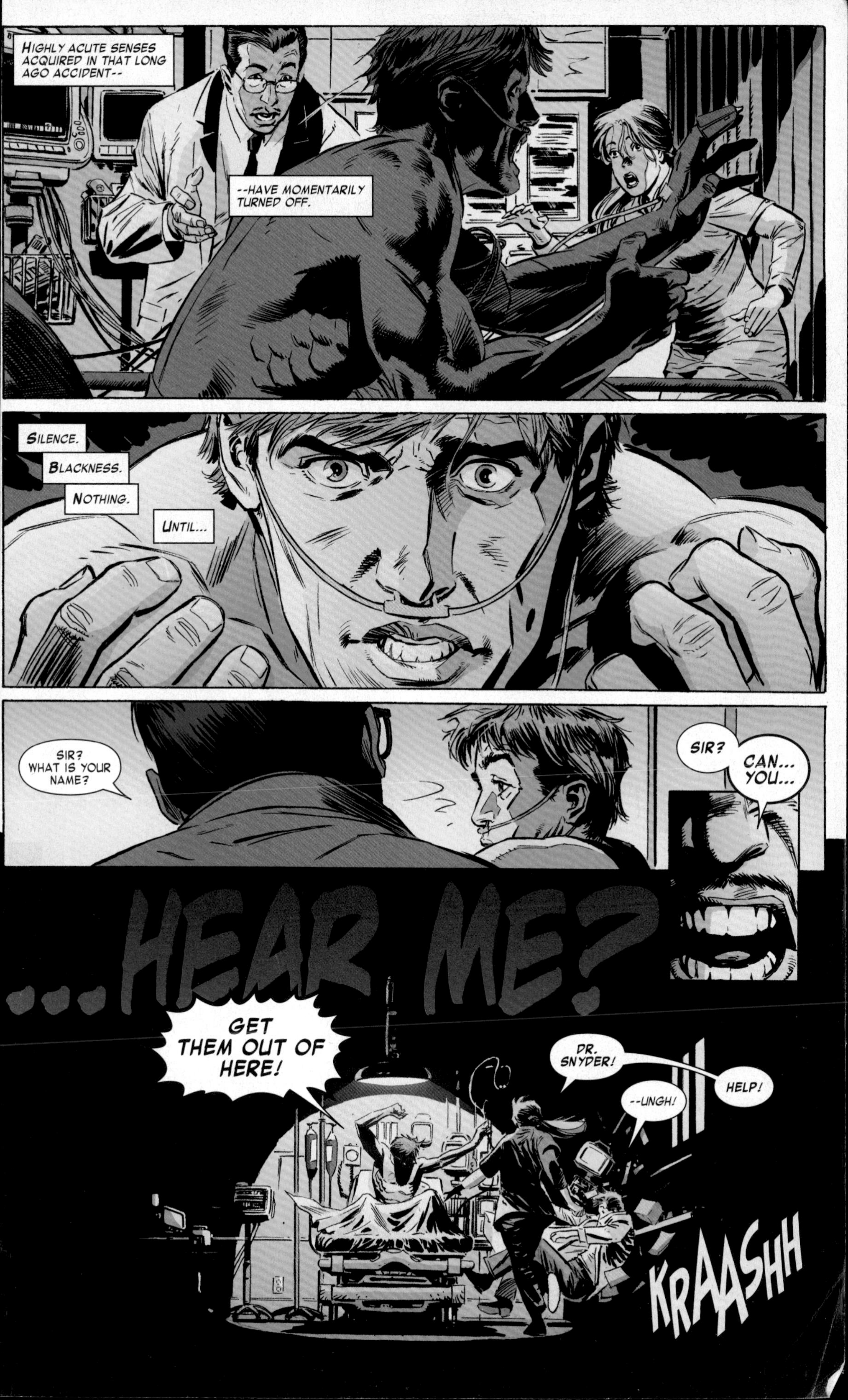
HIGHLY ACUTE SENSES ACQUIRED IN THAT LONG AGO ACCIDENT--
--HAVE MOMENTARILY TURNED OFF.
SILENCE.
BLACKNESS.
NOTHING.
UNTIL...
SIR? WHAT IS YOUR NAME?
SIR?
CAN... YOU...
...HEAR ME?
GET THEM OUT OF HERE!
DR. SNYDER!
HELP!
--UNGH!
KRAASHH

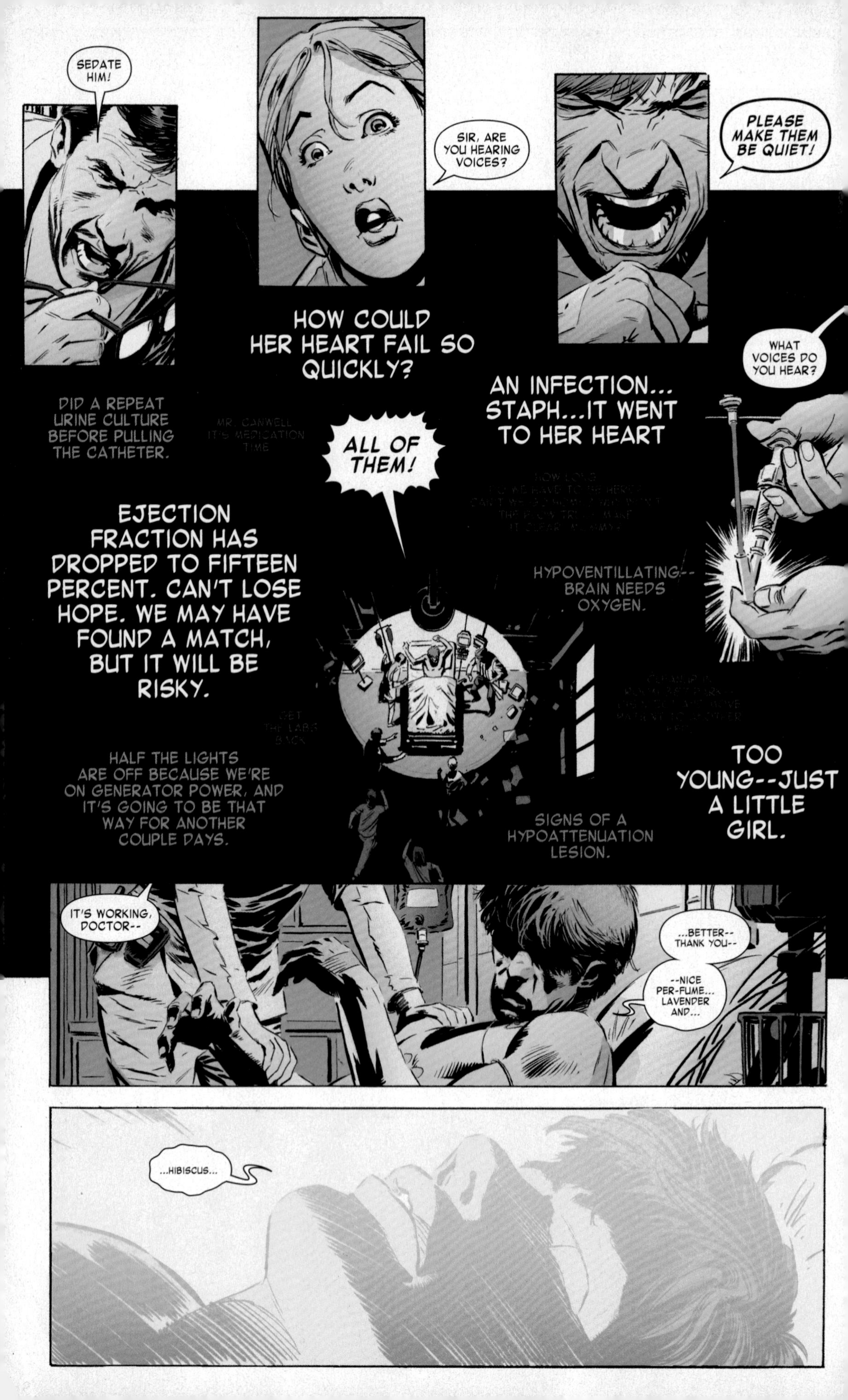

SEDATE HIM!
SIR, ARE YOU HEARING VOICES?
PLEASE MAKE THEM BE QUIET!
HOW COULD HER HEART FAIL SO QUICKLY?
WHAT VOICES DO YOU HEAR?
AN INFECTION... STAPH...IT WENT TO HER HEART
DID A REPEAT URINE CULTURE BEFORE PULLING THE CATHETER.
MR. CANWELL IT'S MEDICATION TIME
ALL OF THEM!
EJECTION FRACTION HAS DROPPED TO FIFTEEN PERCENT. CAN'T LOSE HOPE. WE MAY HAVE FOUND A MATCH, BUT IT WILL BE RISKY.
HYPOVENTILLATING--BRAIN NEEDS OXYGEN.
GET THE LABS BACK
HALF THE LIGHTS ARE OFF BECAUSE WE'RE ON GENERATOR POWER, AND IT'S GOING TO BE THAT WAY FOR ANOTHER COUPLE DAYS.
SIGNS OF A HYPOATTENUATION LESION.
TOO YOUNG--JUST A LITTLE GIRL.
IT'S WORKING, DOCTOR--
...BETTER--THANK YOU--
--NICE PER-FUME... LAVENDER AND...
...HIBISCUS...

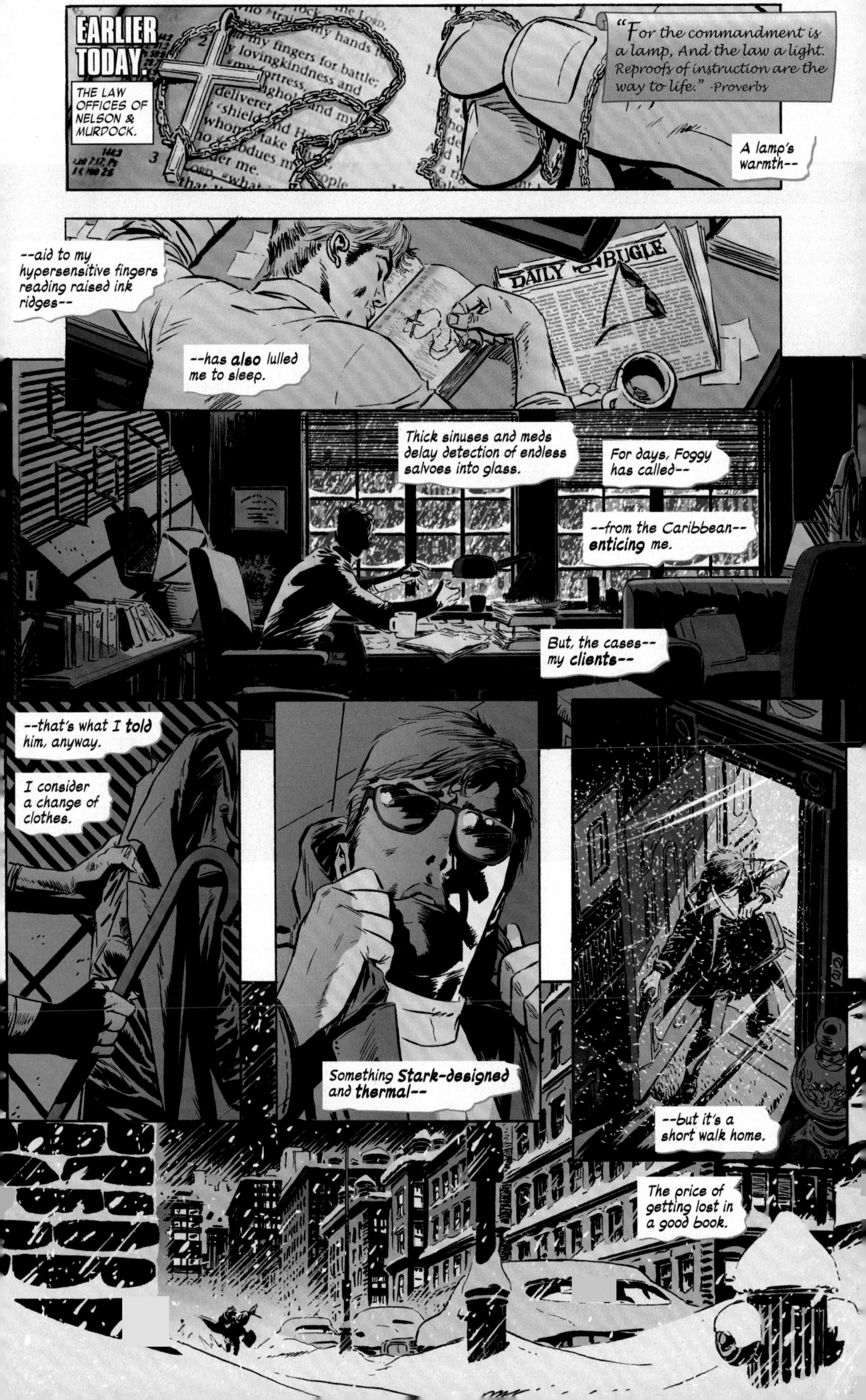
EARLIER TODAY.
THE LAW OFFICES OF NELSON & MURDOCK.
"For the commandment is a lamp, And the law a light. Reproofs of instruction are the way to life." -Proverbs
A lamp's warmth--
--aid to my hypersensitive fingers reading raised ink ridges--
DAILY BUGLE
--has also lulled me to sleep.
Thick sinuses and meds delay detection of endless salvoes into glass.
For days, Foggy has called--
--from the Caribbean-- enticing me.
But, the cases-- my clients--
--that's what I told him, anyway.
I consider a change of clothes.
Something Stark-designed and thermal--
--but it's a short walk home.
The price of getting lost in a good book.

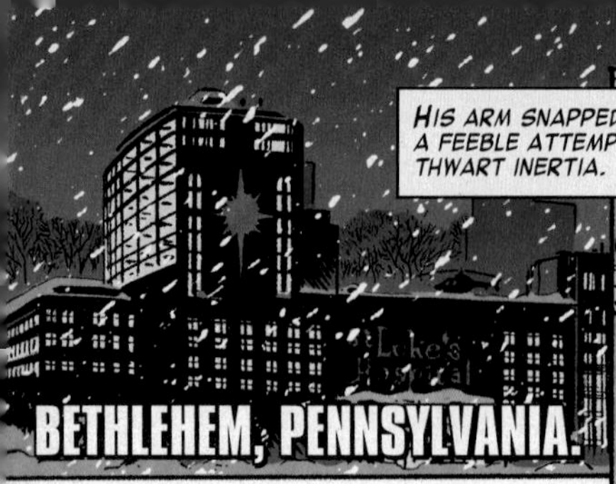
BETHLEHEM, PENNSYLVANIA.

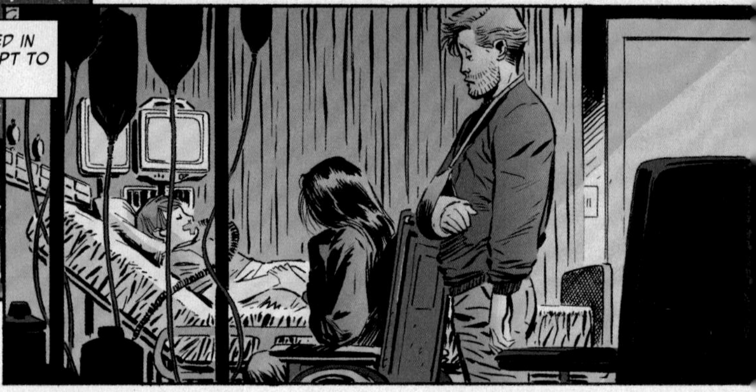
HIS ARM SNAPPED IN A FEEBLE ATTEMPT TO THWART INERTIA.

EVERY OTHER BODY PART--WHILE INTACT--**SCREAMS** WITH A PAIN HE'S TOO **NUMB** TO FEEL.

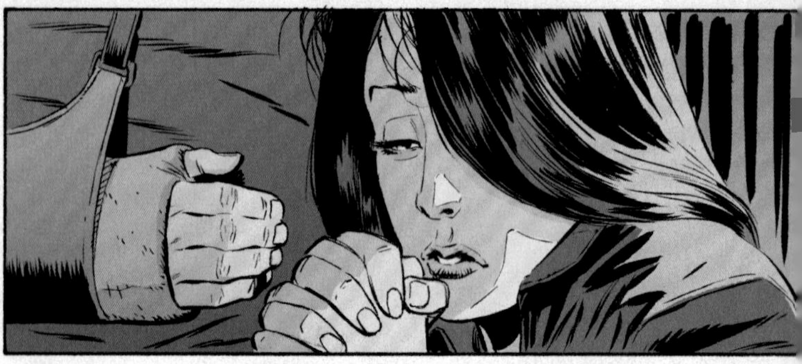

BOTH HER LEGS BROKE, AND THERE'S MORE GLASS TO BE REMOVED.

INCREDIBLY, THE DAUGHTER WAS **UNSCATHED**--

--NOT A SCRATCH ON HER OR HER BEAR.

A MIRACLE.

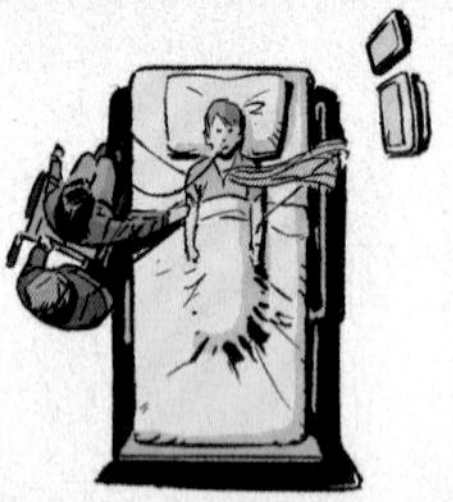

A MIRACLE NOT DUPLICATED IN NATHAN.

THE INJURIES TO HIS SMALL BRAIN SO SEVERE, HE'S BEING KEPT ALIVE--FOR A SHORT TIME.

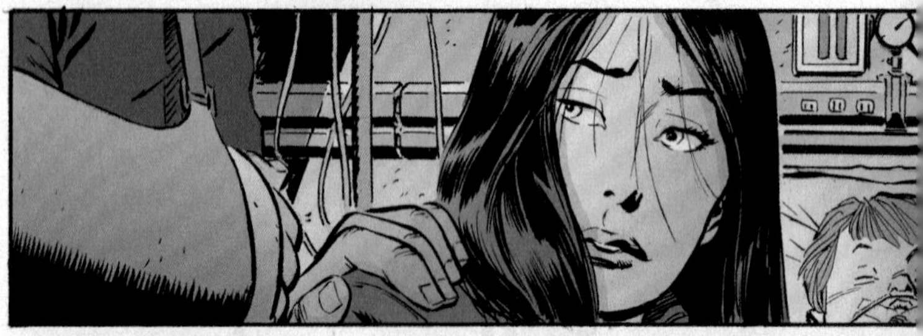

IF HE CAN'T **LIVE**, THEN MAYBE HIS DEATH CAN BECOME A SECOND CHANCE FOR SOMEONE ELSE.

PERHAPS, THEY THINK, THE GIVING OF THEIR **ONLY SON** WILL BE LIFE TO ANOTHER.

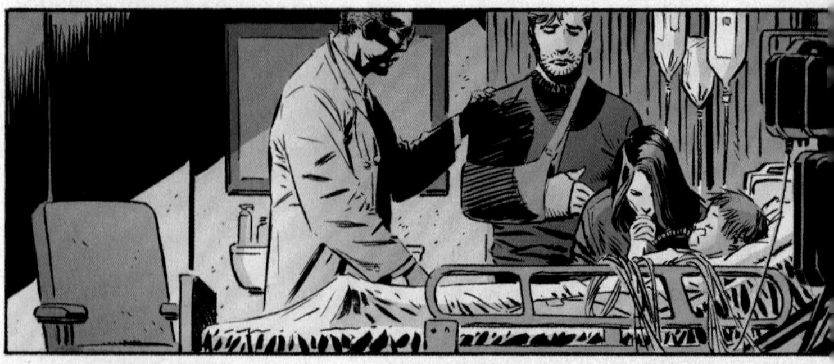

THERE'S A **MATCH**--A GIRL IN NEW YORK. A LETUP IN THE STORM HAS CREATED A WINDOW OF TIME.

A WINDOW OF **HOPE.**

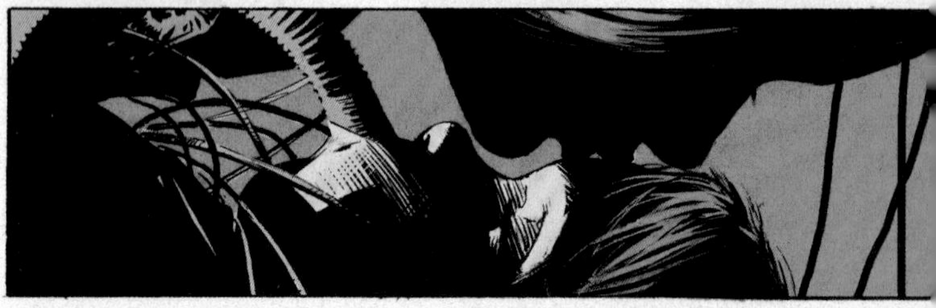

OFFERING UP ONE MORE PRAYER, THEY COMMIT NATHAN'S SOUL TO GOD--

--HIS **BODY** THEY RELEASE TO THE TRANSPLANT TEAM.

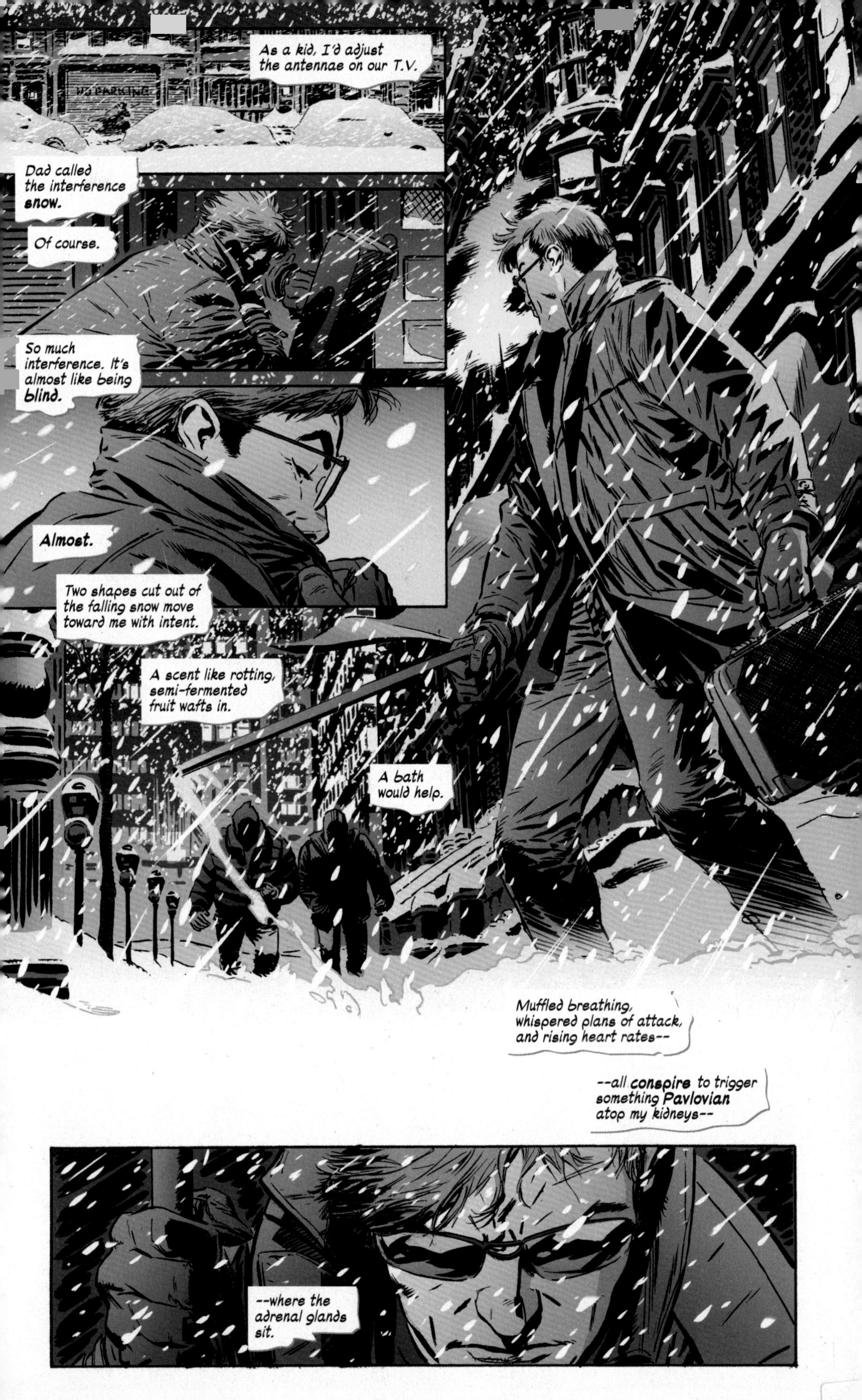

As a kid, I'd adjust the antennae on our T.V.
Dad called the interference snow.
Of course.
So much interference. It's almost like being blind.
Almost.
Two shapes cut out of the falling snow move toward me with intent.
A scent like rotting, semi-fermented fruit wafts in.
A bath would help.
Muffled breathing, whispered plans of attack, and rising heart rates--
--all conspire to trigger something Pavlovian atop my kidneys--
--where the adrenal glands sit.

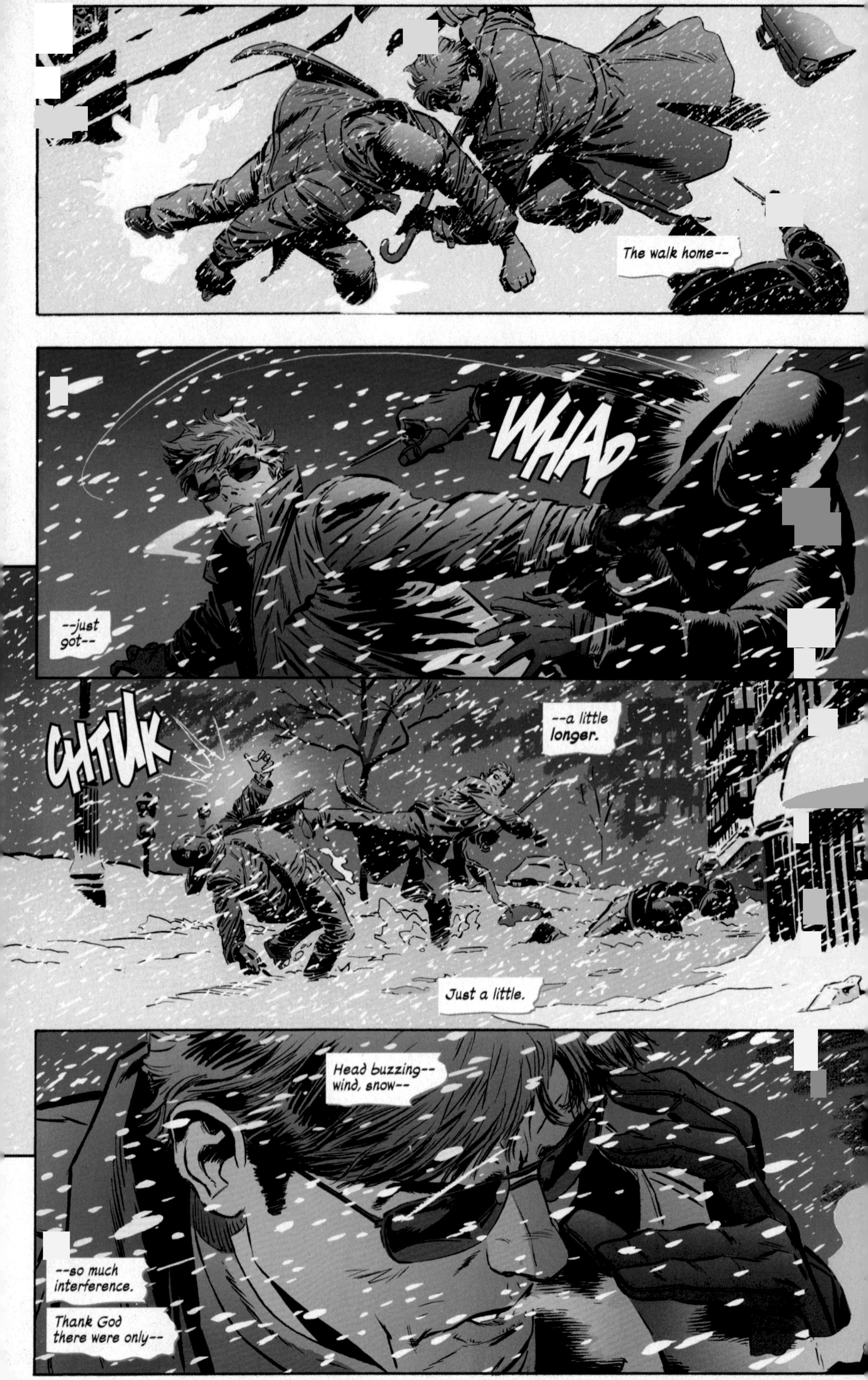
The walk home--
WHAP
--just got--
CHTUK
--a little longer.
Just a little.
Head buzzing-- wind, snow--
--so much interference.
Thank God there were only--

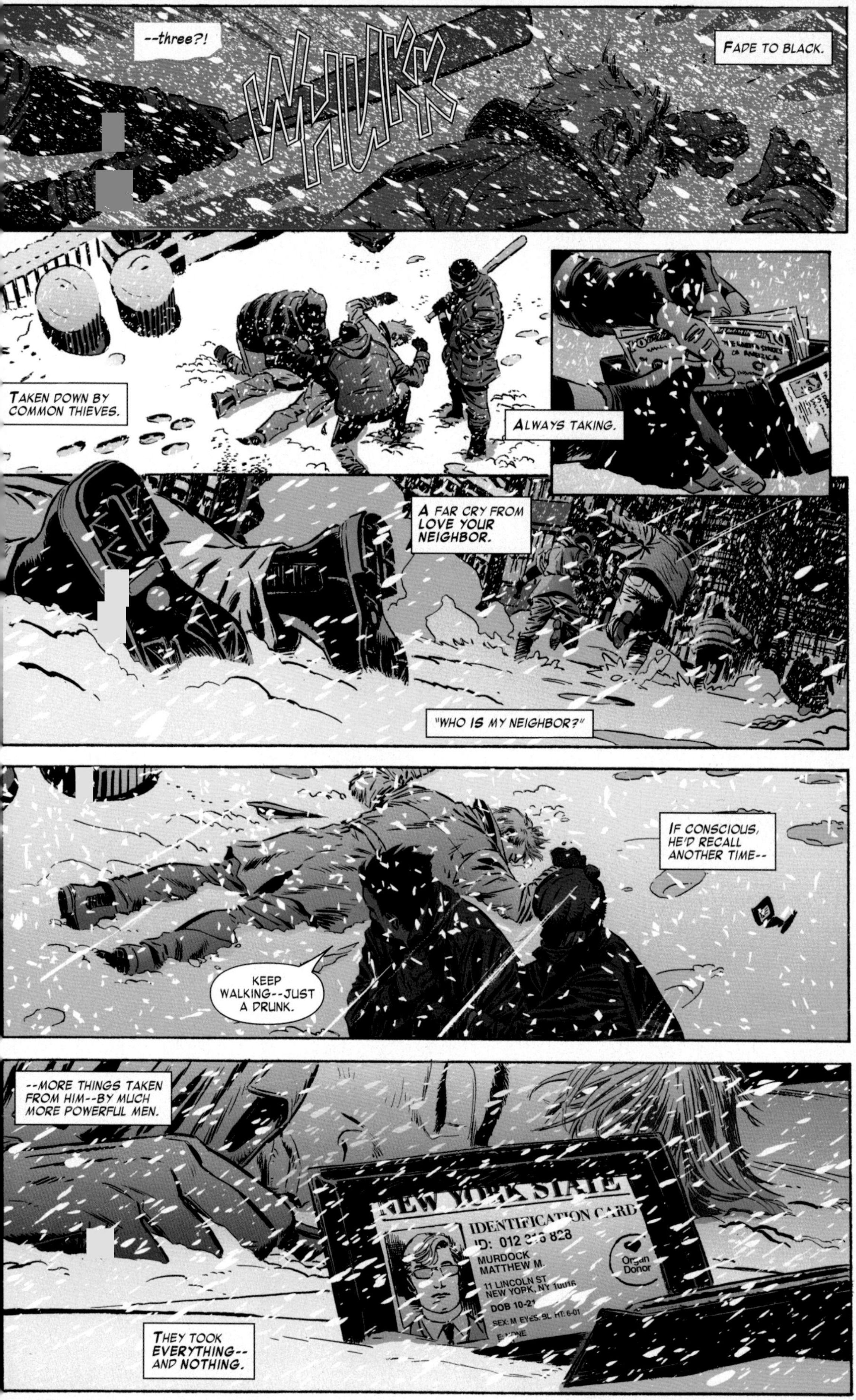
--three?!
WHUK!
FADE TO BLACK.
TAKEN DOWN BY COMMON THIEVES.
ALWAYS TAKING.
A FAR CRY FROM LOVE YOUR NEIGHBOR.
"WHO IS MY NEIGHBOR?"
IF CONSCIOUS, HE'D RECALL ANOTHER TIME--
KEEP WALKING--JUST A DRUNK.
--MORE THINGS TAKEN FROM HIM--BY MUCH MORE POWERFUL MEN.
NEW YORK STATE
IDENTIFICATION CARD
MURDOCK
MATTHEW M.
Organ Donor
THEY TOOK EVERYTHING--AND NOTHING.

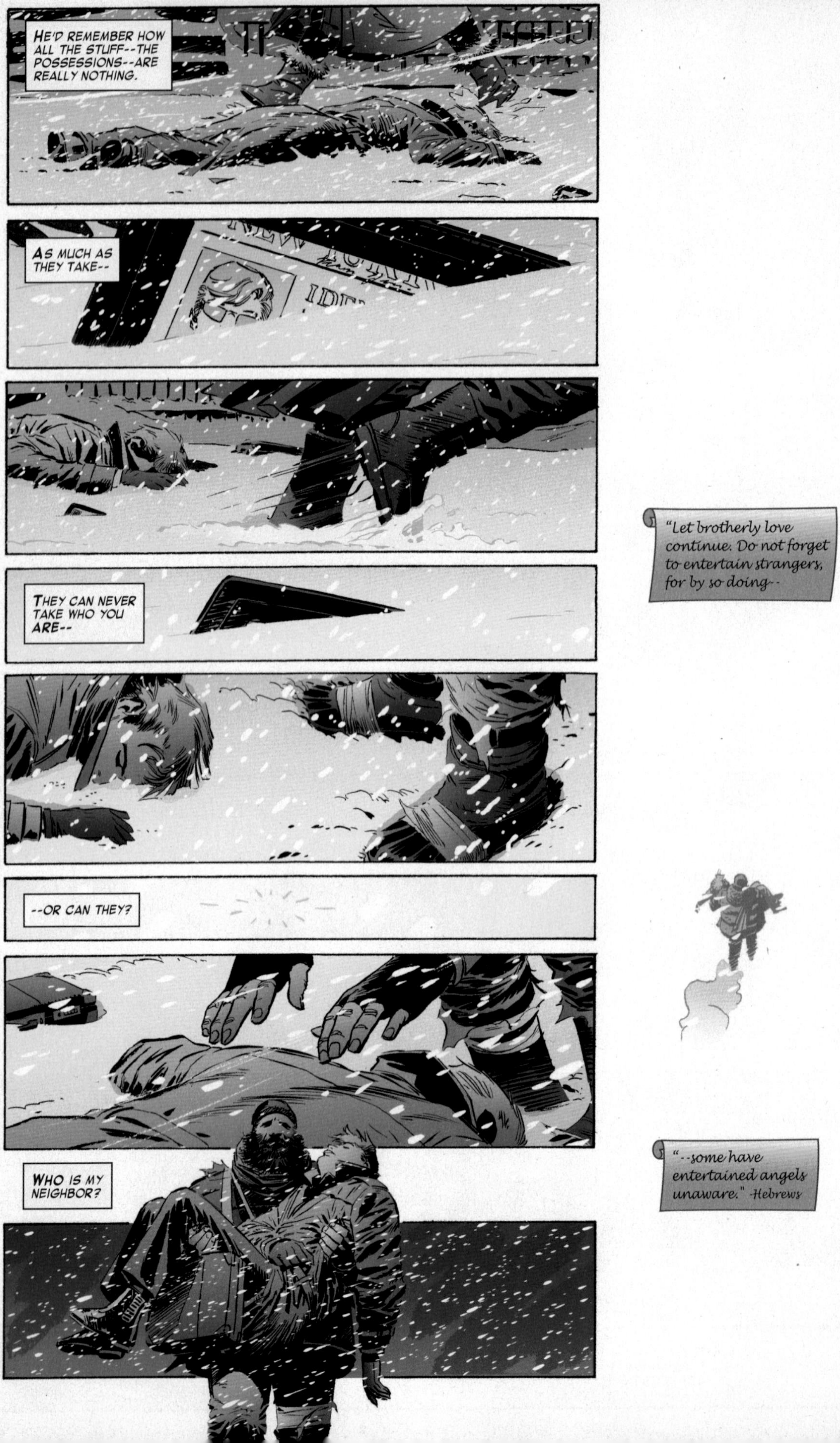
HE'D REMEMBER HOW ALL THE STUFF--THE POSSESSIONS--ARE REALLY NOTHING.
AS MUCH AS THEY TAKE--
THEY CAN NEVER TAKE WHO YOU ARE--
--OR CAN THEY?
WHO IS MY NEIGHBOR?
"Let brotherly love continue. Do not forget to entertain strangers, for by so doing--
"--some have entertained angels unaware." -Hebrews

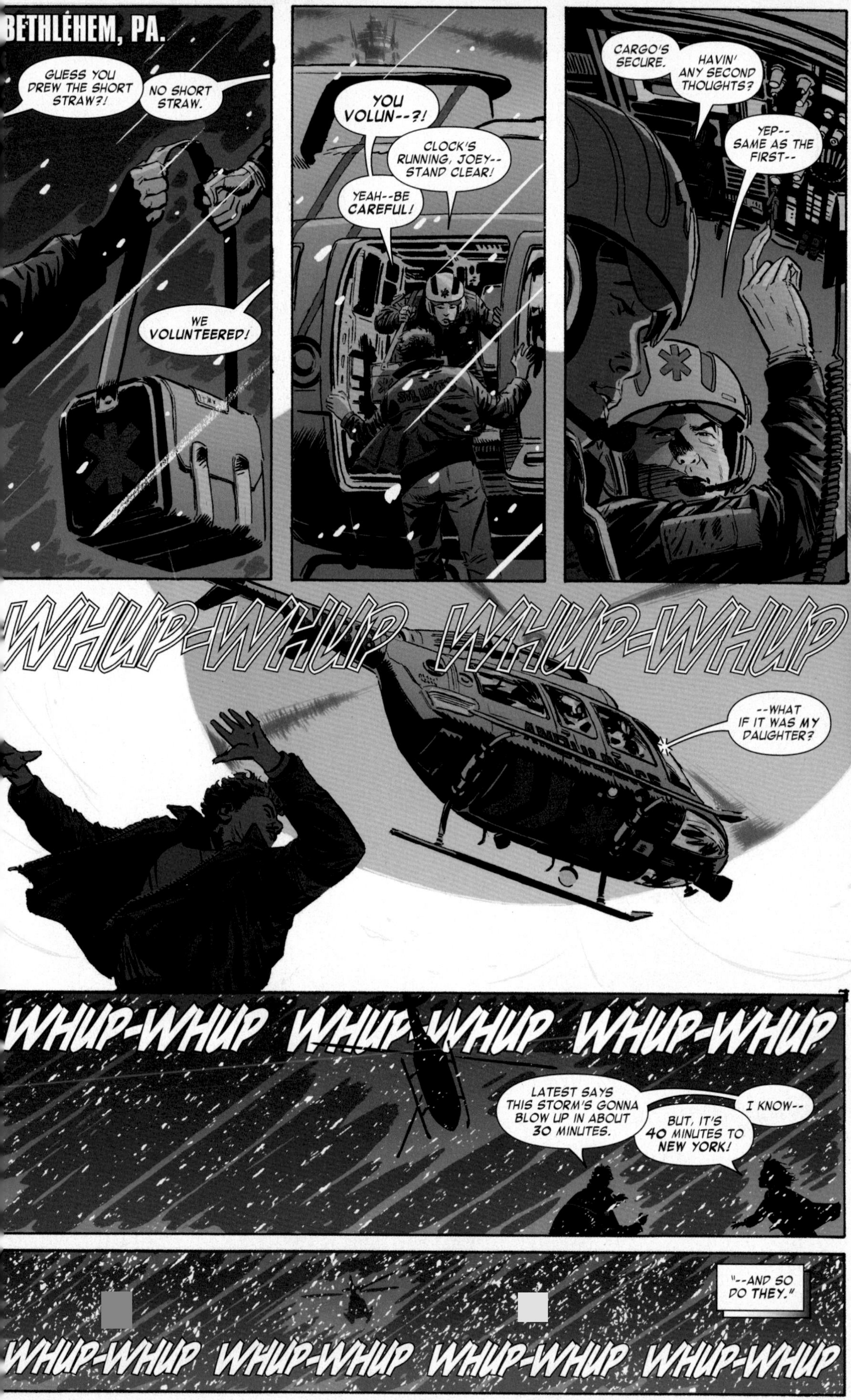
BETHLEHEM, PA.
GUESS YOU DREW THE SHORT STRAW?!
NO SHORT STRAW.
WE VOLUNTEERED!
YOU VOLUN--?!
CLOCK'S RUNNING, JOEY-- STAND CLEAR!
YEAH--BE CAREFUL!
CARGO'S SECURE.
HAVIN' ANY SECOND THOUGHTS?
YEP-- SAME AS THE FIRST--
WHUP-WHUP WHUP-WHUP
--WHAT IF IT WAS MY DAUGHTER?
WHUP-WHUP WHUP-WHUP WHUP-WHUP
LATEST SAYS THIS STORM'S GONNA BLOW UP IN ABOUT 30 MINUTES.
I KNOW--
BUT, IT'S 40 MINUTES TO NEW YORK!
"--AND SO DO THEY."
WHUP-WHUP WHUP-WHUP WHUP-WHUP WHUP-WHUP

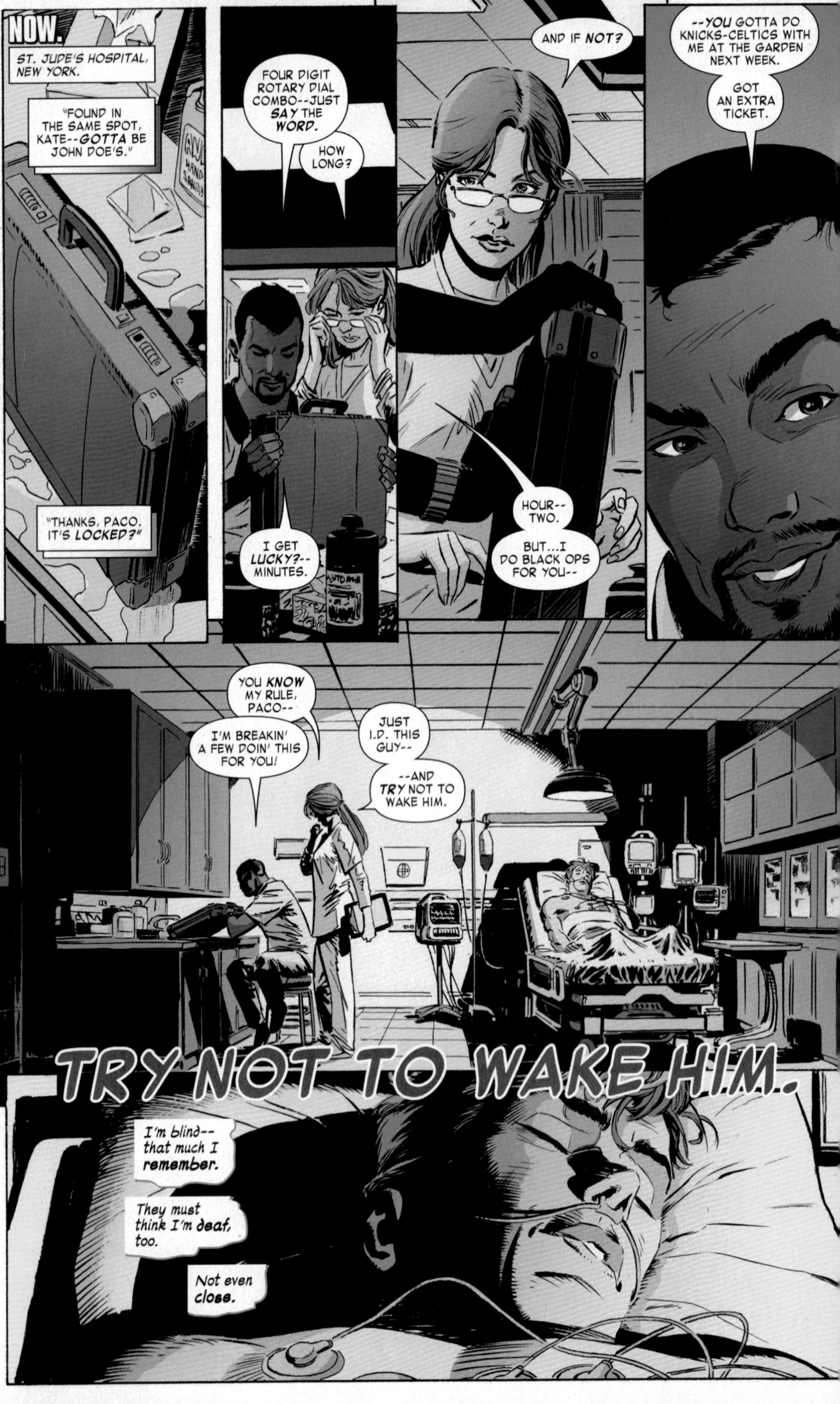
NOW.
ST. JUDE'S HOSPITAL, NEW YORK.
"FOUND IN THE SAME SPOT, KATE--GOTTA BE JOHN DOE'S."
"THANKS, PACO. IT'S LOCKED?"
FOUR DIGIT ROTARY DIAL COMBO--JUST SAY THE WORD.
HOW LONG?
I GET LUCKY?--MINUTES.
AND IF NOT?
HOUR--TWO.
BUT...I DO BLACK OPS FOR YOU--
--YOU GOTTA DO KNICKS-CELTICS WITH ME AT THE GARDEN NEXT WEEK.
GOT AN EXTRA TICKET.
YOU KNOW MY RULE, PACO--
I'M BREAKIN' A FEW DOIN' THIS FOR YOU!
JUST I.D. THIS GUY--
--AND TRY NOT TO WAKE HIM.
TRY NOT TO WAKE HIM.
I'm blind--that much I remember.
They must think I'm deaf, too.
Not even close.

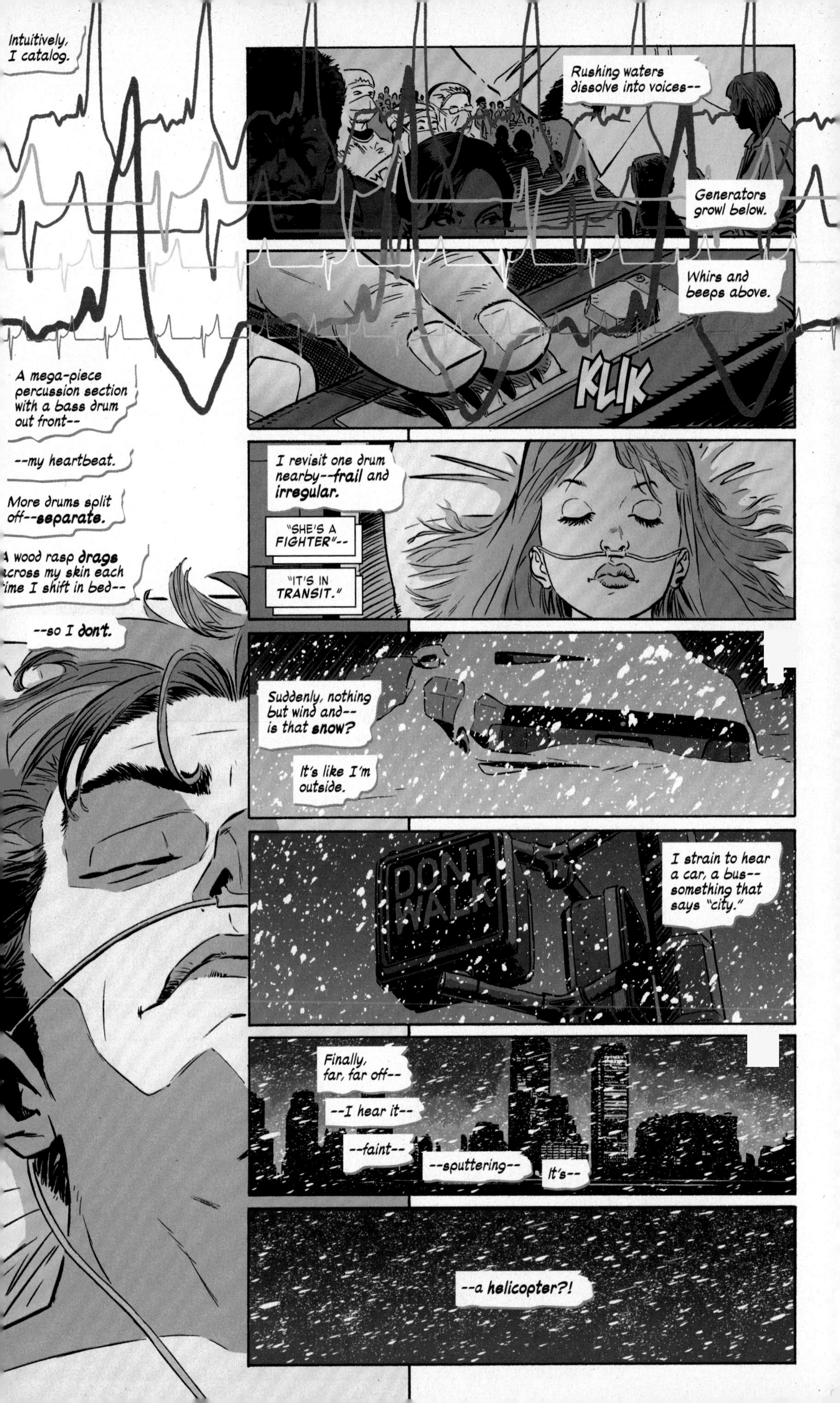

Intuitively, I catalog.
Rushing waters dissolve into voices--
Generators growl below.
Whirs and beeps above.
KLIK
A mega-piece percussion section with a bass drum out front--
--my heartbeat.
I revisit one drum nearby--frail and irregular.
"SHE'S A FIGHTER"--
"IT'S IN TRANSIT."
More drums split off--separate.
A wood rasp drags across my skin each time I shift in bed--
--so I don't.
Suddenly, nothing but wind and-- is that snow?
It's like I'm outside.
DONT WALK
I strain to hear a car, a bus-- something that says "city."
Finally, far, far off--
--I hear it--
--faint--
--sputtering--
It's--
--a helicopter?!

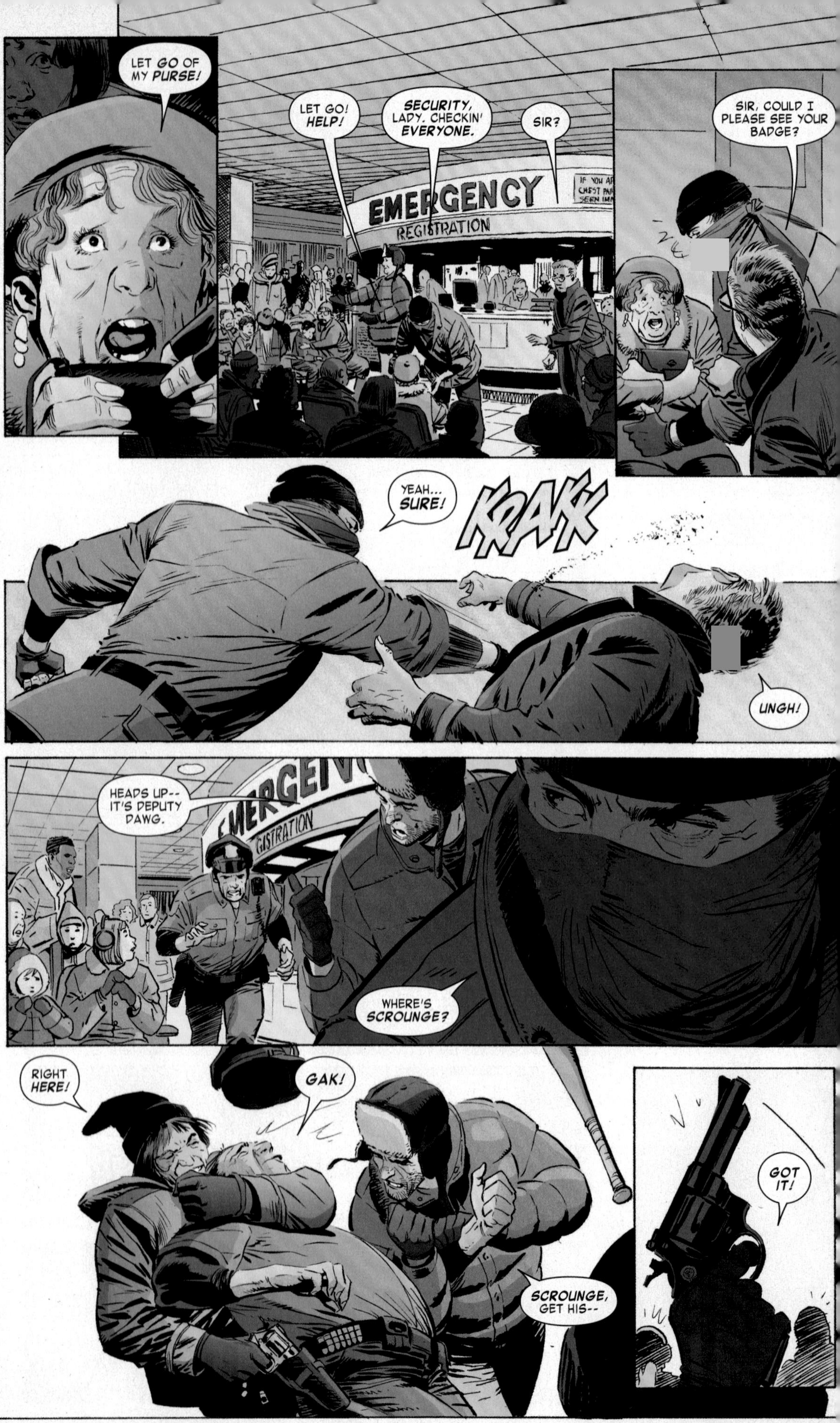
LET GO OF MY PURSE!
LET GO! HELP!
SECURITY, LADY. CHECKIN' EVERYONE.
SIR?
EMERGENCY
REGISTRATION
SIR, COULD I PLEASE SEE YOUR BADGE?
YEAH... SURE!
KRAKK
UNGH!
HEADS UP-- IT'S DEPUTY DAWG.
WHERE'S SCROUNGE?
RIGHT HERE!
GAK!
SCROUNGE, GET HIS--
GOT IT!

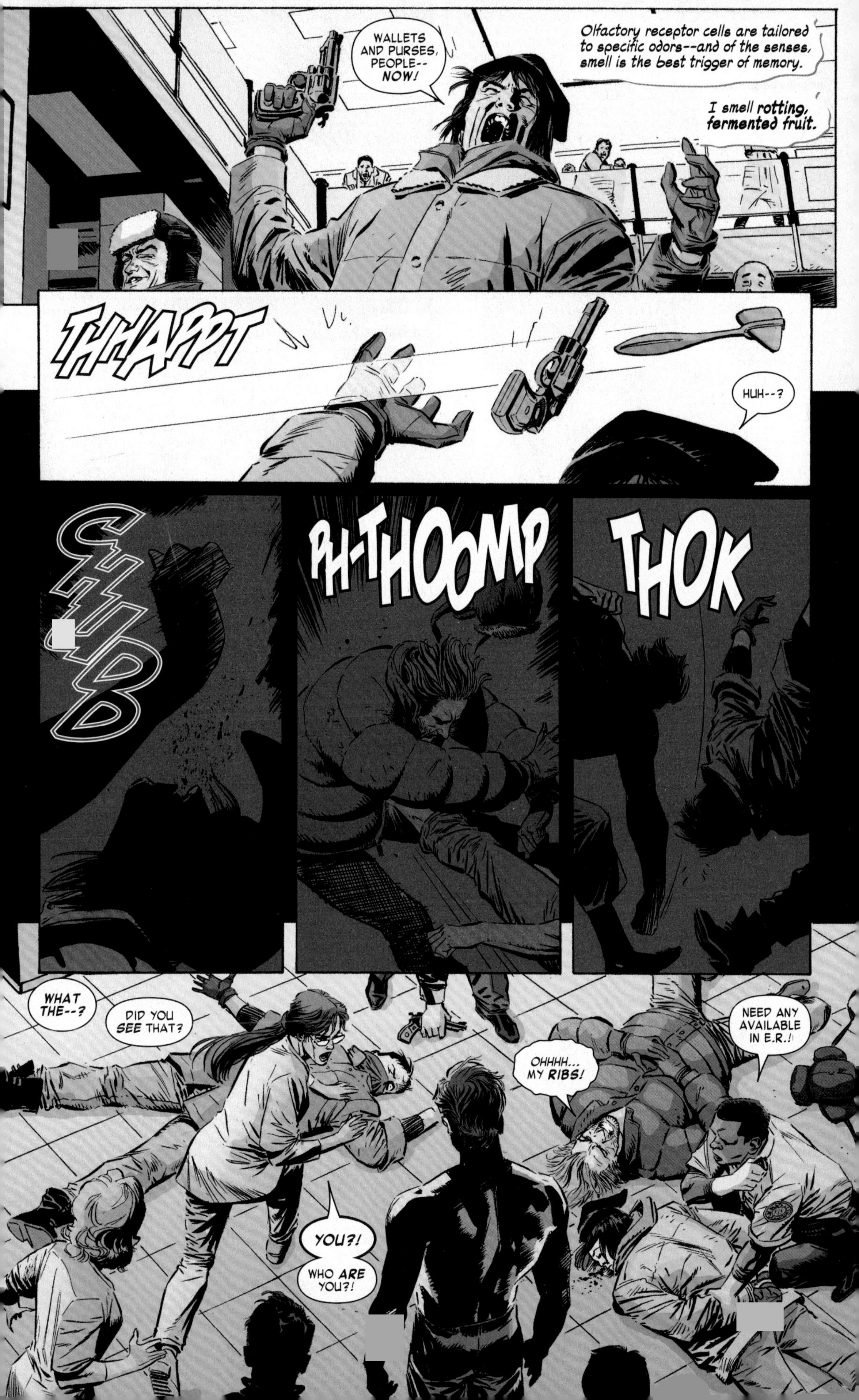

WALLETS AND PURSES, PEOPLE-- NOW!
Olfactory receptor cells are tailored to specific odors--and of the senses, smell is the best trigger of memory.
I smell rotting, fermented fruit.
THHAPPT
HUH--?
CHUD
PH-THOOMP
THOK
WHAT THE--?
DID YOU SEE THAT?
OHHHH... MY RIBS!
NEED ANY AVAILABLE IN E.R.!
YOU?!
WHO ARE YOU?!

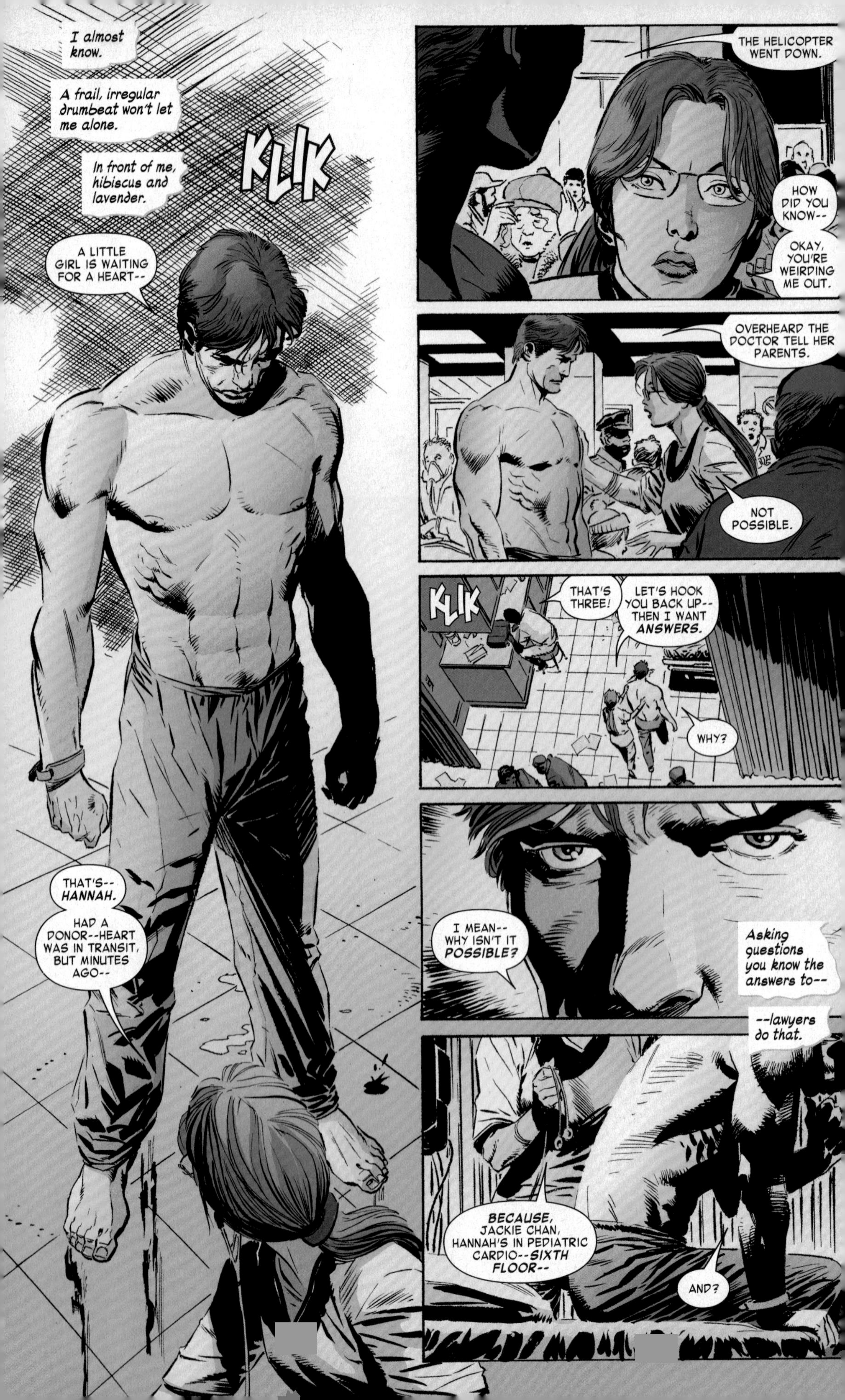
I almost know.
A frail, irregular drumbeat won't let me alone.
KLIK
In front of me, hibiscus and lavender.
A LITTLE GIRL IS WAITING FOR A HEART--
THAT'S-- HANNAH.
HAD A DONOR--HEART WAS IN TRANSIT, BUT MINUTES AGO--
THE HELICOPTER WENT DOWN.
HOW DID YOU KNOW--
OKAY, YOU'RE WEIRDING ME OUT.
OVERHEARD THE DOCTOR TELL HER PARENTS.
NOT POSSIBLE.
KLIK
THAT'S THREE!
LET'S HOOK YOU BACK UP-- THEN I WANT ANSWERS.
WHY?
I MEAN-- WHY ISN'T IT POSSIBLE?
Asking questions you know the answers to--
--lawyers do that.
BECAUSE, JACKIE CHAN, HANNAH'S IN PEDIATRIC CARDIO--SIXTH FLOOR--
AND?

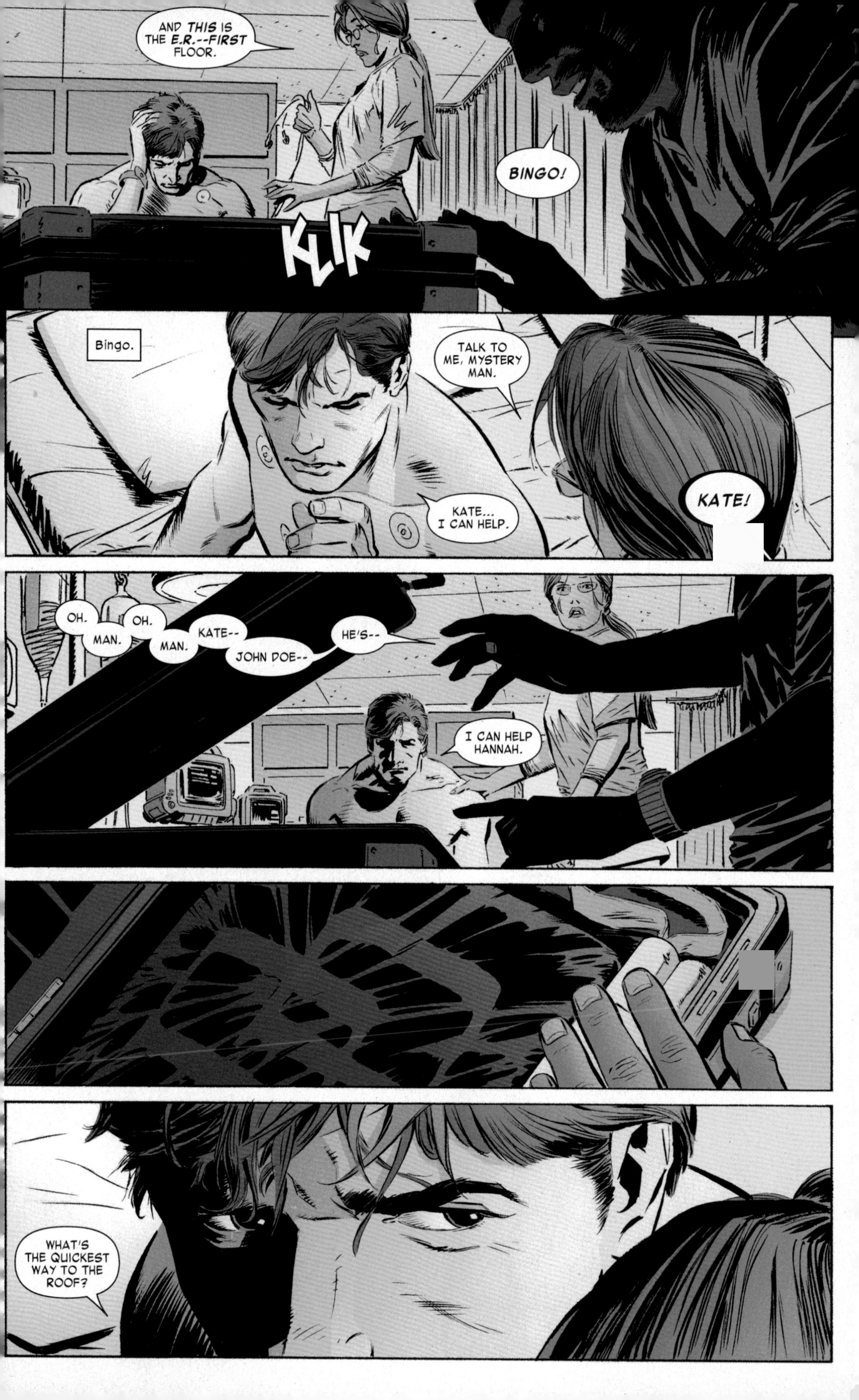
AND THIS IS THE E.R.--FIRST FLOOR.
BINGO!
KLIK
Bingo.
TALK TO ME, MYSTERY MAN.
KATE... I CAN HELP.
KATE!
OH. MAN.
OH. MAN.
KATE--
JOHN DOE--
HE'S--
I CAN HELP HANNAH.
WHAT'S THE QUICKEST WAY TO THE ROOF?

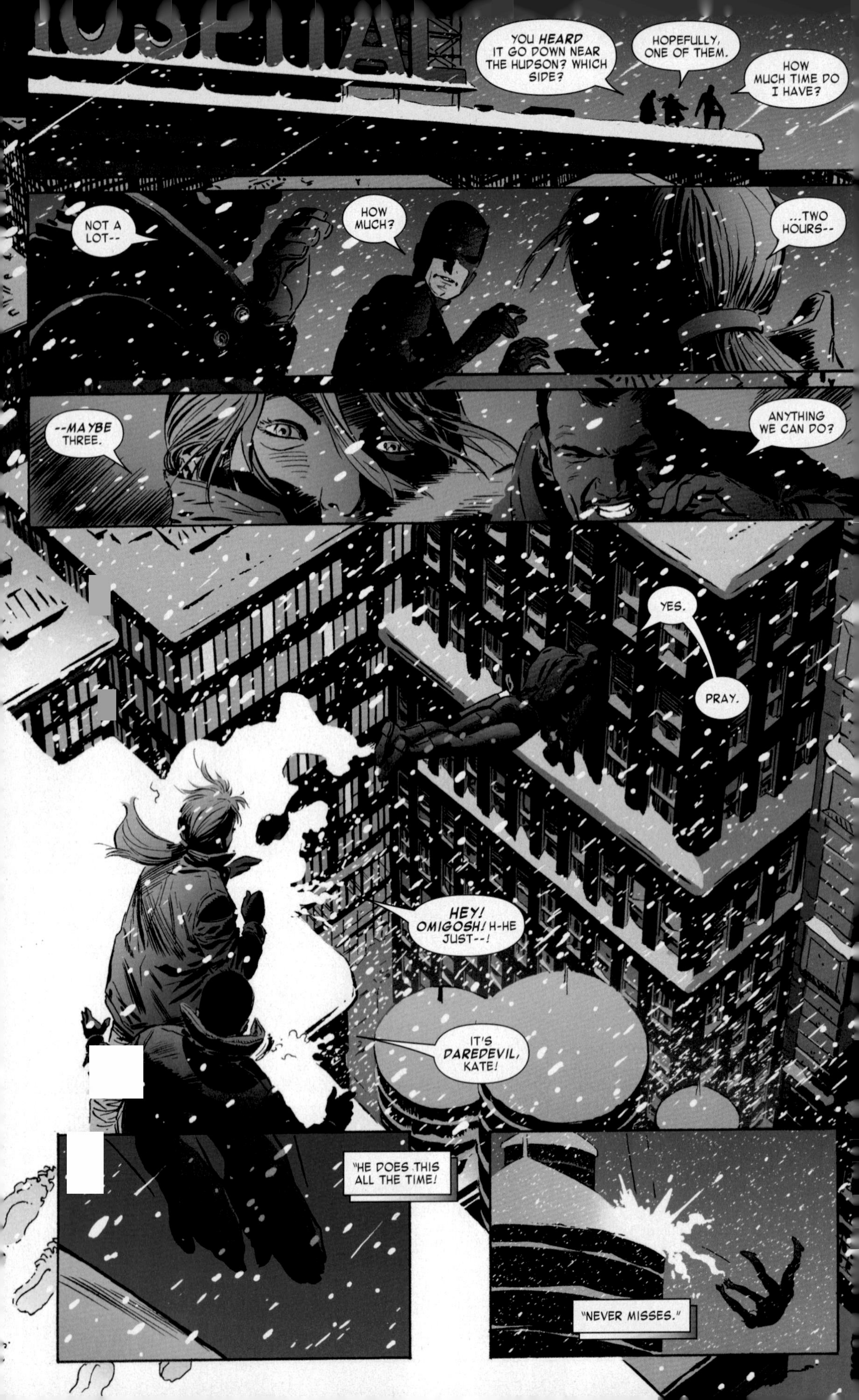
YOU HEARD IT GO DOWN NEAR THE HUDSON? WHICH SIDE?
HOPEFULLY, ONE OF THEM.
HOW MUCH TIME DO I HAVE?
NOT A LOT--
HOW MUCH?
...TWO HOURS--
--MAYBE THREE.
ANYTHING WE CAN DO?
YES.
PRAY.
HEY! OMIGOSH! H-HE JUST--!
IT'S DAREDEVIL, KATE!
"HE DOES THIS ALL THE TIME!
"NEVER MISSES."

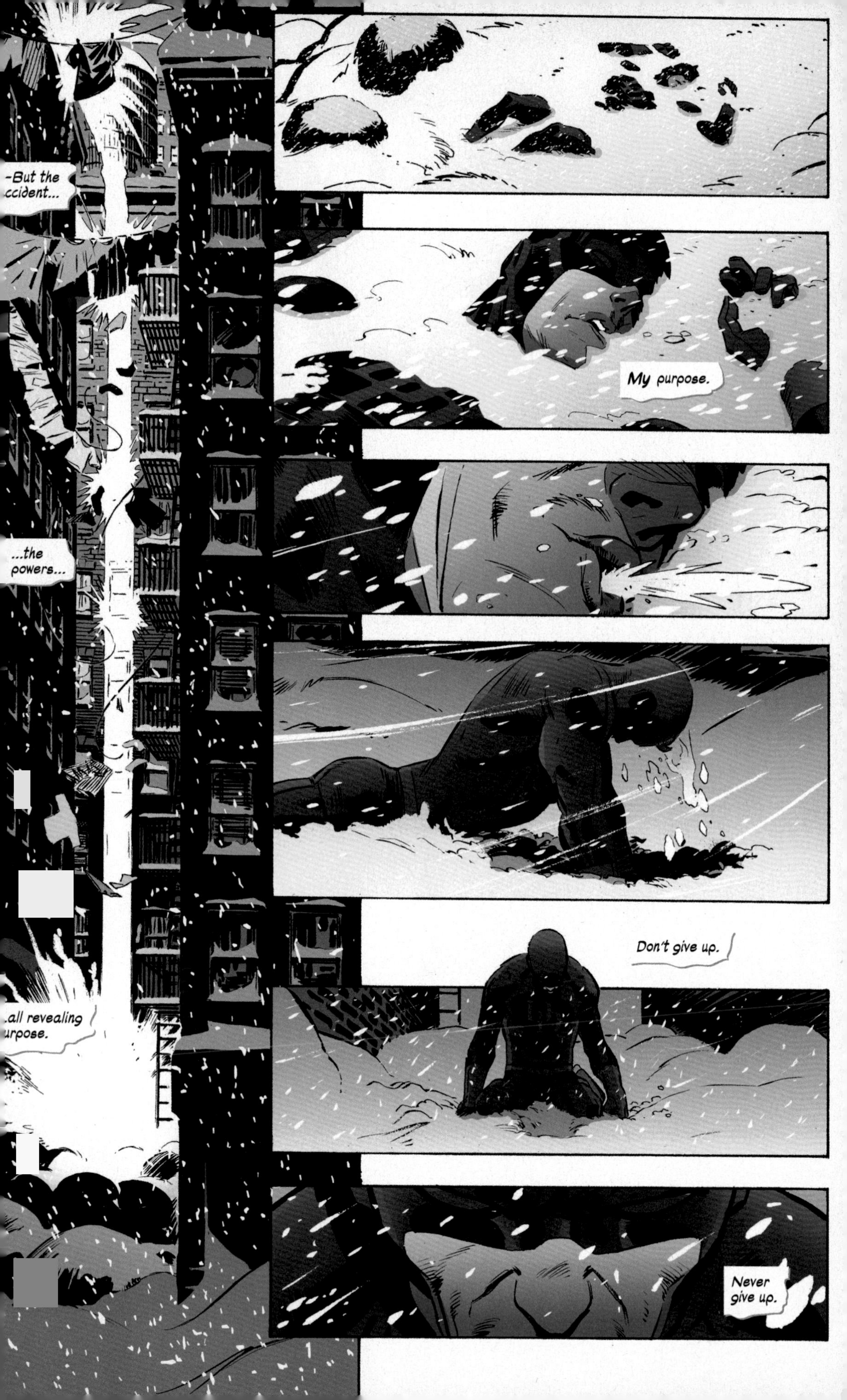
-But the
ccident...
...the
powers...
.all revealing
urpose.
My purpose.
Don't give up.
Never
give up.

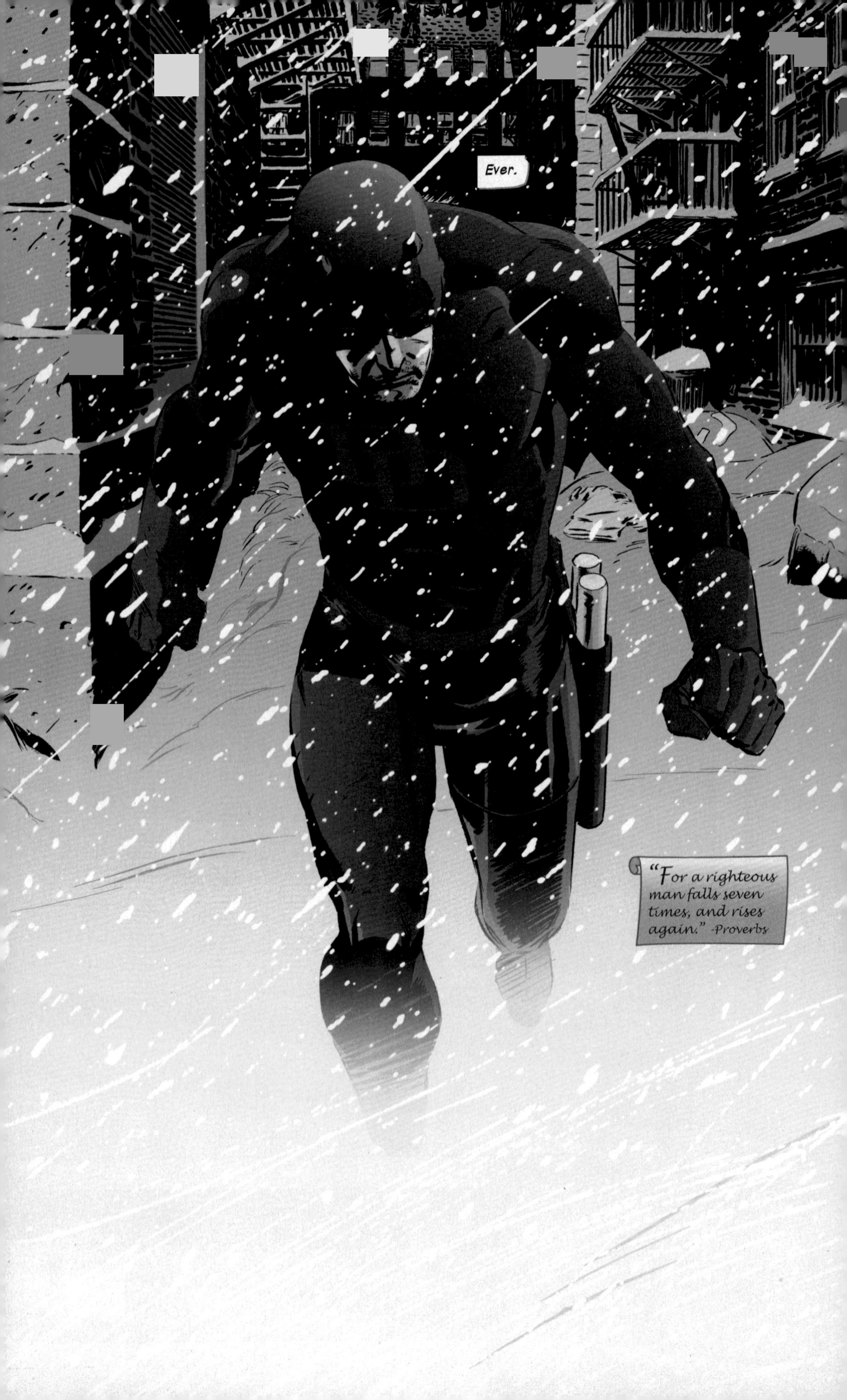
Ever.
"For a righteous man falls seven times, and rises again." -Proverbs

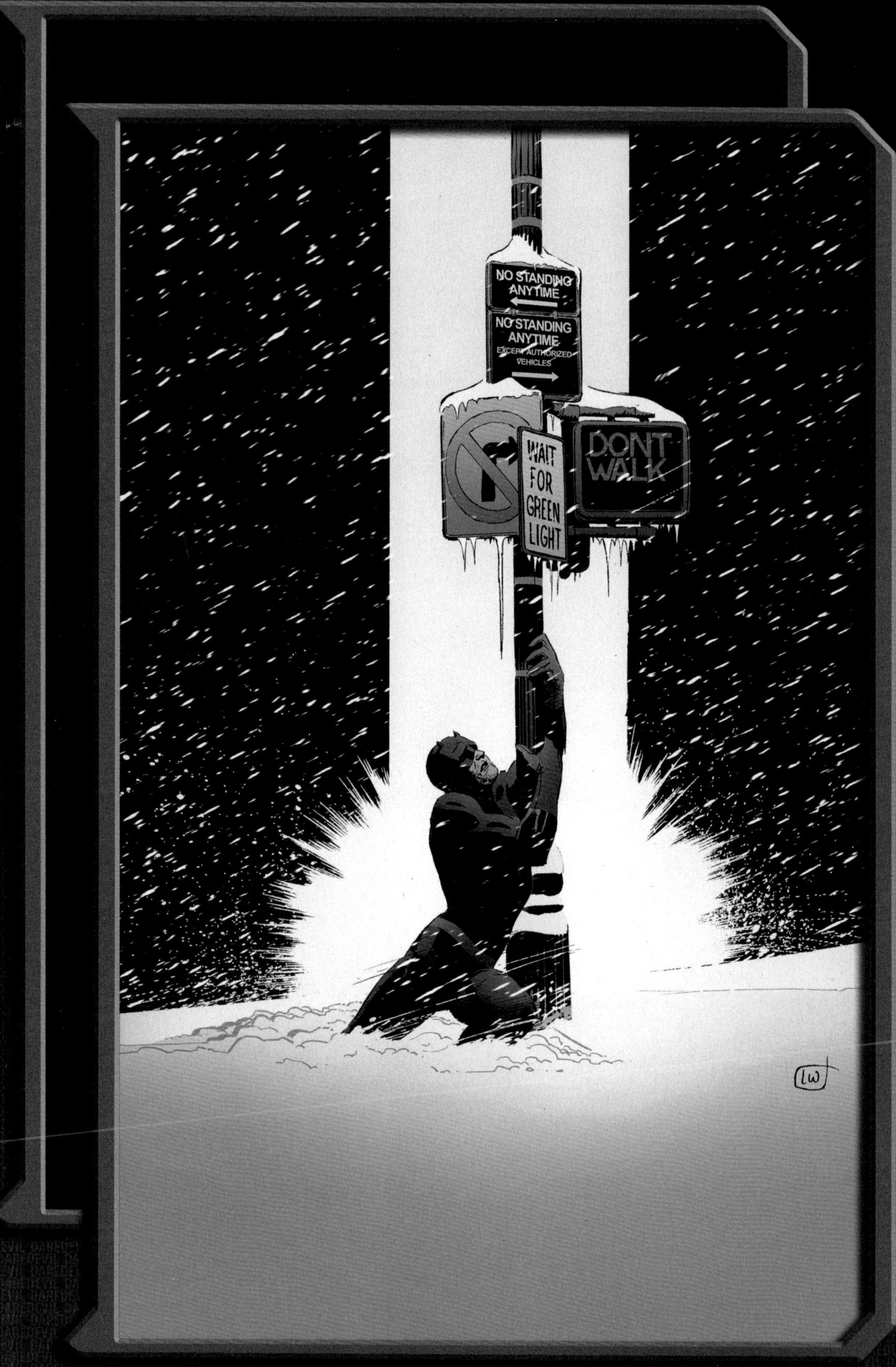
NO STANDING ANYTIME
NO STANDING ANYTIME EXCEPT AUTHORIZED VEHICLES
WAIT FOR GREEN LIGHT
DONT WALK

#2 — ANGELS UNAWARE
PART TWO: HANNAH'S HEART, HANNAH'S HOPE

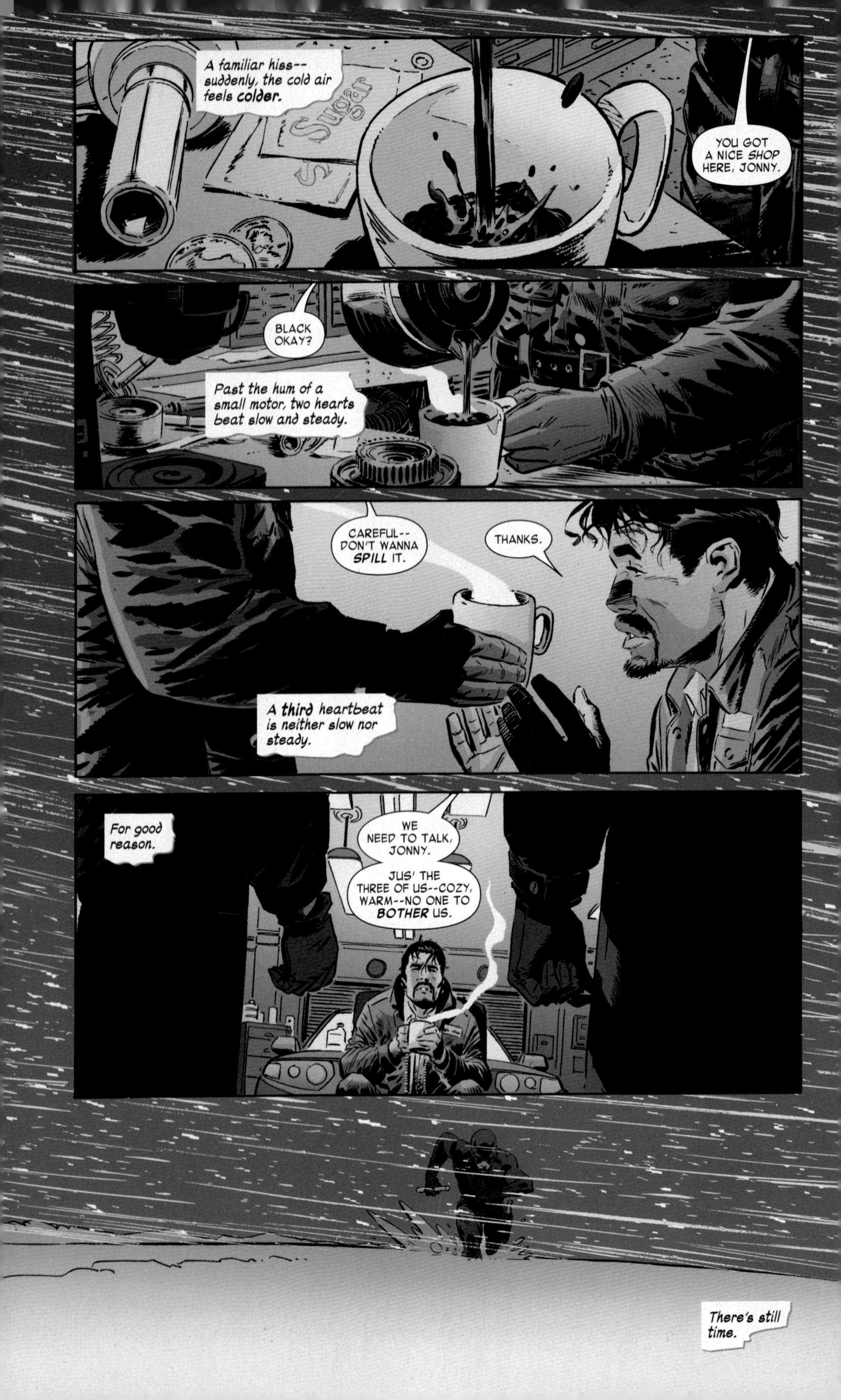
A familiar hiss--suddenly, the cold air feels colder.
YOU GOT A NICE SHOP HERE, JONNY.
BLACK OKAY?
Past the hum of a small motor, two hearts beat slow and steady.
CAREFUL--DON'T WANNA SPILL IT.
THANKS.
A third heartbeat is neither slow nor steady.
For good reason.
WE NEED TO TALK, JONNY.
JUS' THE THREE OF US--COZY, WARM--NO ONE TO BOTHER US.
There's still time.

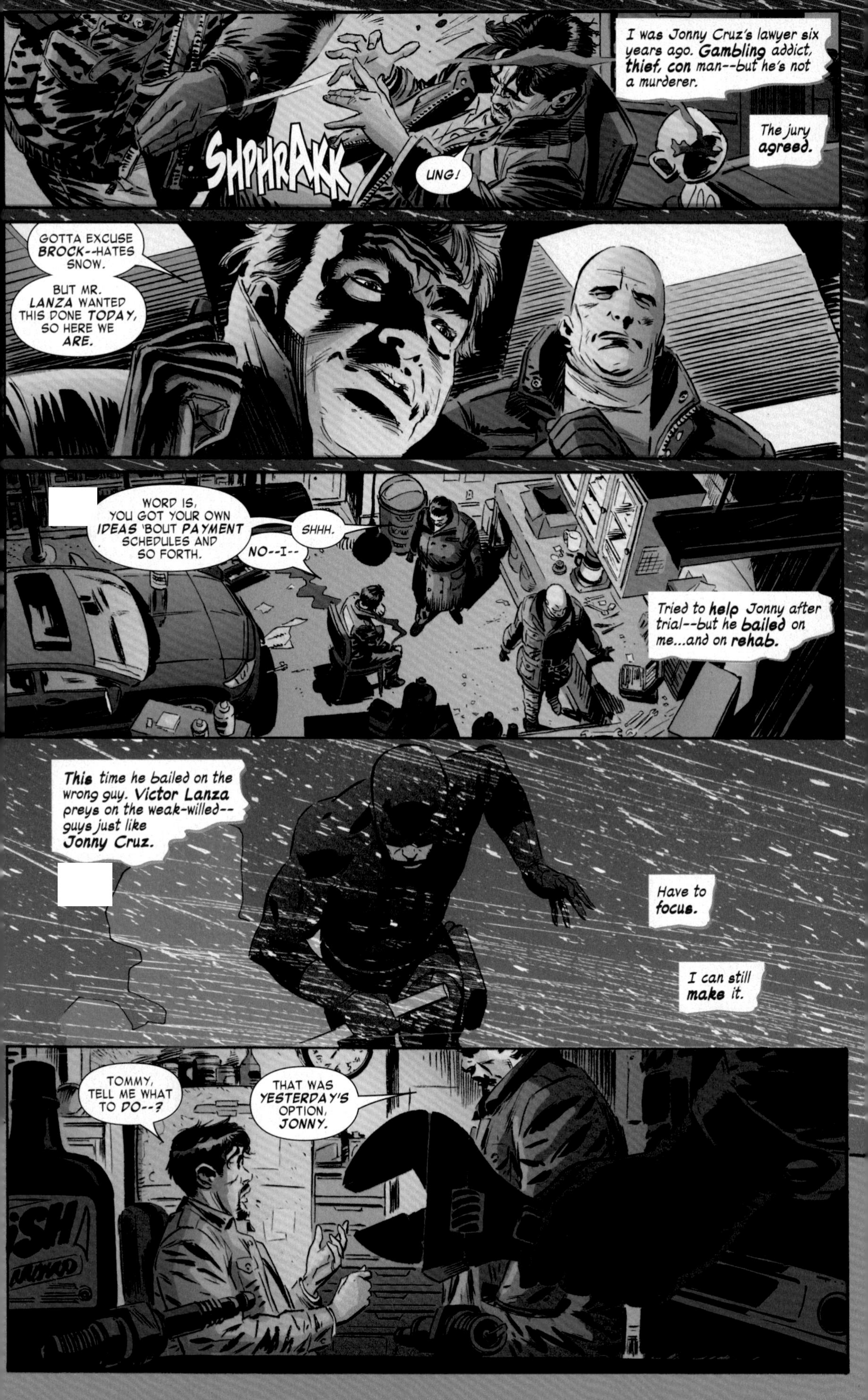

I was Jonny Cruz's lawyer six years ago. Gambling addict, thief, con man--but he's not a murderer.
The jury agreed.
SHPHRAKK
UNG!
GOTTA EXCUSE BROCK--HATES SNOW.
BUT MR. LANZA WANTED THIS DONE TODAY, SO HERE WE ARE.
WORD IS, YOU GOT YOUR OWN IDEAS 'BOUT PAYMENT SCHEDULES AND SO FORTH.
SHHH.
NO--I--
Tried to help Jonny after trial--but he bailed on me...and on rehab.
This time he bailed on the wrong guy. Victor Lanza preys on the weak-willed--guys just like Jonny Cruz.
Have to focus.
I can still make it.
TOMMY, TELL ME WHAT TO DO--?
THAT WAS YESTERDAY'S OPTION, JONNY.

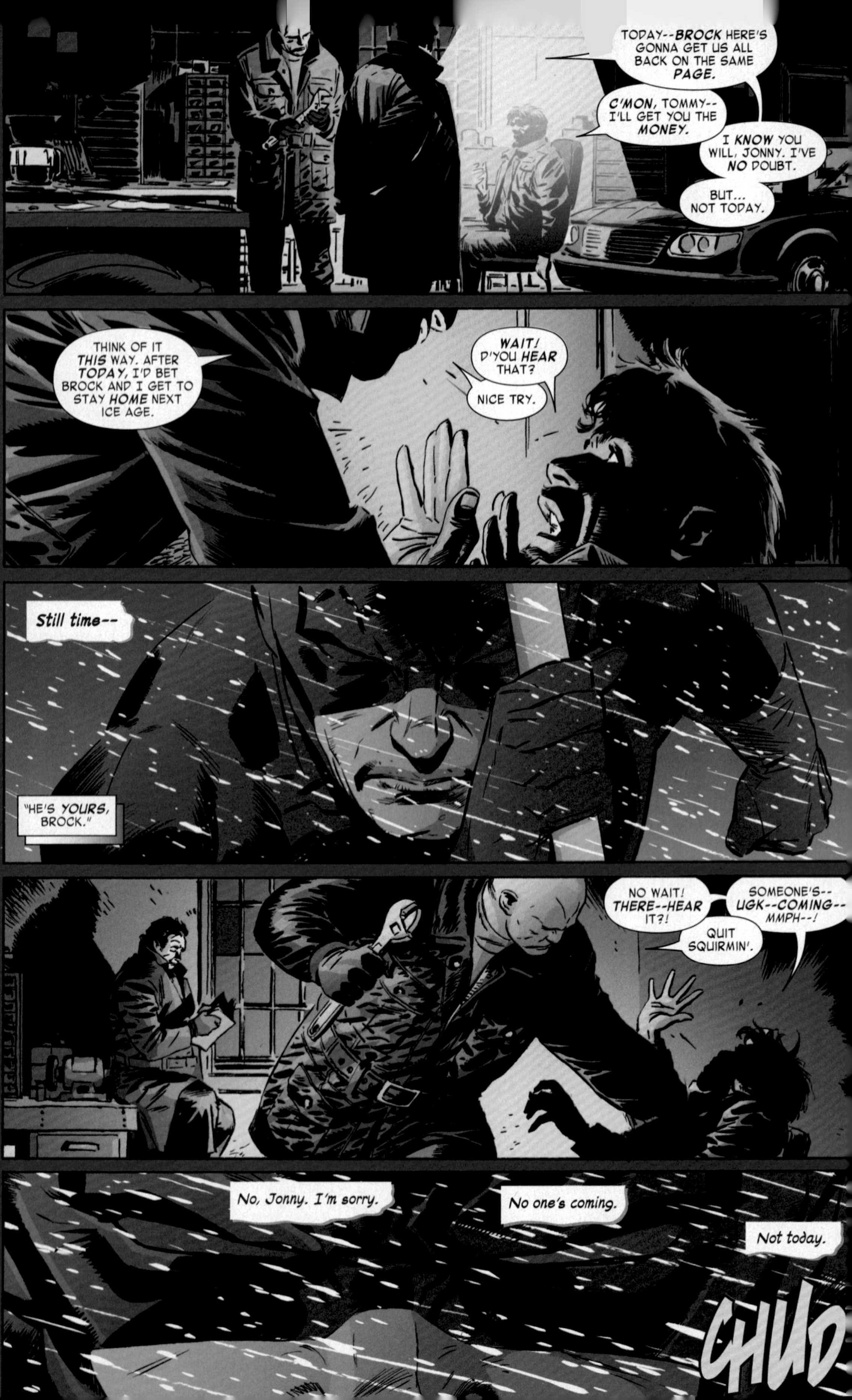
TODAY--BROCK HERE'S GONNA GET US ALL BACK ON THE SAME PAGE.
C'MON, TOMMY--I'LL GET YOU THE MONEY.
I KNOW YOU WILL, JONNY. I'VE NO DOUBT.
BUT... NOT TODAY.
THINK OF IT THIS WAY. AFTER TODAY, I'D BET BROCK AND I GET TO STAY HOME NEXT ICE AGE.
WAIT! D'YOU HEAR THAT?
NICE TRY.
Still time--
"HE'S YOURS, BROCK."
NO WAIT! THERE--HEAR IT?!
SOMEONE'S--UGK--COMING--MMPH--!
QUIT SQUIRMIN'.
No, Jonny. I'm sorry.
No one's coming.
Not today.
CHUD

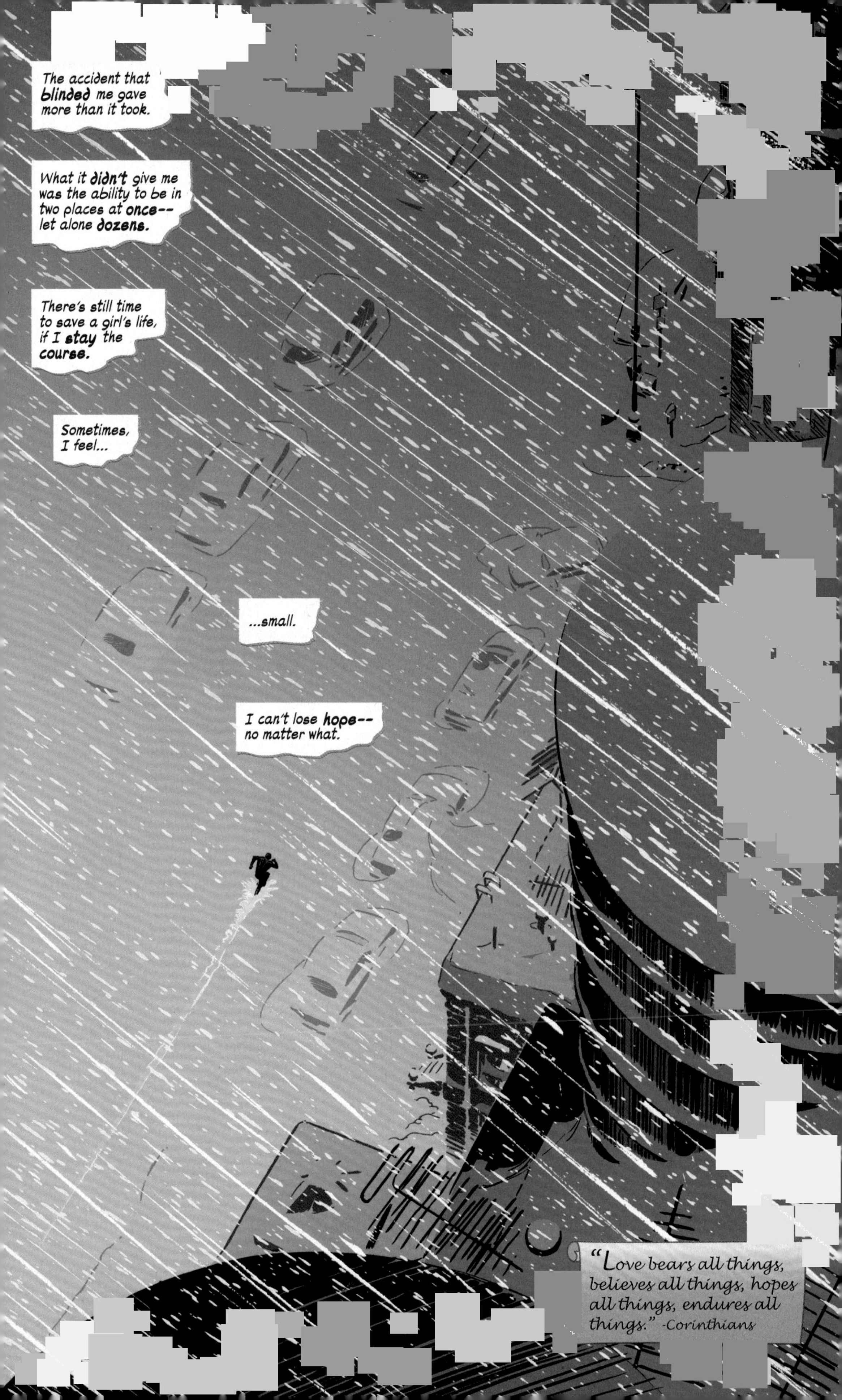
The accident that blinded me gave more than it took.
What it didn't give me was the ability to be in two places at once--let alone dozens.
There's still time to save a girl's life, if I stay the course.
Sometimes, I feel...
...small.
I can't lose hope--no matter what.
"Love bears all things, believes all things, hopes all things, endures all things." -Corinthians

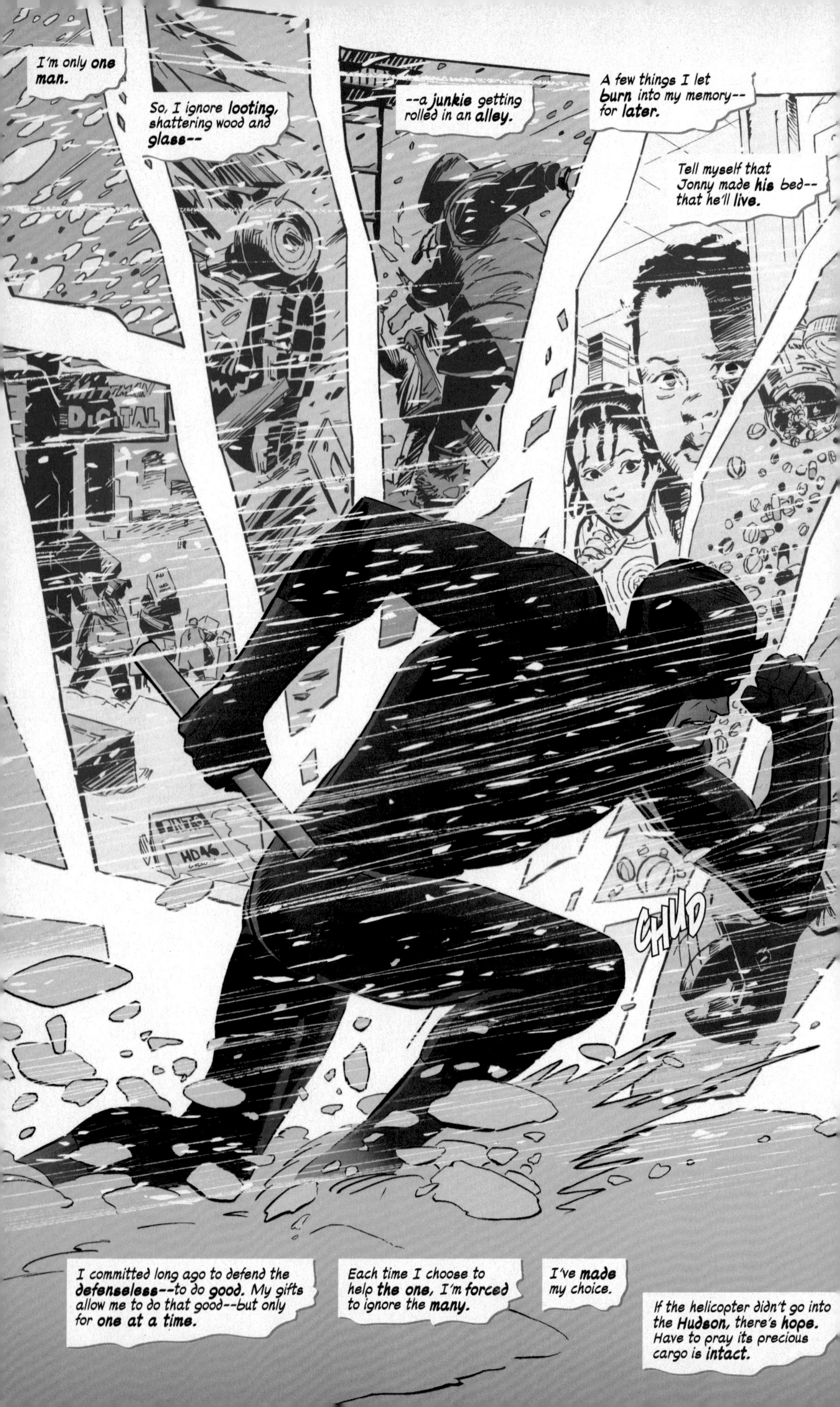
I'm only one man.
So, I ignore looting, shattering wood and glass--
--a junkie getting rolled in an alley.
A few things I let burn into my memory--for later.
Tell myself that Jonny made his bed--that he'll live.
DIGITAL
CHUD
I committed long ago to defend the defenseless--to do good. My gifts allow me to do that good--but only for one at a time.
Each time I choose to help the one, I'm forced to ignore the many.
I've made my choice.
If the helicopter didn't go into the Hudson, there's hope. Have to pray its precious cargo is intact.

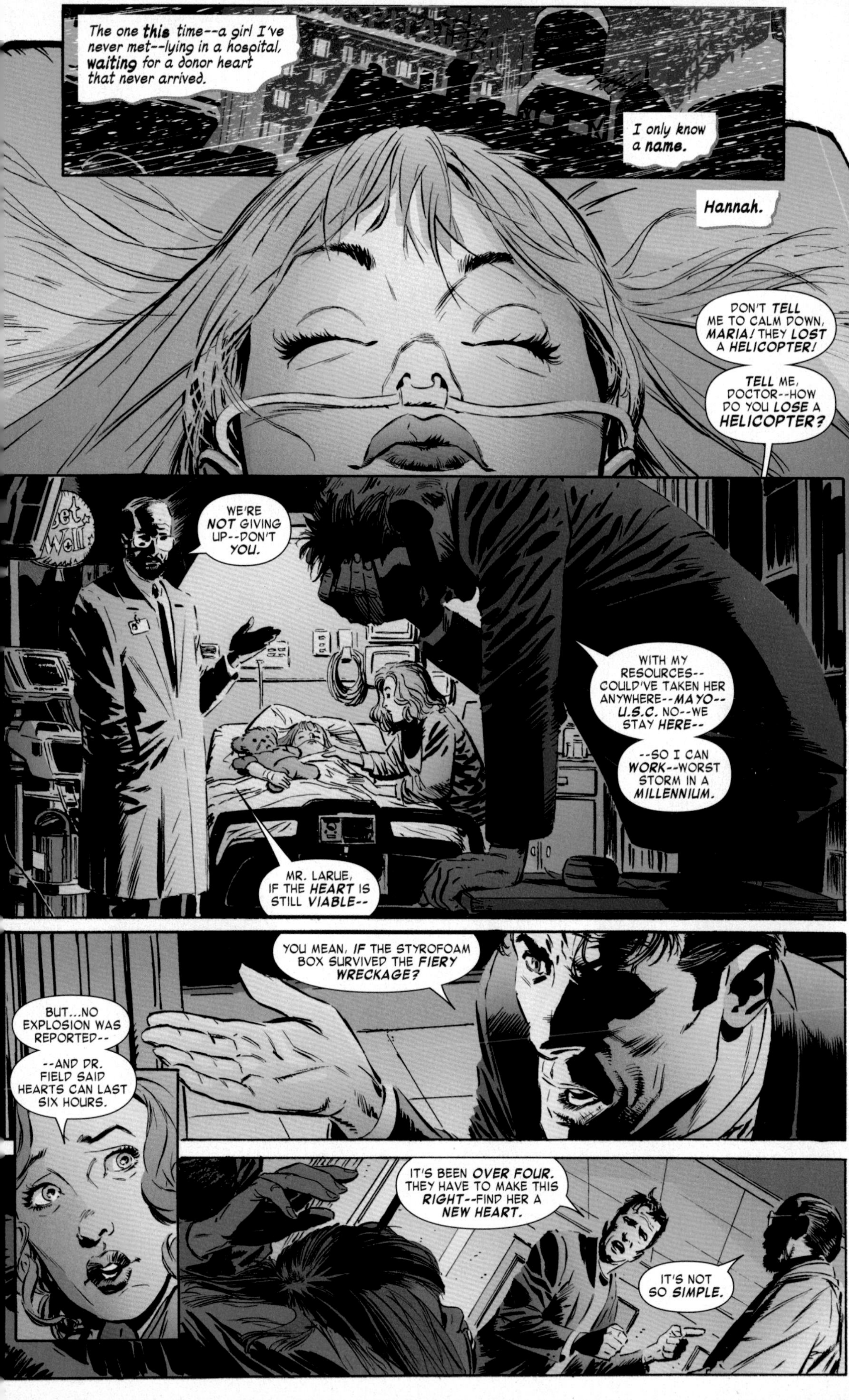
The one this time--a girl I've never met--lying in a hospital, waiting for a donor heart that never arrived.
I only know a name.
Hannah.
DON'T TELL ME TO CALM DOWN, MARIA! THEY LOST A HELICOPTER!
TELL ME, DOCTOR--HOW DO YOU LOSE A HELICOPTER?
WE'RE NOT GIVING UP--DON'T YOU.
WITH MY RESOURCES--COULD'VE TAKEN HER ANYWHERE--MAYO--U.S.C. NO--WE STAY HERE--
--SO I CAN WORK--WORST STORM IN A MILLENNIUM.
MR. LARUE, IF THE HEART IS STILL VIABLE--
YOU MEAN, IF THE STYROFOAM BOX SURVIVED THE FIERY WRECKAGE?
BUT...NO EXPLOSION WAS REPORTED--
--AND DR. FIELD SAID HEARTS CAN LAST SIX HOURS.
IT'S BEEN OVER FOUR. THEY HAVE TO MAKE THIS RIGHT--FIND HER A NEW HEART.
IT'S NOT SO SIMPLE.

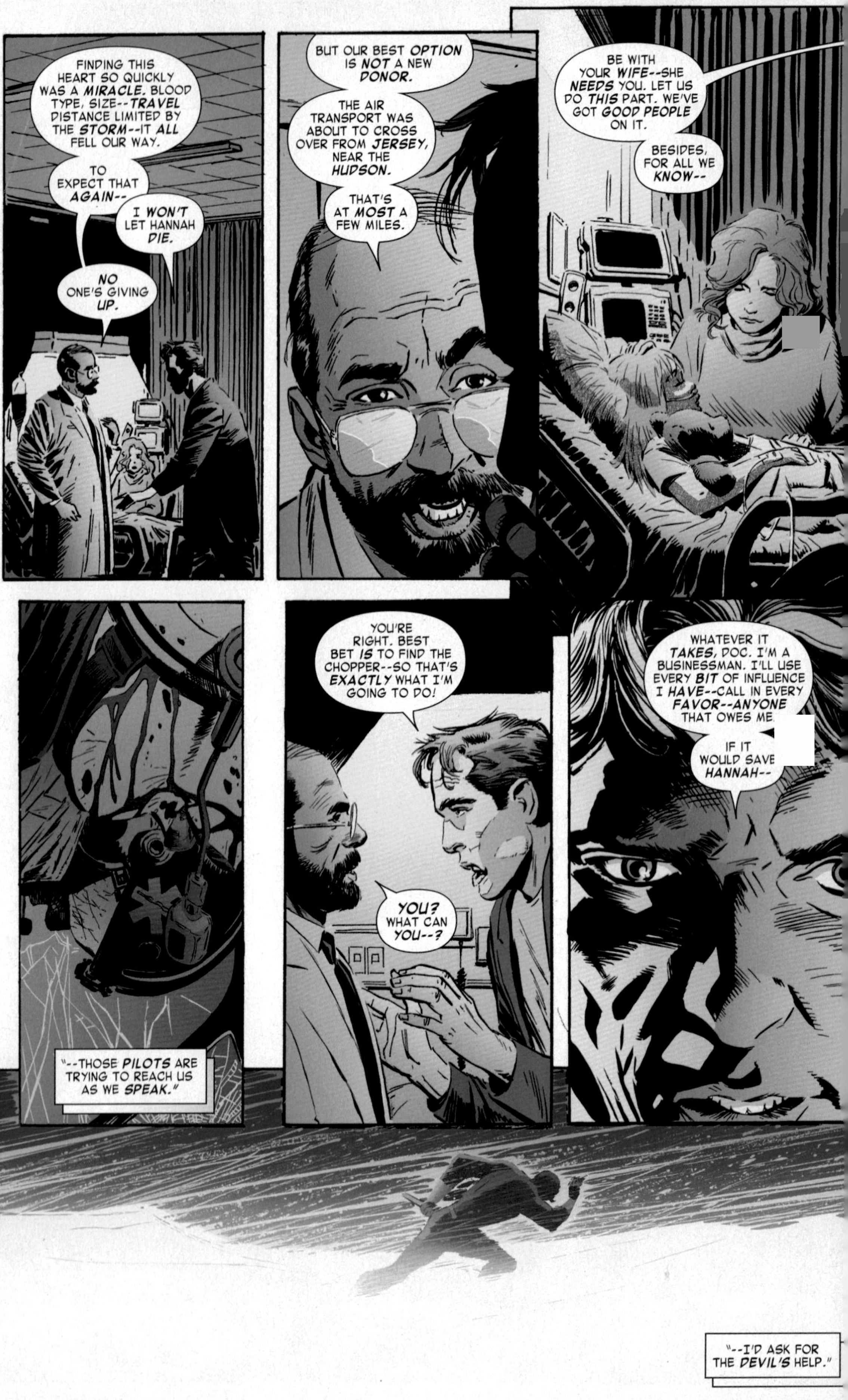
FINDING THIS HEART SO QUICKLY WAS A MIRACLE. BLOOD TYPE, SIZE--TRAVEL DISTANCE LIMITED BY THE STORM--IT ALL FELL OUR WAY.
TO EXPECT THAT AGAIN--
I WON'T LET HANNAH DIE.
NO ONE'S GIVING UP.
BUT OUR BEST OPTION IS NOT A NEW DONOR.
THE AIR TRANSPORT WAS ABOUT TO CROSS OVER FROM JERSEY, NEAR THE HUDSON.
THAT'S AT MOST A FEW MILES.
BE WITH YOUR WIFE--SHE NEEDS YOU. LET US DO THIS PART. WE'VE GOT GOOD PEOPLE ON IT.
BESIDES, FOR ALL WE KNOW--
"--THOSE PILOTS ARE TRYING TO REACH US AS WE SPEAK."
YOU'RE RIGHT. BEST BET IS TO FIND THE CHOPPER--SO THAT'S EXACTLY WHAT I'M GOING TO DO!
YOU? WHAT CAN YOU--?
WHATEVER IT TAKES, DOC. I'M A BUSINESSMAN. I'LL USE EVERY BIT OF INFLUENCE I HAVE--CALL IN EVERY FAVOR--ANYONE THAT OWES ME.
IF IT WOULD SAVE HANNAH--
"--I'D ASK FOR THE DEVIL'S HELP."

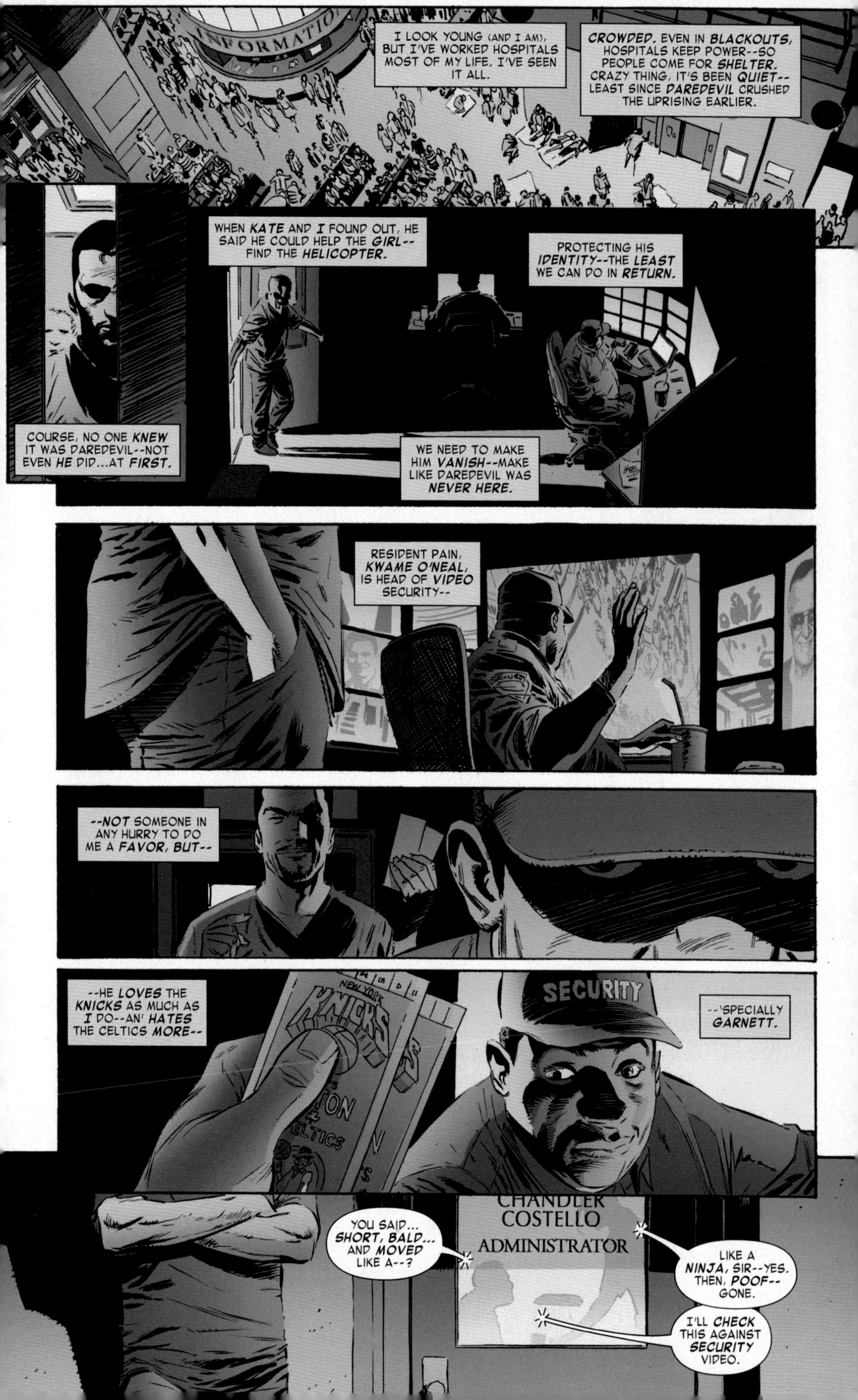

I LOOK YOUNG (AND I AM), BUT I'VE WORKED HOSPITALS MOST OF MY LIFE. I'VE SEEN IT ALL.
CROWDED. EVEN IN BLACKOUTS, HOSPITALS KEEP POWER--SO PEOPLE COME FOR SHELTER. CRAZY THING, IT'S BEEN QUIET--LEAST SINCE DAREDEVIL CRUSHED THE UPRISING EARLIER.
INFORMATIO
COURSE, NO ONE KNEW IT WAS DAREDEVIL--NOT EVEN HE DID...AT FIRST.
WHEN KATE AND I FOUND OUT, HE SAID HE COULD HELP THE GIRL--FIND THE HELICOPTER.
PROTECTING HIS IDENTITY--THE LEAST WE CAN DO IN RETURN.
WE NEED TO MAKE HIM VANISH--MAKE LIKE DAREDEVIL WAS NEVER HERE.
RESIDENT PAIN, KWAME O'NEAL, IS HEAD OF VIDEO SECURITY--
--NOT SOMEONE IN ANY HURRY TO DO ME A FAVOR, BUT--
--HE LOVES THE KNICKS AS MUCH AS I DO--AN' HATES THE CELTICS MORE--
NEW YORK KNICKS
SECURITY
--'SPECIALLY GARNETT.
CHANDLER COSTELLO
ADMINISTRATOR
YOU SAID... SHORT, BALD... AND MOVED LIKE A--?
LIKE A NINJA, SIR--YES. THEN, POOF--GONE.
I'LL CHECK THIS AGAINST SECURITY VIDEO.

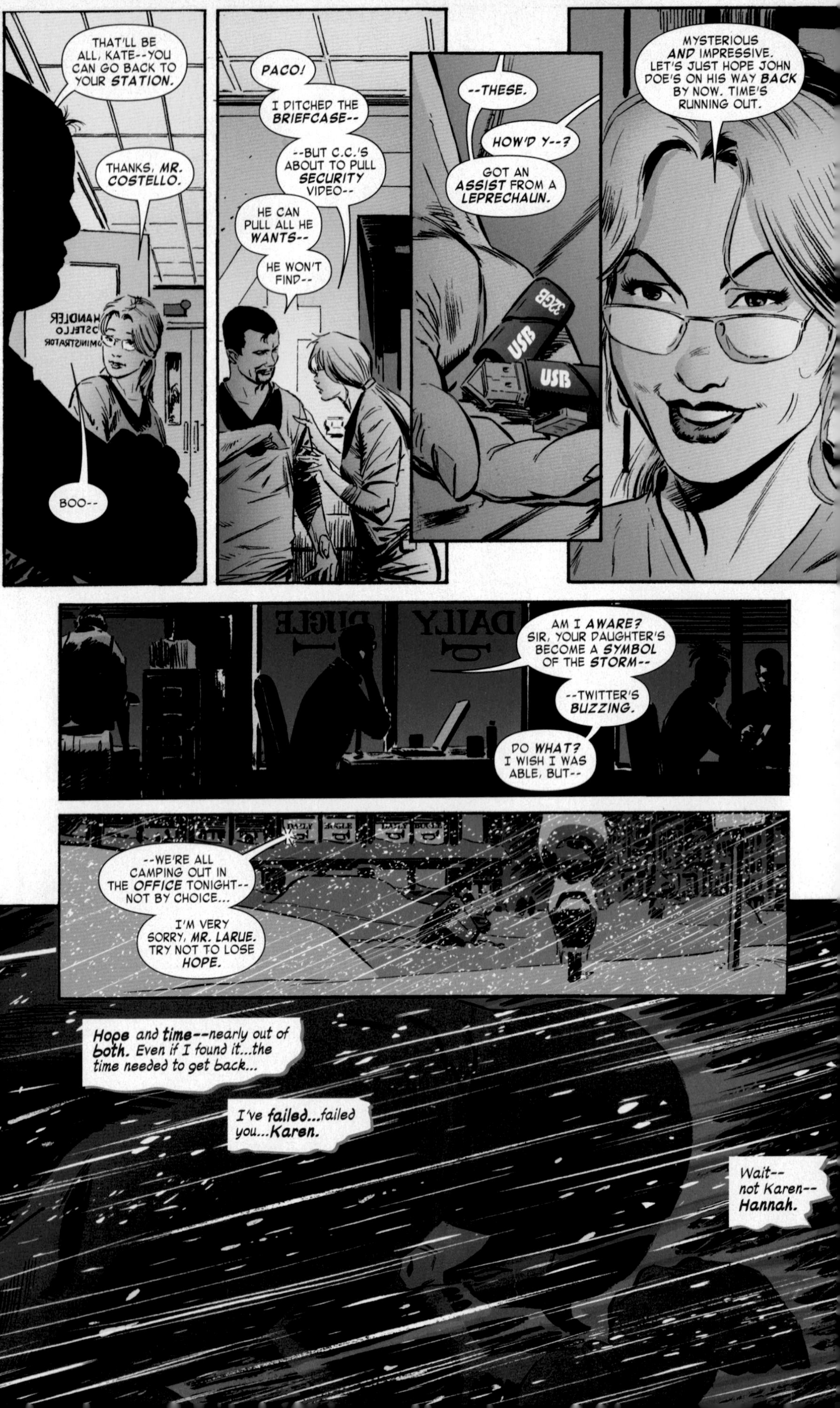
THAT'LL BE ALL, KATE--YOU CAN GO BACK TO YOUR STATION.
THANKS, MR. COSTELLO.
BOO--
PACO!
I DITCHED THE BRIEFCASE--
--BUT C.C.'S ABOUT TO PULL SECURITY VIDEO--
HE CAN PULL ALL HE WANTS--
HE WON'T FIND--
--THESE.
HOW'D Y--?
GOT AN ASSIST FROM A LEPRECHAUN.
USB
32GB
MYSTERIOUS AND IMPRESSIVE. LET'S JUST HOPE JOHN DOE'S ON HIS WAY BACK BY NOW. TIME'S RUNNING OUT.
AM I AWARE? SIR, YOUR DAUGHTER'S BECOME A SYMBOL OF THE STORM--
--TWITTER'S BUZZING.
DO WHAT? I WISH I WAS ABLE, BUT--
--WE'RE ALL CAMPING OUT IN THE OFFICE TONIGHT--NOT BY CHOICE...
I'M VERY SORRY, MR. LARUE. TRY NOT TO LOSE HOPE.
Hope and time--nearly out of both. Even if I found it...the time needed to get back...
I've failed...failed you...Karen.
Wait--not Karen--Hannah.

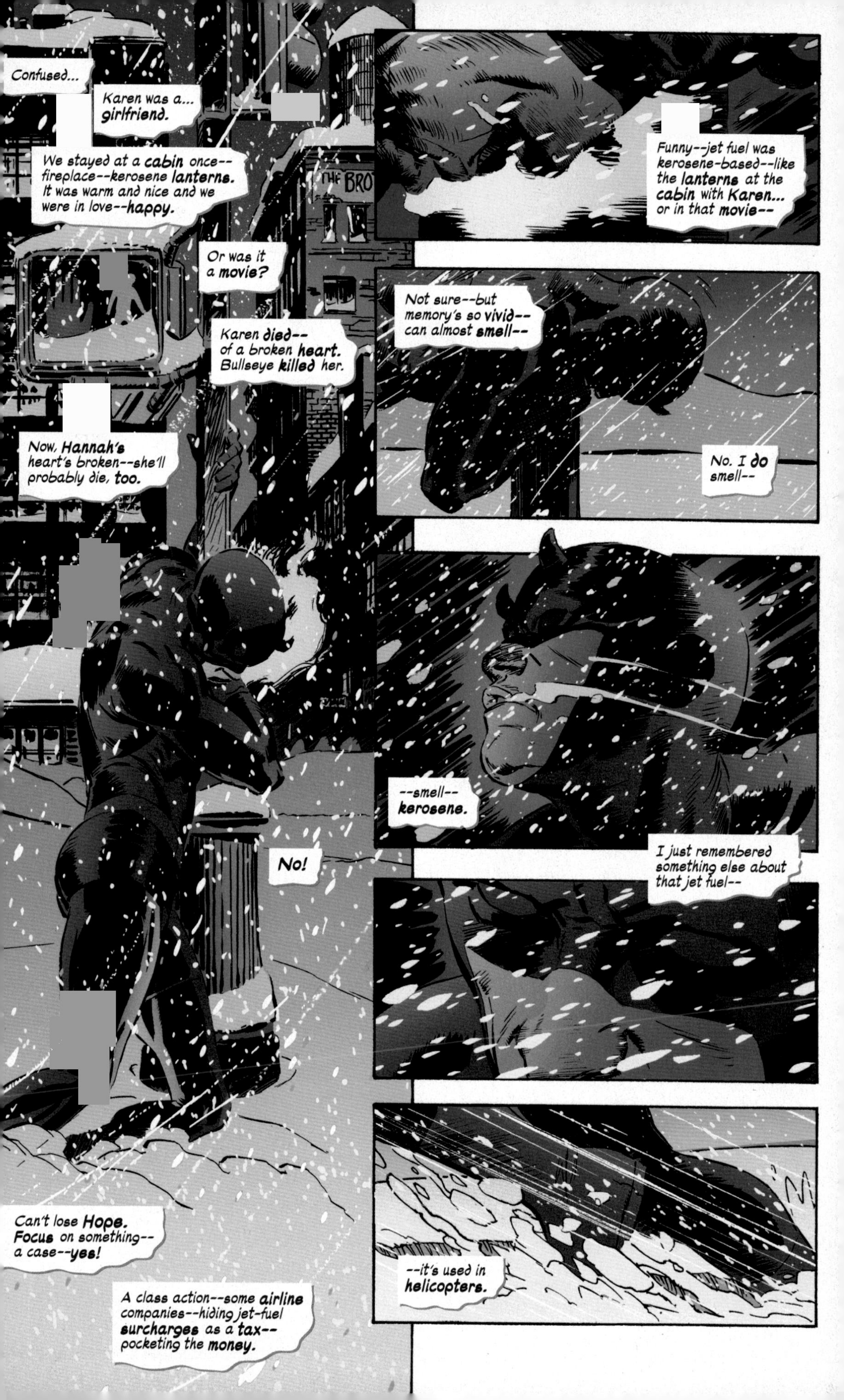

Confused...
Karen was a... girlfriend.
We stayed at a cabin once--fireplace--kerosene lanterns. It was warm and nice and we were in love--happy.
Or was it a movie?
Karen died--of a broken heart. Bullseye killed her.
Now, Hannah's heart's broken--she'll probably die, too.
No!
Can't lose Hope. Focus on something--a case--yes!
A class action--some airline companies--hiding jet-fuel surcharges as a tax--pocketing the money.
Funny--jet fuel was kerosene-based--like the lanterns at the cabin with Karen... or in that movie--
Not sure--but memory's so vivid--can almost smell--
No. I do smell--
--smell--kerosene.
I just remembered something else about that jet fuel--
--it's used in helicopters.

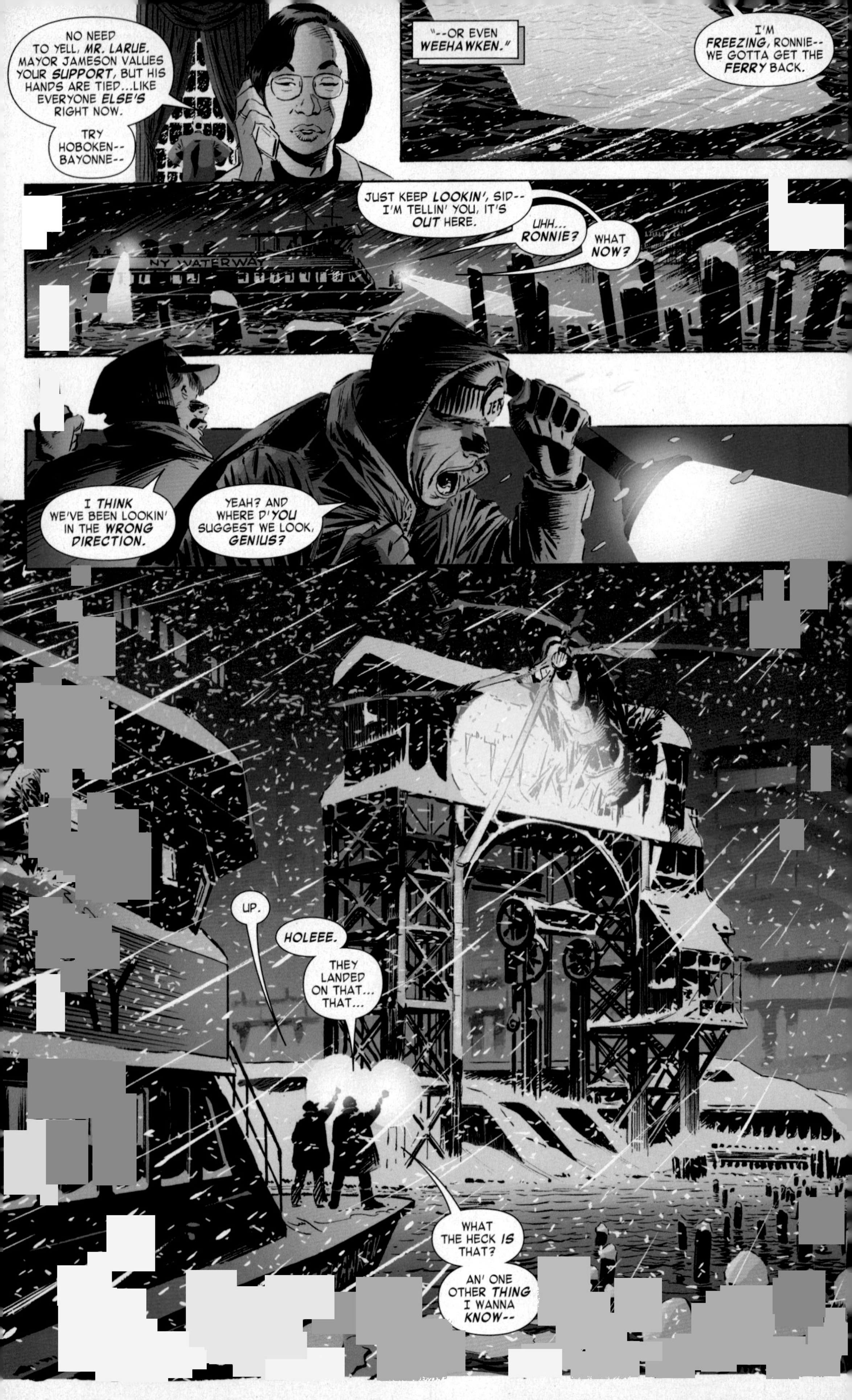
NO NEED TO YELL, MR. LARUE. MAYOR JAMESON VALUES YOUR SUPPORT, BUT HIS HANDS ARE TIED...LIKE EVERYONE ELSE'S RIGHT NOW.
TRY HOBOKEN-- BAYONNE--
"--OR EVEN WEEHAWKEN."
I'M FREEZING, RONNIE-- WE GOTTA GET THE FERRY BACK.
JUST KEEP LOOKIN', SID-- I'M TELLIN' YOU, IT'S OUT HERE.
UHH... RONNIE?
WHAT NOW?
NY WATERWAY
I THINK WE'VE BEEN LOOKIN' IN THE WRONG DIRECTION.
YEAH? AND WHERE D'YOU SUGGEST WE LOOK, GENIUS?
UP.
HOLEEE.
THEY LANDED ON THAT... THAT...
WHAT THE HECK IS THAT?
AN' ONE OTHER THING I WANNA KNOW--

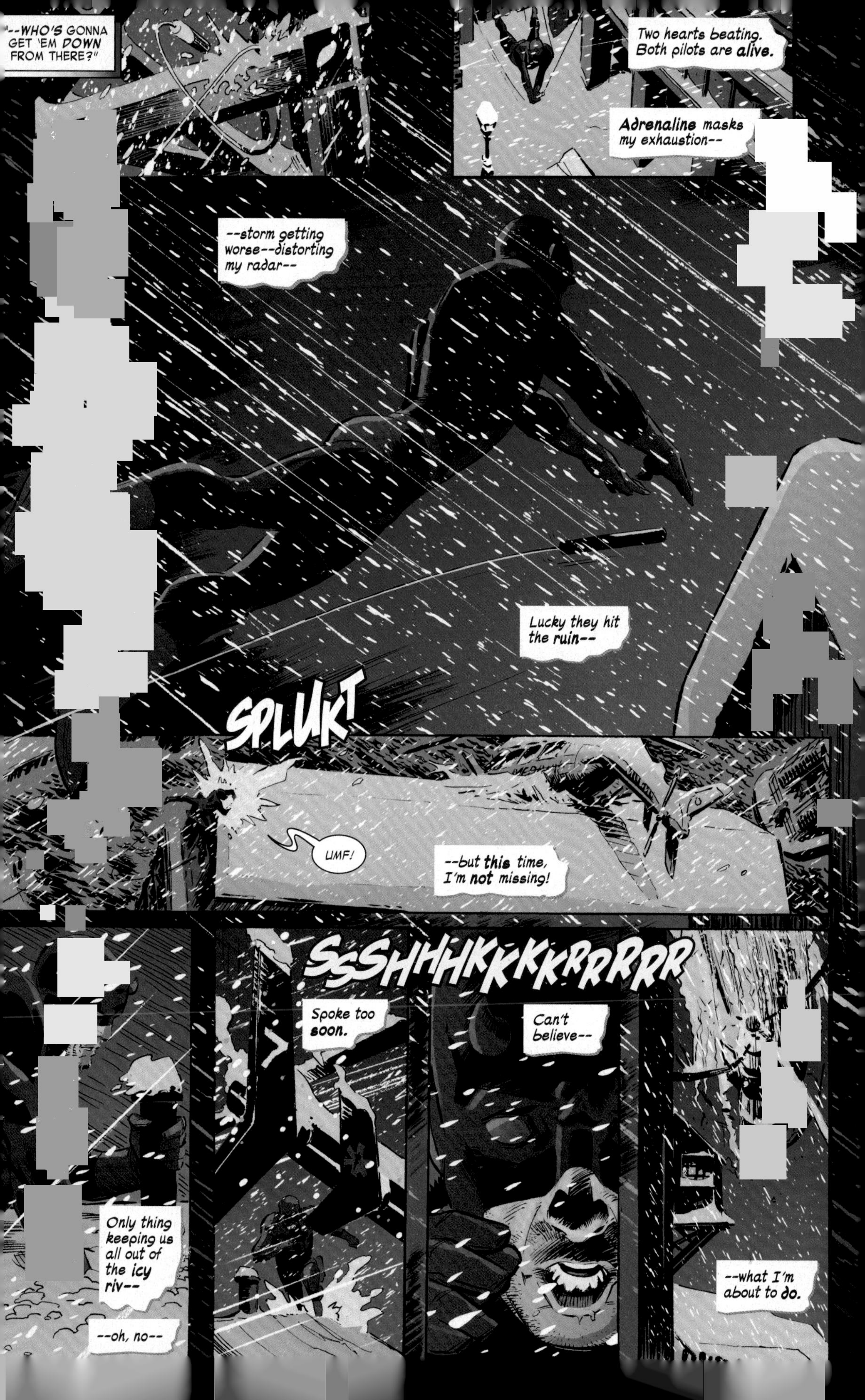
"--WHO'S GONNA GET 'EM DOWN FROM THERE?"
Two hearts beating. Both pilots are alive.
Adrenaline masks my exhaustion--
--storm getting worse--distorting my radar--
Lucky they hit the ruin--
SPLUKT
UMF!
--but this time, I'm not missing!
SSSHHHKKKKRRRRR
Only thing keeping us all out of the icy riv--
--oh, no--
Spoke too soon.
Can't believe--
--what I'm about to do.

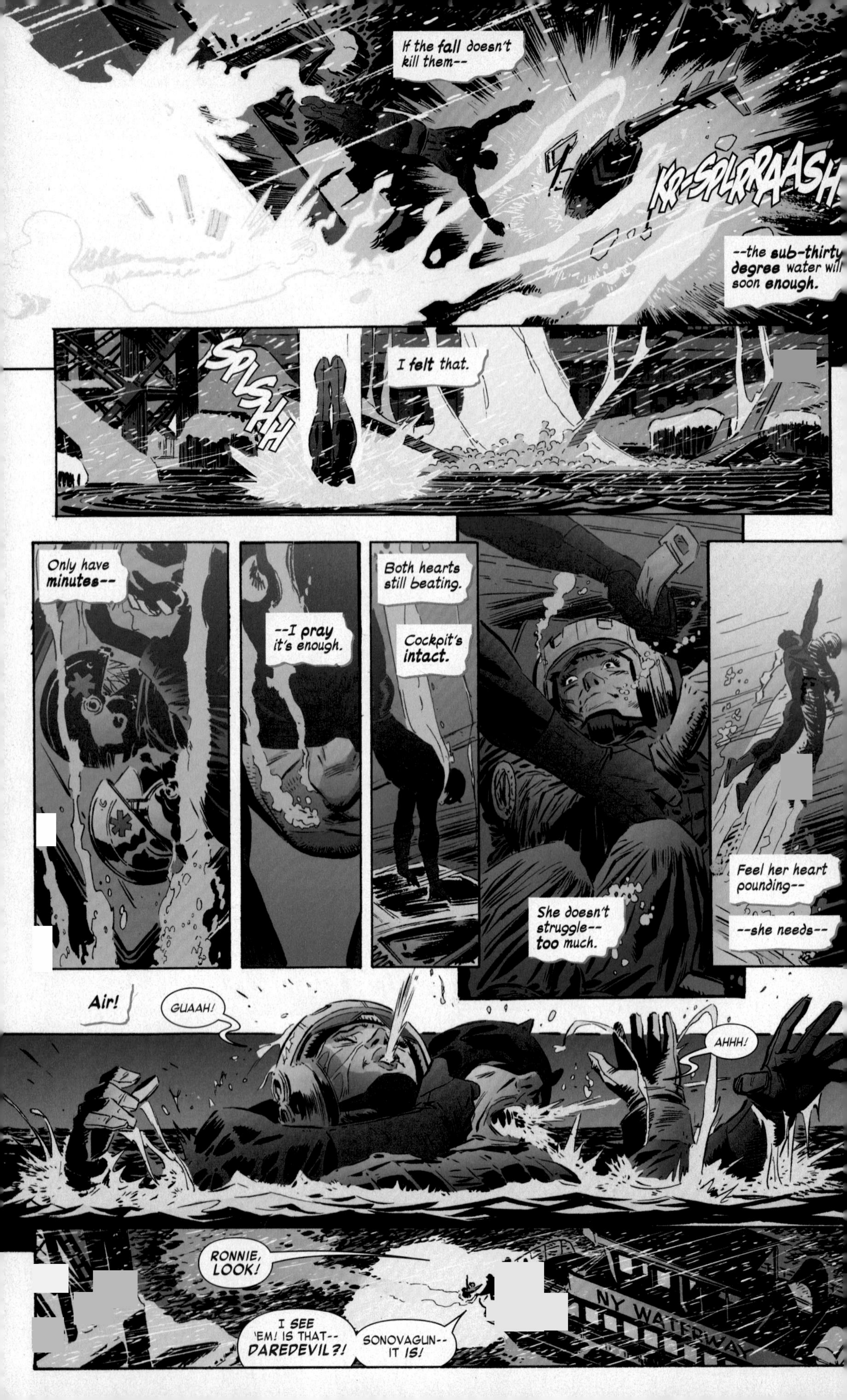
If the fall doesn't kill them--
KR-SPLRRAASH
--the sub-thirty degree water will soon enough.
SPLSHH
I felt that.
Only have minutes--
--I pray it's enough.
Both hearts still beating.
Cockpit's intact.
She doesn't struggle-- too much.
Feel her heart pounding--
--she needs--
Air!
GUAAH!
AHHH!
RONNIE, LOOK!
I SEE 'EM! IS THAT-- DAREDEVIL?!
SONOVAGUN-- IT IS!
NY WATERWA

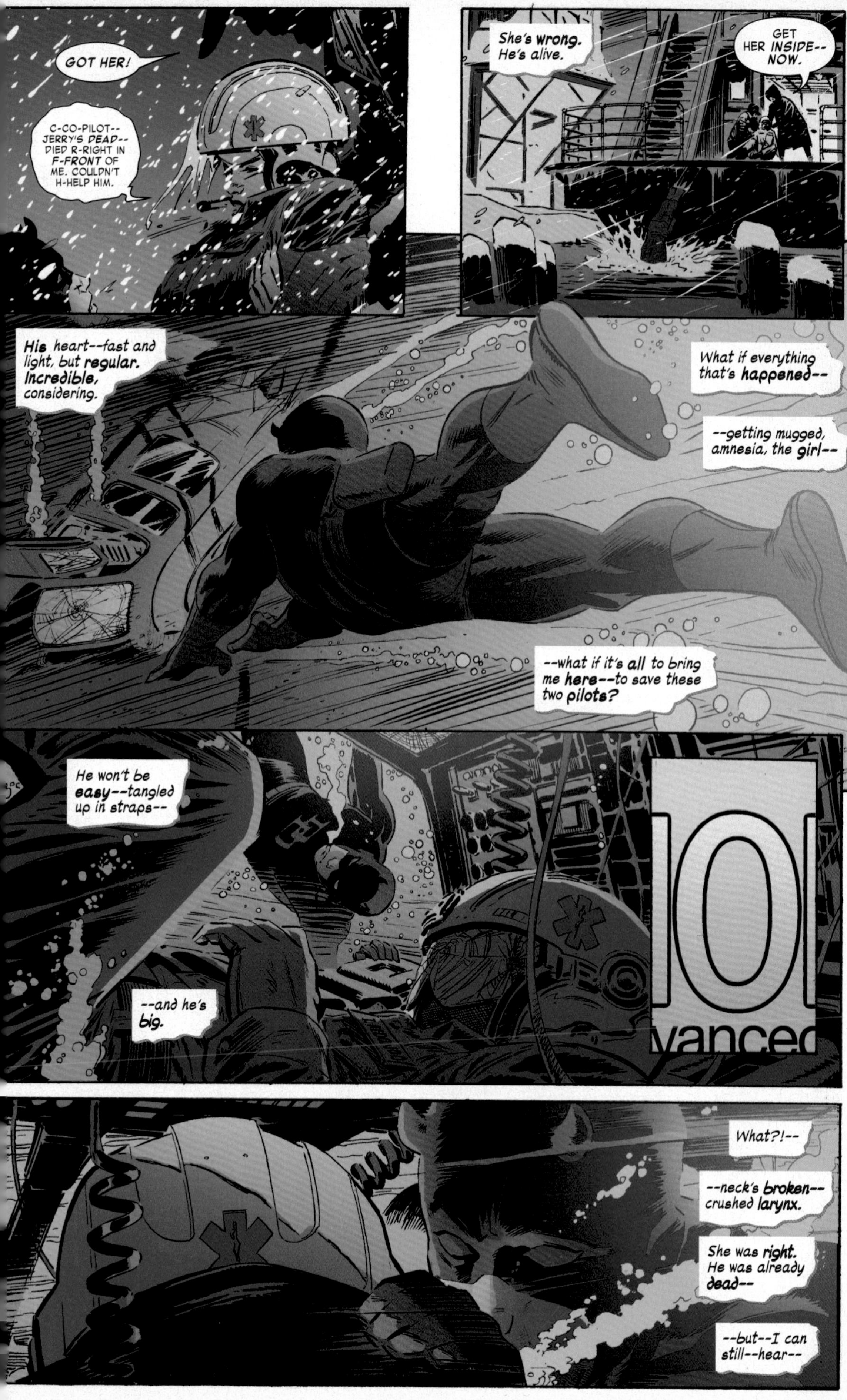

GOT HER!
C-CO-PILOT--
JERRY'S DEAD--
DIED R-RIGHT IN
F-FRONT OF
ME. COULDN'T
H-HELP HIM.
She's wrong.
He's alive.
GET
HER INSIDE--
NOW.
His heart--fast and
light, but regular.
Incredible,
considering.
What if everything
that's happened--
--getting mugged,
amnesia, the girl--
--what if it's all to bring
me here--to save these
two pilots?
He won't be
easy--tangled
up in straps--
--and he's
big.
What?!--
--neck's broken--
crushed larynx.
She was right.
He was already
dead--
--but--I can
still--hear--

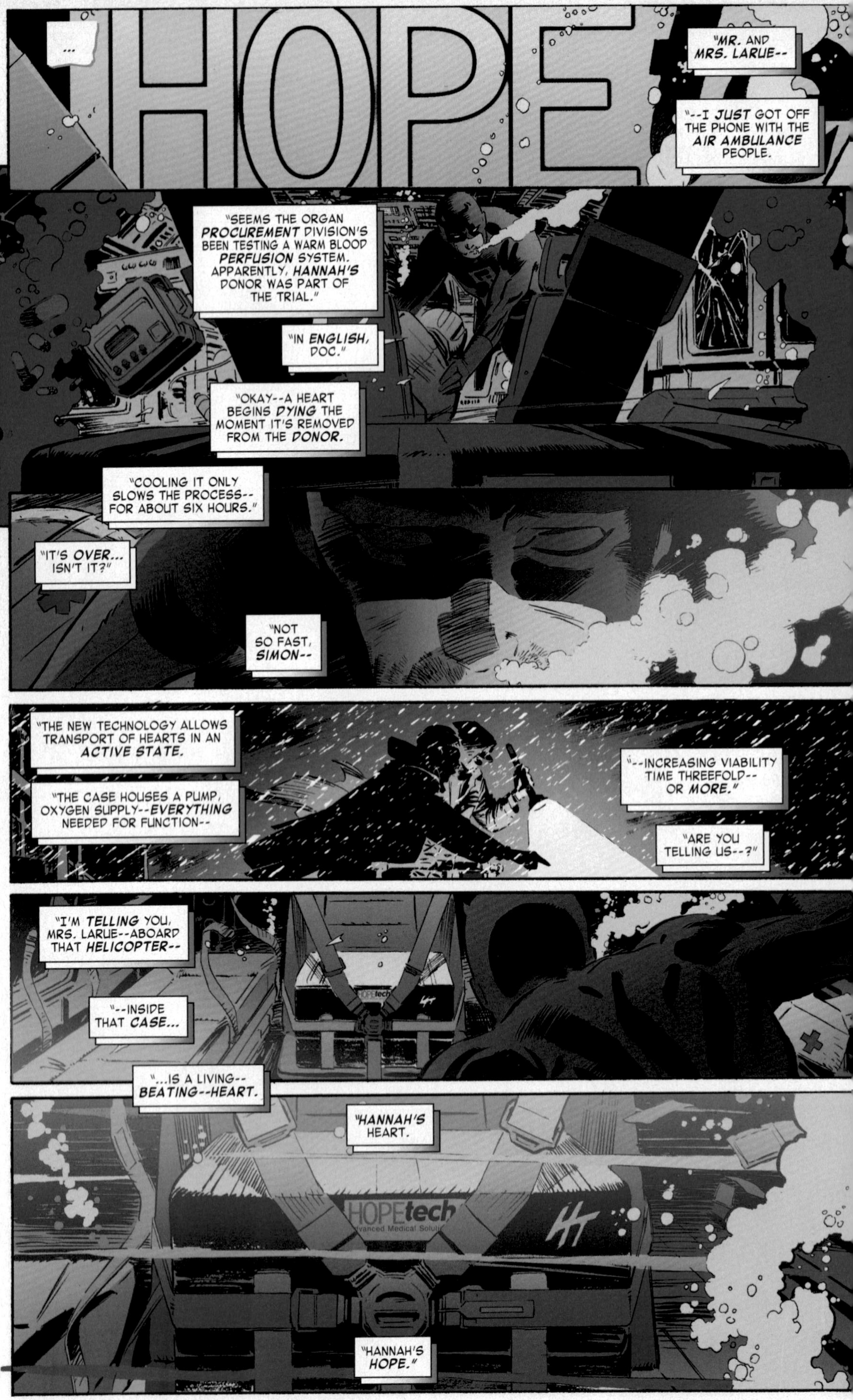
...
HOPE
"MR. AND MRS. LARUE--
"--I JUST GOT OFF THE PHONE WITH THE AIR AMBULANCE PEOPLE.
"SEEMS THE ORGAN PROCUREMENT DIVISION'S BEEN TESTING A WARM BLOOD PERFUSION SYSTEM. APPARENTLY, HANNAH'S DONOR WAS PART OF THE TRIAL."
"IN ENGLISH, DOC."
"OKAY--A HEART BEGINS DYING THE MOMENT IT'S REMOVED FROM THE DONOR.
"COOLING IT ONLY SLOWS THE PROCESS--FOR ABOUT SIX HOURS."
"IT'S OVER... ISN'T IT?"
"NOT SO FAST, SIMON--
"THE NEW TECHNOLOGY ALLOWS TRANSPORT OF HEARTS IN AN ACTIVE STATE.
"THE CASE HOUSES A PUMP, OXYGEN SUPPLY--EVERYTHING NEEDED FOR FUNCTION--
"--INCREASING VIABILITY TIME THREEFOLD--OR MORE."
"ARE YOU TELLING US--?"
"I'M TELLING YOU, MRS. LARUE--ABOARD THAT HELICOPTER--
"--INSIDE THAT CASE...
"...IS A LIVING--BEATING--HEART.
"HANNAH'S HEART.
HOPEtech
"HANNAH'S HOPE."

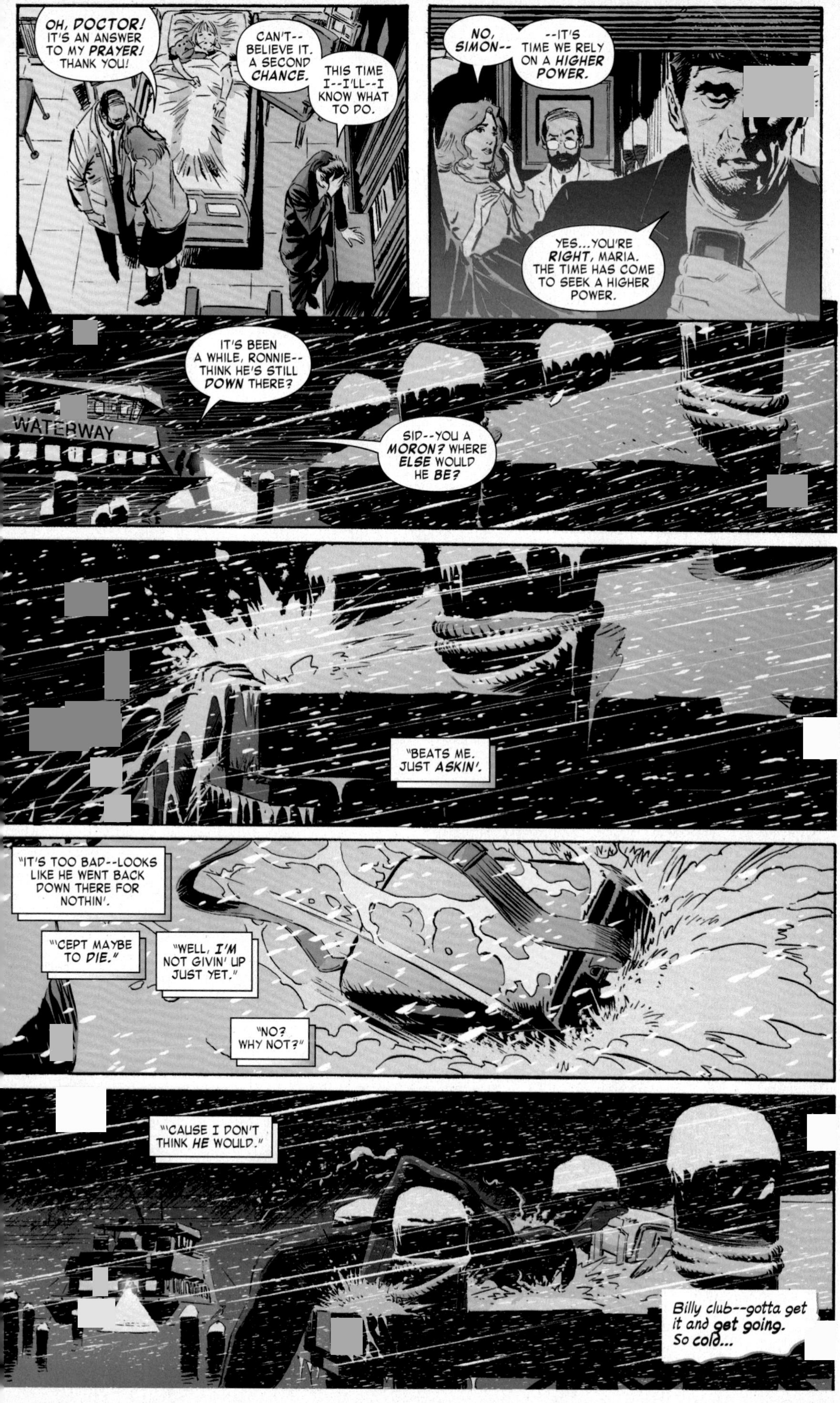
OH, DOCTOR! IT'S AN ANSWER TO MY PRAYER! THANK YOU!
CAN'T-- BELIEVE IT. A SECOND CHANCE.
THIS TIME I--I'LL--I KNOW WHAT TO DO.
NO, SIMON--
--IT'S TIME WE RELY ON A HIGHER POWER.
YES...YOU'RE RIGHT, MARIA. THE TIME HAS COME TO SEEK A HIGHER POWER.
WATERWAY
IT'S BEEN A WHILE, RONNIE-- THINK HE'S STILL DOWN THERE?
SID--YOU A MORON? WHERE ELSE WOULD HE BE?
"BEATS ME. JUST ASKIN'.
"IT'S TOO BAD--LOOKS LIKE HE WENT BACK DOWN THERE FOR NOTHIN'.
"'CEPT MAYBE TO DIE."
"WELL, I'M NOT GIVIN' UP JUST YET."
"NO? WHY NOT?"
"'CAUSE I DON'T THINK HE WOULD."
Billy club--gotta get it and get going. So cold...

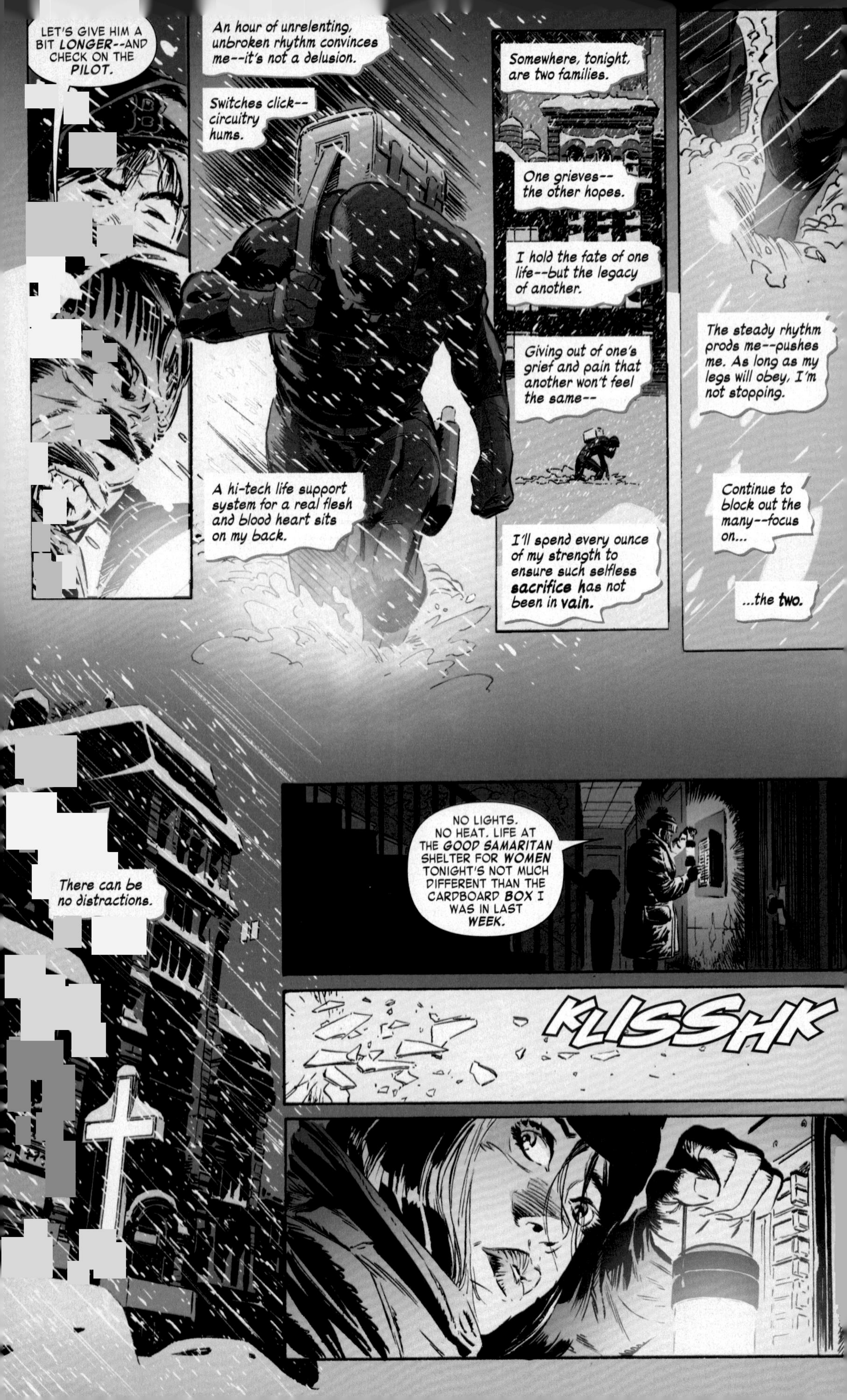

LET'S GIVE HIM A BIT LONGER--AND CHECK ON THE PILOT.
An hour of unrelenting, unbroken rhythm convinces me--it's not a delusion.
Switches click--circuitry hums.
A hi-tech life support system for a real flesh and blood heart sits on my back.
Somewhere, tonight, are two families.
One grieves--the other hopes.
I hold the fate of one life--but the legacy of another.
Giving out of one's grief and pain that another won't feel the same--
I'll spend every ounce of my strength to ensure such selfless sacrifice has not been in vain.
The steady rhythm prods me--pushes me. As long as my legs will obey, I'm not stopping.
Continue to block out the many--focus on...
...the two.
There can be no distractions.
NO LIGHTS. NO HEAT. LIFE AT THE GOOD SAMARITAN SHELTER FOR WOMEN TONIGHT'S NOT MUCH DIFFERENT THAN THE CARDBOARD BOX I WAS IN LAST WEEK.
KLISSHK

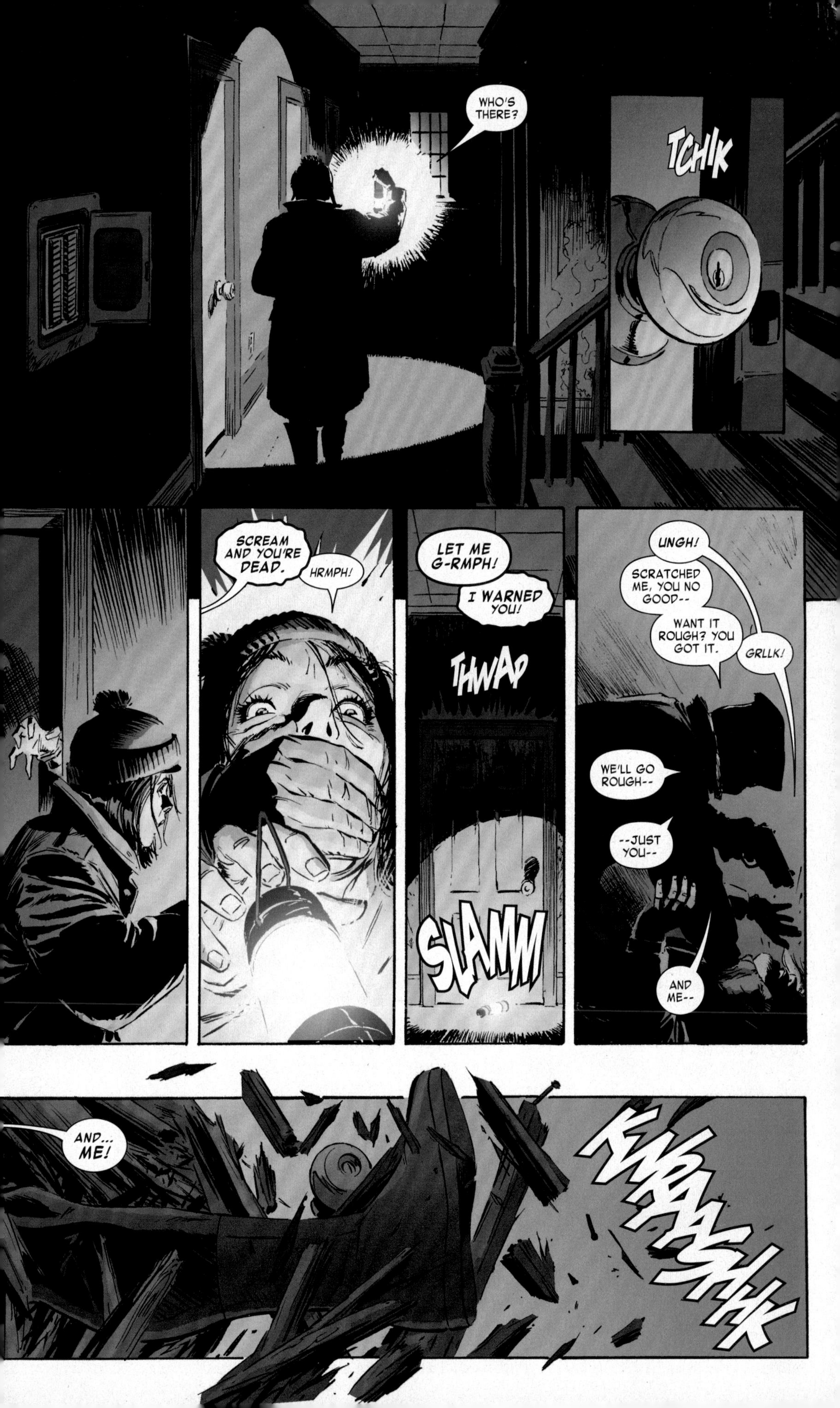
WHO'S THERE?
TCHIK
SCREAM AND YOU'RE DEAD.
HRMPH!
LET ME G-RMPH!
I WARNED YOU!
THWAP
SLAMM
UNGH!
SCRATCHED ME, YOU NO GOOD--
WANT IT ROUGH? YOU GOT IT.
GRLLK!
WE'LL GO ROUGH--
--JUST YOU--
AND ME--
AND... ME!
KRASHHK

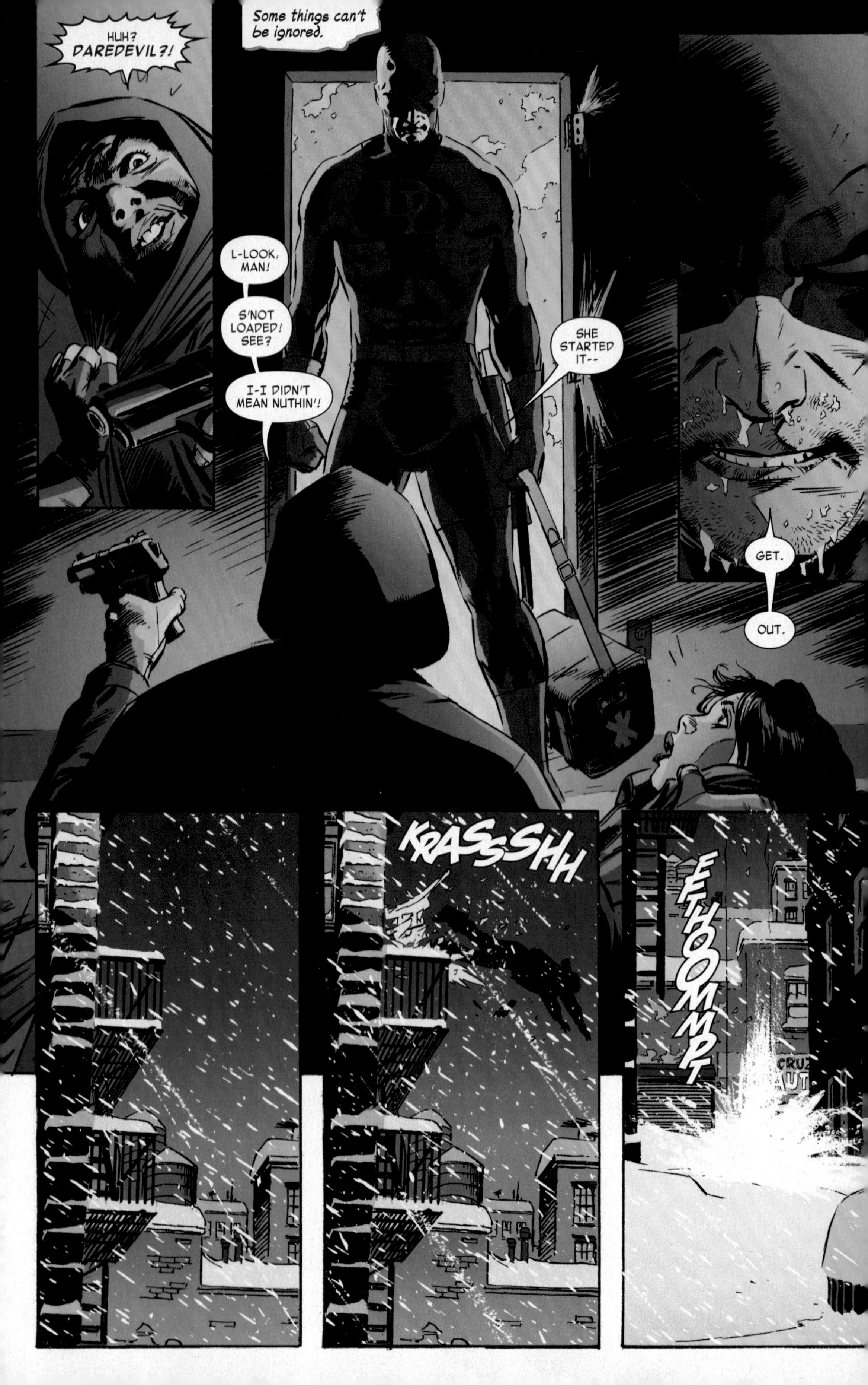
HUH? DAREDEVIL?!
Some things can't be ignored.
L-LOOK, MAN!
S'NOT LOADED! SEE?
I-I DIDN'T MEAN NUTHIN'!
SHE STARTED IT--
GET.
OUT.
KRASSSHH
FTHOOMMPT

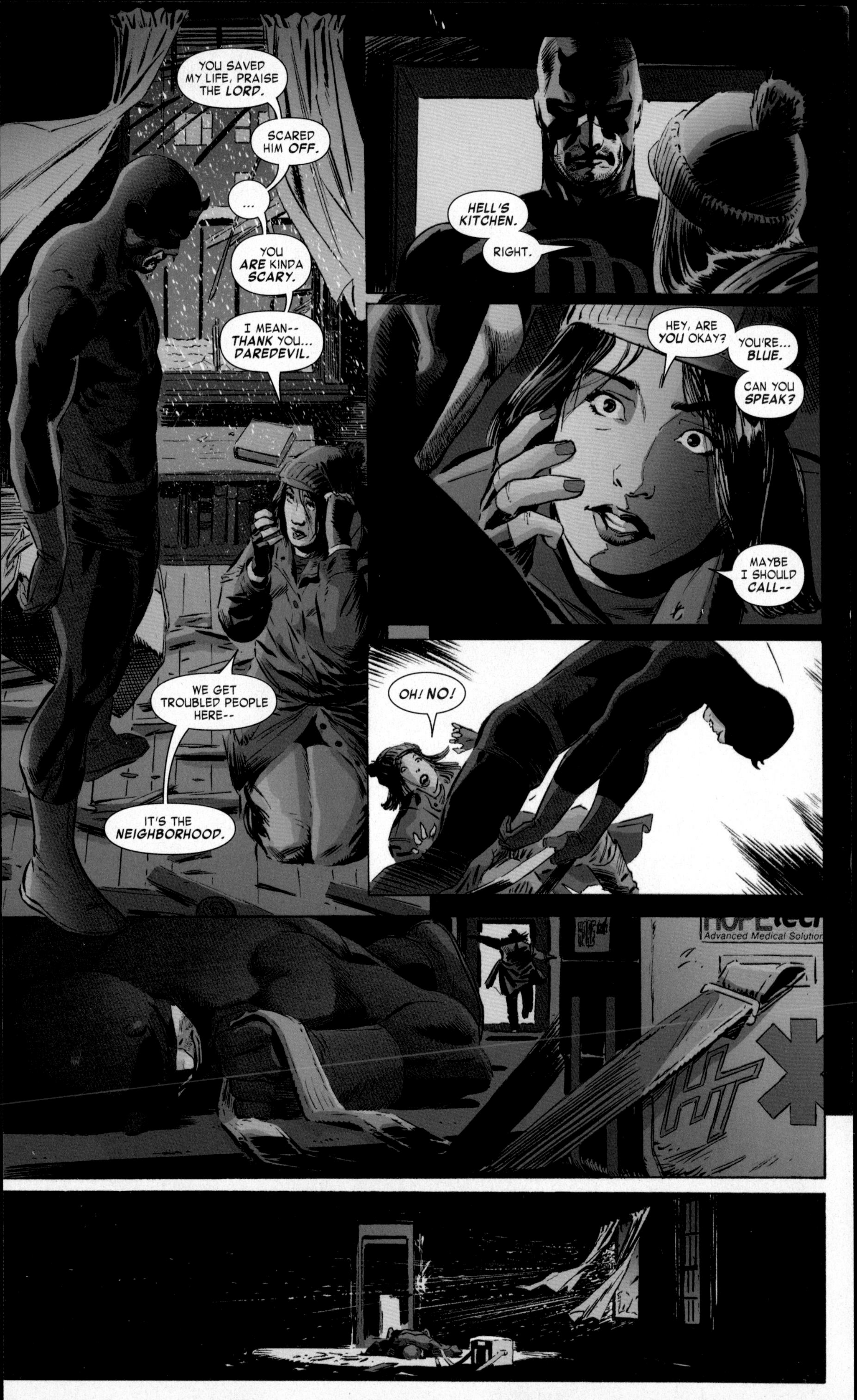

YOU SAVED MY LIFE, PRAISE THE LORD.
SCARED HIM OFF.
...
YOU ARE KINDA SCARY.
I MEAN-- THANK YOU... DAREDEVIL.
WE GET TROUBLED PEOPLE HERE--
IT'S THE NEIGHBORHOOD.
HELL'S KITCHEN.
RIGHT.
HEY, ARE YOU OKAY?
YOU'RE... BLUE.
CAN YOU SPEAK?
MAYBE I SHOULD CALL--
OH! NO!
Advanced Medical Solution

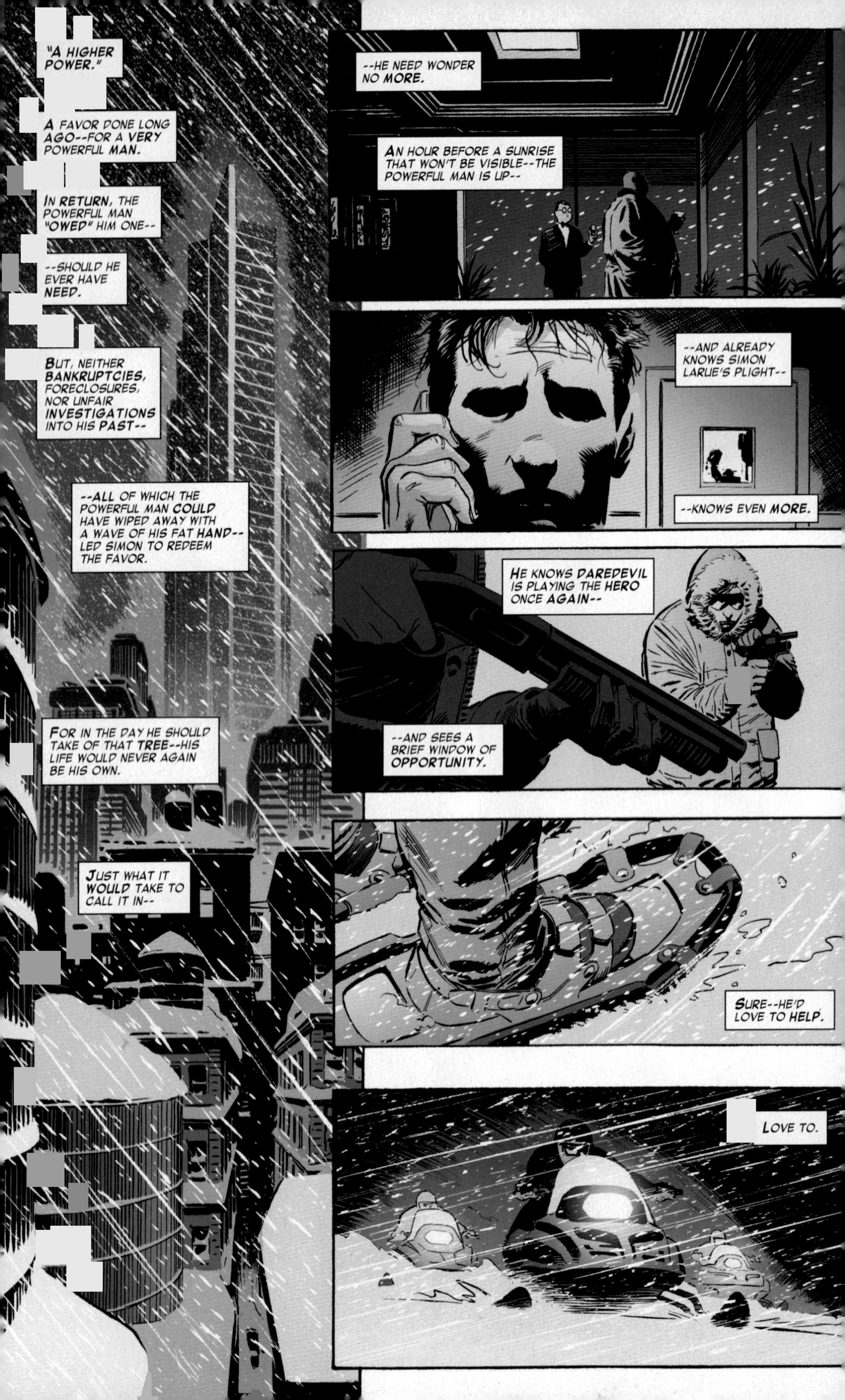
"A HIGHER POWER."
A FAVOR DONE LONG AGO--FOR A VERY POWERFUL MAN.
IN RETURN, THE POWERFUL MAN "OWED" HIM ONE--
--SHOULD HE EVER HAVE NEED.
BUT, NEITHER BANKRUPTCIES, FORECLOSURES, NOR UNFAIR INVESTIGATIONS INTO HIS PAST--
--ALL OF WHICH THE POWERFUL MAN COULD HAVE WIPED AWAY WITH A WAVE OF HIS FAT HAND--LED SIMON TO REDEEM THE FAVOR.
FOR IN THE DAY HE SHOULD TAKE OF THAT TREE--HIS LIFE WOULD NEVER AGAIN BE HIS OWN.
JUST WHAT IT WOULD TAKE TO CALL IT IN--
--HE NEED WONDER NO MORE.
AN HOUR BEFORE A SUNRISE THAT WON'T BE VISIBLE--THE POWERFUL MAN IS UP--
--AND ALREADY KNOWS SIMON LARUE'S PLIGHT--
--KNOWS EVEN MORE.
HE KNOWS DAREDEVIL IS PLAYING THE HERO ONCE AGAIN--
--AND SEES A BRIEF WINDOW OF OPPORTUNITY.
SURE--HE'D LOVE TO HELP.
LOVE TO.

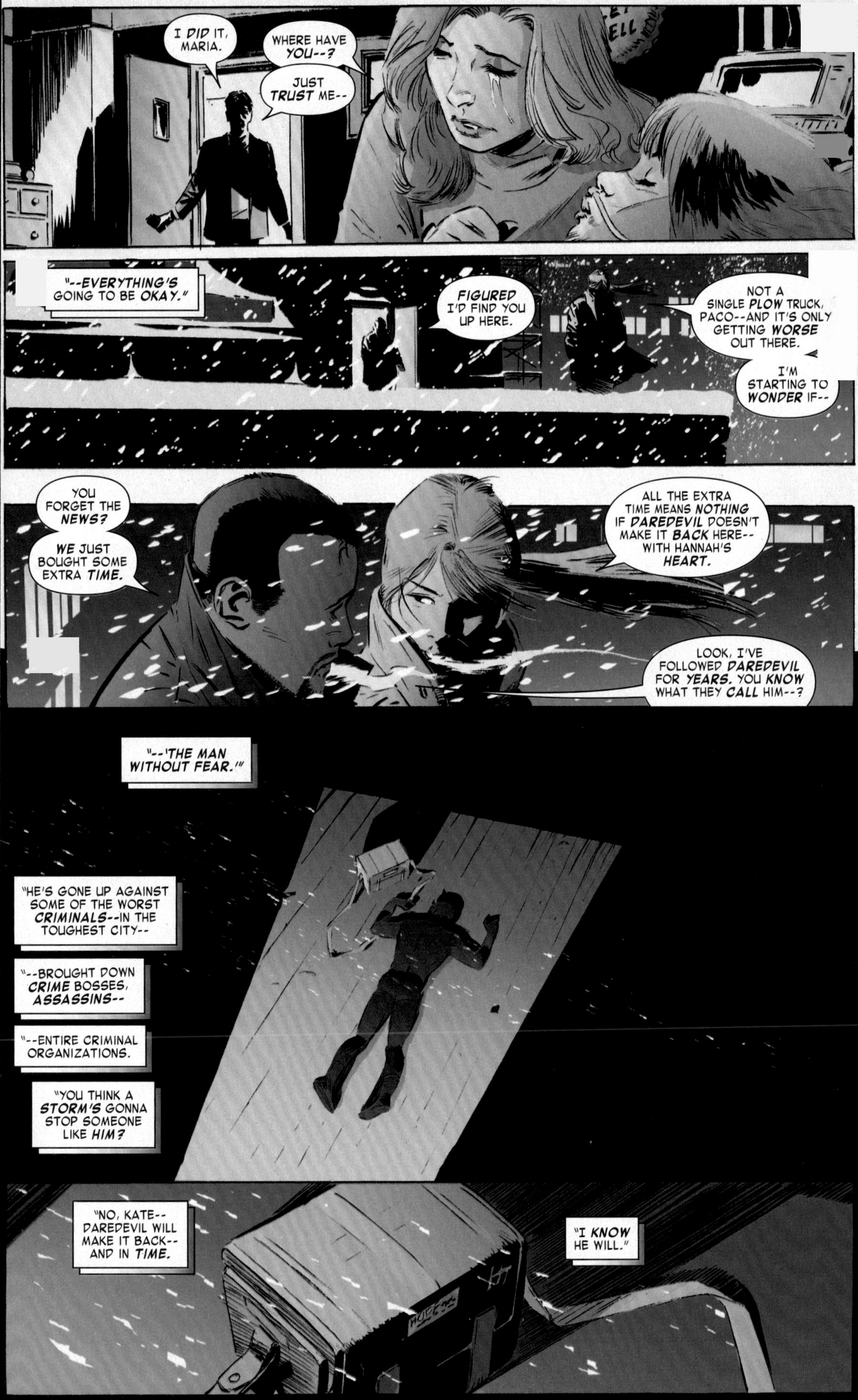
I DID IT, MARIA.
WHERE HAVE YOU--?
JUST TRUST ME--
"--EVERYTHING'S GOING TO BE OKAY."
FIGURED I'D FIND YOU UP HERE.
NOT A SINGLE PLOW TRUCK, PACO--AND IT'S ONLY GETTING WORSE OUT THERE.
I'M STARTING TO WONDER IF--
YOU FORGET THE NEWS?
WE JUST BOUGHT SOME EXTRA TIME.
ALL THE EXTRA TIME MEANS NOTHING IF DAREDEVIL DOESN'T MAKE IT BACK HERE--WITH HANNAH'S HEART.
LOOK, I'VE FOLLOWED DAREDEVIL FOR YEARS. YOU KNOW WHAT THEY CALL HIM--?
"--'THE MAN WITHOUT FEAR.'"
"HE'S GONE UP AGAINST SOME OF THE WORST CRIMINALS--IN THE TOUGHEST CITY--
"--BROUGHT DOWN CRIME BOSSES, ASSASSINS--
"--ENTIRE CRIMINAL ORGANIZATIONS.
"YOU THINK A STORM'S GONNA STOP SOMEONE LIKE HIM?
"NO, KATE--DAREDEVIL WILL MAKE IT BACK--AND IN TIME.
"I KNOW HE WILL."

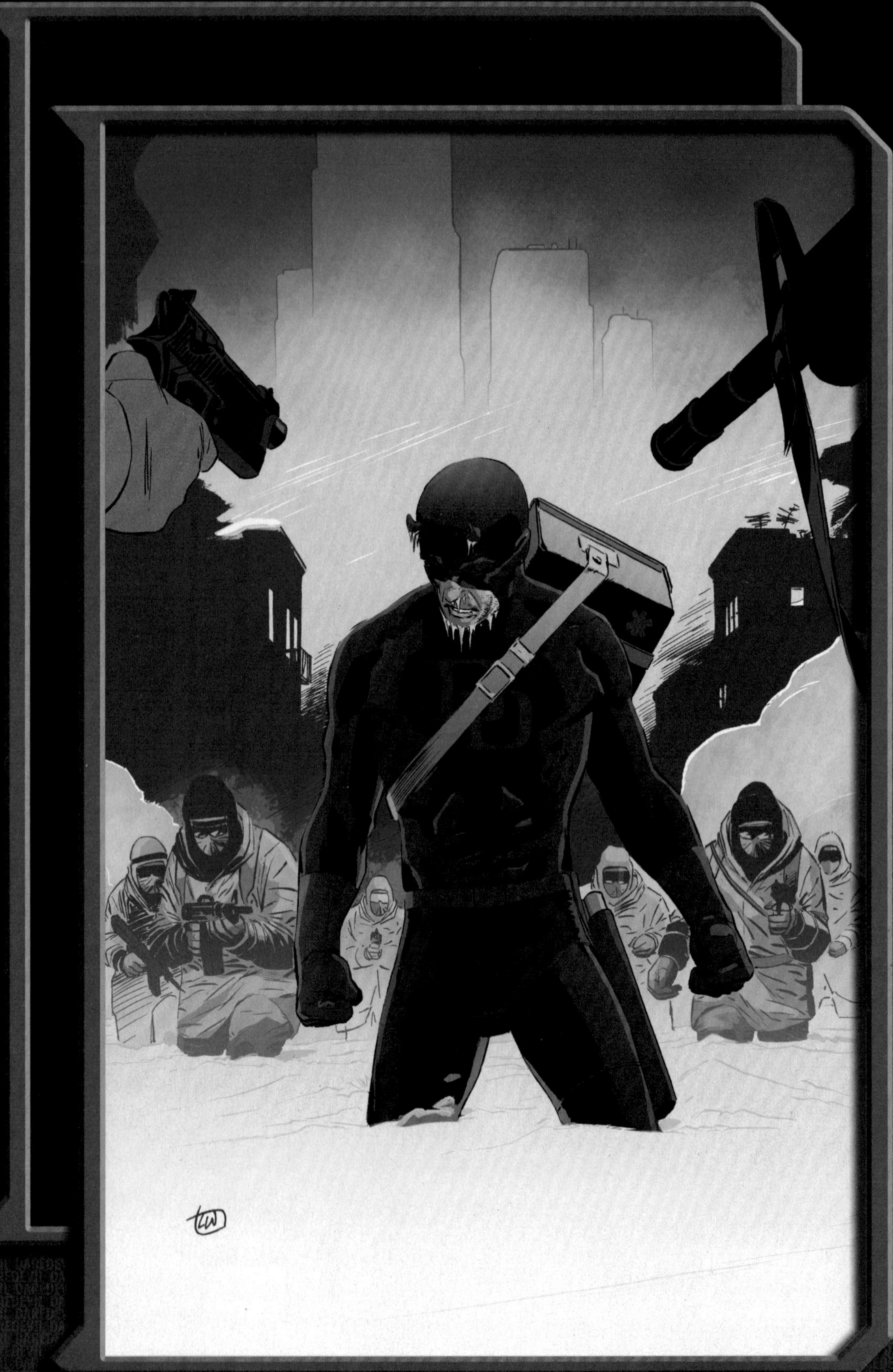

#3 — ANGELS UNAWARE
PART THREE: CHANGE OF HEART

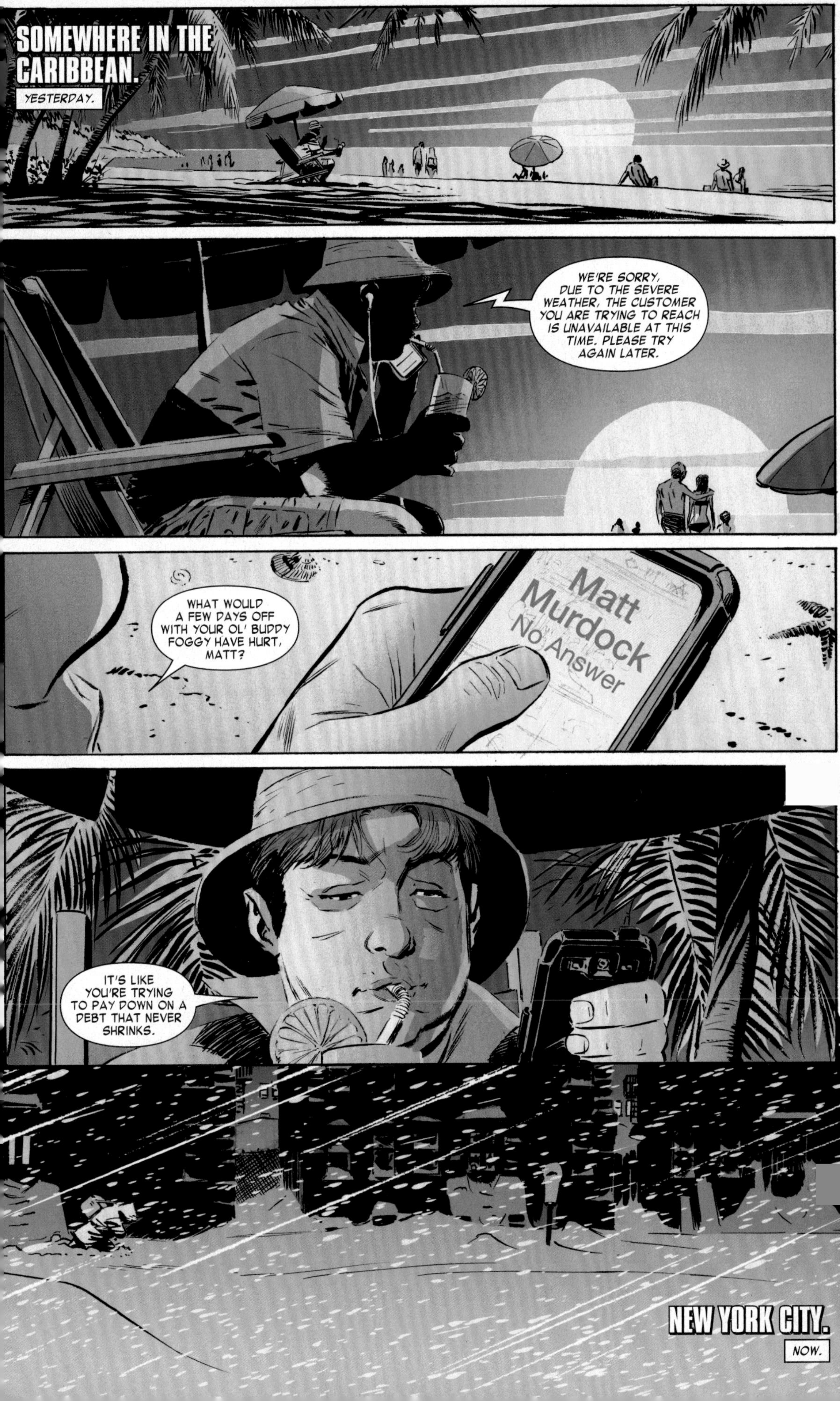
SOMEWHERE IN THE CARIBBEAN.
YESTERDAY.
WE'RE SORRY, DUE TO THE SEVERE WEATHER, THE CUSTOMER YOU ARE TRYING TO REACH IS UNAVAILABLE AT THIS TIME. PLEASE TRY AGAIN LATER.
Matt Murdock
No Answer
WHAT WOULD A FEW DAYS OFF WITH YOUR OL' BUDDY FOGGY HAVE HURT, MATT?
IT'S LIKE YOU'RE TRYING TO PAY DOWN ON A DEBT THAT NEVER SHRINKS.
NEW YORK CITY.
NOW.

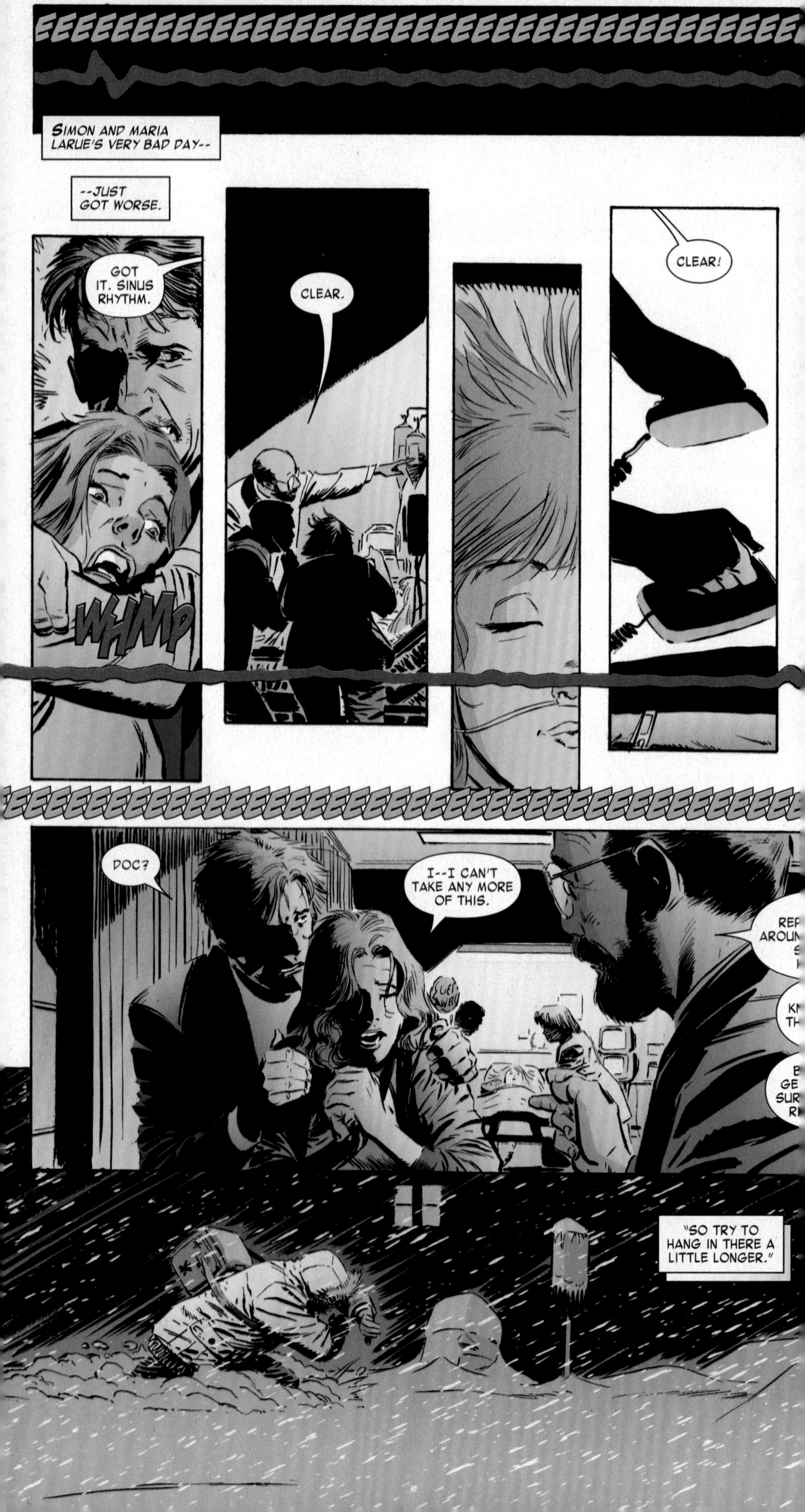
SIMON AND MARIA LARUE'S VERY BAD DAY--
--JUST GOT WORSE.
GOT IT. SINUS RHYTHM.
WHMP
CLEAR.
CLEAR!
DOC?
I--I CAN'T TAKE ANY MORE OF THIS.
"SO TRY TO HANG IN THERE A LITTLE LONGER."

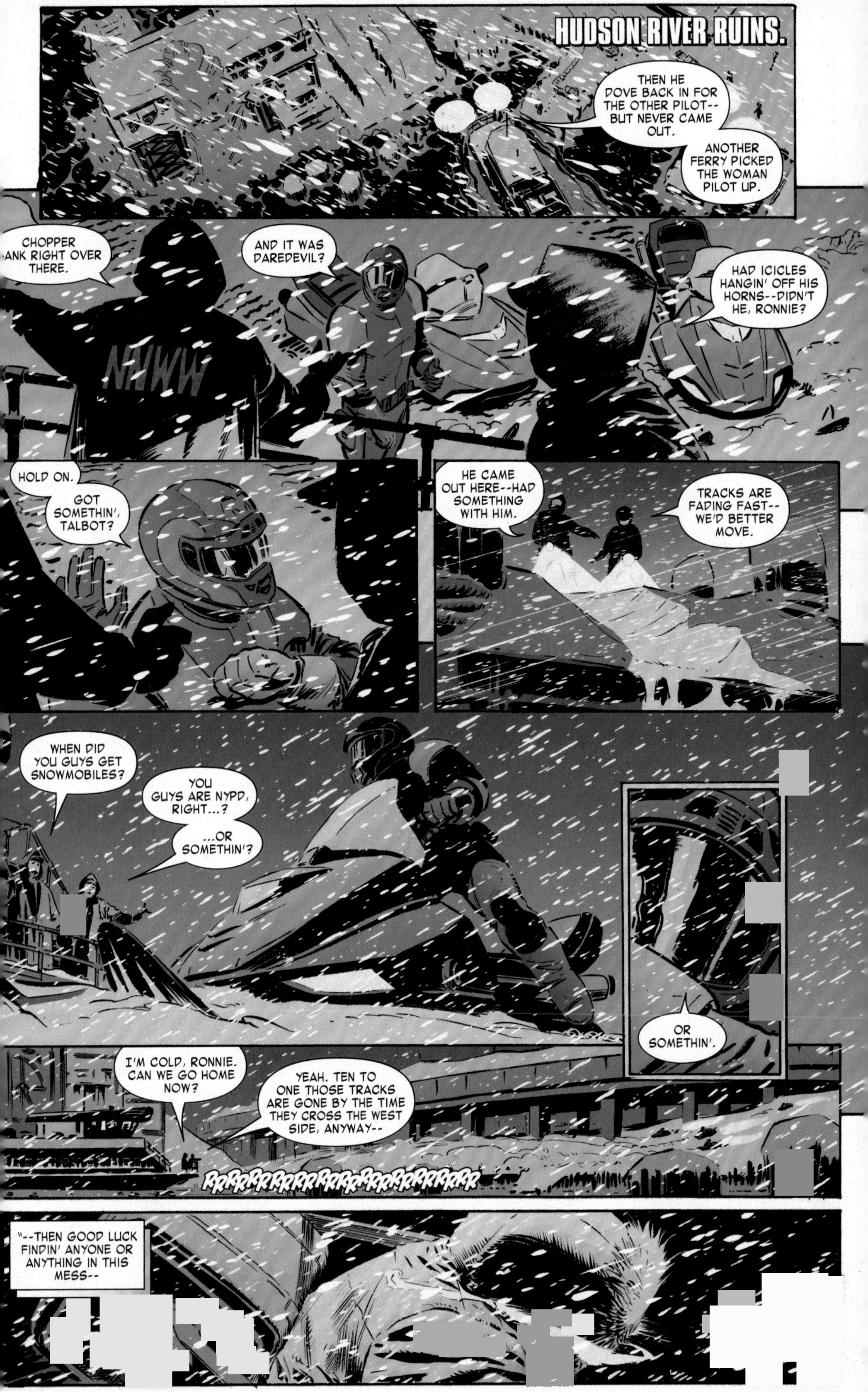
HUDSON RIVER RUINS.
THEN HE DOVE BACK IN FOR THE OTHER PILOT--BUT NEVER CAME OUT.
ANOTHER FERRY PICKED THE WOMAN PILOT UP.
CHOPPER ANK RIGHT OVER THERE.
AND IT WAS DAREDEVIL?
HAD ICICLES HANGIN' OFF HIS HORNS--DIDN'T HE, RONNIE?
NHWW
HOLD ON.
GOT SOMETHIN', TALBOT?
HE CAME OUT HERE--HAD SOMETHING WITH HIM.
TRACKS ARE FADING FAST--WE'D BETTER MOVE.
WHEN DID YOU GUYS GET SNOWMOBILES?
YOU GUYS ARE NYPD, RIGHT...?
...OR SOMETHIN'?
OR SOMETHIN'.
I'M COLD, RONNIE. CAN WE GO HOME NOW?
YEAH. TEN TO ONE THOSE TRACKS ARE GONE BY THE TIME THEY CROSS THE WEST SIDE, ANYWAY--
RRRRRRRRRRRRRRRRRRRRRRRRRRR
"--THEN GOOD LUCK FINDIN' ANYONE OR ANYTHING IN THIS MESS--

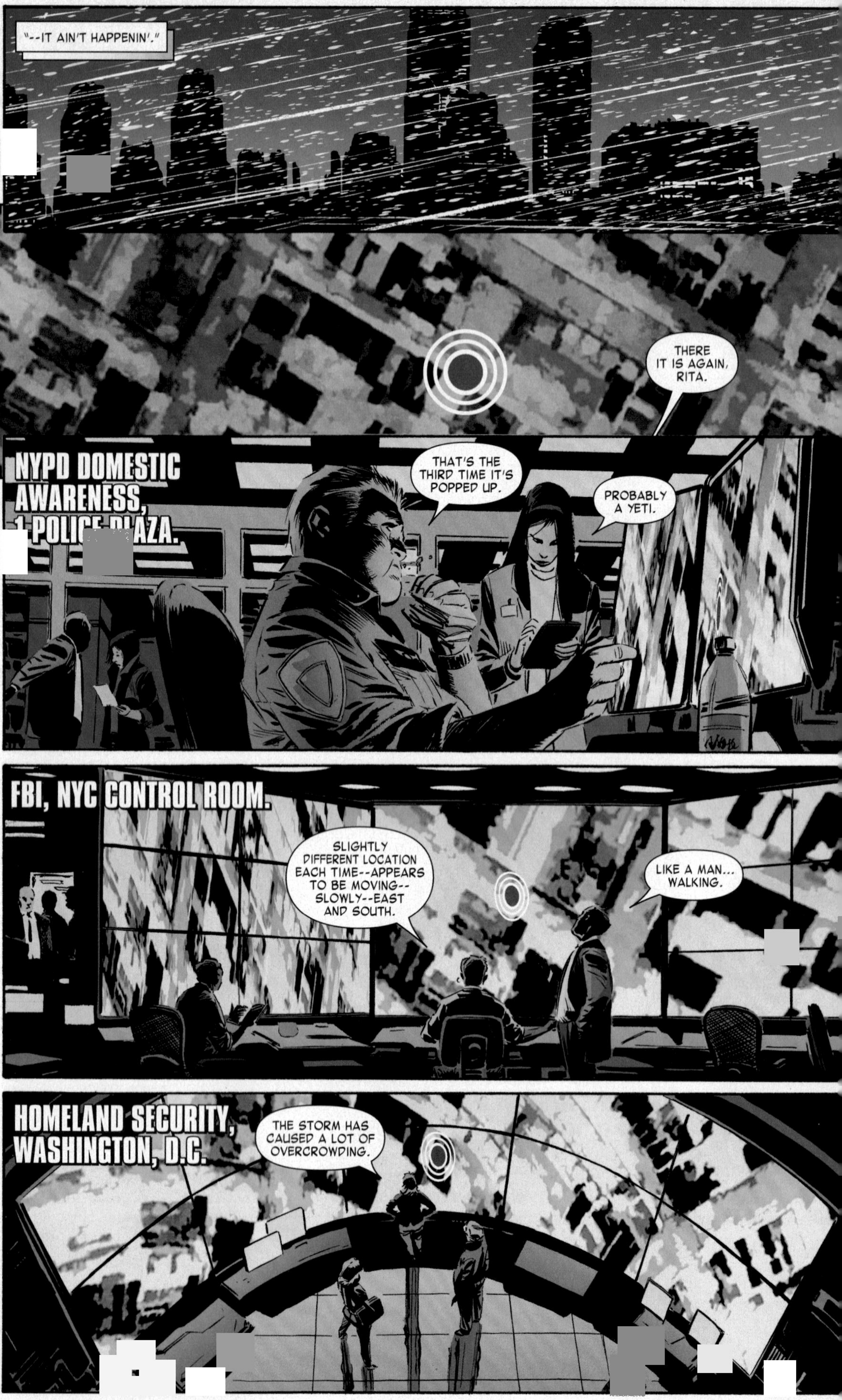
"--IT AIN'T HAPPENIN'."
THERE IT IS AGAIN, RITA.
NYPD DOMESTIC AWARENESS, 1 POLICE PLAZA.
THAT'S THE THIRD TIME IT'S POPPED UP.
PROBABLY A YETI.
FBI, NYC CONTROL ROOM.
SLIGHTLY DIFFERENT LOCATION EACH TIME--APPEARS TO BE MOVING--SLOWLY--EAST AND SOUTH.
LIKE A MAN... WALKING.
HOMELAND SECURITY, WASHINGTON, D.C.
THE STORM HAS CAUSED A LOT OF OVERCROWDING.

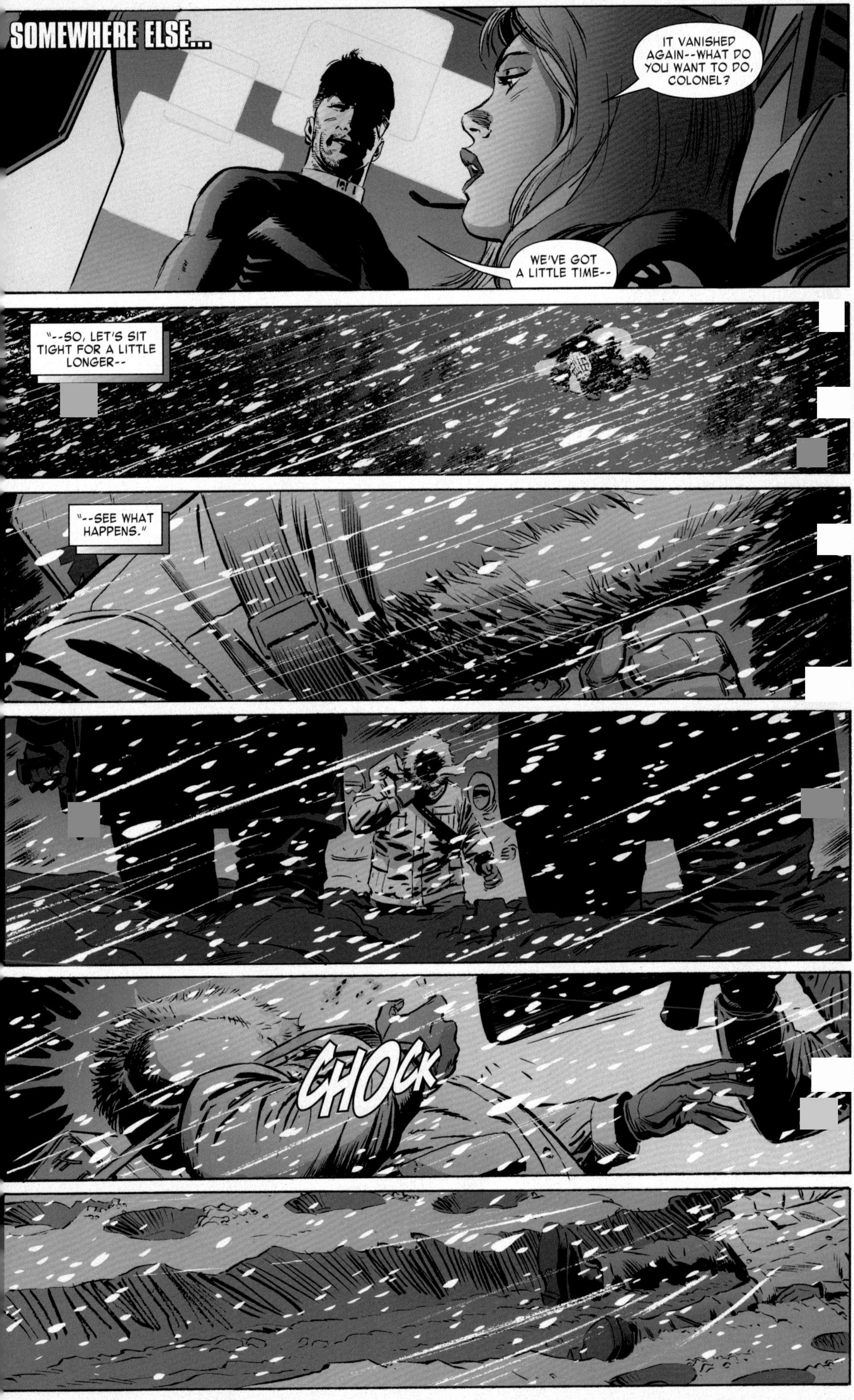
SOMEWHERE ELSE...
IT VANISHED AGAIN--WHAT DO YOU WANT TO DO, COLONEL?
WE'VE GOT A LITTLE TIME--
"--SO, LET'S SIT TIGHT FOR A LITTLE LONGER--
"--SEE WHAT HAPPENS."
CHOCK

Dreams can tell you things.
And the one I just had is a doozy.

Countless times, my life has
replayed in my dreams. Those
early years with my dad--

--spending hours at
my favorite place--
the gym.

I wouldn't tell dad about
that, though--he didn't want
me to wind up like him.

He was a fighter.

And each time there's the
accident--a single moment
that changes my life forever--

--and the last day
I ever saw anything.

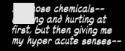ose chemicals--
ng and hurting at
first, but then giving me
my hyper acute senses--

--and my radar.

I always like when mom
comes back to me--briefly.

I didn't know it was her
back then. In the dream,
I do.

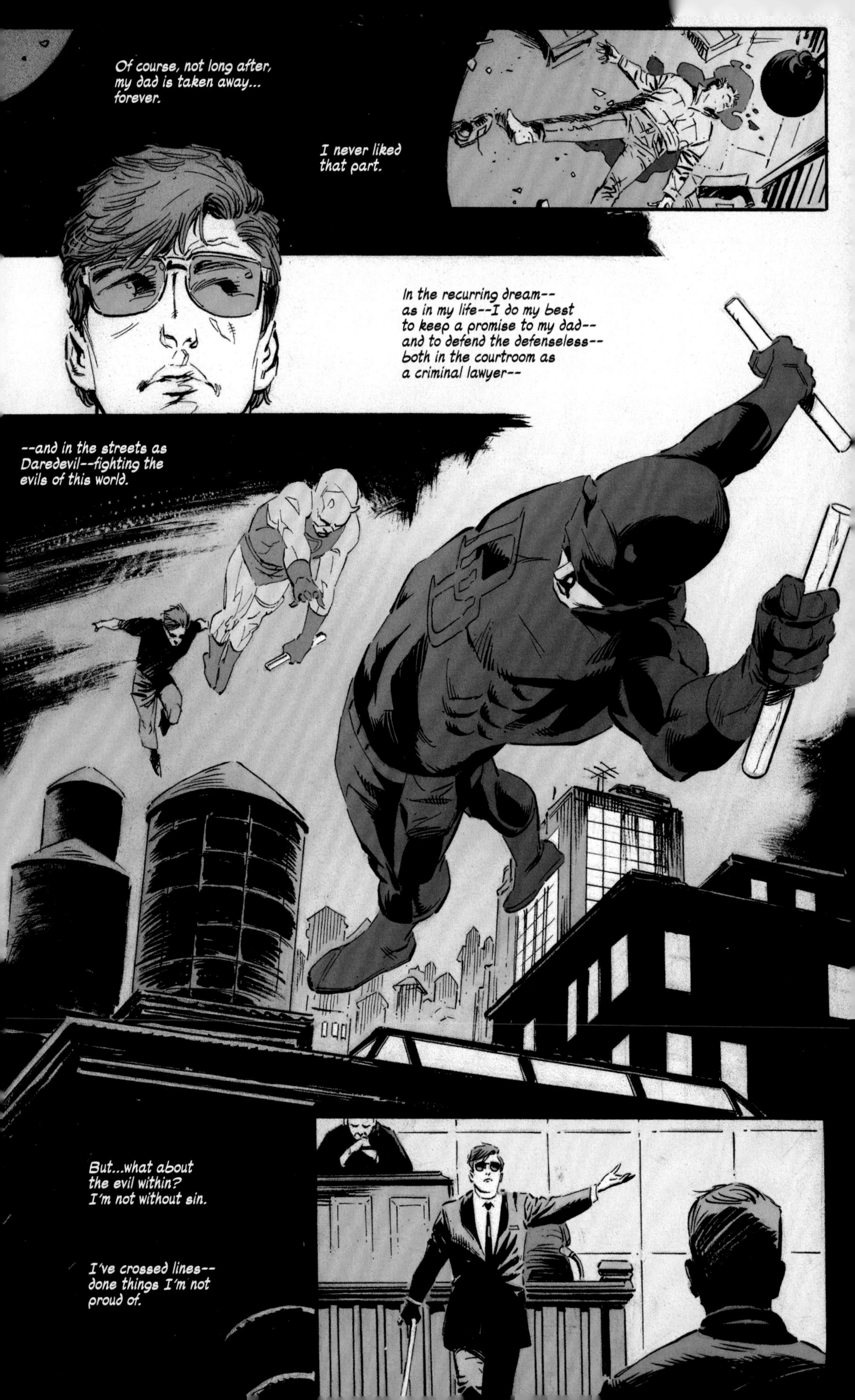
Of course, not long after, my dad is taken away... forever.
I never liked that part.
In the recurring dream-- as in my life--I do my best to keep a promise to my dad-- and to defend the defenseless-- both in the courtroom as a criminal lawyer--
--and in the streets as Daredevil--fighting the evils of this world.
But...what about the evil within? I'm not without sin.
I've crossed lines-- done things I'm not proud of.

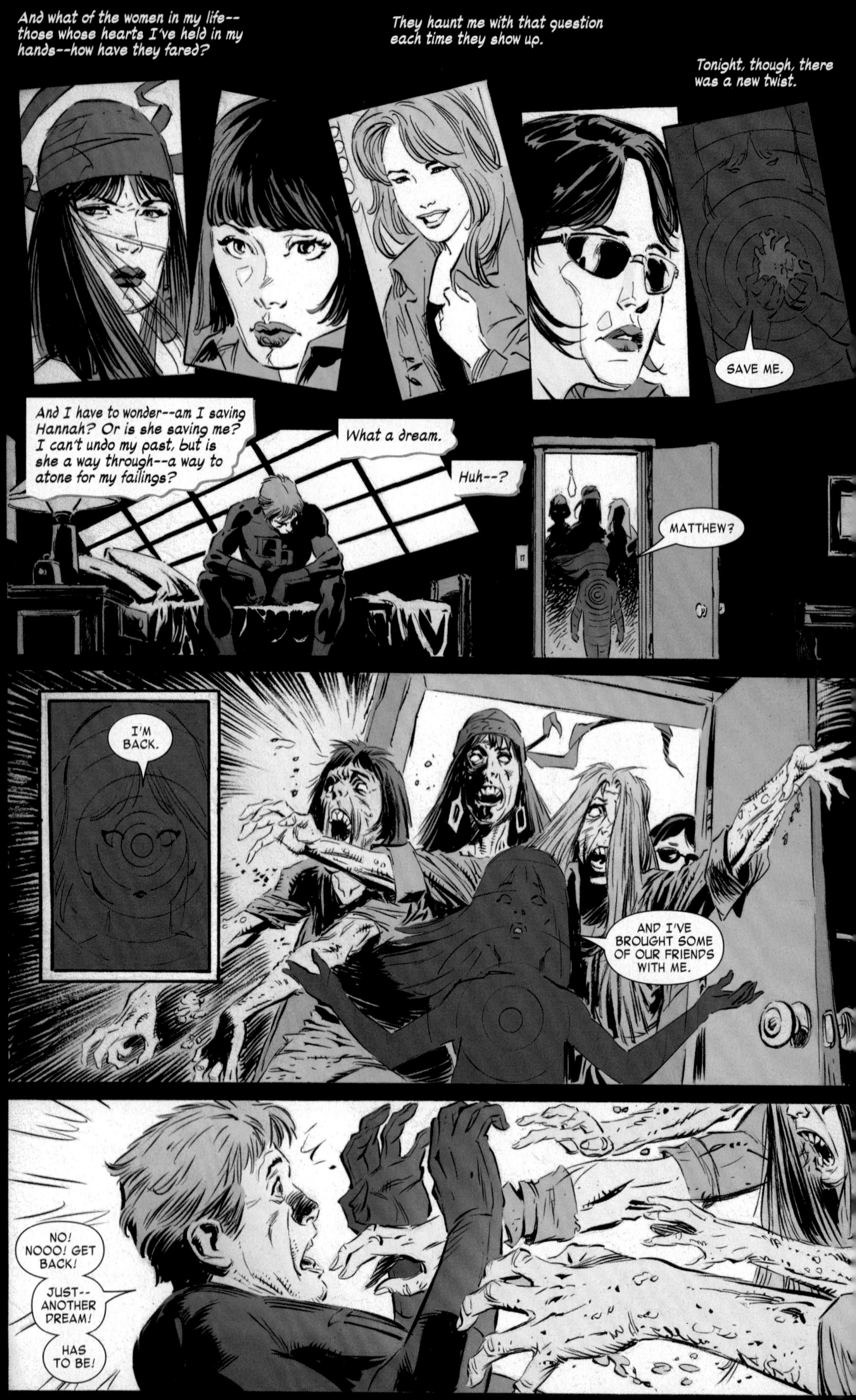

And what of the women in my life--those whose hearts I've held in my hands--how have they fared?
They haunt me with that question each time they show up.
Tonight, though, there was a new twist.
SAVE ME.
And I have to wonder--am I saving Hannah? Or is she saving me? I can't undo my past, but is she a way through--a way to atone for my failings?
What a dream.
Huh--?
MATTHEW?
I'M BACK.
AND I'VE BROUGHT SOME OF OUR FRIENDS WITH ME.
NO! NOOO! GET BACK!
JUST--ANOTHER DREAM!
HAS TO BE!

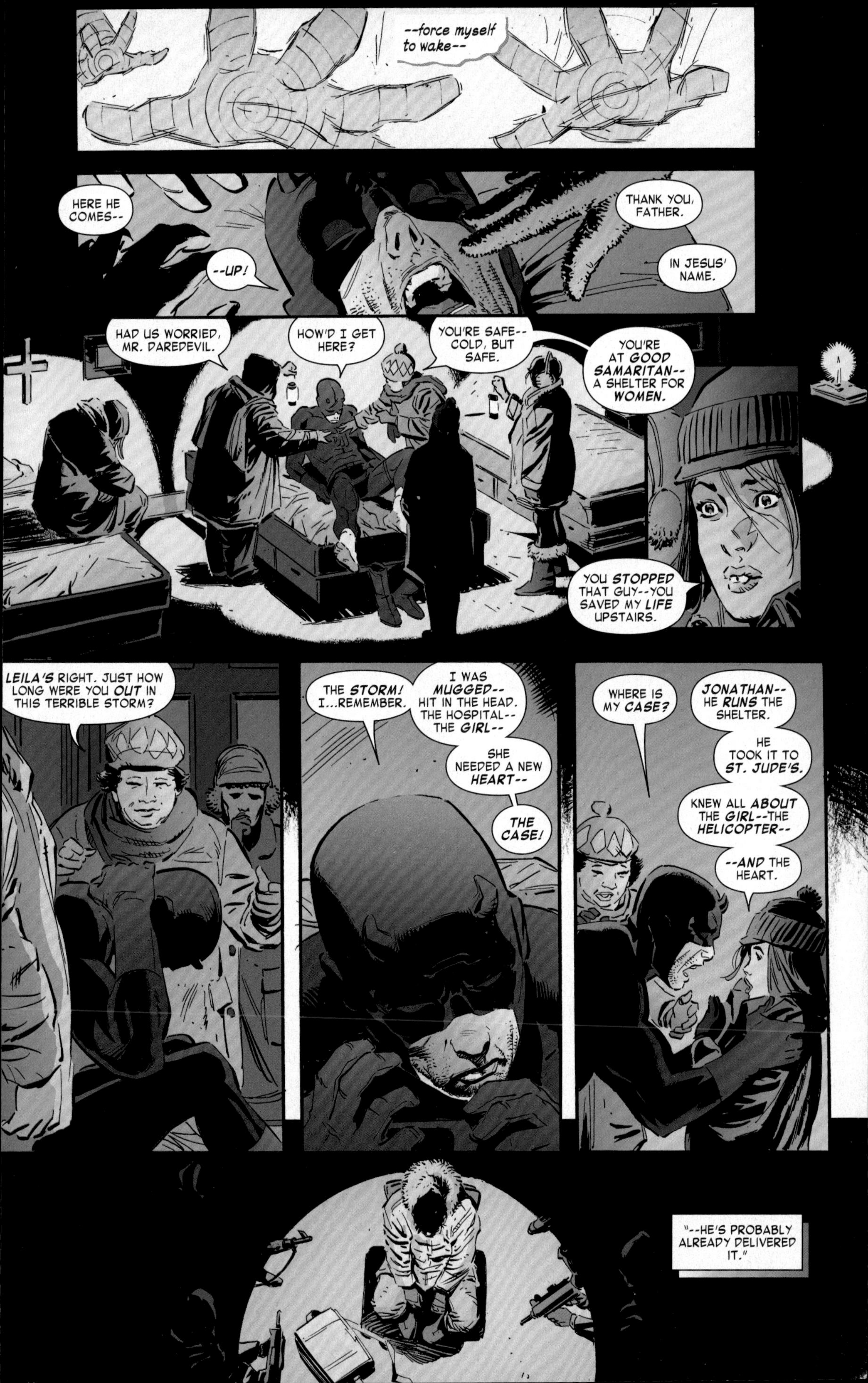
--force myself to wake--
HERE HE COMES--
--UP!
THANK YOU, FATHER.
IN JESUS' NAME.
HAD US WORRIED, MR. DAREDEVIL.
HOW'D I GET HERE?
YOU'RE SAFE-- COLD, BUT SAFE.
YOU'RE AT GOOD SAMARITAN-- A SHELTER FOR WOMEN.
YOU STOPPED THAT GUY--YOU SAVED MY LIFE UPSTAIRS.
LEILA'S RIGHT. JUST HOW LONG WERE YOU OUT IN THIS TERRIBLE STORM?
THE STORM! I...REMEMBER.
I WAS MUGGED-- HIT IN THE HEAD. THE HOSPITAL-- THE GIRL--
SHE NEEDED A NEW HEART--
THE CASE!
WHERE IS MY CASE?
JONATHAN-- HE RUNS THE SHELTER.
HE TOOK IT TO ST. JUDE'S.
KNEW ALL ABOUT THE GIRL--THE HELICOPTER--
--AND THE HEART.
"--HE'S PROBABLY ALREADY DELIVERED IT."

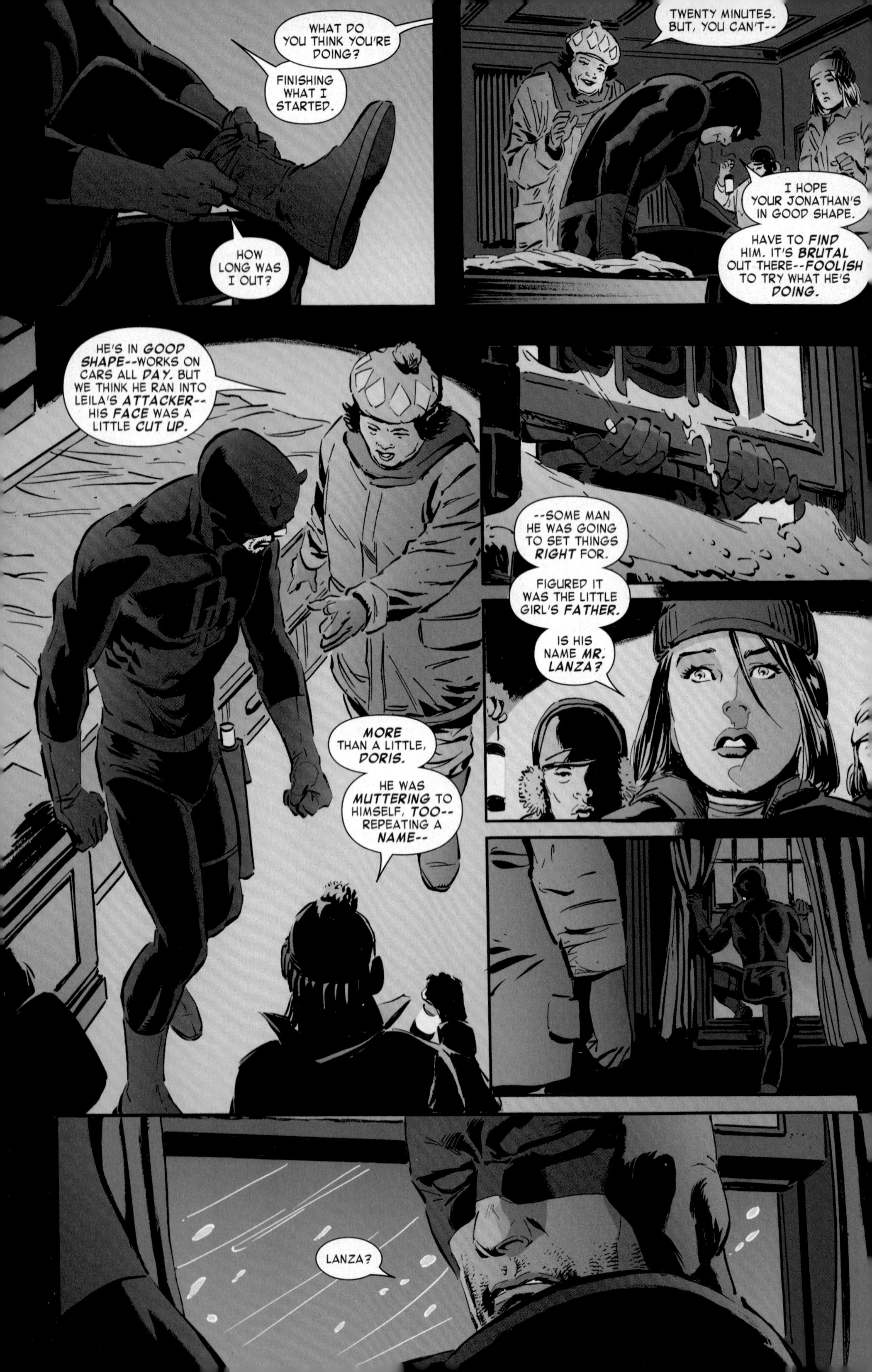
WHAT DO YOU THINK YOU'RE DOING?
FINISHING WHAT I STARTED.
HOW LONG WAS I OUT?
TWENTY MINUTES. BUT, YOU CAN'T--
I HOPE YOUR JONATHAN'S IN GOOD SHAPE.
HAVE TO FIND HIM. IT'S BRUTAL OUT THERE--FOOLISH TO TRY WHAT HE'S DOING.
HE'S IN GOOD SHAPE--WORKS ON CARS ALL DAY. BUT WE THINK HE RAN INTO LEILA'S ATTACKER--HIS FACE WAS A LITTLE CUT UP.
MORE THAN A LITTLE, DORIS.
HE WAS MUTTERING TO HIMSELF, TOO--REPEATING A NAME--
--SOME MAN HE WAS GOING TO SET THINGS RIGHT FOR.
FIGURED IT WAS THE LITTLE GIRL'S FATHER.
IS HIS NAME MR. LANZA?
LANZA?

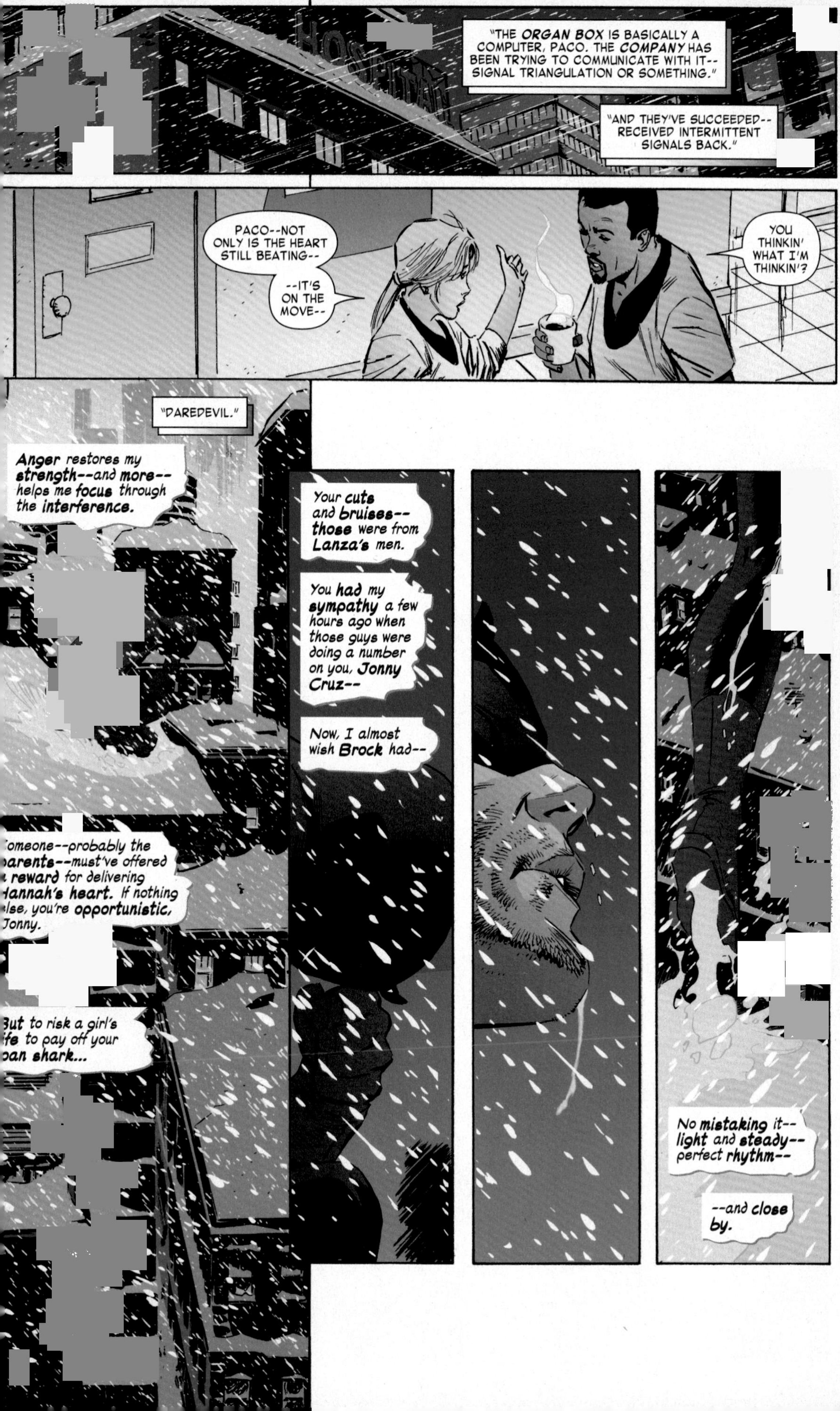

"THE ORGAN BOX IS BASICALLY A COMPUTER, PACO. THE COMPANY HAS BEEN TRYING TO COMMUNICATE WITH IT-- SIGNAL TRIANGULATION OR SOMETHING."
"AND THEY'VE SUCCEEDED-- RECEIVED INTERMITTENT SIGNALS BACK."
PACO--NOT ONLY IS THE HEART STILL BEATING--
--IT'S ON THE MOVE--
YOU THINKIN' WHAT I'M THINKIN'?
"DAREDEVIL."
Anger restores my strength--and more--helps me focus through the interference.
omeone--probably the arents--must've offered reward for delivering Hannah's heart. If nothing lse, you're opportunistic, Jonny.
But to risk a girl's ife to pay off your oan shark...
Your cuts and bruises-- those were from Lanza's men.
You had my sympathy a few hours ago when those guys were doing a number on you, Jonny Cruz--
Now, I almost wish Brock had--
No mistaking it-- light and steady-- perfect rhythm--
--and close by.

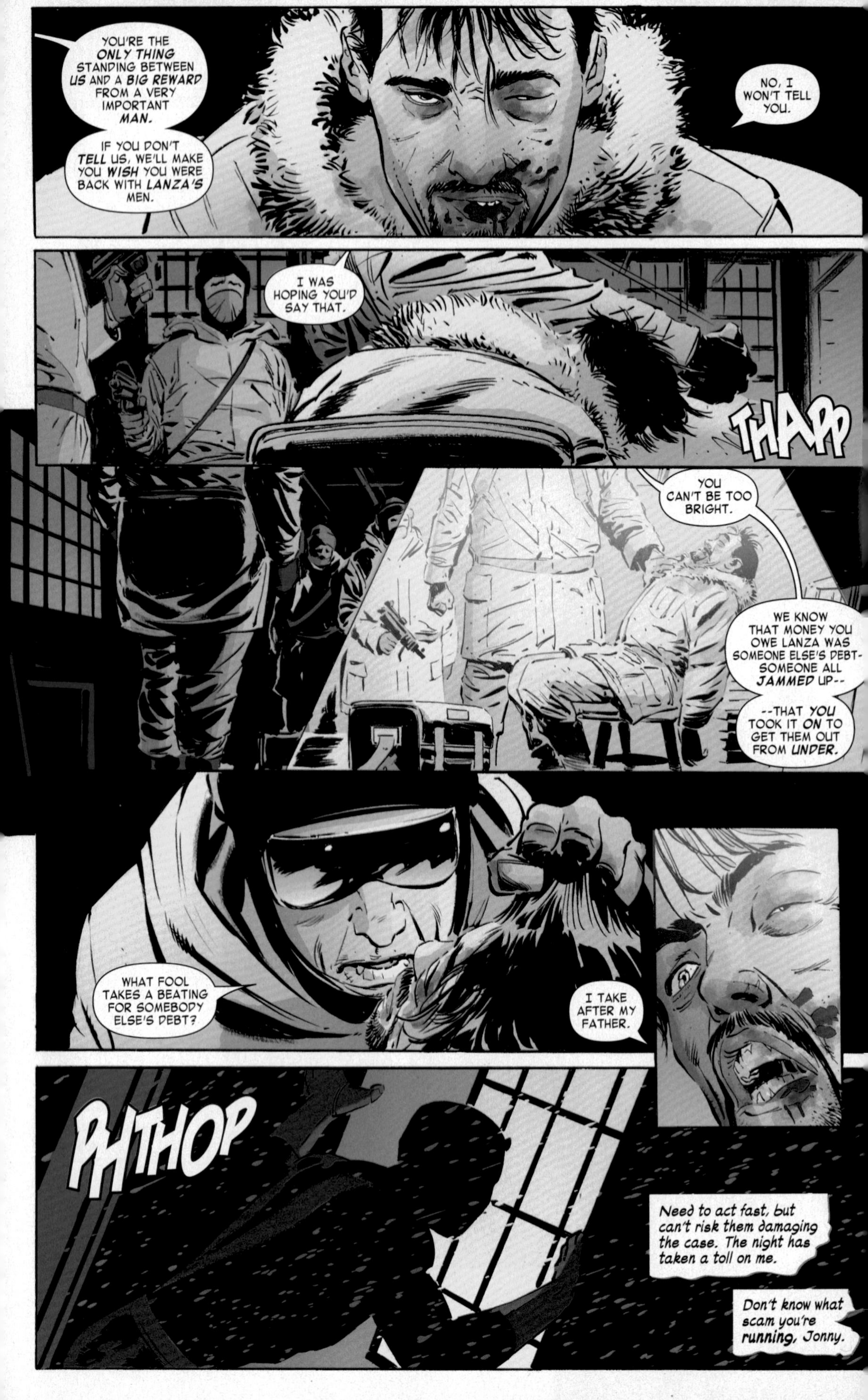
YOU'RE THE ONLY THING STANDING BETWEEN US AND A BIG REWARD FROM A VERY IMPORTANT MAN.
IF YOU DON'T TELL US, WE'LL MAKE YOU WISH YOU WERE BACK WITH LANZA'S MEN.
NO, I WON'T TELL YOU.
I WAS HOPING YOU'D SAY THAT.
THAPP
YOU CAN'T BE TOO BRIGHT.
WE KNOW THAT MONEY YOU OWE LANZA WAS SOMEONE ELSE'S DEBT-SOMEONE ALL JAMMED UP--
--THAT YOU TOOK IT ON TO GET THEM OUT FROM UNDER.
WHAT FOOL TAKES A BEATING FOR SOMEBODY ELSE'S DEBT?
I TAKE AFTER MY FATHER.
PHTHOP
Need to act fast, but can't risk them damaging the case. The night has taken a toll on me.
Don't know what scam you're running, Jonny.

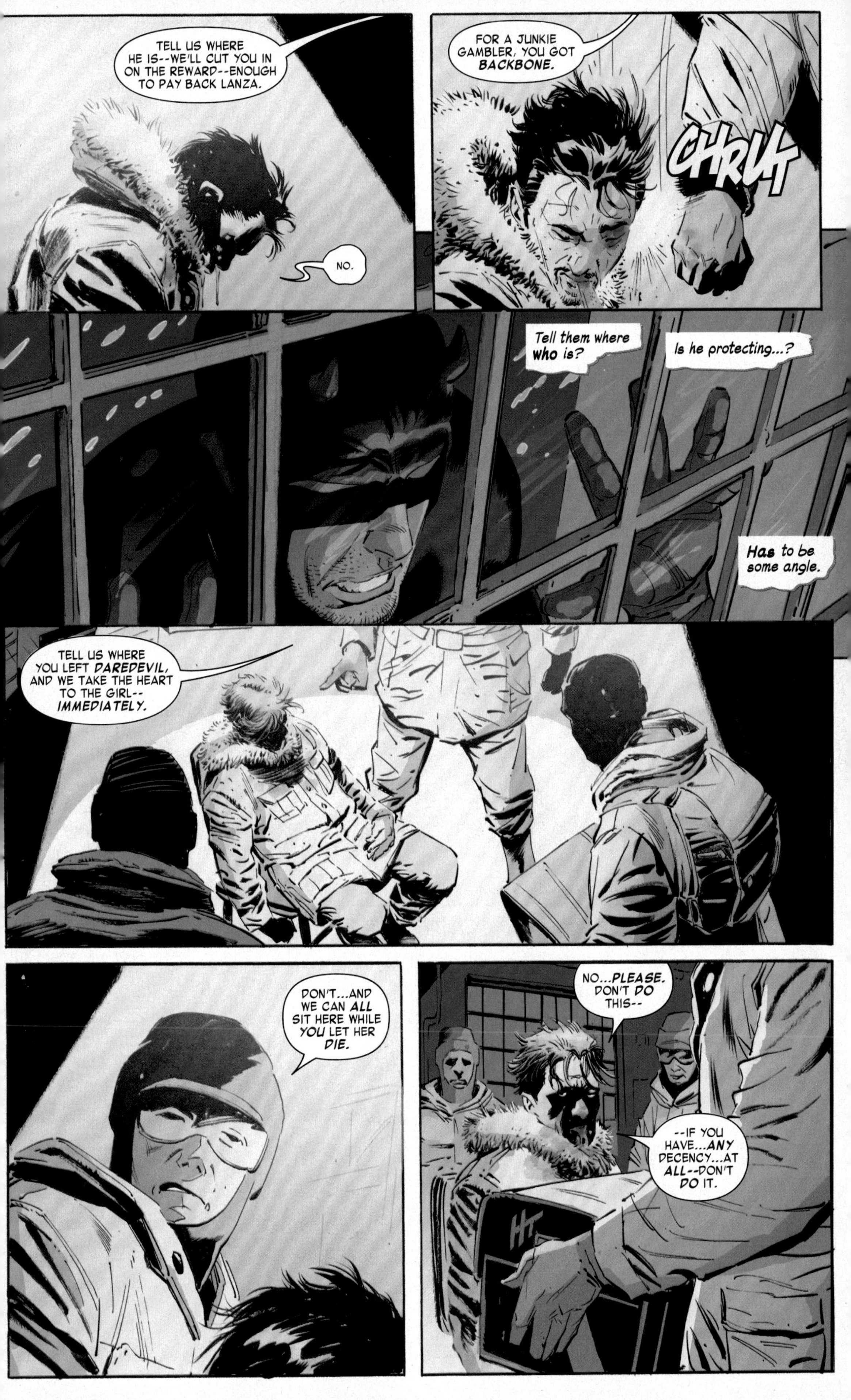

TELL US WHERE HE IS--WE'LL CUT YOU IN ON THE REWARD--ENOUGH TO PAY BACK LANZA.
NO.
FOR A JUNKIE GAMBLER, YOU GOT BACKBONE.
CHRUK
Tell them where who is?
Is he protecting...?
Has to be some angle.
TELL US WHERE YOU LEFT DAREDEVIL, AND WE TAKE THE HEART TO THE GIRL-- IMMEDIATELY.
DON'T...AND WE CAN ALL SIT HERE WHILE YOU LET HER DIE.
NO...PLEASE. DON'T DO THIS--
--IF YOU HAVE...ANY DECENCY...AT ALL--DON'T DO IT.

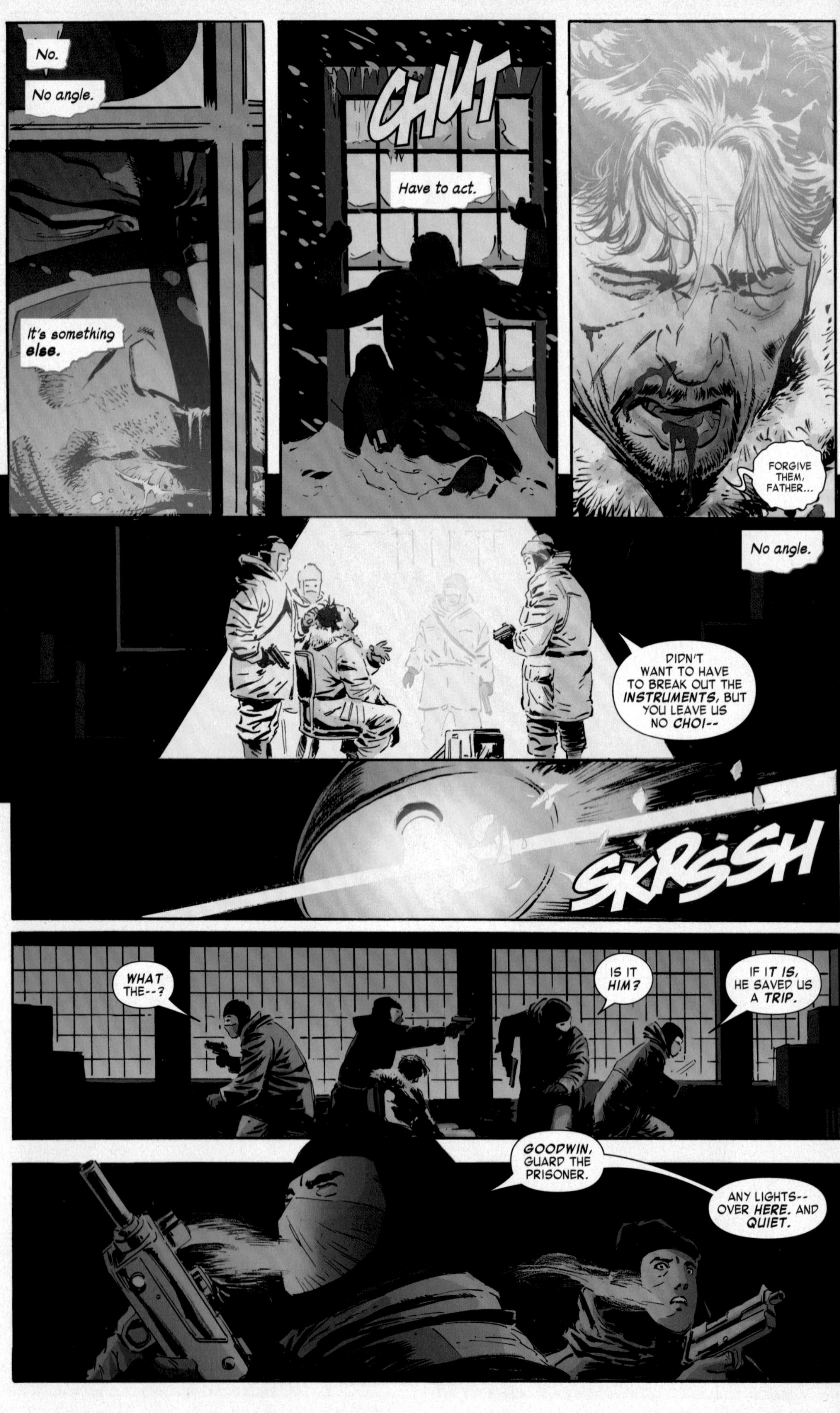
No.
No angle.
It's something else.
CHUT
Have to act.
FORGIVE THEM, FATHER...
No angle.
DIDN'T WANT TO HAVE TO BREAK OUT THE INSTRUMENTS, BUT YOU LEAVE US NO CHOI--
SKRSSH
WHAT THE--?
IS IT HIM?
IF IT IS, HE SAVED US A TRIP.
GOODWIN, GUARD THE PRISONER.
ANY LIGHTS-- OVER HERE. AND QUIET.

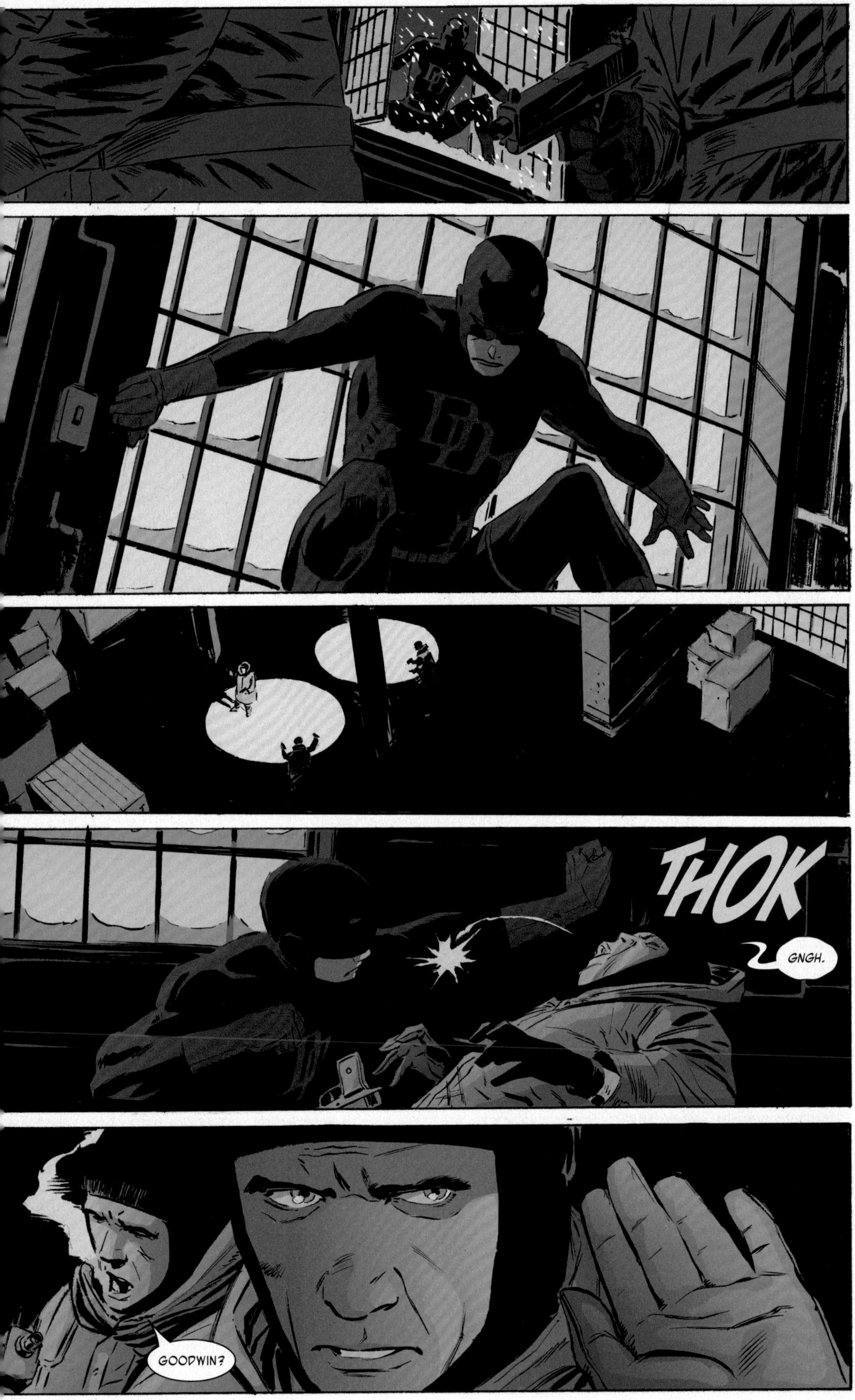
THOK
GNGH.
GOODWIN?

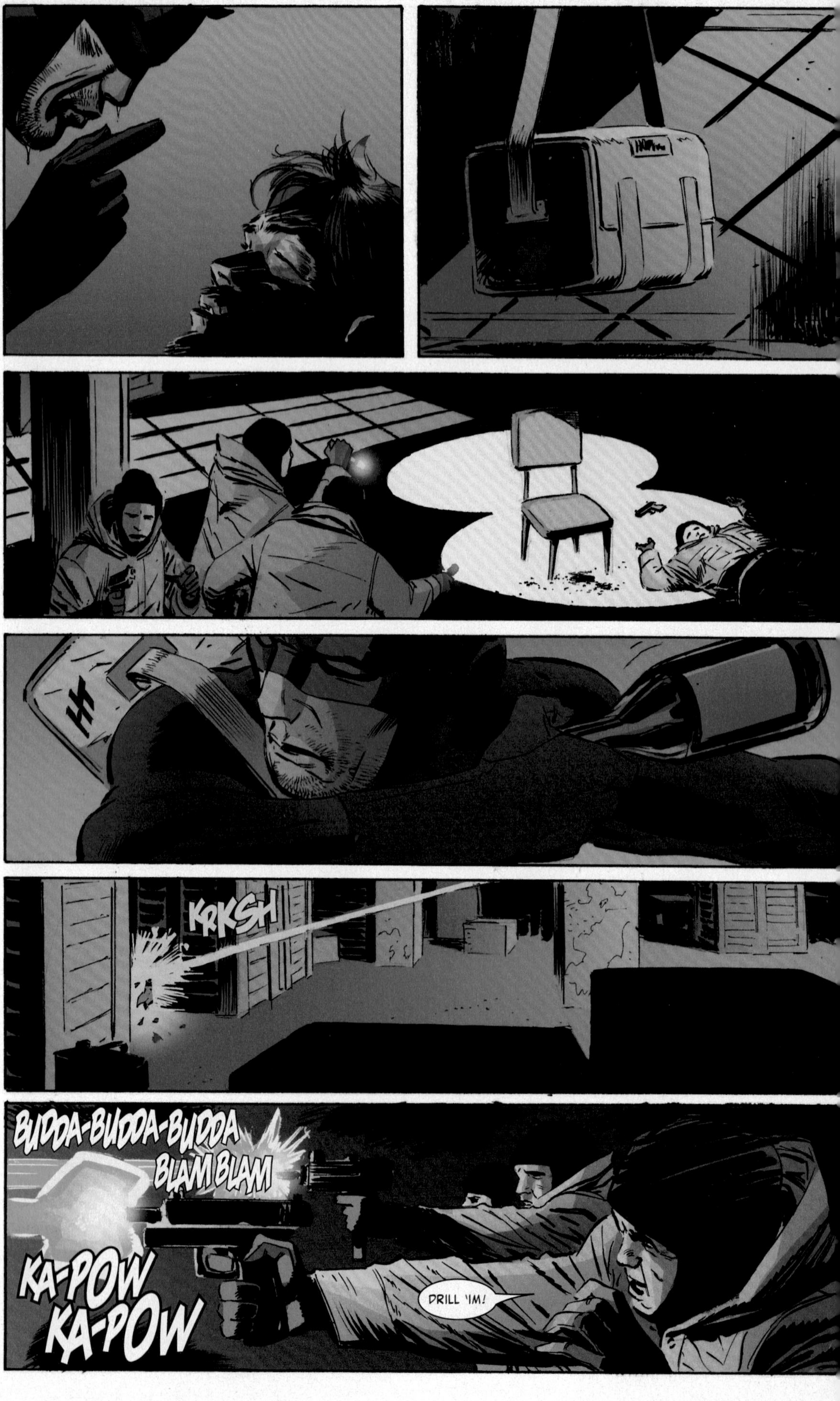
KRKSH
BUDDA-BUDDA-BUDDA
BLAM BLAM
KA-POW
KA-POW
DRILL 'IM!

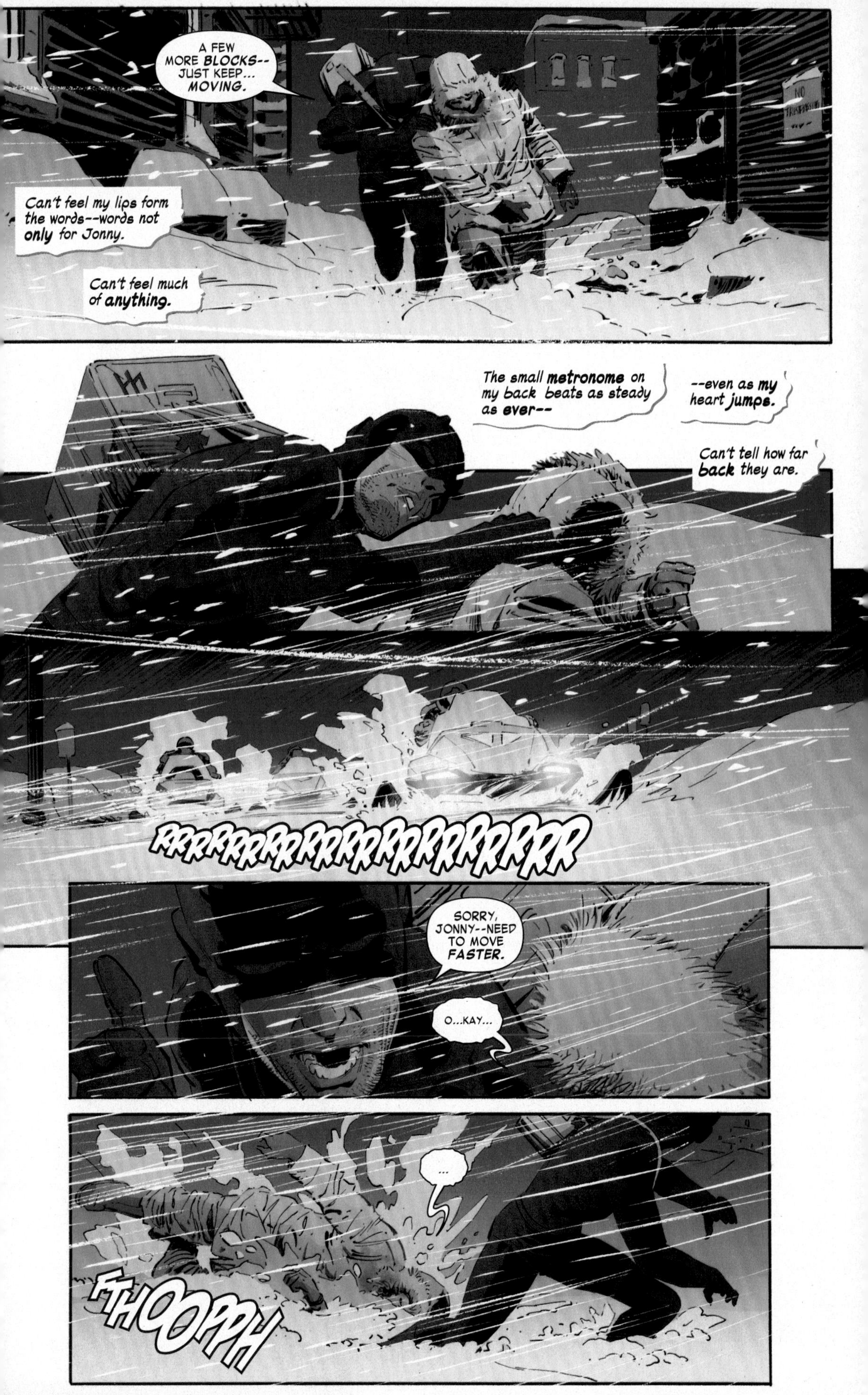
A FEW MORE BLOCKS-- JUST KEEP... MOVING.
Can't feel my lips form the words--words not only for Jonny.
Can't feel much of anything.
The small metronome on my back beats as steady as ever--
--even as my heart jumps.
Can't tell how far back they are.
RRRRRRRRRRRRRRRRRRRRRRRR
SORRY, JONNY--NEED TO MOVE FASTER.
O...KAY...
...
FTHOOPPH

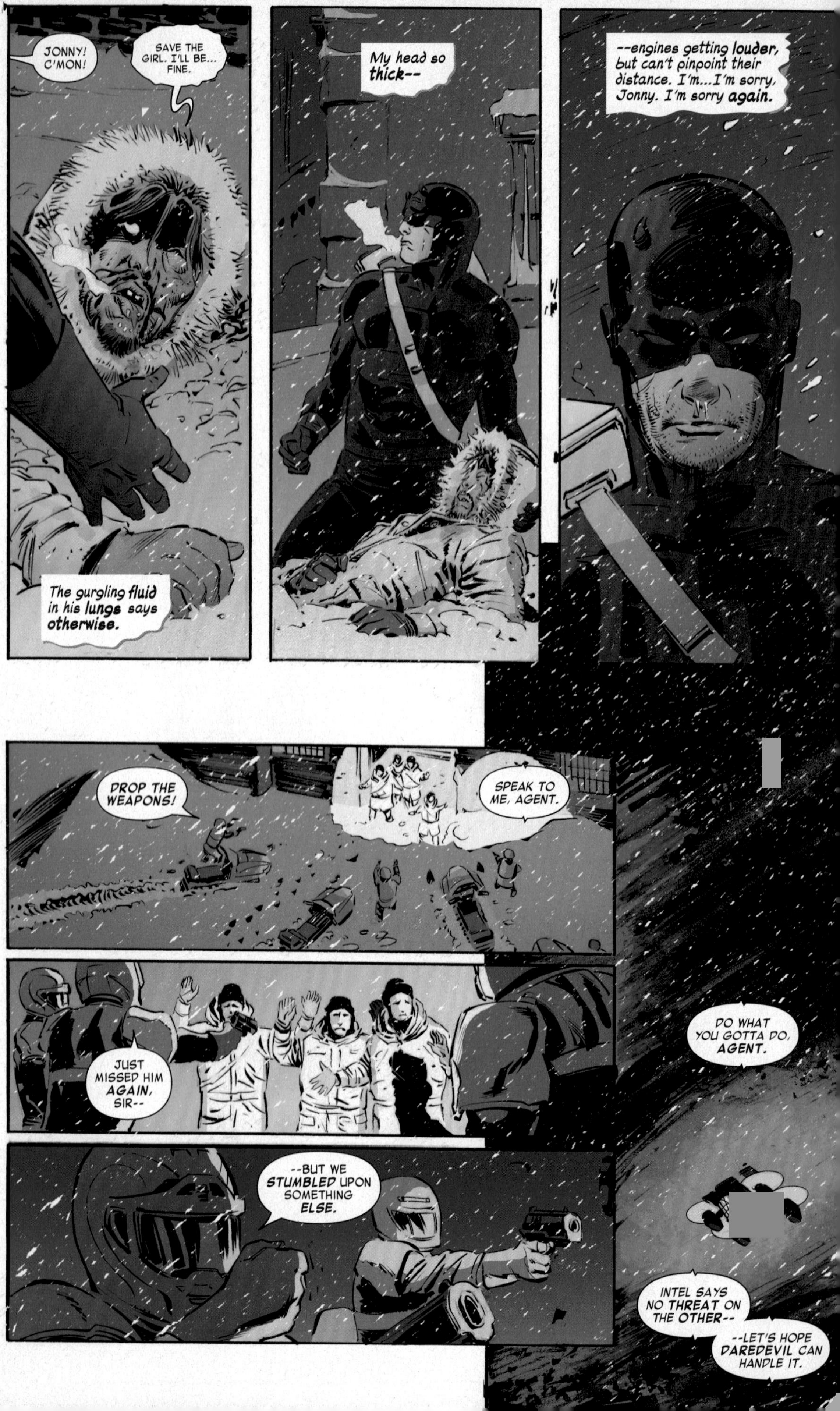
JONNY! C'MON!
SAVE THE GIRL. I'LL BE... FINE.
The gurgling fluid in his lungs says otherwise.
My head so thick--
--engines getting louder, but can't pinpoint their distance. I'm...I'm sorry, Jonny. I'm sorry again.
DROP THE WEAPONS!
SPEAK TO ME, AGENT.
JUST MISSED HIM AGAIN, SIR--
--BUT WE STUMBLED UPON SOMETHING ELSE.
DO WHAT YOU GOTTA DO, AGENT.
INTEL SAYS NO THREAT ON THE OTHER--
--LET'S HOPE DAREDEVIL CAN HANDLE IT.

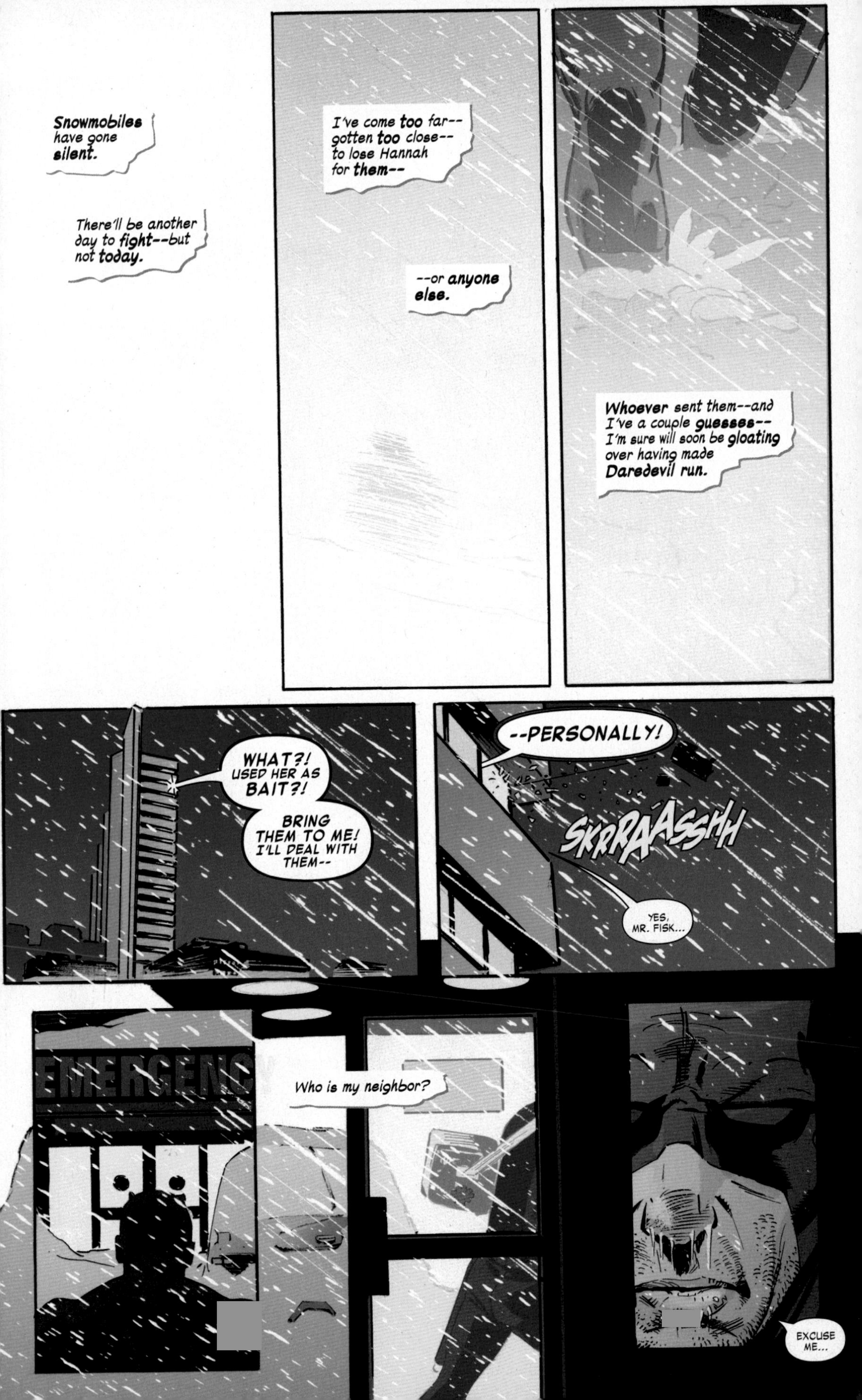
Snowmobiles have gone silent.
There'll be another day to fight--but not today.
I've come too far--gotten too close--to lose Hannah for them--
--or anyone else.
Whoever sent them--and I've a couple guesses--I'm sure will soon be gloating over having made Daredevil run.
WHAT?! USED HER AS BAIT?!
BRING THEM TO ME! I'LL DEAL WITH THEM--
--PERSONALLY!
SKRRAASSHH
YES, MR. FISK...
EMERGENC
Who is my neighbor?
EXCUSE ME...

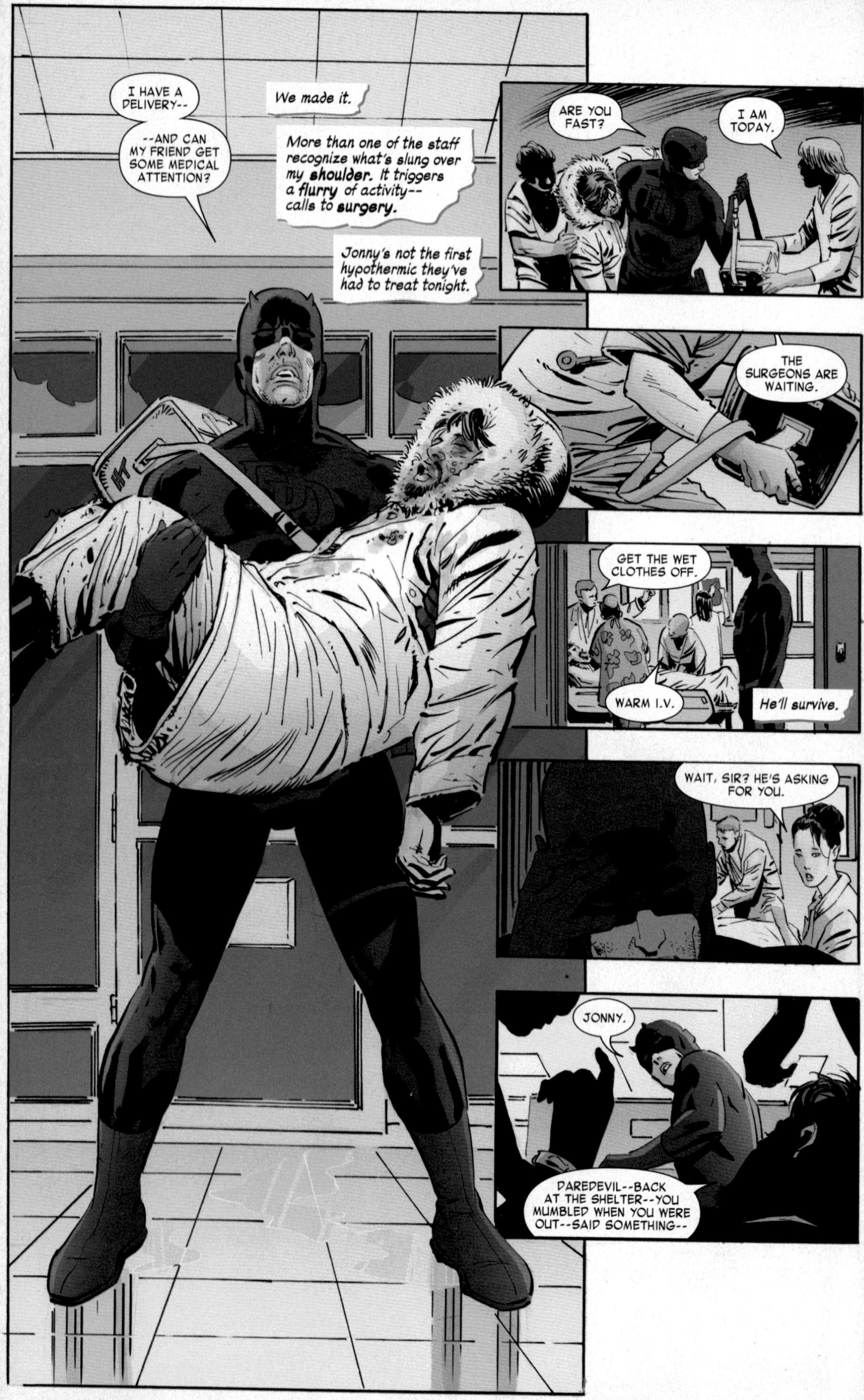
I HAVE A DELIVERY--
--AND CAN MY FRIEND GET SOME MEDICAL ATTENTION?
We made it.
More than one of the staff recognize what's slung over my **shoulder.** It triggers a **flurry** of activity-- calls to **surgery.**
Jonny's not the first hypothermic they've had to treat tonight.
ARE YOU FAST?
I AM TODAY.
THE SURGEONS ARE WAITING.
GET THE WET CLOTHES OFF.
WARM I.V.
He'll survive.
WAIT, SIR? HE'S ASKING FOR YOU.
JONNY.
DAREDEVIL--BACK AT THE SHELTER--YOU MUMBLED WHEN YOU WERE OUT--SAID SOMETHING--

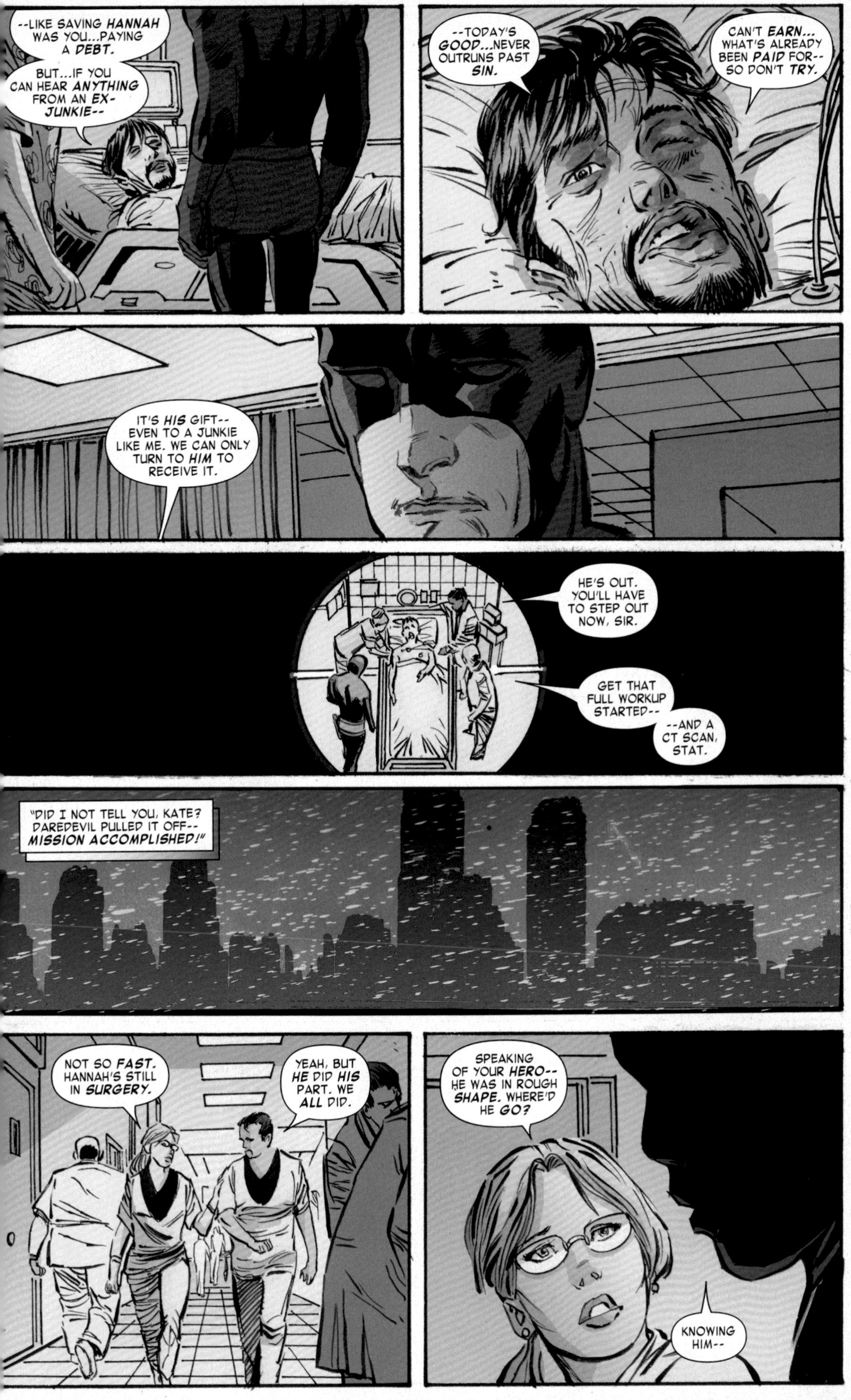
--LIKE SAVING HANNAH WAS YOU...PAYING A DEBT.
BUT...IF YOU CAN HEAR ANYTHING FROM AN EX-JUNKIE--
--TODAY'S GOOD...NEVER OUTRUNS PAST SIN.
CAN'T EARN... WHAT'S ALREADY BEEN PAID FOR--SO DON'T TRY.
IT'S HIS GIFT--EVEN TO A JUNKIE LIKE ME. WE CAN ONLY TURN TO HIM TO RECEIVE IT.
HE'S OUT. YOU'LL HAVE TO STEP OUT NOW, SIR.
GET THAT FULL WORKUP STARTED--
--AND A CT SCAN, STAT.
"DID I NOT TELL YOU, KATE? DAREDEVIL PULLED IT OFF--MISSION ACCOMPLISHED!"
NOT SO FAST. HANNAH'S STILL IN SURGERY.
YEAH, BUT HE DID HIS PART. WE ALL DID.
SPEAKING OF YOUR HERO--HE WAS IN ROUGH SHAPE. WHERE'D HE GO?
KNOWING HIM--

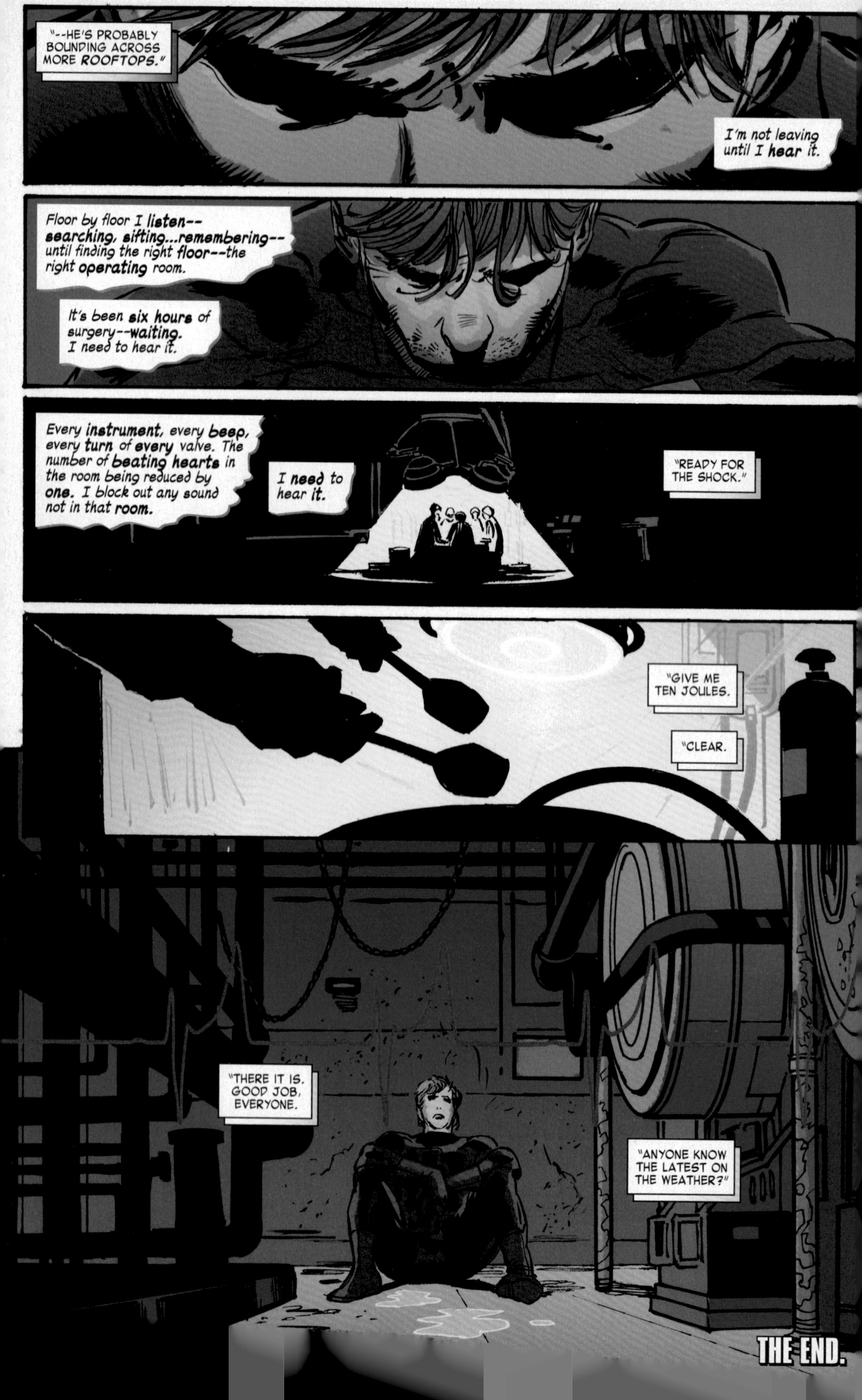
"--HE'S PROBABLY BOUNDING ACROSS MORE ROOFTOPS."
I'm not leaving until I hear it.
Floor by floor I listen--searching, sifting...remembering--until finding the right floor--the right operating room.
It's been six hours of surgery--waiting. I need to hear it.
Every instrument, every beep, every turn of every valve. The number of beating hearts in the room being reduced by one. I block out any sound not in that room.
I need to hear it.
"READY FOR THE SHOCK."
"GIVE ME TEN JOULES.
"CLEAR.
"THERE IT IS. GOOD JOB, EVERYONE.
"ANYONE KNOW THE LATEST ON THE WEATHER?"
THE END.

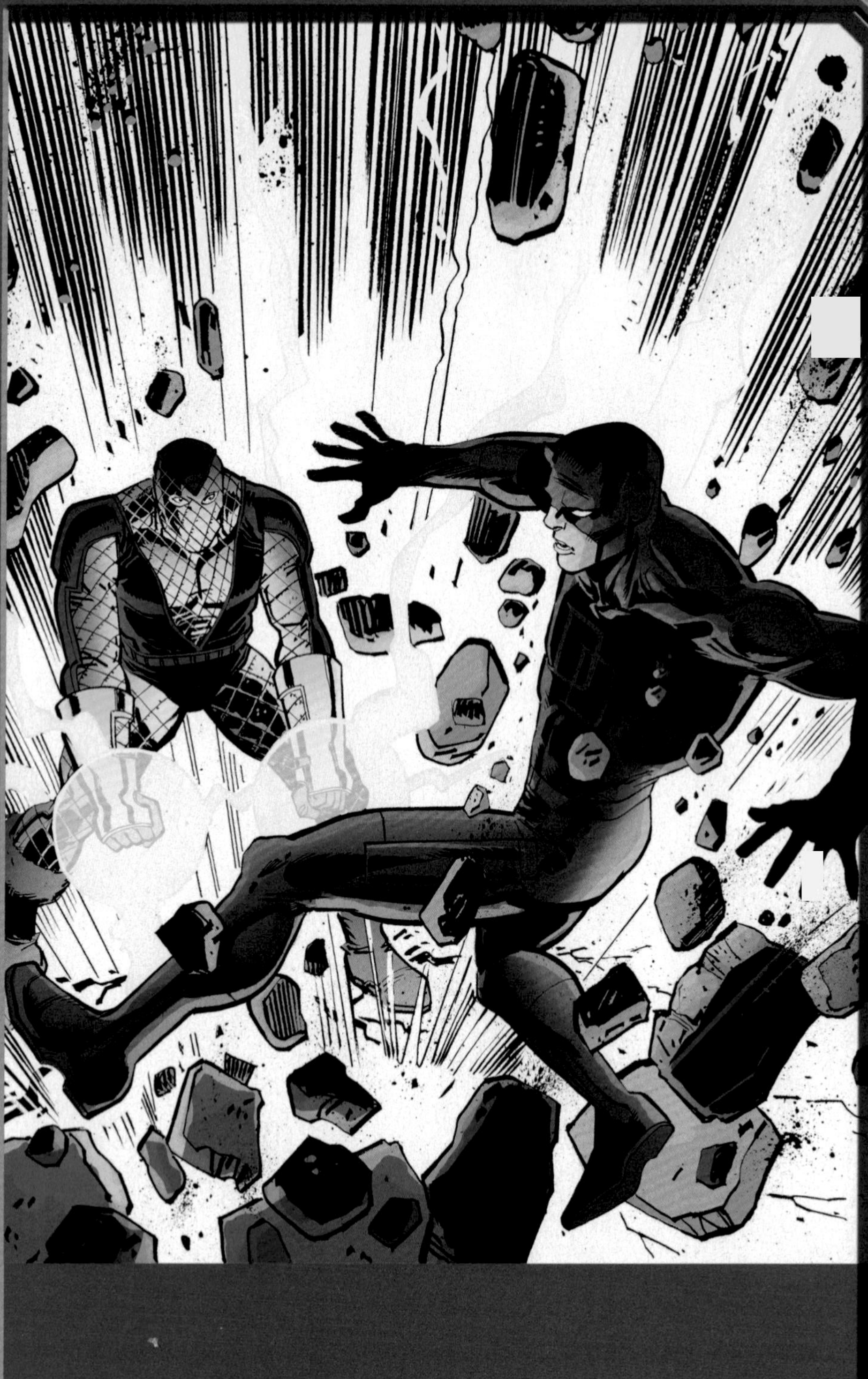

#4 — A MAN NAMED BUGGIT
PART ONE: WHAT A NICE DAY

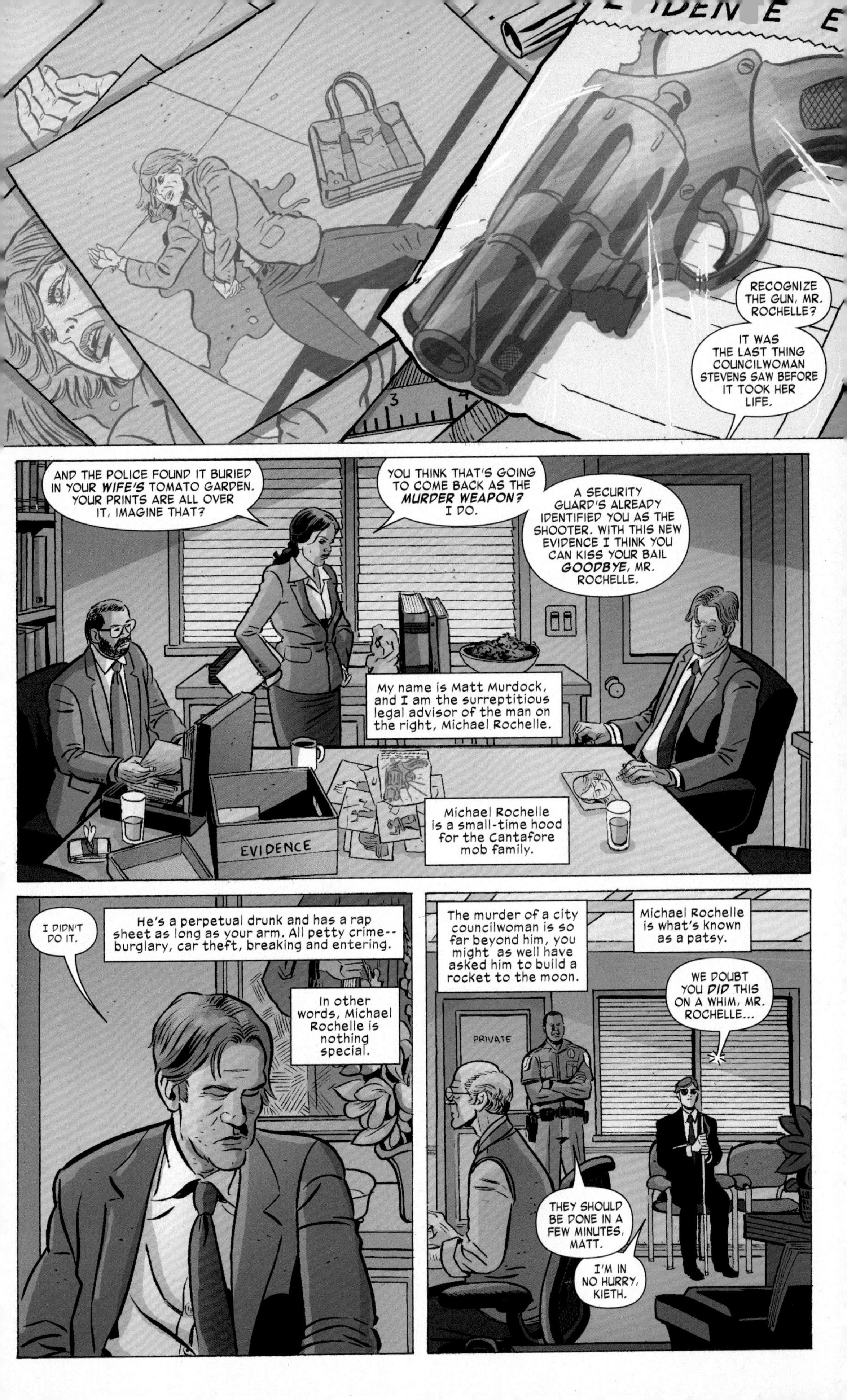
EVIDENCE
RECOGNIZE THE GUN, MR. ROCHELLE?
IT WAS THE LAST THING COUNCILWOMAN STEVENS SAW BEFORE IT TOOK HER LIFE.
AND THE POLICE FOUND IT BURIED IN YOUR WIFE'S TOMATO GARDEN. YOUR PRINTS ARE ALL OVER IT, IMAGINE THAT?
YOU THINK THAT'S GOING TO COME BACK AS THE MURDER WEAPON? I DO.
A SECURITY GUARD'S ALREADY IDENTIFIED YOU AS THE SHOOTER. WITH THIS NEW EVIDENCE I THINK YOU CAN KISS YOUR BAIL GOODBYE, MR. ROCHELLE.
My name is Matt Murdock, and I am the surreptitious legal advisor of the man on the right, Michael Rochelle.
Michael Rochelle is a small-time hood for the Cantafore mob family.
EVIDENCE
I DIDN'T DO IT.
He's a perpetual drunk and has a rap sheet as long as your arm. All petty crime--burglary, car theft, breaking and entering.
In other words, Michael Rochelle is nothing special.
The murder of a city councilwoman is so far beyond him, you might as well have asked him to build a rocket to the moon.
Michael Rochelle is what's known as a patsy.
WE DOUBT YOU DID THIS ON A WHIM, MR. ROCHELLE...
PRIVATE
THEY SHOULD BE DONE IN A FEW MINUTES, MATT.
I'M IN NO HURRY, KIETH.

WE BELIEVE YOU WERE HIRED BY FRANK MILO.

BUT RIGHT NOW, THE BUCK STOPS WITH *YOU.*

I have my own methods for determining the truth, and I know beyond a shadow of a doubt Rochelle is innocent.

NOW MIGHT BE A GOOD TIME TO STOP ACTING AS YOUR OWN ATTORNEY, AND ALLOW A PUBLIC DEFENDER TO BE APPOINTED ON YOUR *BEHALF.*

IF ONLY SO THAT THEY CAN CONFIRM WHAT AN UNTENABLE SPOT YOU'RE IN.

PERHAPS ADVISE YOU TO CUT A *DEAL,* MR. ROCHELLE...?

So I agreed to advise Michael in his own defense.

MR. ROCHELLE...?

Of course, he's not doing a thing I told him.

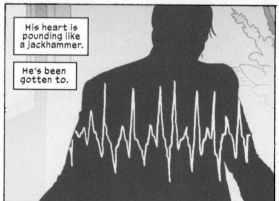

His heart is pounding like a jackhammer.

He's been gotten to.

MAKE SURE HE'S IN JUDGE WILSON'S COURT IN 15 MINUTES.

YES, MA'AM.

YOU KNOW HE DIDN'T DO IT, RIGHT?

MIDTOWN TRAFFIC IS AT A STANDSTILL AS A GIANT SUBTERRANEAN MONSTER IS RAMPAGING THROUGH THE...

EVIDENCE

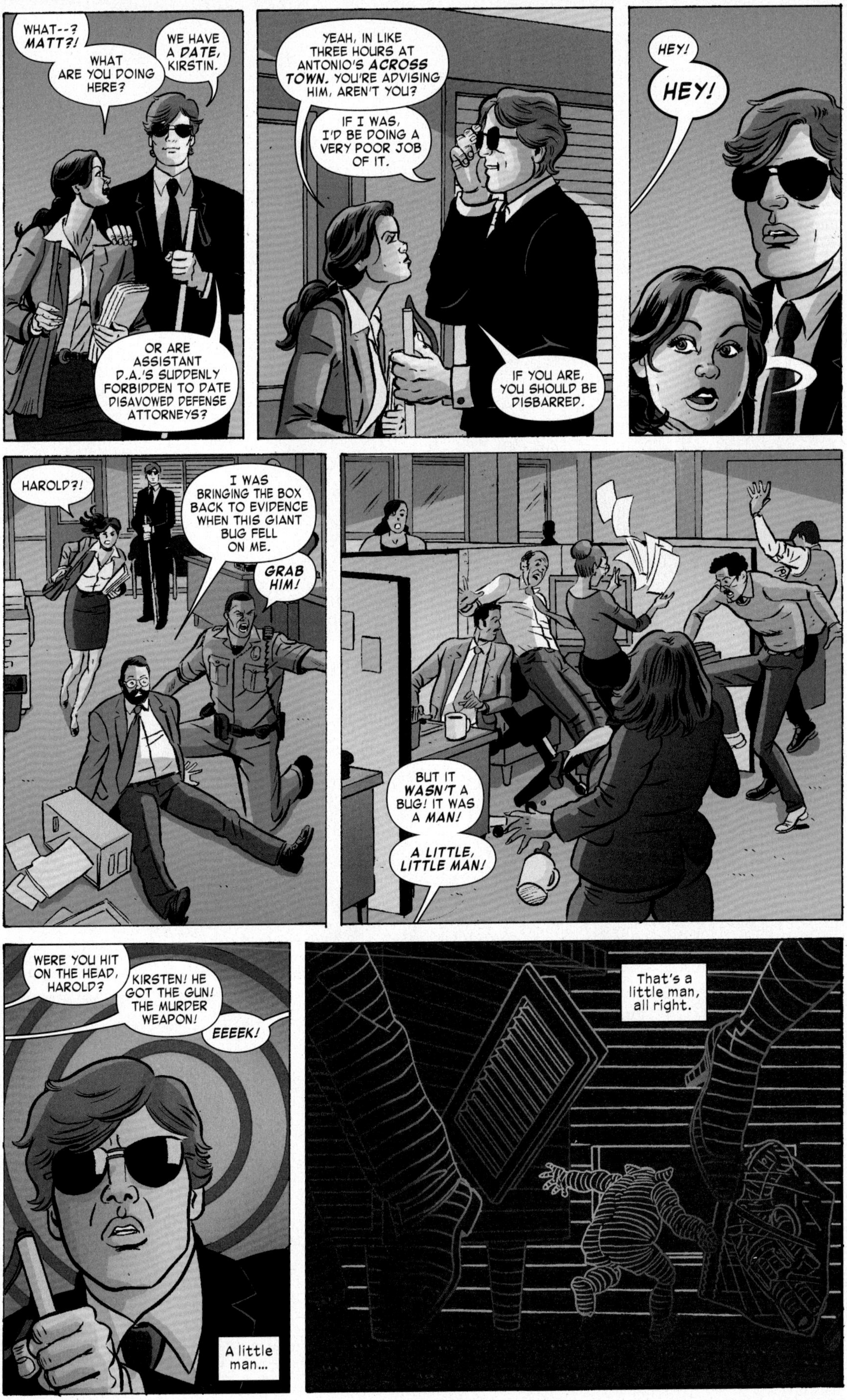
WHAT--? MATT?!
WHAT ARE YOU DOING HERE?
WE HAVE A DATE, KIRSTIN.
OR ARE ASSISTANT D.A.'S SUDDENLY FORBIDDEN TO DATE DISAVOWED DEFENSE ATTORNEYS?
YEAH, IN LIKE THREE HOURS AT ANTONIO'S ACROSS TOWN. YOU'RE ADVISING HIM, AREN'T YOU?
IF I WAS, I'D BE DOING A VERY POOR JOB OF IT.
IF YOU ARE, YOU SHOULD BE DISBARRED.
HEY!
HEY!
HAROLD?!
I WAS BRINGING THE BOX BACK TO EVIDENCE WHEN THIS GIANT BUG FELL ON ME.
GRAB HIM!
BUT IT WASN'T A BUG! IT WAS A MAN!
A LITTLE, LITTLE MAN!
WERE YOU HIT ON THE HEAD, HAROLD?
KIRSTEN! HE GOT THE GUN! THE MURDER WEAPON!
EEEEK!
A little man...
That's a little man, all right.

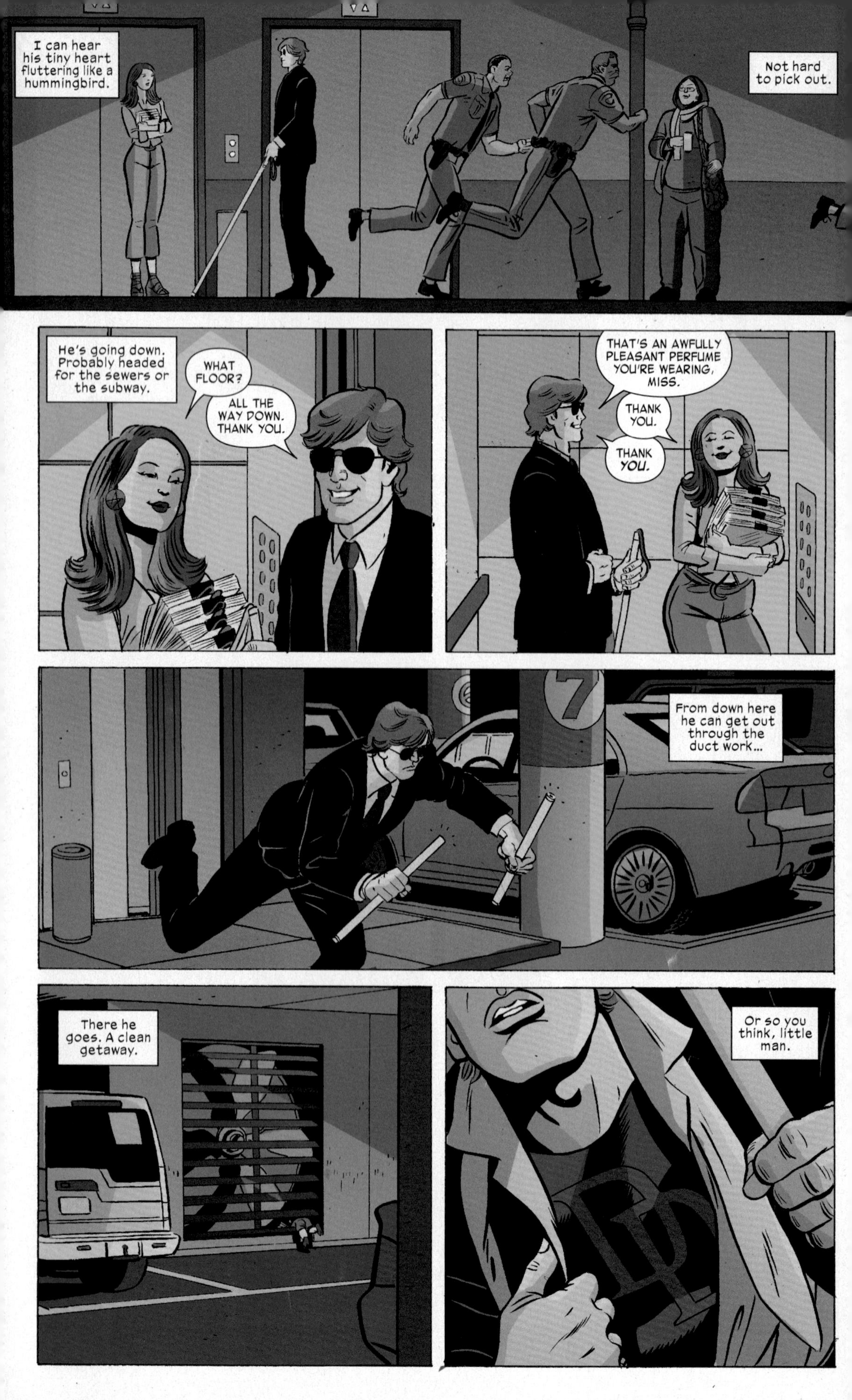

I can hear his tiny heart fluttering like a hummingbird.
Not hard to pick out.
He's going down. Probably headed for the sewers or the subway.
WHAT FLOOR?
ALL THE WAY DOWN. THANK YOU.
THAT'S AN AWFULLY PLEASANT PERFUME YOU'RE WEARING, MISS.
THANK YOU.
THANK *YOU.*
From down here he can get out through the duct work...
There he goes. A clean getaway.
Or so you think, little man.

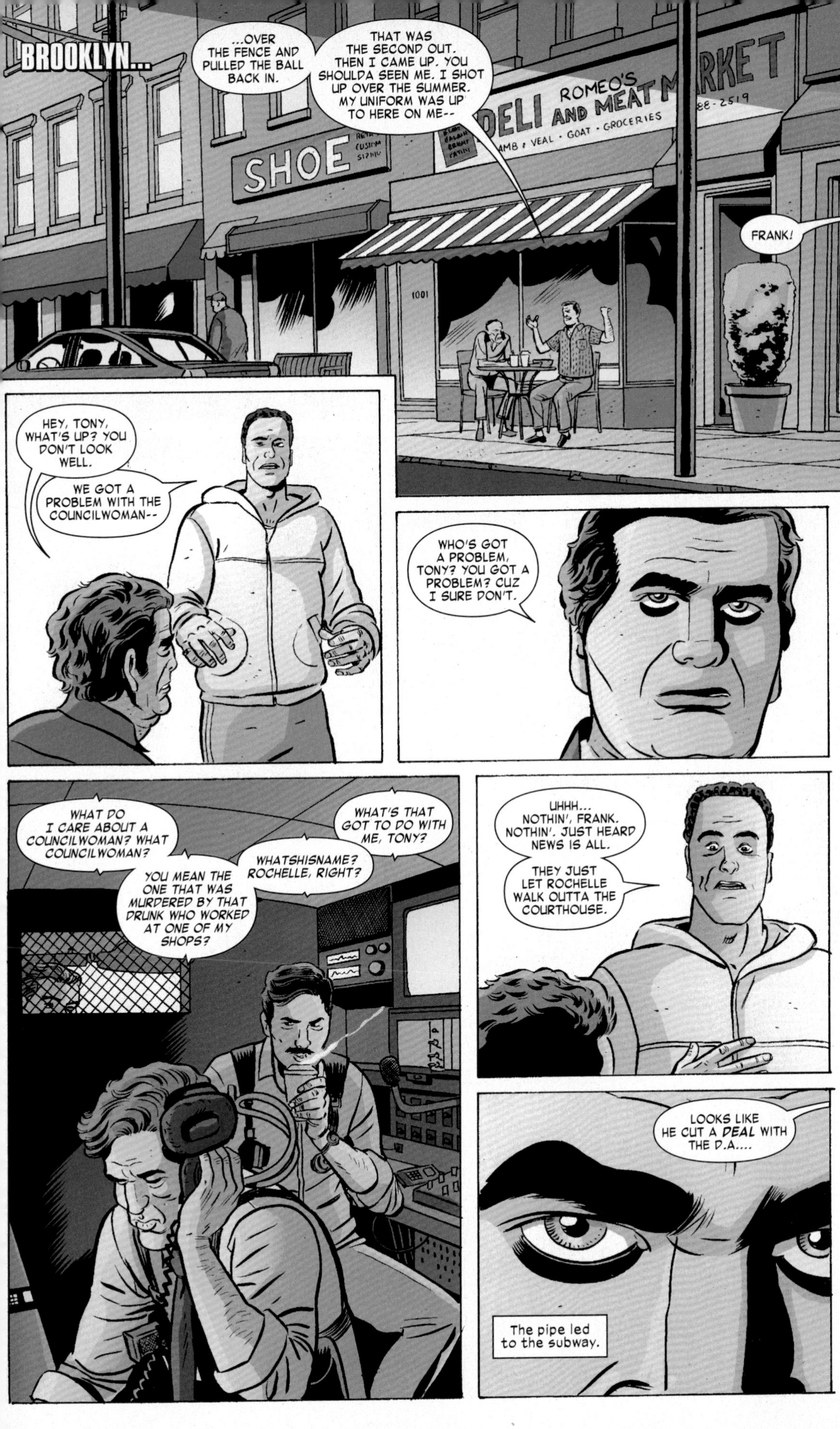
BROOKLYN...
...OVER THE FENCE AND PULLED THE BALL BACK IN.
THAT WAS THE SECOND OUT. THEN I CAME UP. YOU SHOULDA SEEN ME. I SHOT UP OVER THE SUMMER. MY UNIFORM WAS UP TO HERE ON ME--
SHOE
DELI ROMEO'S AND MEAT MARKET
LAMB • VEAL • GOAT • GROCERIES
1001
FRANK!
HEY, TONY, WHAT'S UP? YOU DON'T LOOK WELL.
WE GOT A PROBLEM WITH THE COUNCILWOMAN--
WHO'S GOT A PROBLEM, TONY? YOU GOT A PROBLEM? CUZ I SURE DON'T.
WHAT DO I CARE ABOUT A COUNCILWOMAN? WHAT COUNCILWOMAN?
YOU MEAN THE ONE THAT WAS MURDERED BY THAT DRUNK WHO WORKED AT ONE OF MY SHOPS?
WHATSHISNAME? ROCHELLE, RIGHT?
WHAT'S THAT GOT TO DO WITH ME, TONY?
UHHH... NOTHIN', FRANK. NOTHIN'. JUST HEARD NEWS IS ALL.
THEY JUST LET ROCHELLE WALK OUTTA THE COURTHOUSE.
LOOKS LIKE HE CUT A DEAL WITH THE D.A....
The pipe led to the subway.

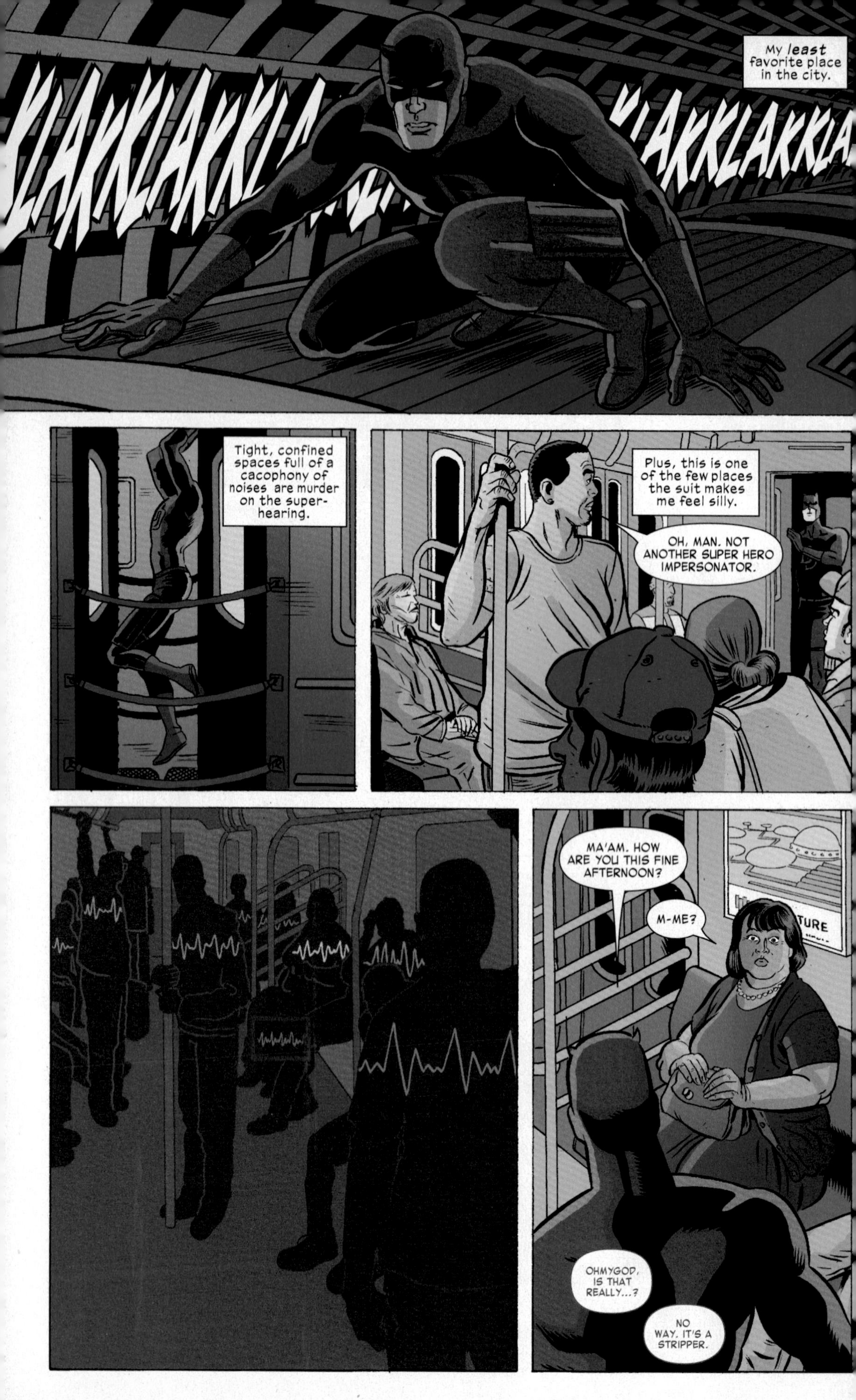
My least favorite place in the city.
KLAKKLAKKLA...
KLAKKLAKKLA
Tight, confined spaces full of a cacophony of noises are murder on the super-hearing.
Plus, this is one of the few places the suit makes me feel silly.
OH, MAN. NOT ANOTHER SUPER HERO IMPERSONATOR.
MA'AM. HOW ARE YOU THIS FINE AFTERNOON?
M-ME?
OHMYGOD, IS THAT REALLY...?
NO WAY. IT'S A STRIPPER.

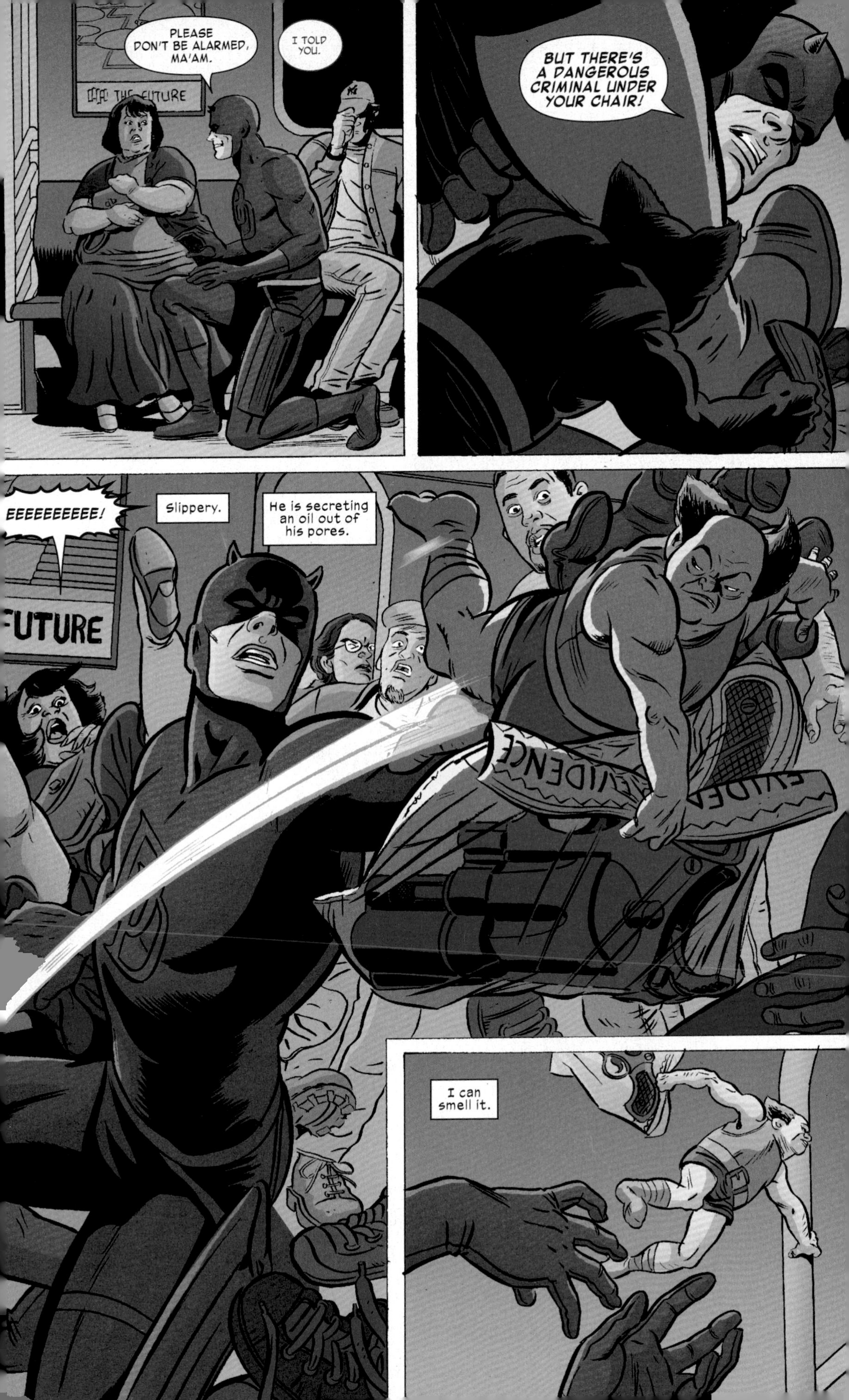
THE FUTURE
PLEASE DON'T BE ALARMED, MA'AM.
I TOLD YOU.
BUT THERE'S A DANGEROUS CRIMINAL UNDER YOUR CHAIR!
EEEEEEEEEE!
Slippery.
He is secreting an oil out of his pores.
FUTURE
EVIDENCE
EVIDEN
I can smell it.

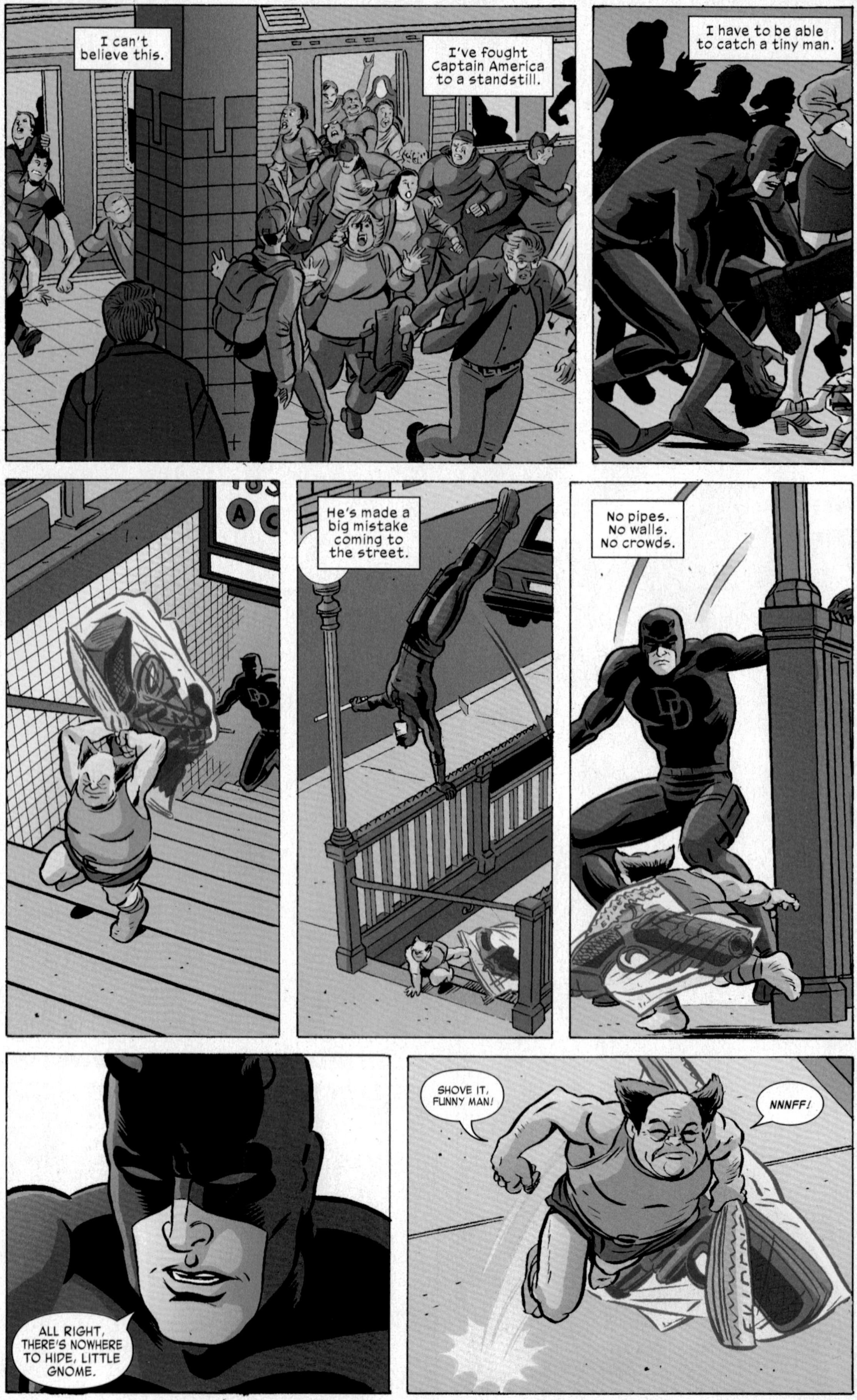
I can't believe this.
I've fought Captain America to a standstill.
I have to be able to catch a tiny man.
He's made a big mistake coming to the street.
No pipes. No walls. No crowds.
ALL RIGHT, THERE'S NOWHERE TO HIDE, LITTLE GNOME.
SHOVE IT, FUNNY MAN!
NNNFF!

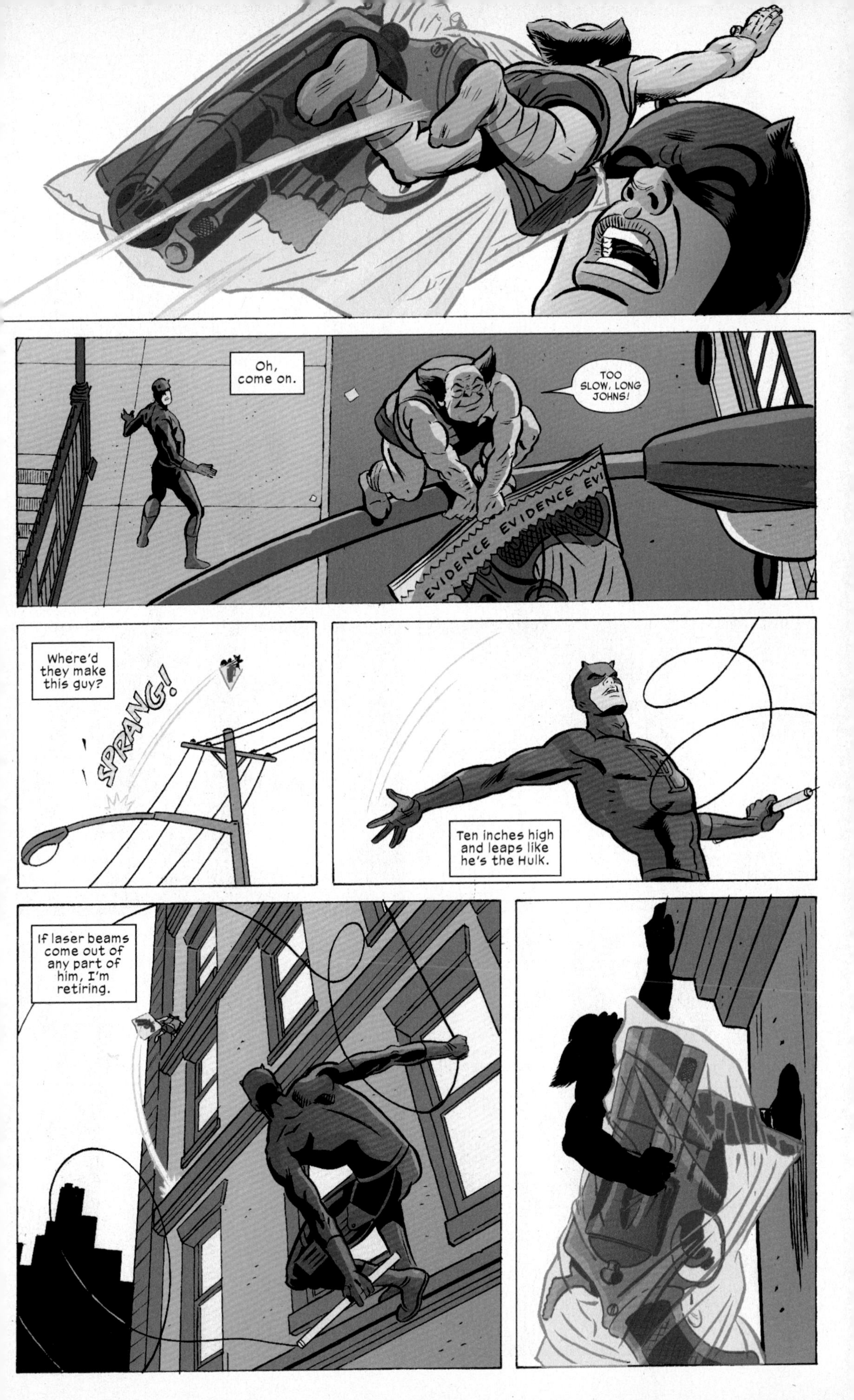
Oh, come on.
TOO SLOW, LONG JOHNS!
EVIDENCE EVIDENCE EVI
Where'd they make this guy?
SPRANG!
Ten inches high and leaps like he's the Hulk.
If laser beams come out of any part of him, I'm retiring.

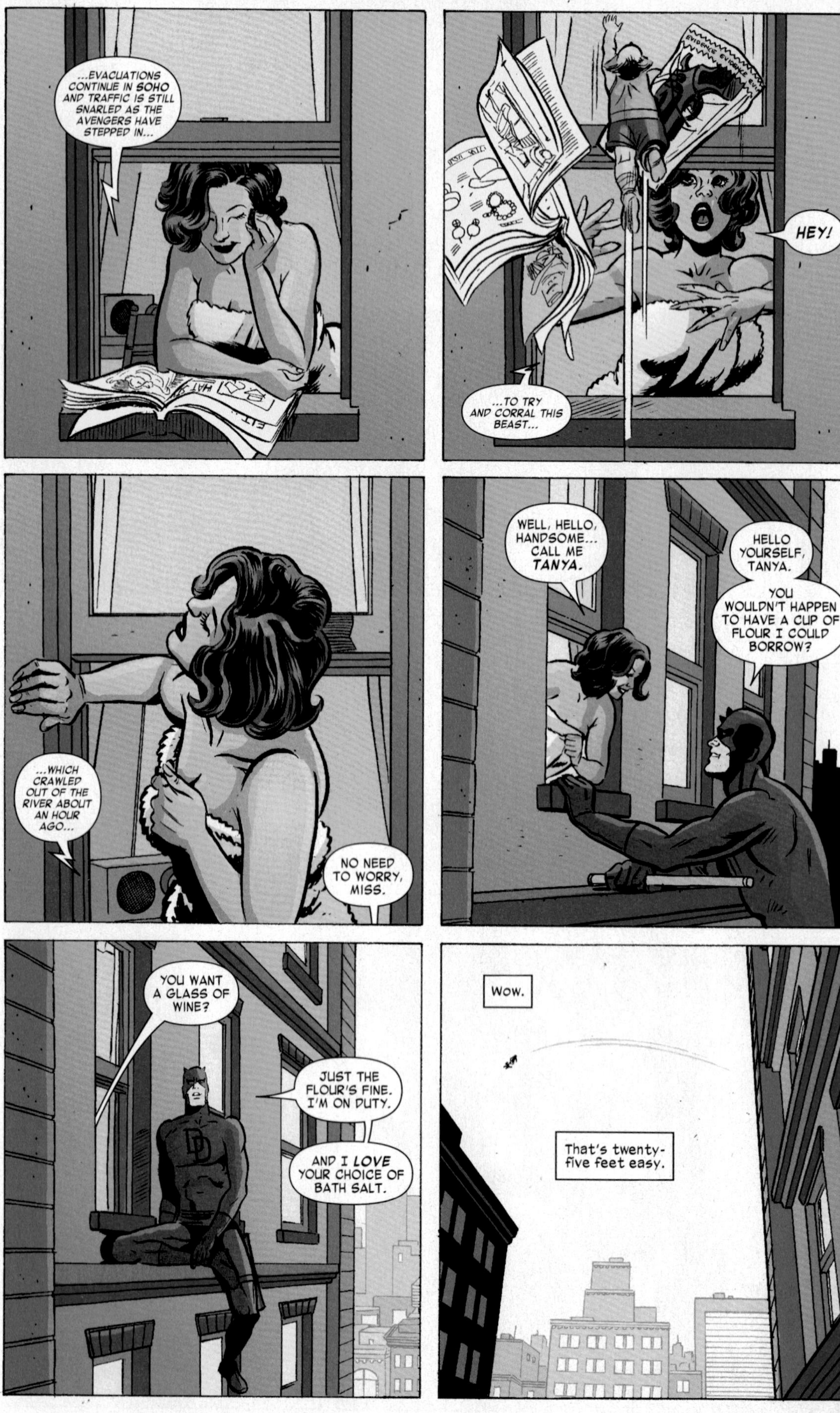
...EVACUATIONS CONTINUE IN SOHO AND TRAFFIC IS STILL SNARLED AS THE AVENGERS HAVE STEPPED IN...
HEY!
...TO TRY AND CORRAL THIS BEAST...
...WHICH CRAWLED OUT OF THE RIVER ABOUT AN HOUR AGO...
NO NEED TO WORRY, MISS.
WELL, HELLO, HANDSOME... CALL ME TANYA.
HELLO YOURSELF, TANYA.
YOU WOULDN'T HAPPEN TO HAVE A CUP OF FLOUR I COULD BORROW?
YOU WANT A GLASS OF WINE?
JUST THE FLOUR'S FINE. I'M ON DUTY.
AND I LOVE YOUR CHOICE OF BATH SALT.
Wow.
That's twenty-five feet easy.

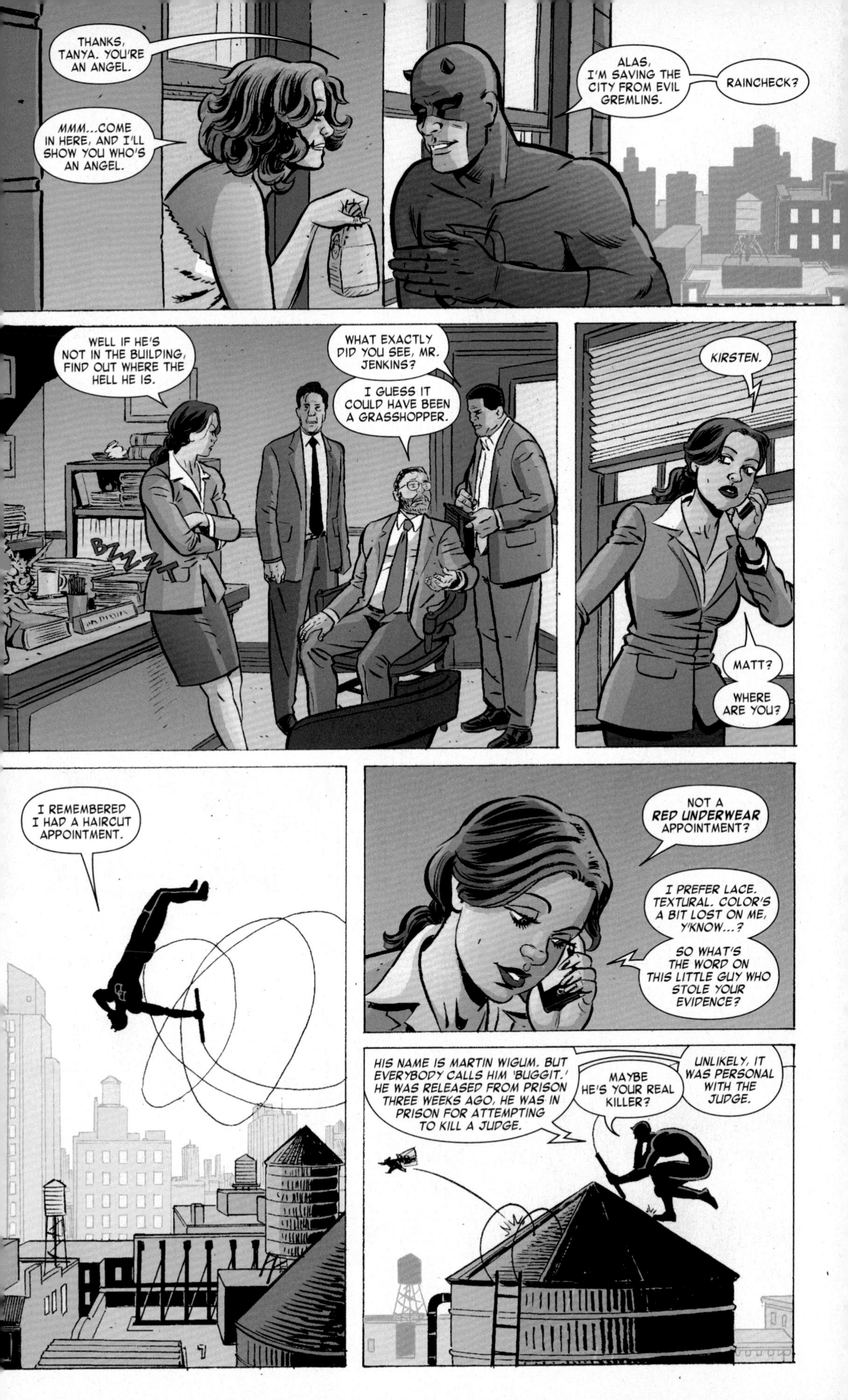
THANKS, TANYA. YOU'RE AN ANGEL.
MMM...COME IN HERE, AND I'LL SHOW YOU WHO'S AN ANGEL.
ALAS, I'M SAVING THE CITY FROM EVIL GREMLINS.
RAINCHECK?
WELL IF HE'S NOT IN THE BUILDING, FIND OUT WHERE THE HELL HE IS.
WHAT EXACTLY DID YOU SEE, MR. JENKINS?
I GUESS IT COULD HAVE BEEN A GRASSHOPPER.
BZZZT
KIRSTEN.
MATT?
WHERE ARE YOU?
I REMEMBERED I HAD A HAIRCUT APPOINTMENT.
NOT A **RED UNDERWEAR** APPOINTMENT?
I PREFER LACE. TEXTURAL. COLOR'S A BIT LOST ON ME, Y'KNOW...?
SO WHAT'S THE WORD ON THIS LITTLE GUY WHO STOLE YOUR EVIDENCE?
HIS NAME IS MARTIN WIGUM. BUT EVERYBODY CALLS HIM 'BUGGIT.' HE WAS RELEASED FROM PRISON THREE WEEKS AGO, HE WAS IN PRISON FOR ATTEMPTING TO KILL A JUDGE.
MAYBE HE'S YOUR REAL KILLER?
UNLIKELY, IT WAS PERSONAL WITH THE JUDGE.

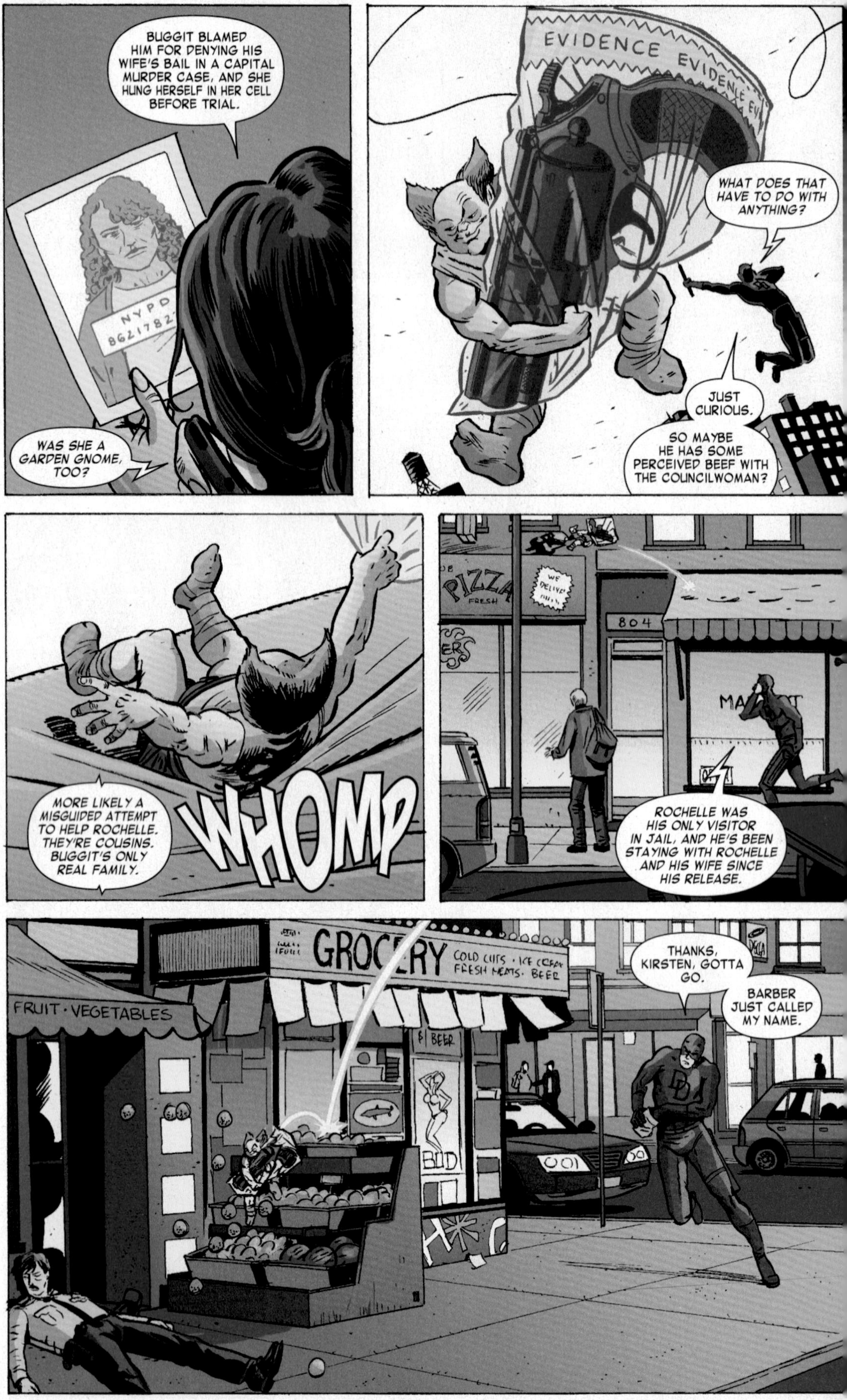
BUGGIT BLAMED HIM FOR DENYING HIS WIFE'S BAIL IN A CAPITAL MURDER CASE, AND SHE HUNG HERSELF IN HER CELL BEFORE TRIAL.
NYPD
8621782
WAS SHE A GARDEN GNOME, TOO?
EVIDENCE EVIDENCE
WHAT DOES THAT HAVE TO DO WITH ANYTHING?
JUST CURIOUS.
SO MAYBE HE HAS SOME PERCEIVED BEEF WITH THE COUNCILWOMAN?
MORE LIKELY A MISGUIDED ATTEMPT TO HELP ROCHELLE. THEY'RE COUSINS. BUGGIT'S ONLY REAL FAMILY.
WHOMP
PIZZA
FRESH
804
ROCHELLE WAS HIS ONLY VISITOR IN JAIL, AND HE'S BEEN STAYING WITH ROCHELLE AND HIS WIFE SINCE HIS RELEASE.
GROCERY
COLD CUTS • ICE CREAM
FRESH MEATS • BEER
FRUIT • VEGETABLES
BEER
BUD
THANKS, KIRSTEN, GOTTA GO.
BARBER JUST CALLED MY NAME.

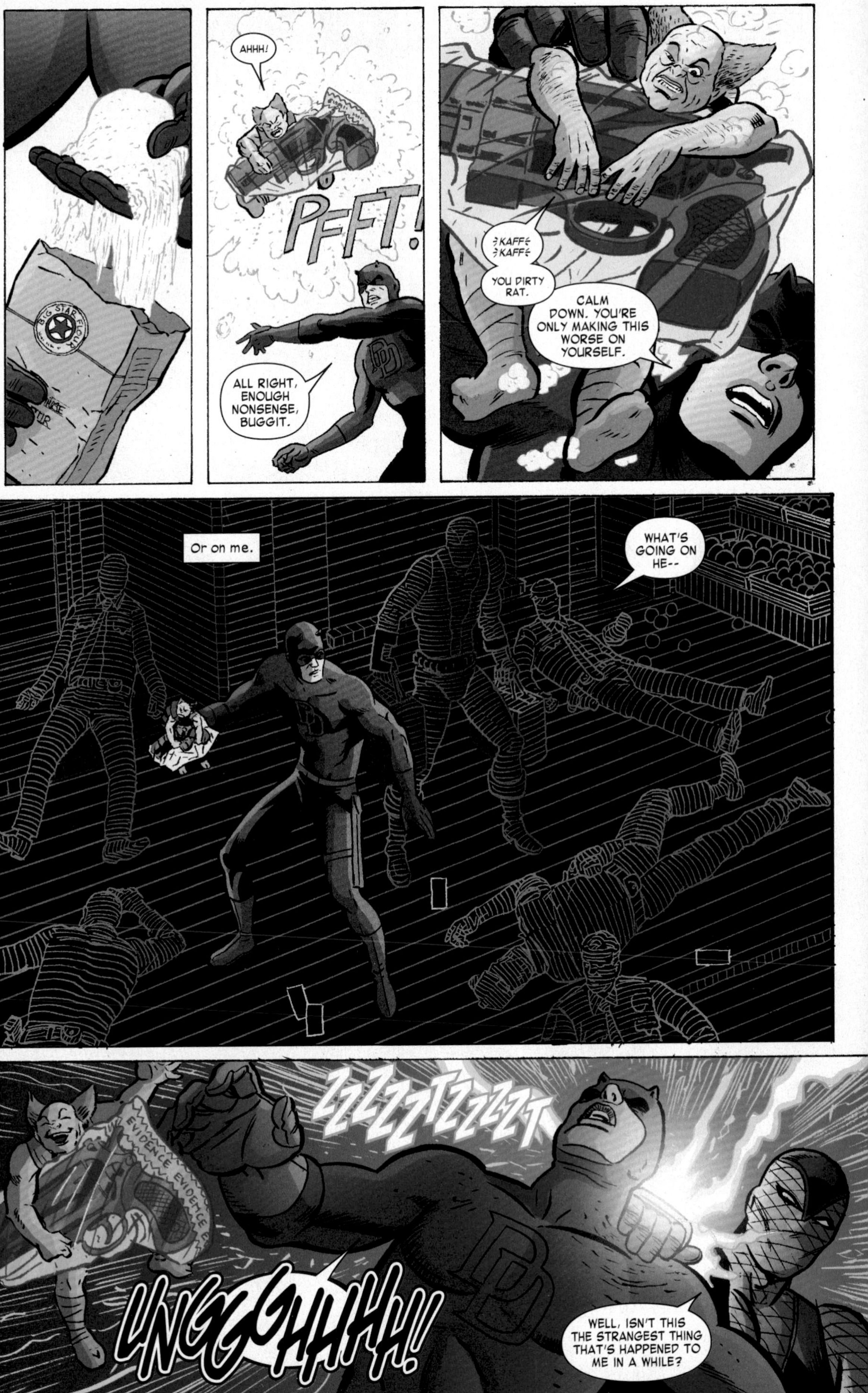
BIG STAR FLOUR
AHHH!
PFFT!
ALL RIGHT, ENOUGH NONSENSE, BUGGIT.
KAFF *KAFF*
YOU DIRTY RAT.
CALM DOWN. YOU'RE ONLY MAKING THIS WORSE ON YOURSELF.
Or on me.
WHAT'S GOING ON HE--
ZZZZTZZZZT
EVIDENCE EVIDENCE EVIDENCE
UNGGHHHH!
WELL, ISN'T THIS THE STRANGEST THING THAT'S HAPPENED TO ME IN A WHILE?

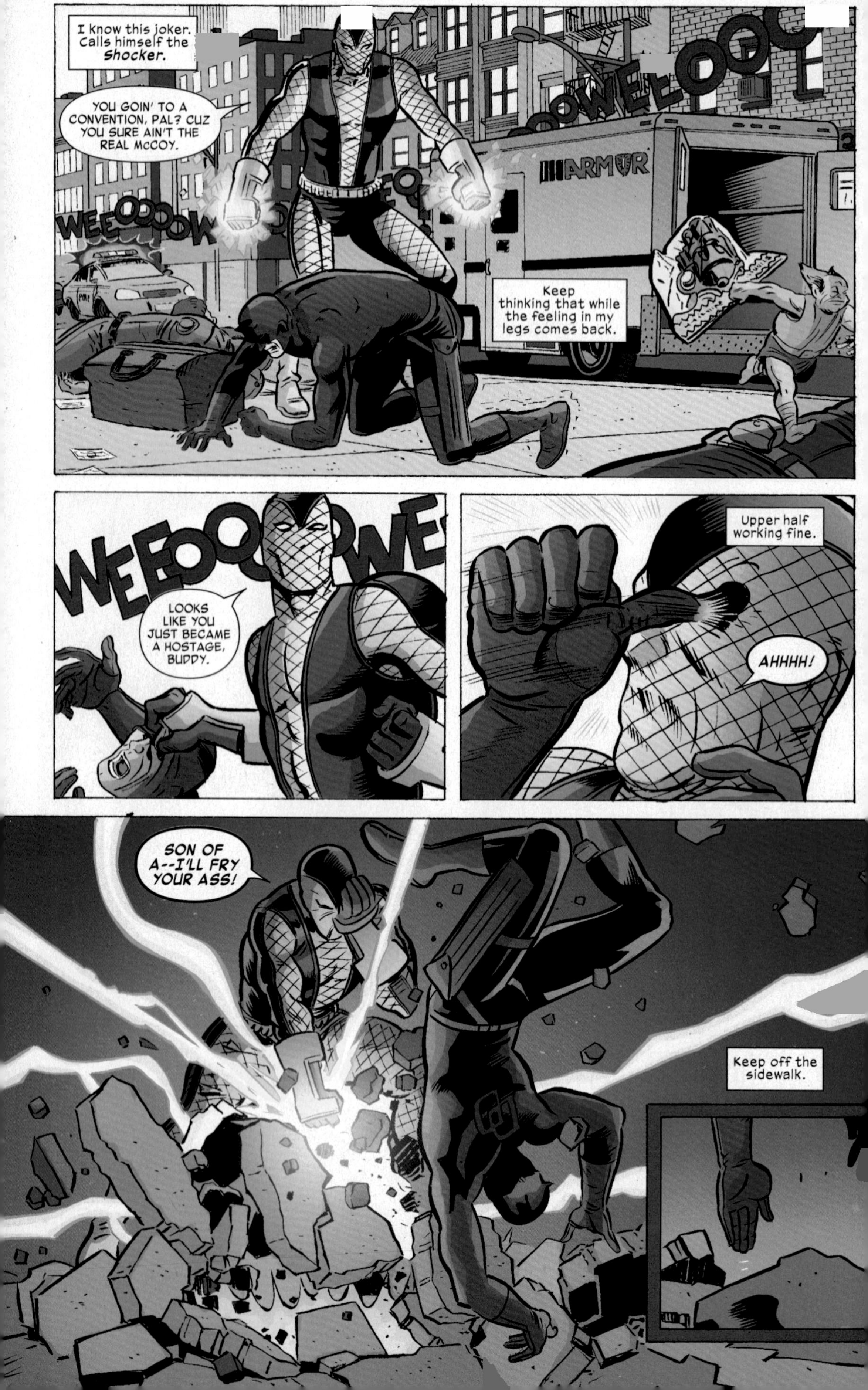
I know this joker. Calls himself the Shocker.
YOU GOIN' TO A CONVENTION, PAL? CUZ YOU SURE AIN'T THE REAL McCOY.
WEEOOOOW
OOWEEOOO
Keep thinking that while the feeling in my legs comes back.
ARMOR
WEEOOOWE
LOOKS LIKE YOU JUST BECAME A HOSTAGE, BUDDY.
Upper half working fine.
AHHHH!
SON OF A--I'LL FRY YOUR ASS!
Keep off the sidewalk.

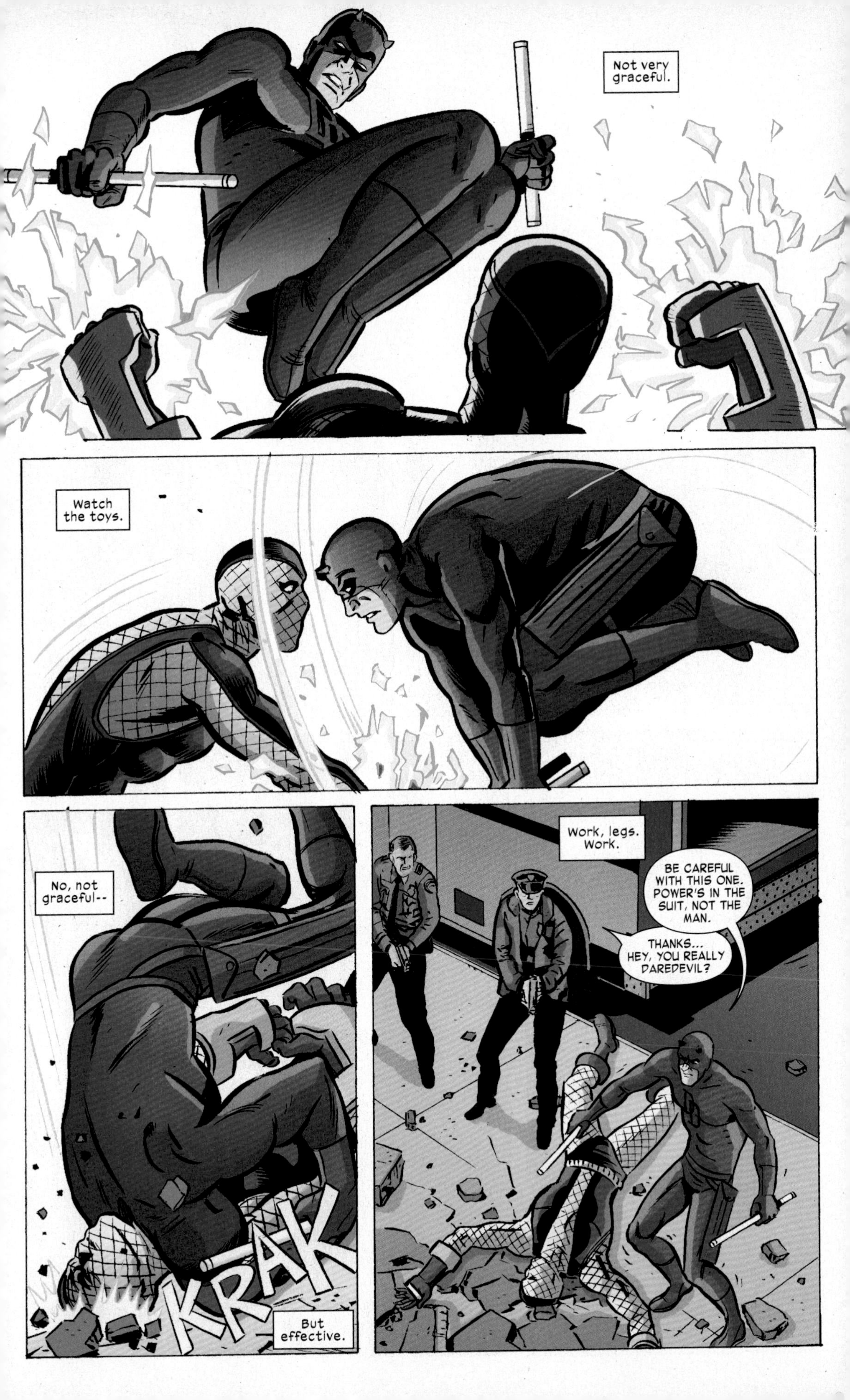
Not very graceful.
Watch the toys.
No, not graceful--
KRAK
But effective.
Work, legs. Work.
BE CAREFUL WITH THIS ONE. POWER'S IN THE SUIT, NOT THE MAN.
THANKS... HEY, YOU REALLY DAREDEVIL?

NEVER HEARD OF HIM.

Damn me.

Was I just outsmarted by a gnome?

Come on, Buggit...

Tell me you didn't stay to watch the action...

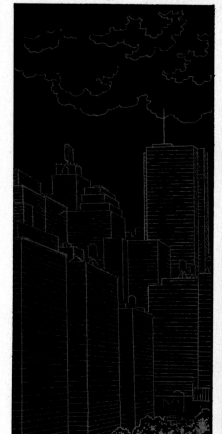

SKTT-SKTT-SKTTR

FLAP FLAP FLAP FLAP

Gotcha.

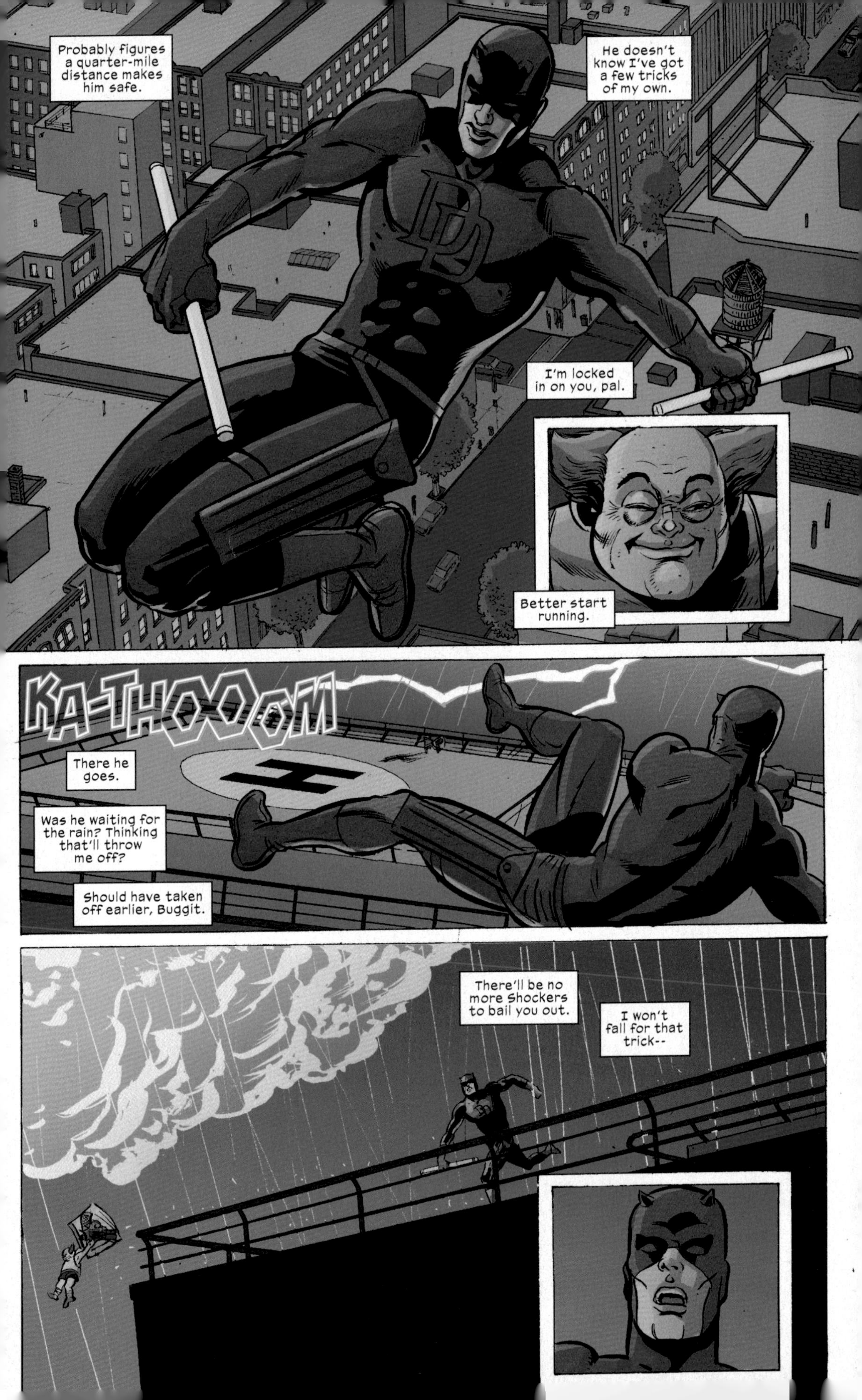
Probably figures a quarter-mile distance makes him safe.
He doesn't know I've got a few tricks of my own.
I'm locked in on you, pal.
Better start running.
KA-THOOOOM
There he goes.
Was he waiting for the rain? Thinking that'll throw me off?
Should have taken off earlier, Buggit.
There'll be no more Shockers to bail you out.
I won't fall for that trick--

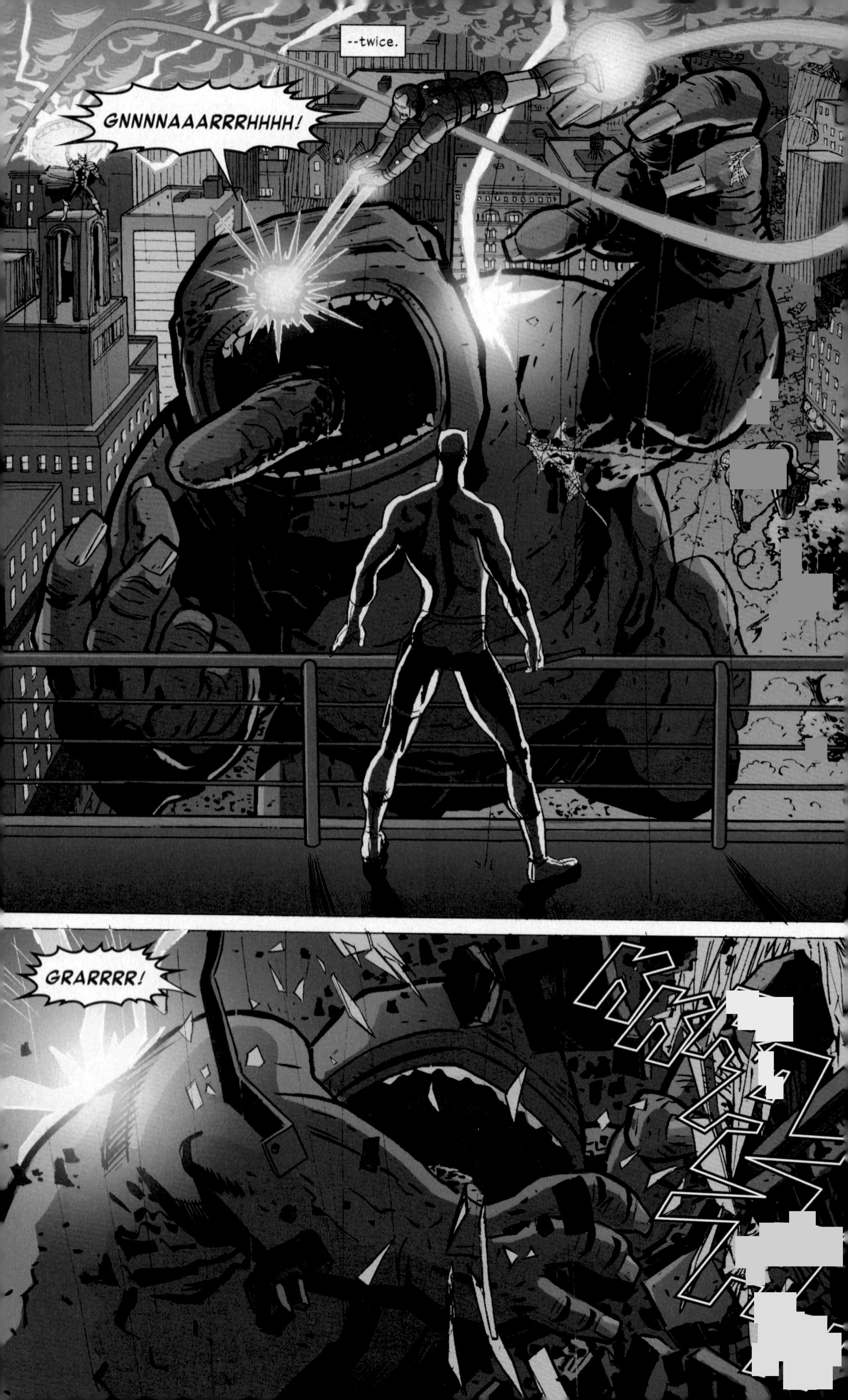
--twice.
GNNNNAAARRRHHHH!
GRARRRR!

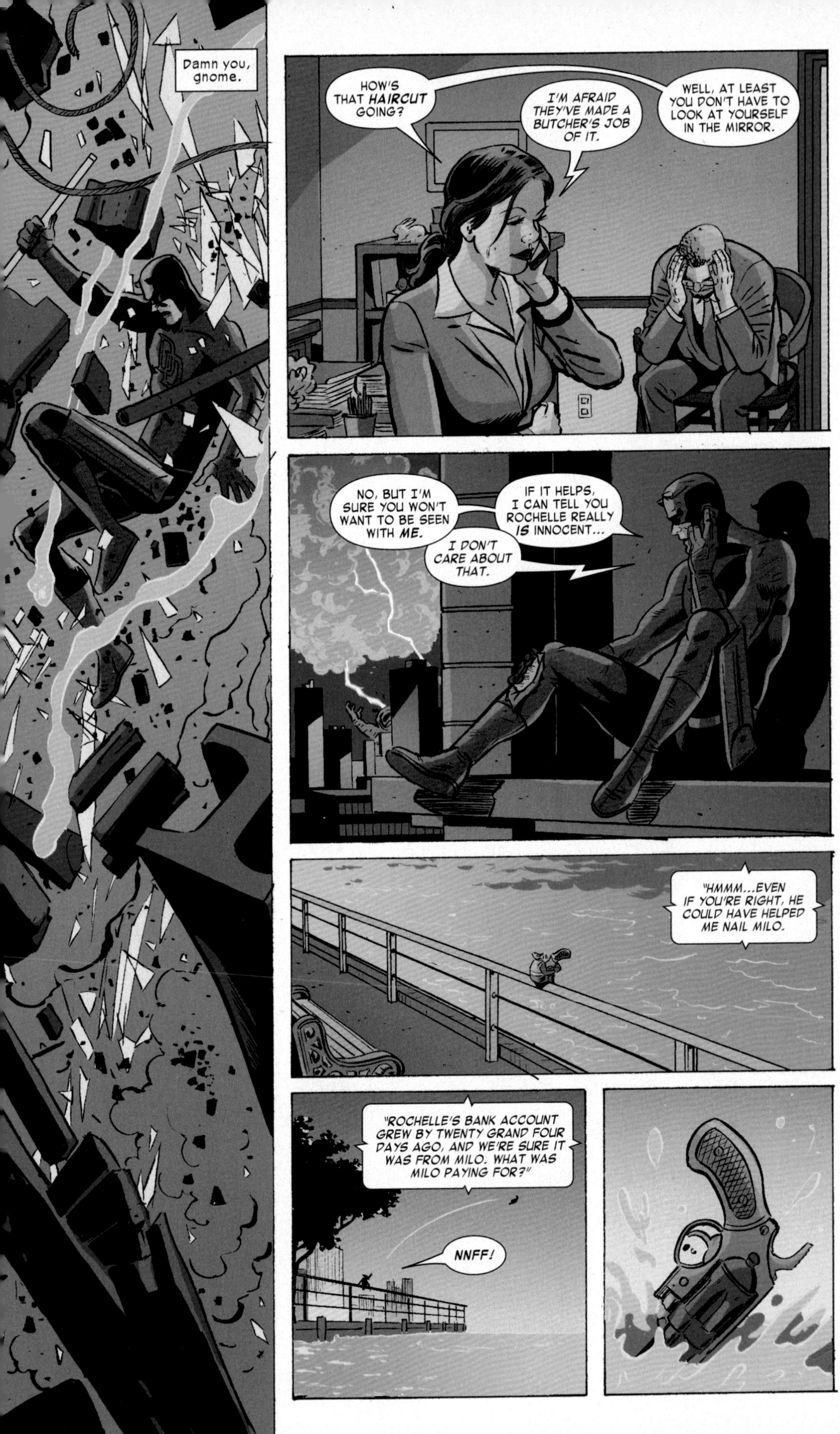
Damn you, gnome.
HOW'S THAT HAIRCUT GOING?
I'M AFRAID THEY'VE MADE A BUTCHER'S JOB OF IT.
WELL, AT LEAST YOU DON'T HAVE TO LOOK AT YOURSELF IN THE MIRROR.
NO, BUT I'M SURE YOU WON'T WANT TO BE SEEN WITH ME.
IF IT HELPS, I CAN TELL YOU ROCHELLE REALLY IS INNOCENT...
I DON'T CARE ABOUT THAT.
"HMMM...EVEN IF YOU'RE RIGHT, HE COULD HAVE HELPED ME NAIL MILO.
"ROCHELLE'S BANK ACCOUNT GREW BY TWENTY GRAND FOUR DAYS AGO, AND WE'RE SURE IT WAS FROM MILO. WHAT WAS MILO PAYING FOR?"
NNFF!

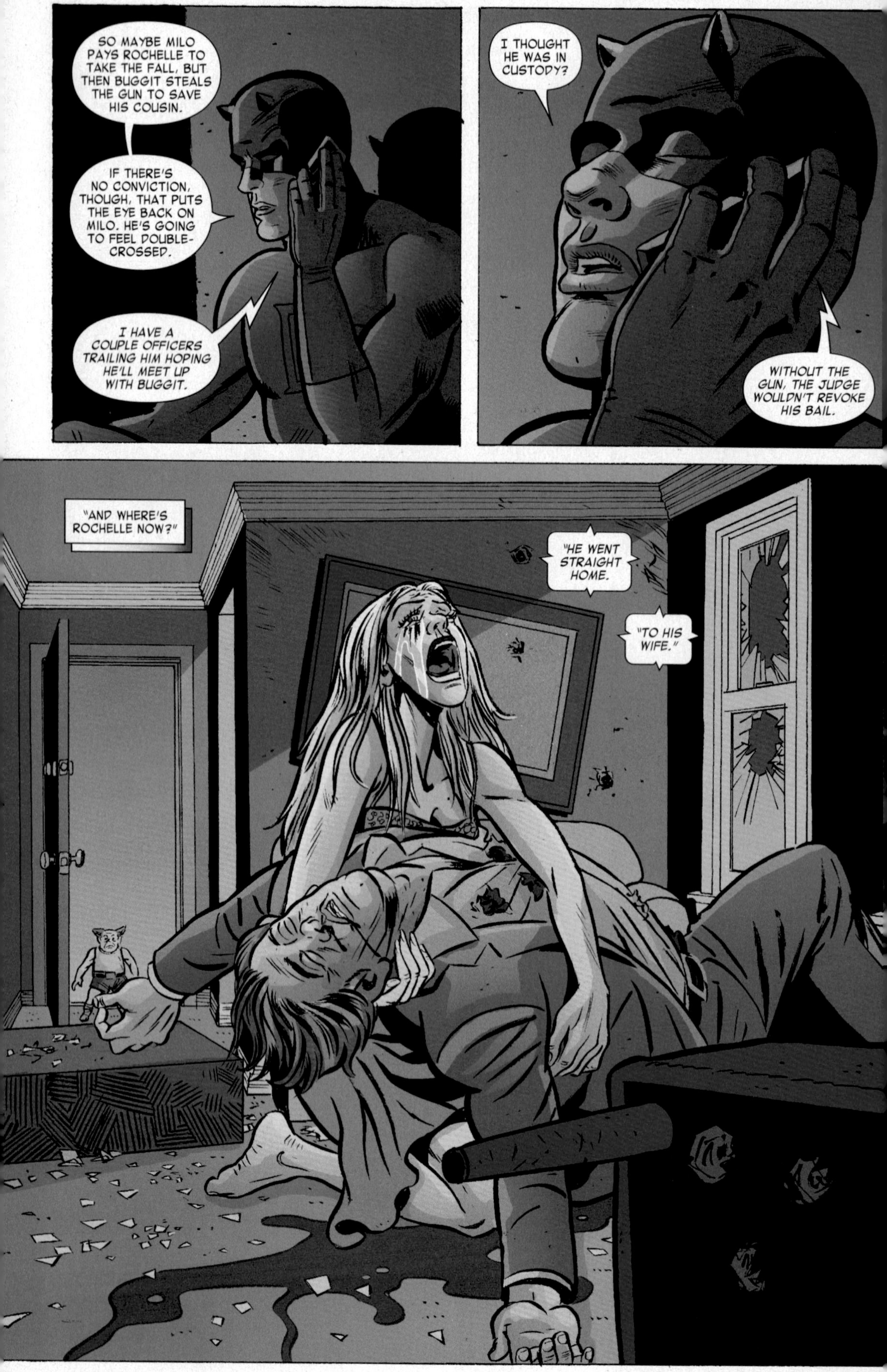

SO MAYBE MILO PAYS ROCHELLE TO TAKE THE FALL, BUT THEN BUGGIT STEALS THE GUN TO SAVE HIS COUSIN.
IF THERE'S NO CONVICTION, THOUGH, THAT PUTS THE EYE BACK ON MILO. HE'S GOING TO FEEL DOUBLE-CROSSED.
I HAVE A COUPLE OFFICERS TRAILING HIM HOPING HE'LL MEET UP WITH BUGGIT.
I THOUGHT HE WAS IN CUSTODY?
WITHOUT THE GUN, THE JUDGE WOULDN'T REVOKE HIS BAIL.
"AND WHERE'S ROCHELLE NOW?"
"HE WENT STRAIGHT HOME.
"TO HIS WIFE."

#5 — A MAN NAMED BUGGIT
PART TWO: WHAT A NIGHT

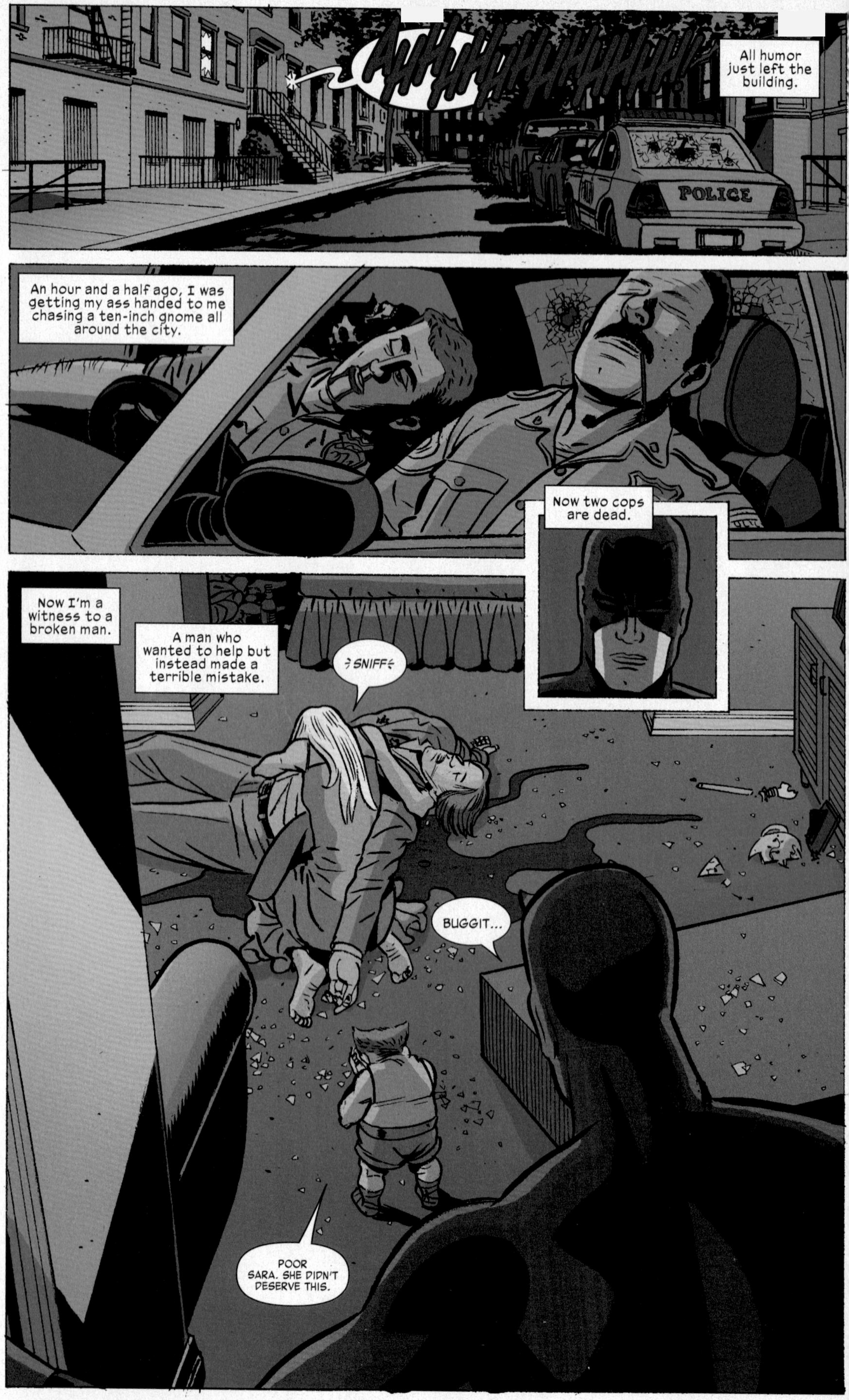
AAHHHHHHHHHHHHH!
All humor just left the building.
POLICE
An hour and a half ago, I was getting my ass handed to me chasing a ten-inch gnome all around the city.
Now two cops are dead.
Now I'm a witness to a broken man.
A man who wanted to help but instead made a terrible mistake.
SNIFF
BUGGIT...
POOR SARA. SHE DIDN'T DESERVE THIS.

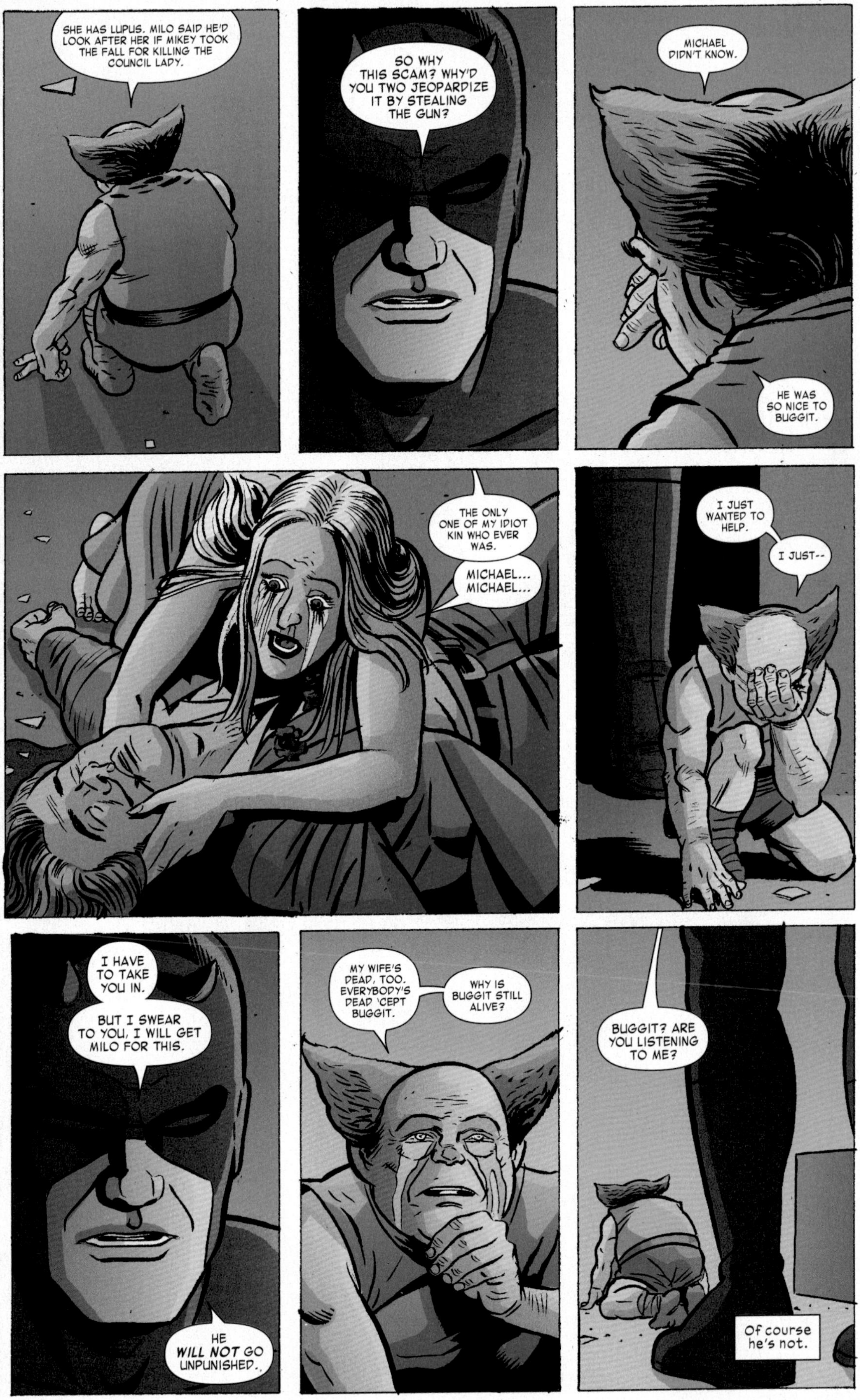
SHE HAS LUPUS. MILO SAID HE'D LOOK AFTER HER IF MIKEY TOOK THE FALL FOR KILLING THE COUNCIL LADY.
SO WHY THIS SCAM? WHY'D YOU TWO JEOPARDIZE IT BY STEALING THE GUN?
MICHAEL DIDN'T KNOW.
HE WAS SO NICE TO BUGGIT.
THE ONLY ONE OF MY IDIOT KIN WHO EVER WAS.
MICHAEL... MICHAEL...
I JUST WANTED TO HELP.
I JUST--
I HAVE TO TAKE YOU IN.
BUT I SWEAR TO YOU, I WILL GET MILO FOR THIS.
HE WILL NOT GO UNPUNISHED.
MY WIFE'S DEAD, TOO. EVERYBODY'S DEAD 'CEPT BUGGIT.
WHY IS BUGGIT STILL ALIVE?
BUGGIT? ARE YOU LISTENING TO ME?
Of course he's not.

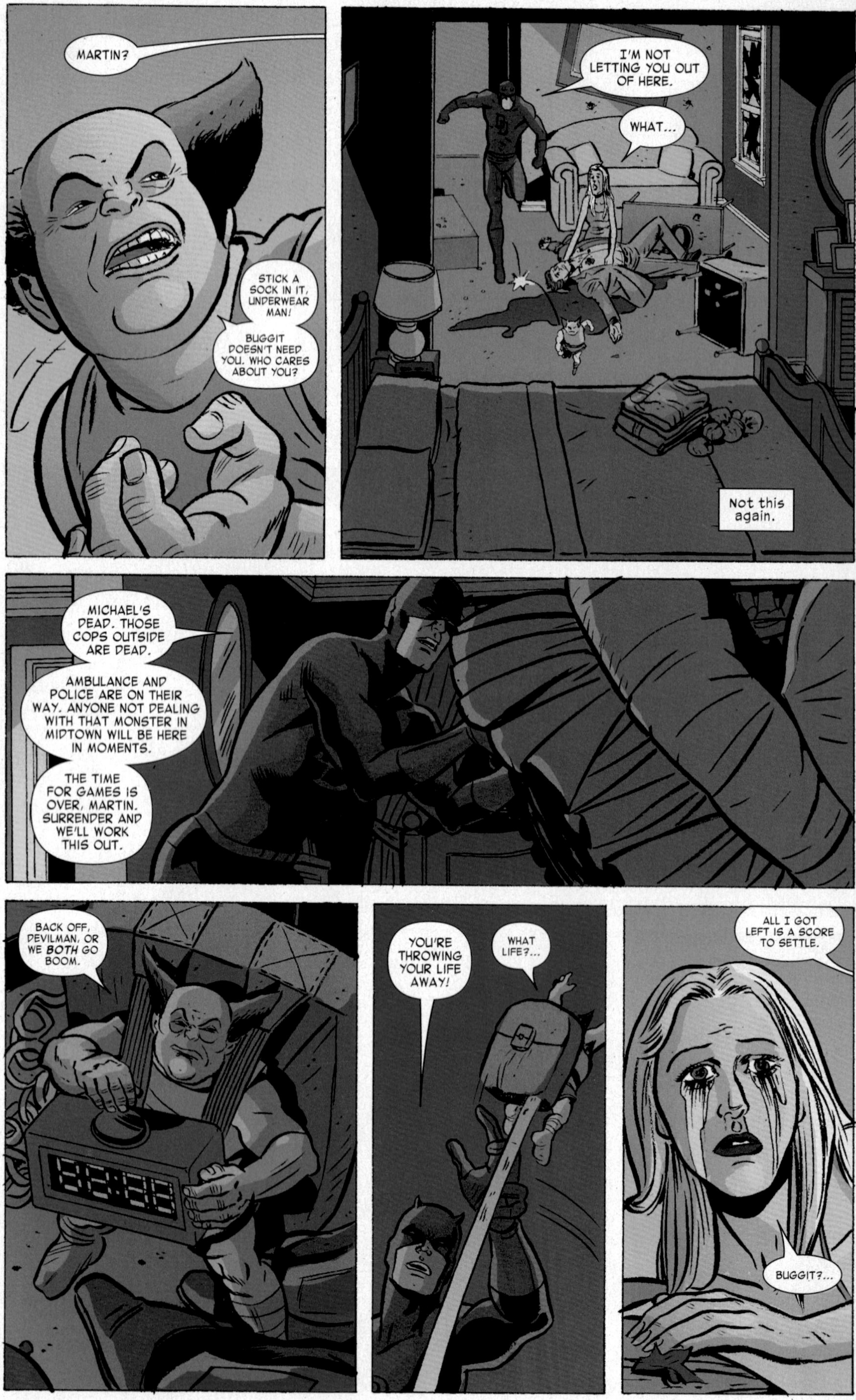
MARTIN?
STICK A SOCK IN IT, UNDERWEAR MAN!
BUGGIT DOESN'T NEED YOU. WHO CARES ABOUT YOU?
I'M NOT LETTING YOU OUT OF HERE.
WHAT...
Not this again.
MICHAEL'S DEAD. THOSE COPS OUTSIDE ARE DEAD.
AMBULANCE AND POLICE ARE ON THEIR WAY. ANYONE NOT DEALING WITH THAT MONSTER IN MIDTOWN WILL BE HERE IN MOMENTS.
THE TIME FOR GAMES IS OVER, MARTIN. SURRENDER AND WE'LL WORK THIS OUT.
BACK OFF, DEVILMAN, OR WE BOTH GO BOOM.
YOU'RE THROWING YOUR LIFE AWAY!
WHAT LIFE?...
ALL I GOT LEFT IS A SCORE TO SETTLE.
BUGGIT?...

GOT A PROBLEM WITH THAT? TRY AND CATCH ME.

That's one stubborn little man.

With the Avengers fighting that subterranean monster in Midtown, it seems crazy to be chasing down a tiny grieving man.

But the harder Buggit's pushed, the harder he pushes back.

He's dead serious, and hell-bent on revenge.

ROAAARRHH!

On a day where New York City has enough *hell* to deal with already.

If I get too close he'll blow us, and anyone else around, sky-high.

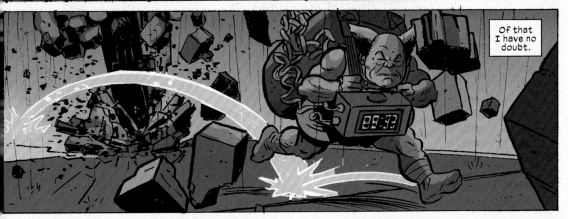

Of that I have no doubt.

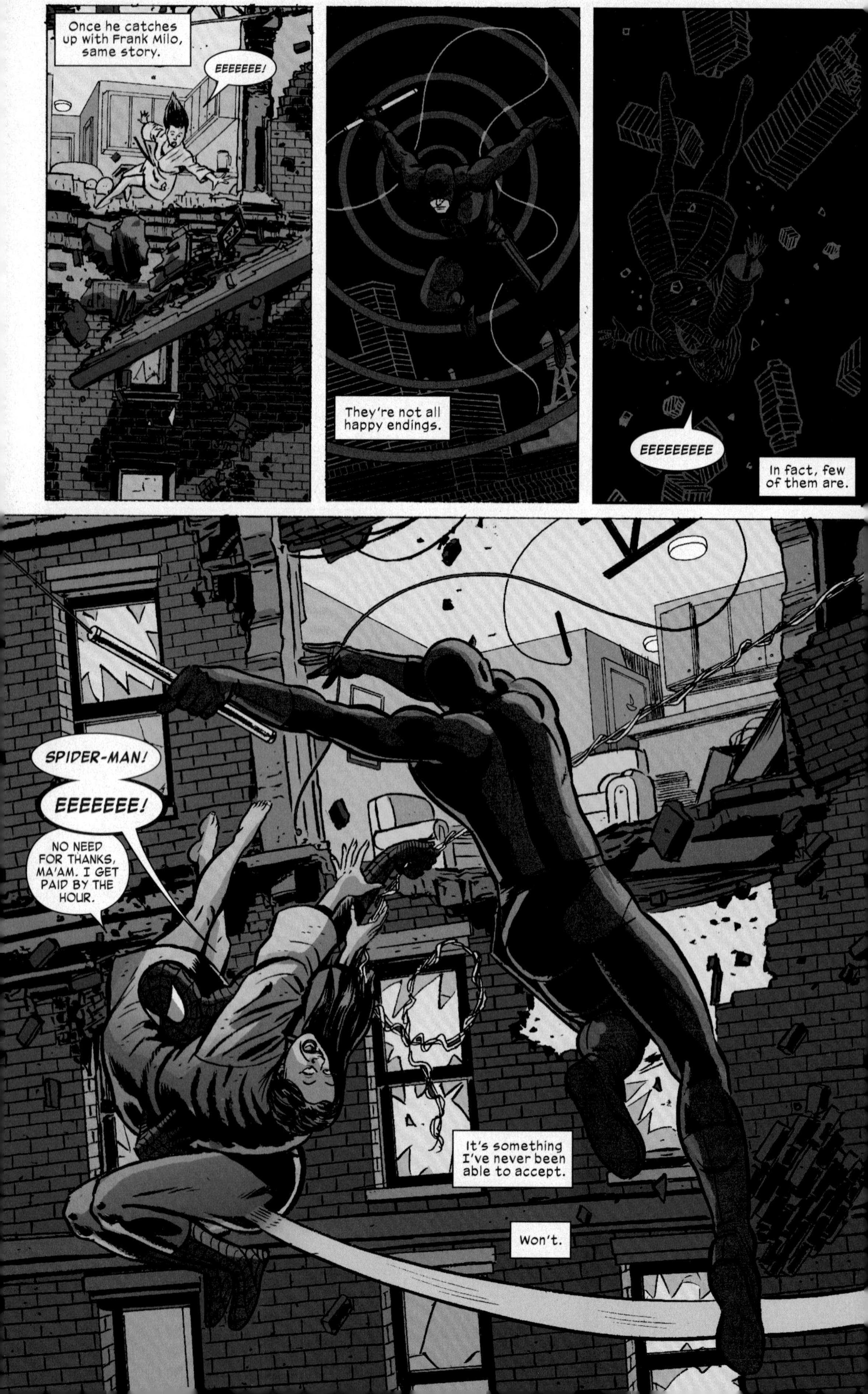

Once he catches up with Frank Milo, same story.
EEEEEEE!
They're not all happy endings.
EEEEEEEEE
In fact, few of them are.
SPIDER-MAN!
EEEEEEE!
NO NEED FOR THANKS, MA'AM. I GET PAID BY THE HOUR.
It's something I've never been able to accept.
Won't.

Not if I have any say in it.

OH, GOD! OH, GOD! GO BACK! GO BACK!

YOU STAY PUT! I'LL GET YOUR BABY.

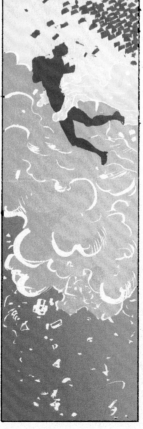

CONNOR!

HE'S FINE, MISS.

WELL, SOMEBODY'S SCORING MAJOR MOM POINTS.

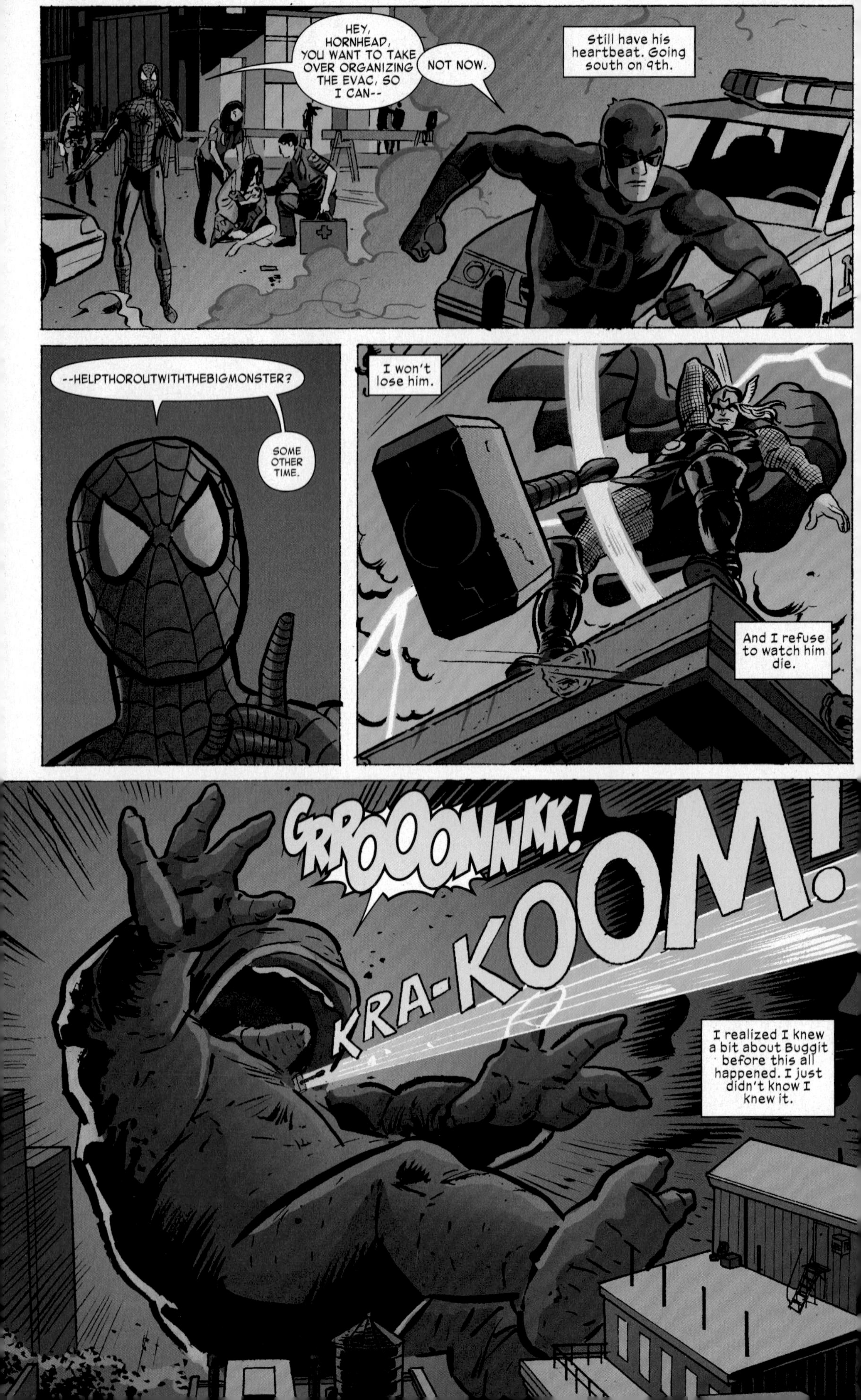
HEY, HORNHEAD, YOU WANT TO TAKE OVER ORGANIZING THE EVAC, SO I CAN--
NOT NOW.
Still have his heartbeat. Going south on 9th.
--HELPTHOROUTWITHTHEBIGMONSTER?
SOME OTHER TIME.
I won't lose him.
And I refuse to watch him die.
GRROOOONNKK!
KRA-KOOOM!
I realized I knew a bit about Buggit before this all happened. I just didn't know I knew it.

Michael Rochelle came to see me a few weeks ago insisting he was being framed for the murder of Councilwoman Stevens...

I CAN'T GO BACK TO JAIL. MY WIFE, SARA'S SICK. I TAKE CARE OF HER, SEE?

I BELIEVE YOU, MR. ROCHELLE, BUT I'M NOT CURRENTLY PRACTICING TRIAL LAW. I CAN ONLY ADVISE YOU IF YOU CHOOSE TO ACT AS YOUR OWN COUNSEL.

AND MY FIRST ADVICE WOULD BE TO GET YOURSELF A FIRST CLASS TRIAL ATTORNEY.

MY COUSIN MARTIN'S JUST GOT OUT OF JAIL. POOR GUY'S WIFE WAS REAL PSYCHO. SHE TWISTED HIS HEAD ALL AROUND.

WHEN SHE KILLED HERSELF, HE KINDA SHUT DOWN INSIDE, SEE? GOT REAL ANGRY AT THE WORLD.

HE DON'T WANNA LISTEN TO NOBODY. BUT HE'LL LISTEN TO ME.

SINCE MARTIN GOT IN TROUBLE I BEEN CLEAN AS A WHISTLE.

HE NEEDS ME, AND I GUESS I NEED HIM, TOO...

I have to admit, at the time, all that schmaltz just washed over me.

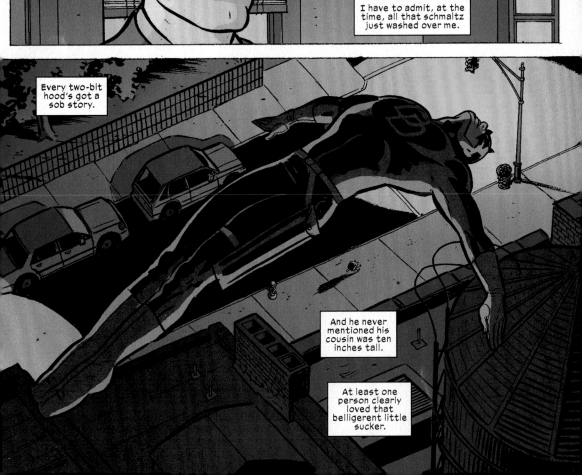

Every two-bit hood's got a sob story.

And he never mentioned his cousin was ten inches tall.

At least one person clearly loved that belligerent little sucker.

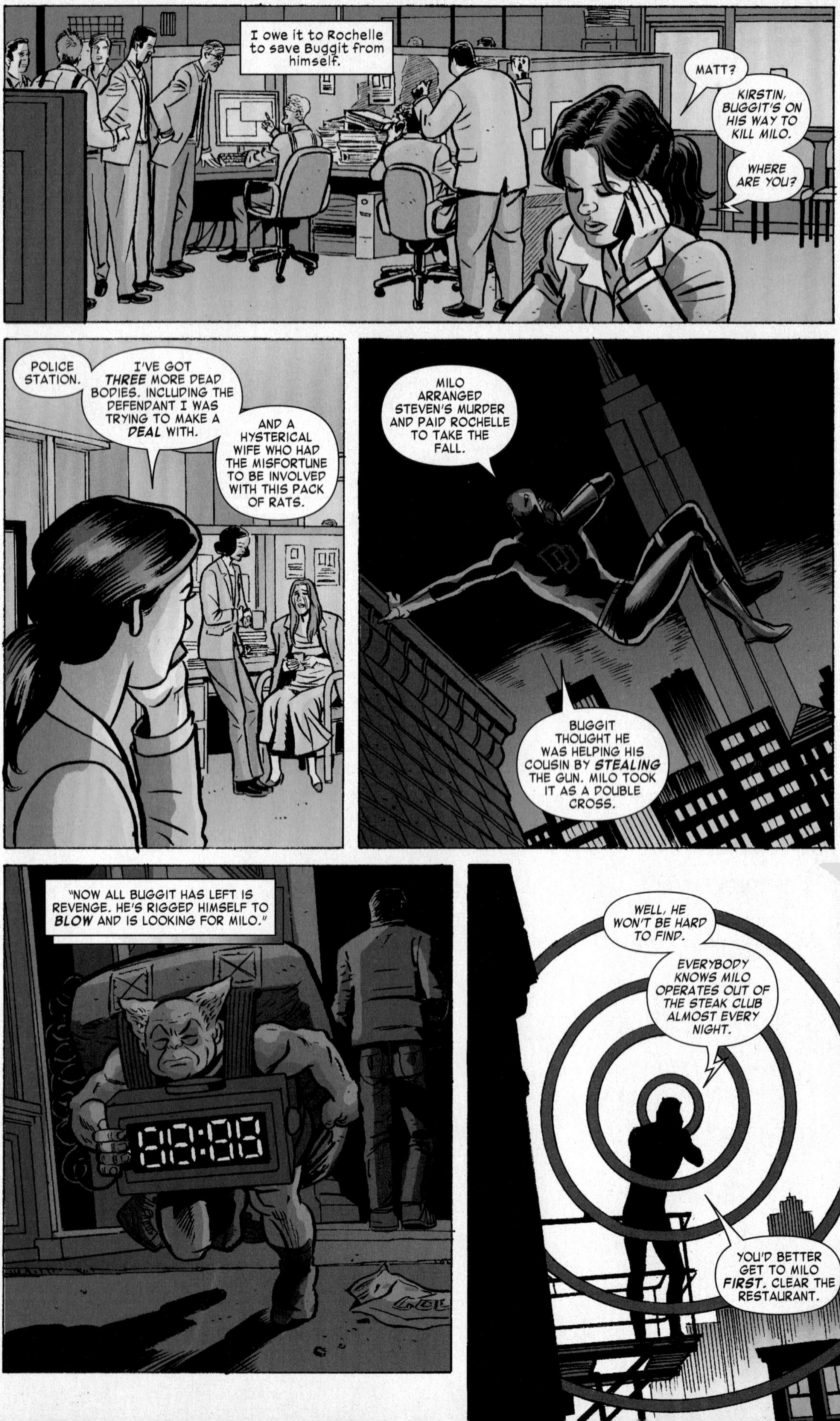
I owe it to Rochelle to save Buggit from himself.
MATT?
KIRSTIN, BUGGIT'S ON HIS WAY TO KILL MILO.
WHERE ARE YOU?
POLICE STATION.
I'VE GOT THREE MORE DEAD BODIES. INCLUDING THE DEFENDANT I WAS TRYING TO MAKE A DEAL WITH.
AND A HYSTERICAL WIFE WHO HAD THE MISFORTUNE TO BE INVOLVED WITH THIS PACK OF RATS.
MILO ARRANGED STEVEN'S MURDER AND PAID ROCHELLE TO TAKE THE FALL.
BUGGIT THOUGHT HE WAS HELPING HIS COUSIN BY STEALING THE GUN. MILO TOOK IT AS A DOUBLE CROSS.
"NOW ALL BUGGIT HAS LEFT IS REVENGE. HE'S RIGGED HIMSELF TO BLOW AND IS LOOKING FOR MILO."
WELL, HE WON'T BE HARD TO FIND.
EVERYBODY KNOWS MILO OPERATES OUT OF THE STEAK CLUB ALMOST EVERY NIGHT.
YOU'D BETTER GET TO MILO FIRST. CLEAR THE RESTAURANT.

PUT MILO UNDER PROTECTION UNTIL I CAN FIGURE OUT SOME WAY TO TALK BUGGIT DOWN.

PROTECT THE MOB BOSS WHO JUST HAD TWO DETECTIVES *GUNNED* DOWN.

MAKES YOU WONDER WHOSE SIDE WE'RE ON.

NOT ME.

I'M ON THE SIDE OF LIFE.

What the hell is going on down there?

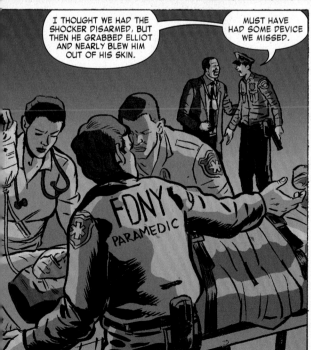

I THOUGHT WE HAD THE SHOCKER DISARMED, BUT THEN HE GRABBED ELLIOT AND NEARLY BLEW HIM OUT OF HIS SKIN.

MUST HAVE HAD SOME DEVICE WE MISSED.

FDNY PARAMEDIC

I FIRED, MISSED, AND SHOCKER RAN INTO THE BUILDING.

ALL RIGHT. COVER ALL THE EXITS AND WAIT FOR S.W.A.T.

I should have made sure Shocker was out for the count.

ELLIOT'S IN BAD SHAPE, CAPTAIN, THEY'RE NOT SURE IF HE'LL MAKE IT.

Now another cop might die tonight.

And this one'll be on me.

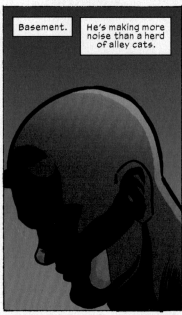

Basement.

He's making more noise than a herd of alley cats.

Tapping the building's power supply.

SPAK

STUPID...STUPID... LET YOUR TEMPER GET THE BEST OF YOU WITH THAT COP....

Shocker's gauntlets project compressed air at such a high frequency they can literally separate matter.

He needs juice to run them.

Apparently a lot--

--for whatever he has planned next.

COME ON, BABY. COME ON...

HIGH VOLTAGE

ZZ

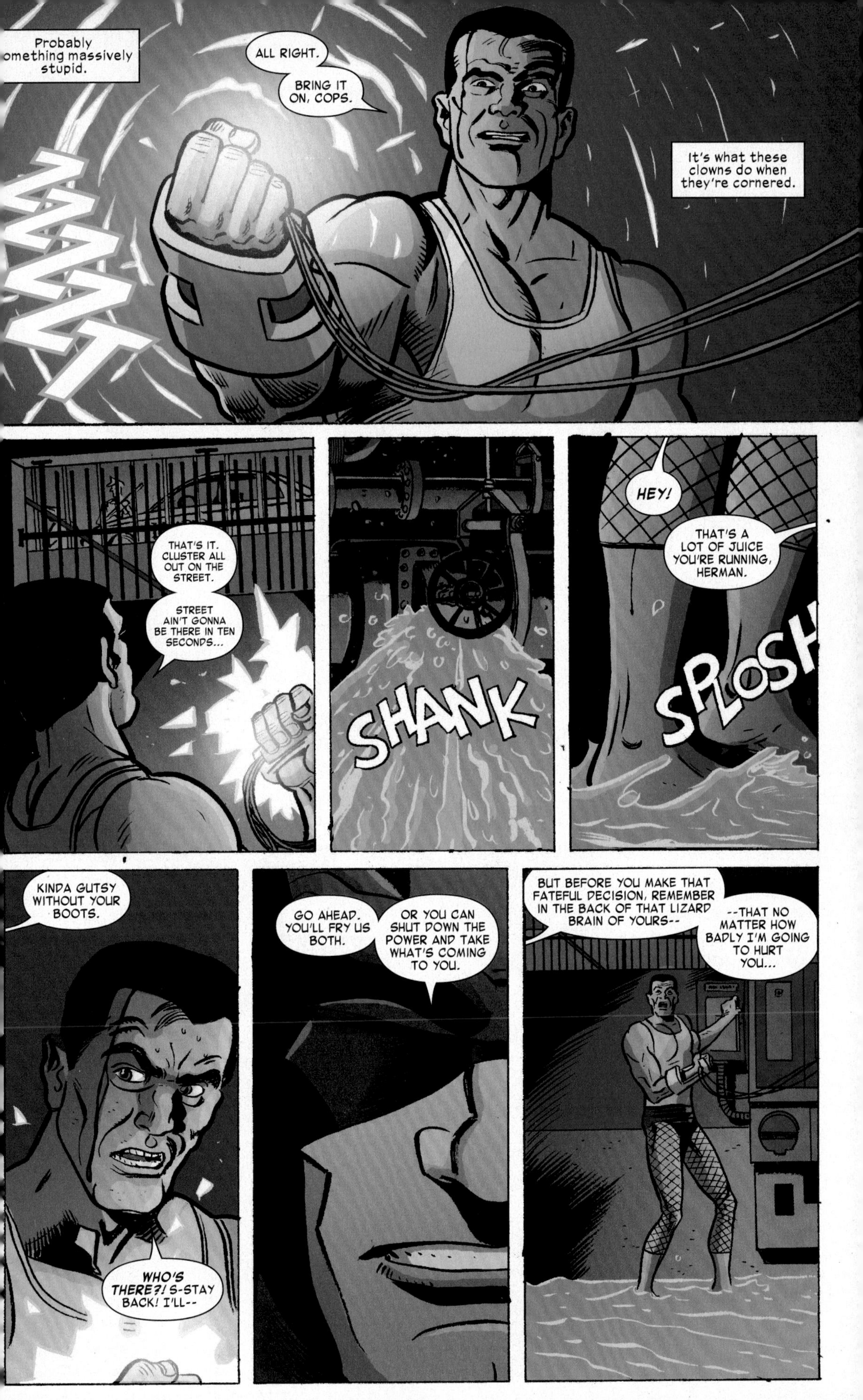

Probably
omething massively
stupid.
ALL RIGHT.
BRING IT ON, COPS.
It's what these clowns do when they're cornered.
ZZZT
THAT'S IT. CLUSTER ALL OUT ON THE STREET.
STREET AIN'T GONNA BE THERE IN TEN SECONDS...
SHANK
HEY!
THAT'S A LOT OF JUICE YOU'RE RUNNING, HERMAN.
SPLOSH
KINDA GUTSY WITHOUT YOUR BOOTS.
WHO'S THERE?! S-STAY BACK! I'LL--
GO AHEAD. YOU'LL FRY US BOTH.
OR YOU CAN SHUT DOWN THE POWER AND TAKE WHAT'S COMING TO YOU.
BUT BEFORE YOU MAKE THAT FATEFUL DECISION, REMEMBER IN THE BACK OF THAT LIZARD BRAIN OF YOURS--
--THAT NO MATTER HOW BADLY I'M GOING TO HURT YOU...

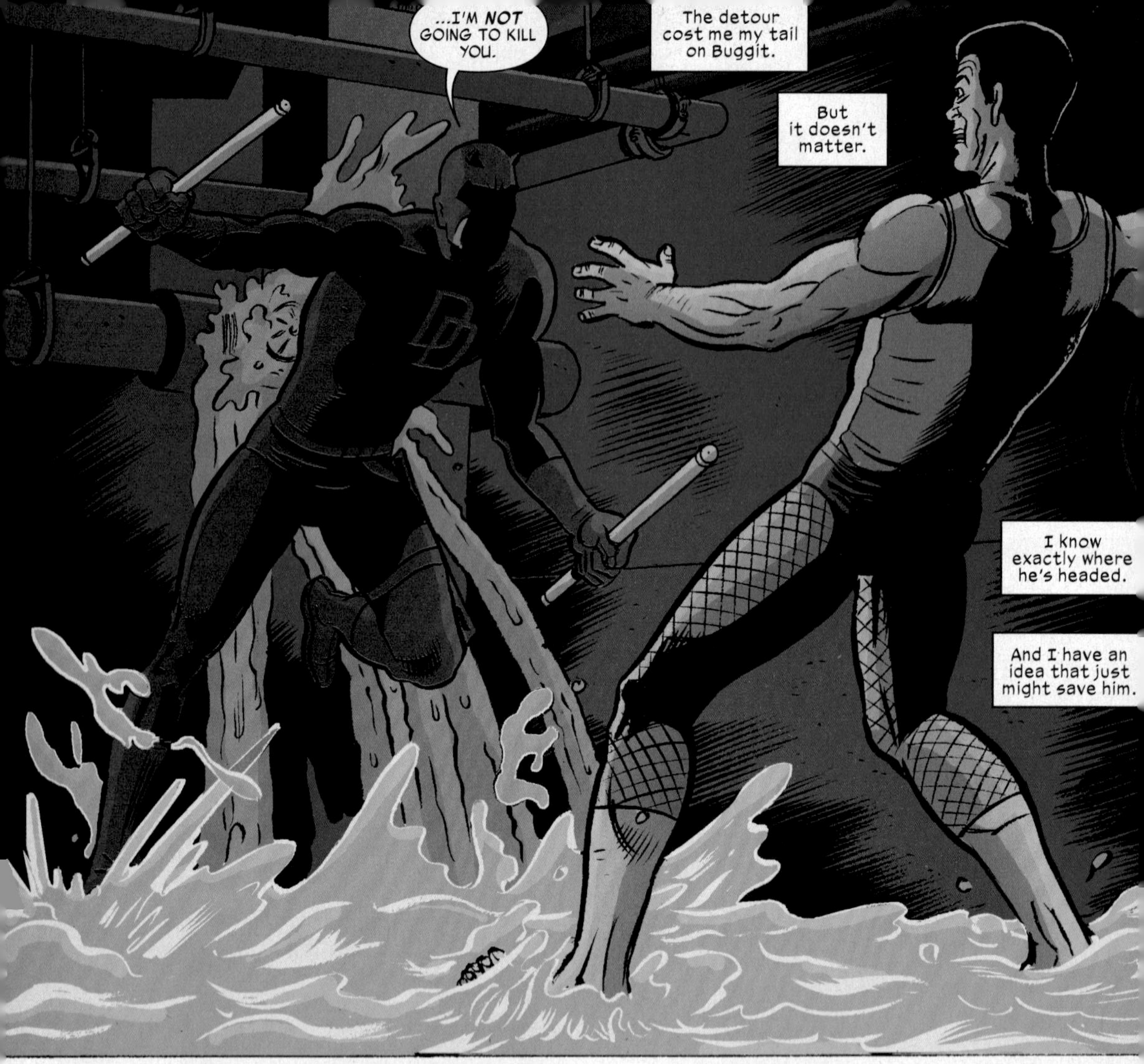
...I'M NOT GOING TO KILL YOU.
The detour cost me my tail on Buggit.
But it doesn't matter.
I know exactly where he's headed.
And I have an idea that just might save him.

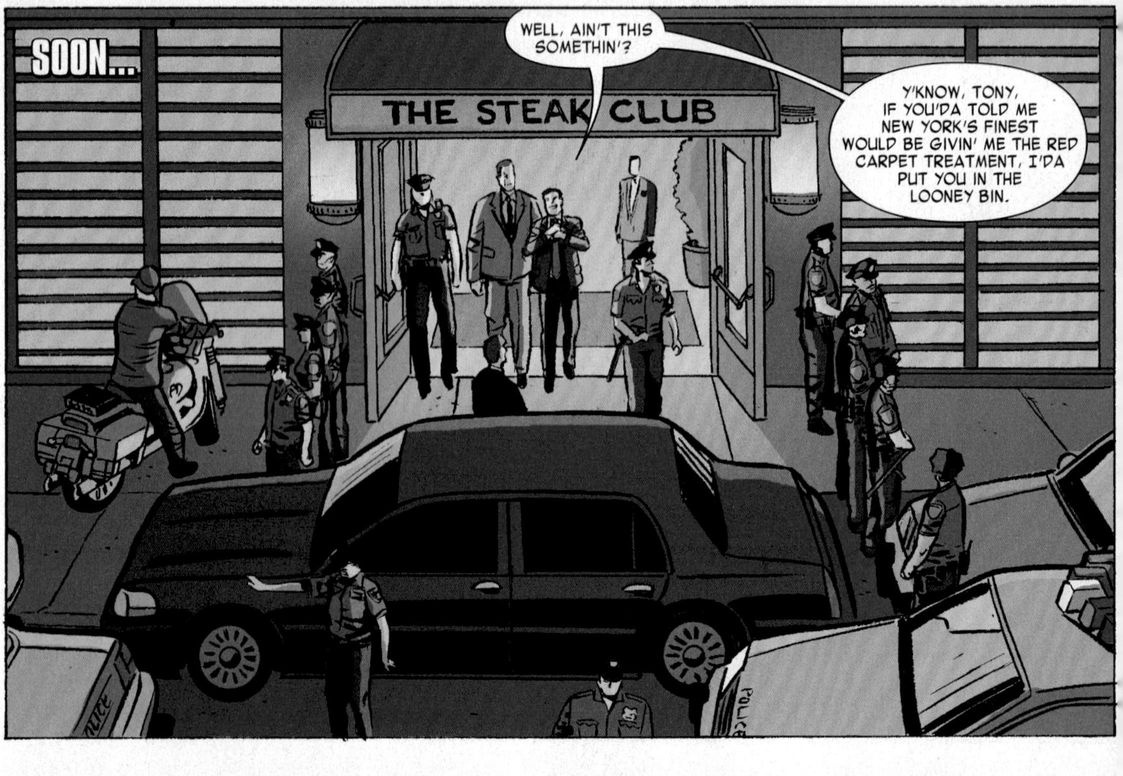
SOON...
THE STEAK CLUB
WELL, AIN'T THIS SOMETHIN'?
Y'KNOW, TONY, IF YOU'DA TOLD ME NEW YORK'S FINEST WOULD BE GIVIN' ME THE RED CARPET TREATMENT, I'DA PUT YOU IN THE LOONEY BIN.

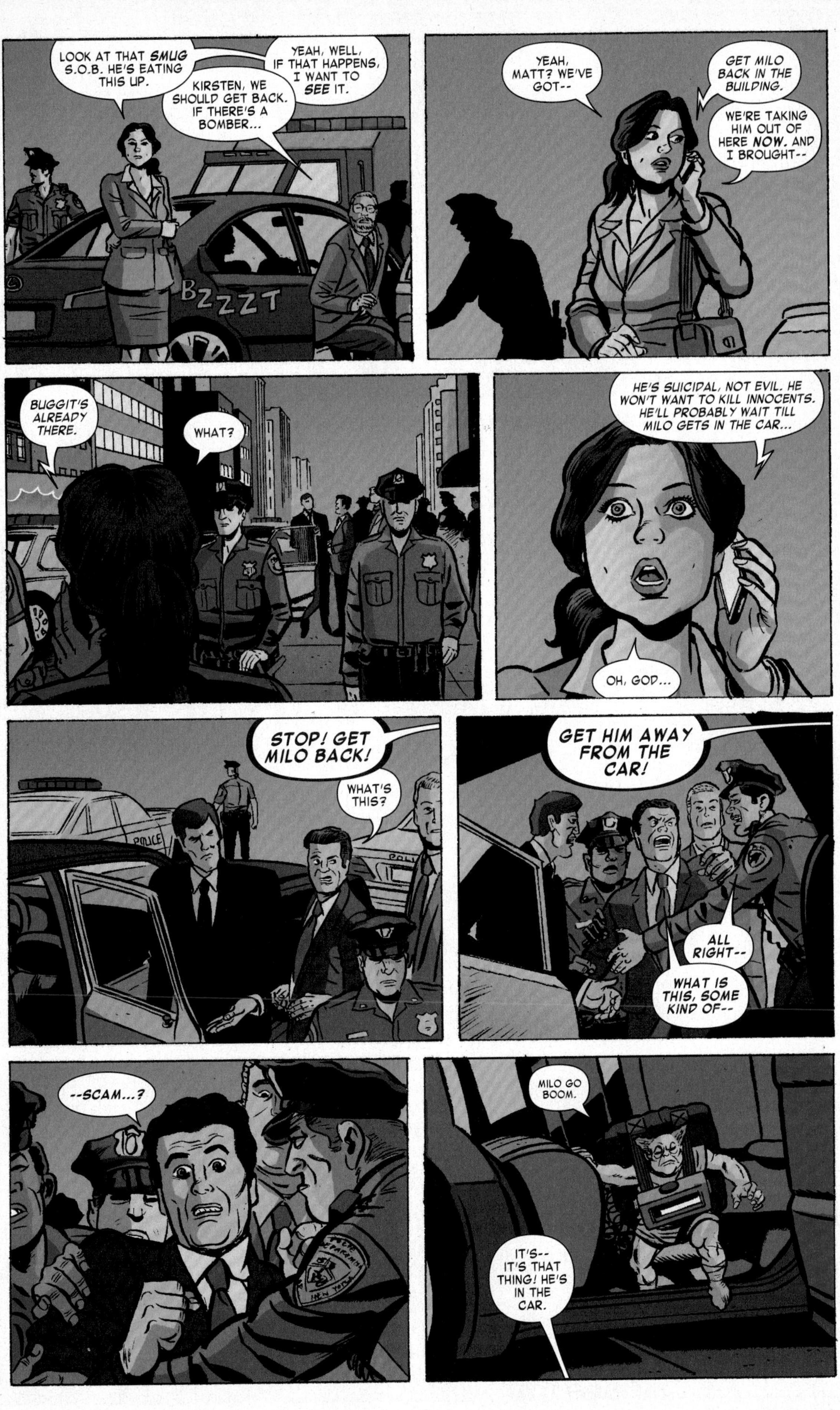
LOOK AT THAT SMUG S.O.B. HE'S EATING THIS UP.
YEAH, WELL, IF THAT HAPPENS, I WANT TO SEE IT.
KIRSTEN, WE SHOULD GET BACK. IF THERE'S A BOMBER...
BZZZT
YEAH, MATT? WE'VE GOT--
GET MILO BACK IN THE BUILDING.
WE'RE TAKING HIM OUT OF HERE NOW. AND I BROUGHT--
BUGGIT'S ALREADY THERE.
WHAT?
HE'S SUICIDAL, NOT EVIL. HE WON'T WANT TO KILL INNOCENTS. HE'LL PROBABLY WAIT TILL MILO GETS IN THE CAR...
OH, GOD...
STOP! GET MILO BACK!
WHAT'S THIS?
POLICE
GET HIM AWAY FROM THE CAR!
ALL RIGHT--
WHAT IS THIS, SOME KIND OF--
--SCAM...?
MILO GO BOOM.
IT'S-- IT'S THAT THING! HE'S IN THE CAR.

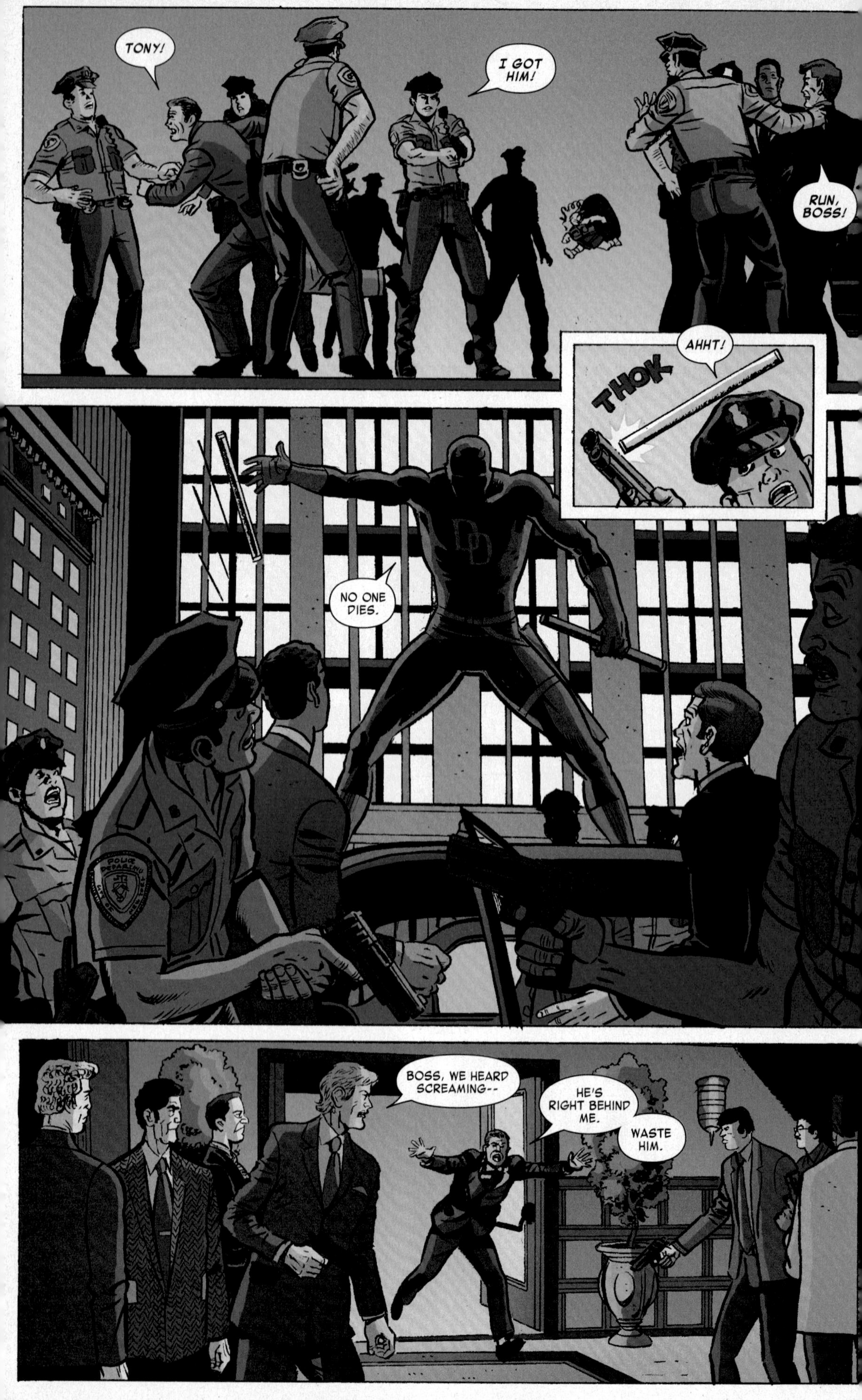
TONY!
I GOT HIM!
RUN, BOSS!
AHHT!
THOK
NO ONE DIES.
BOSS, WE HEARD SCREAMING--
HE'S RIGHT BEHIND ME.
WASTE HIM.

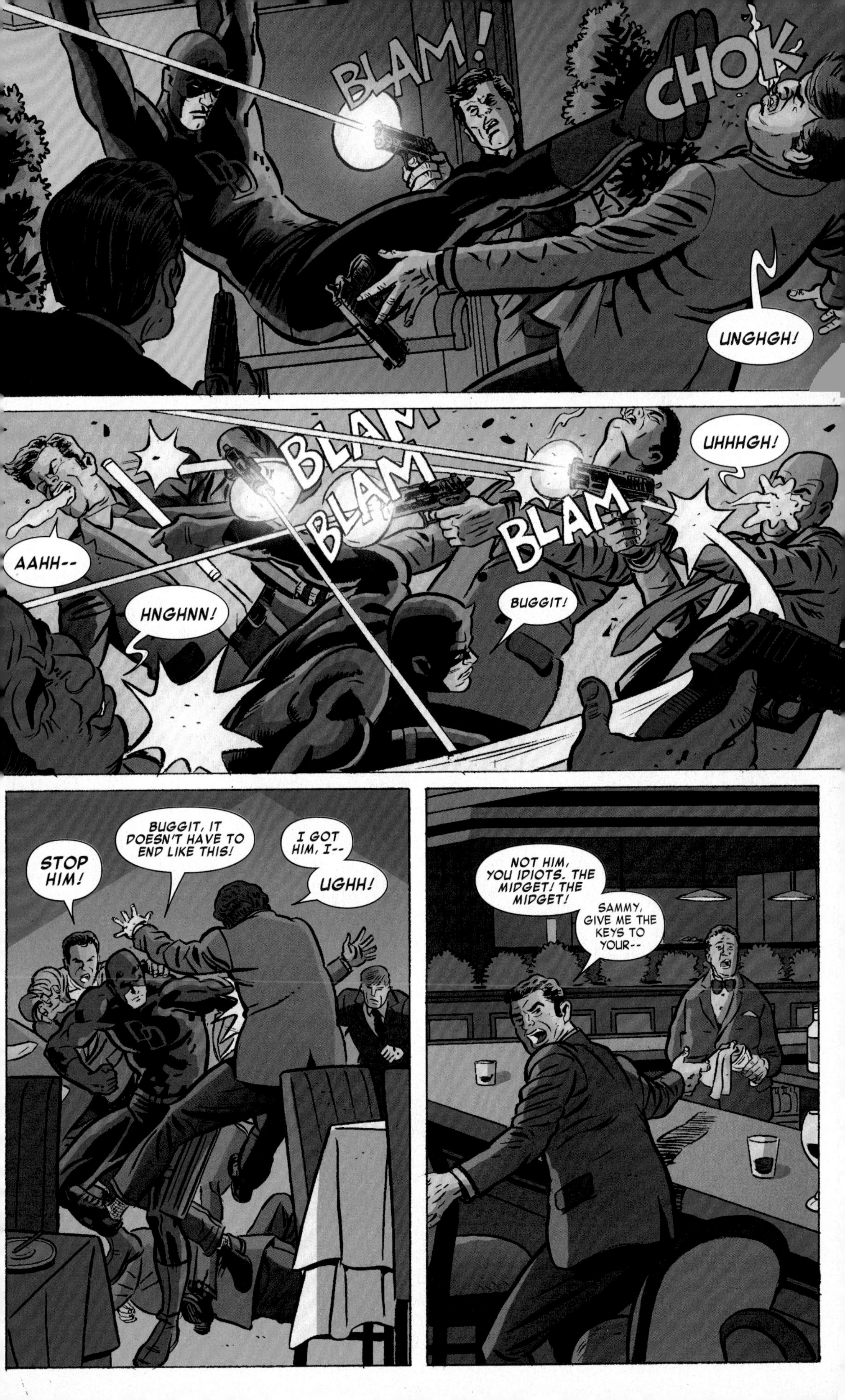
BLAM!
CHOK
UNGHGH!
BLAM
BLAM
BLAM
BLAM
UHHHGH!
AAHH--
HNGHNN!
BUGGIT!
STOP HIM!
BUGGIT, IT DOESN'T HAVE TO END LIKE THIS!
I GOT HIM, I--
UGHH!
NOT HIM, YOU IDIOTS. THE MIDGET! THE MIDGET!
SAMMY, GIVE ME THE KEYS TO YOUR--

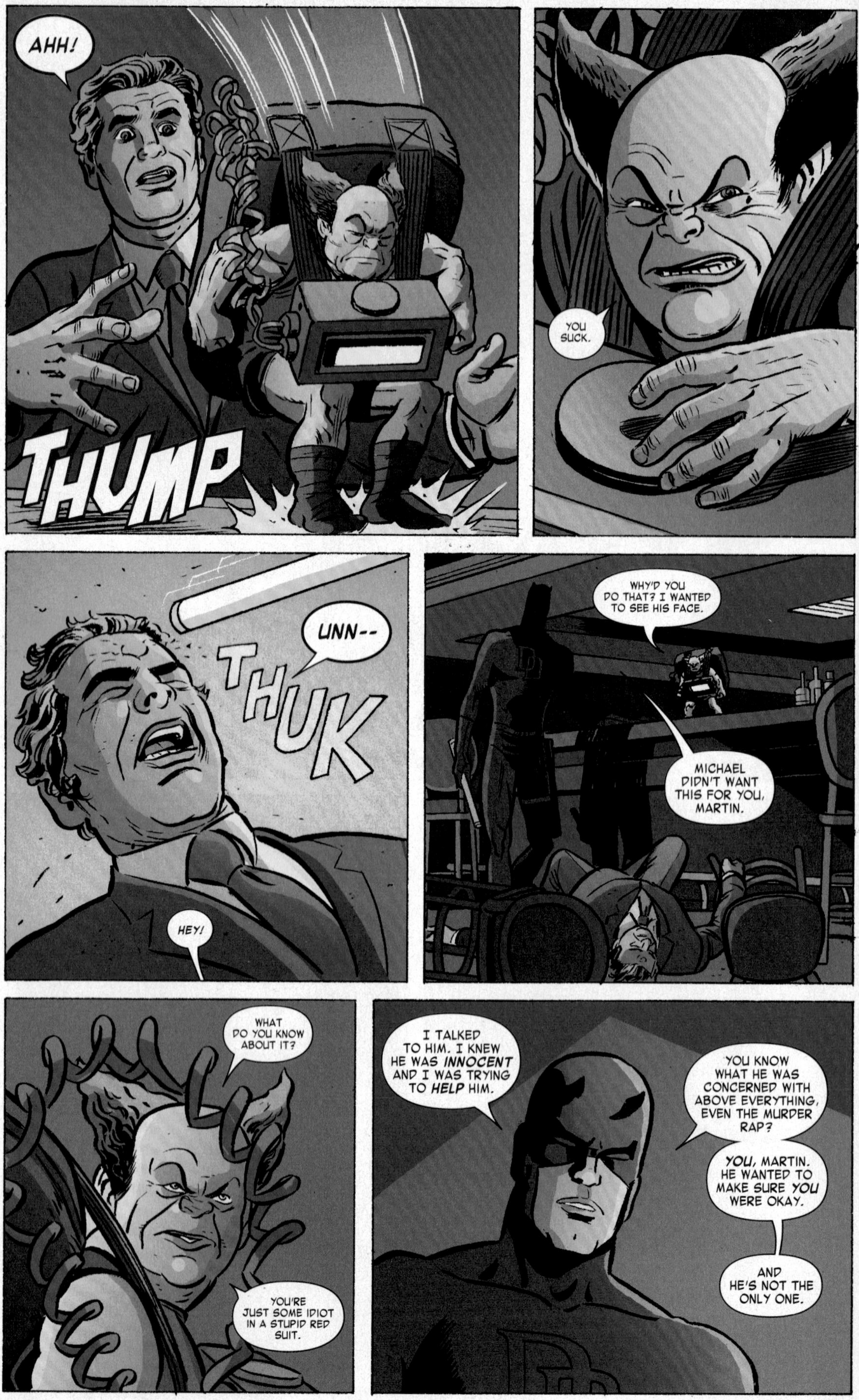
AHH!
THUMP
YOU SUCK.
UNN--
THUK
HEY!
WHY'D YOU DO THAT? I WANTED TO SEE HIS FACE.
MICHAEL DIDN'T WANT THIS FOR YOU, MARTIN.
WHAT DO YOU KNOW ABOUT IT?
YOU'RE JUST SOME IDIOT IN A STUPID RED SUIT.
I TALKED TO HIM. I KNEW HE WAS INNOCENT AND I WAS TRYING TO HELP HIM.
YOU KNOW WHAT HE WAS CONCERNED WITH ABOVE EVERYTHING, EVEN THE MURDER RAP?
YOU, MARTIN. HE WANTED TO MAKE SURE YOU WERE OKAY.
AND HE'S NOT THE ONLY ONE.

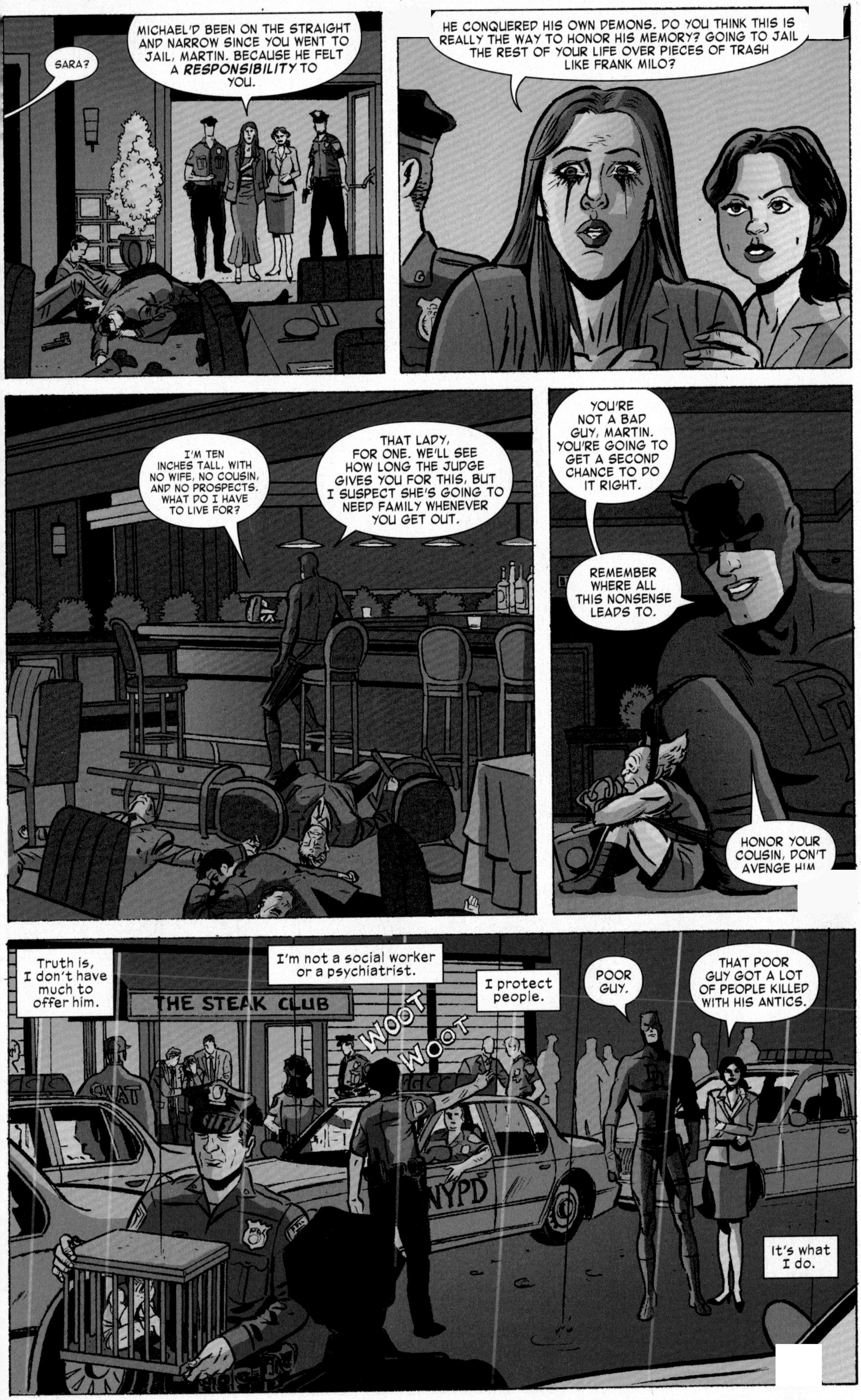
SARA?
MICHAEL'D BEEN ON THE STRAIGHT AND NARROW SINCE YOU WENT TO JAIL, MARTIN. BECAUSE HE FELT A RESPONSIBILITY TO YOU.
HE CONQUERED HIS OWN DEMONS. DO YOU THINK THIS IS REALLY THE WAY TO HONOR HIS MEMORY? GOING TO JAIL THE REST OF YOUR LIFE OVER PIECES OF TRASH LIKE FRANK MILO?
I'M TEN INCHES TALL, WITH NO WIFE, NO COUSIN, AND NO PROSPECTS. WHAT DO I HAVE TO LIVE FOR?
THAT LADY, FOR ONE. WE'LL SEE HOW LONG THE JUDGE GIVES YOU FOR THIS, BUT I SUSPECT SHE'S GOING TO NEED FAMILY WHENEVER YOU GET OUT.
YOU'RE NOT A BAD GUY, MARTIN. YOU'RE GOING TO GET A SECOND CHANCE TO DO IT RIGHT.
REMEMBER WHERE ALL THIS NONSENSE LEADS TO.
HONOR YOUR COUSIN, DON'T AVENGE HIM.
Truth is, I don't have much to offer him.
I'm not a social worker or a psychiatrist.
I protect people.
POOR GUY.
THAT POOR GUY GOT A LOT OF PEOPLE KILLED WITH HIS ANTICS.
THE STEAK CLUB
WOOT WOOT
NYPD
It's what I do.

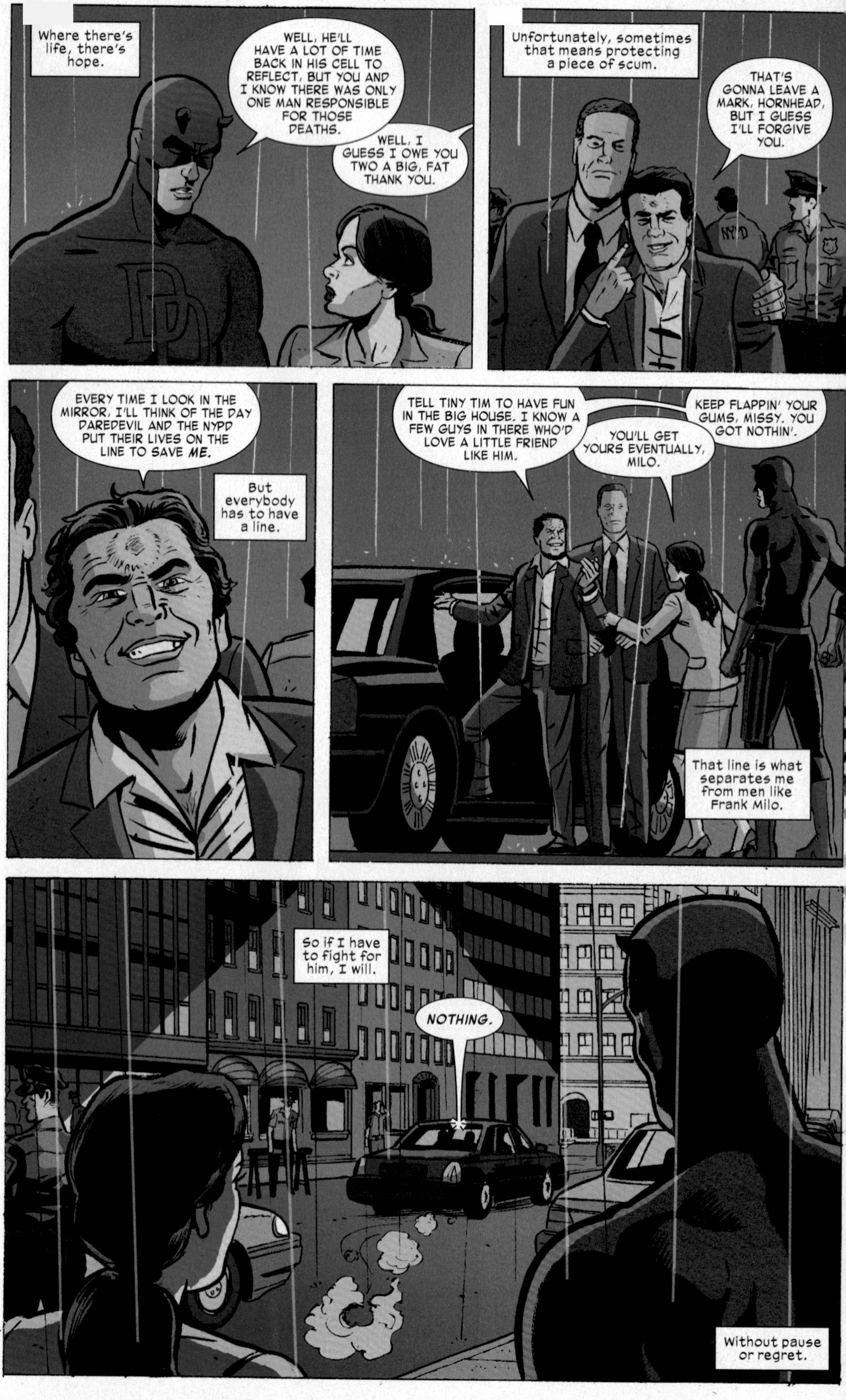
Where there's life, there's hope.
WELL, HE'LL HAVE A LOT OF TIME BACK IN HIS CELL TO REFLECT, BUT YOU AND I KNOW THERE WAS ONLY ONE MAN RESPONSIBLE FOR THOSE DEATHS.
WELL, I GUESS I OWE YOU TWO A BIG, FAT THANK YOU.
Unfortunately, sometimes that means protecting a piece of scum.
THAT'S GONNA LEAVE A MARK, HORNHEAD, BUT I GUESS I'LL FORGIVE YOU.
NYPD
EVERY TIME I LOOK IN THE MIRROR, I'LL THINK OF THE DAY DAREDEVIL AND THE NYPD PUT THEIR LIVES ON THE LINE TO SAVE *ME.*
But everybody has to have a line.
TELL TINY TIM TO HAVE FUN IN THE BIG HOUSE. I KNOW A FEW GUYS IN THERE WHO'D LOVE A LITTLE FRIEND LIKE HIM.
KEEP FLAPPIN' YOUR GUMS, MISSY. YOU GOT NOTHIN'.
YOU'LL GET YOURS EVENTUALLY, MILO.
That line is what separates me from men like Frank Milo.
So if I have to fight for him, I will.
NOTHING.
Without pause or regret.

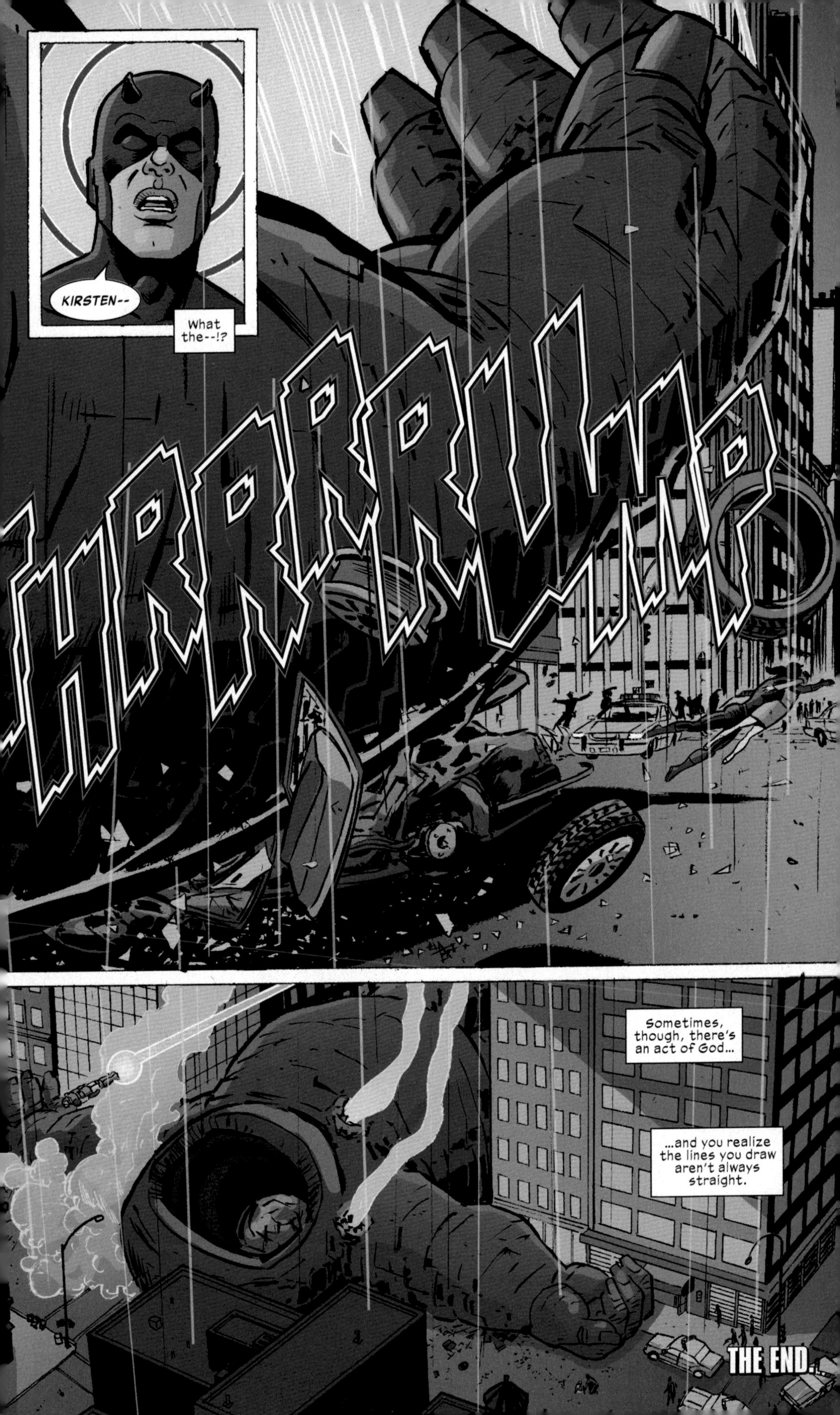

KIRSTEN--
What the--!?
KRRRUNP
Sometimes, though, there's an act of God...
...and you realize the lines you draw aren't always straight.
THE END.

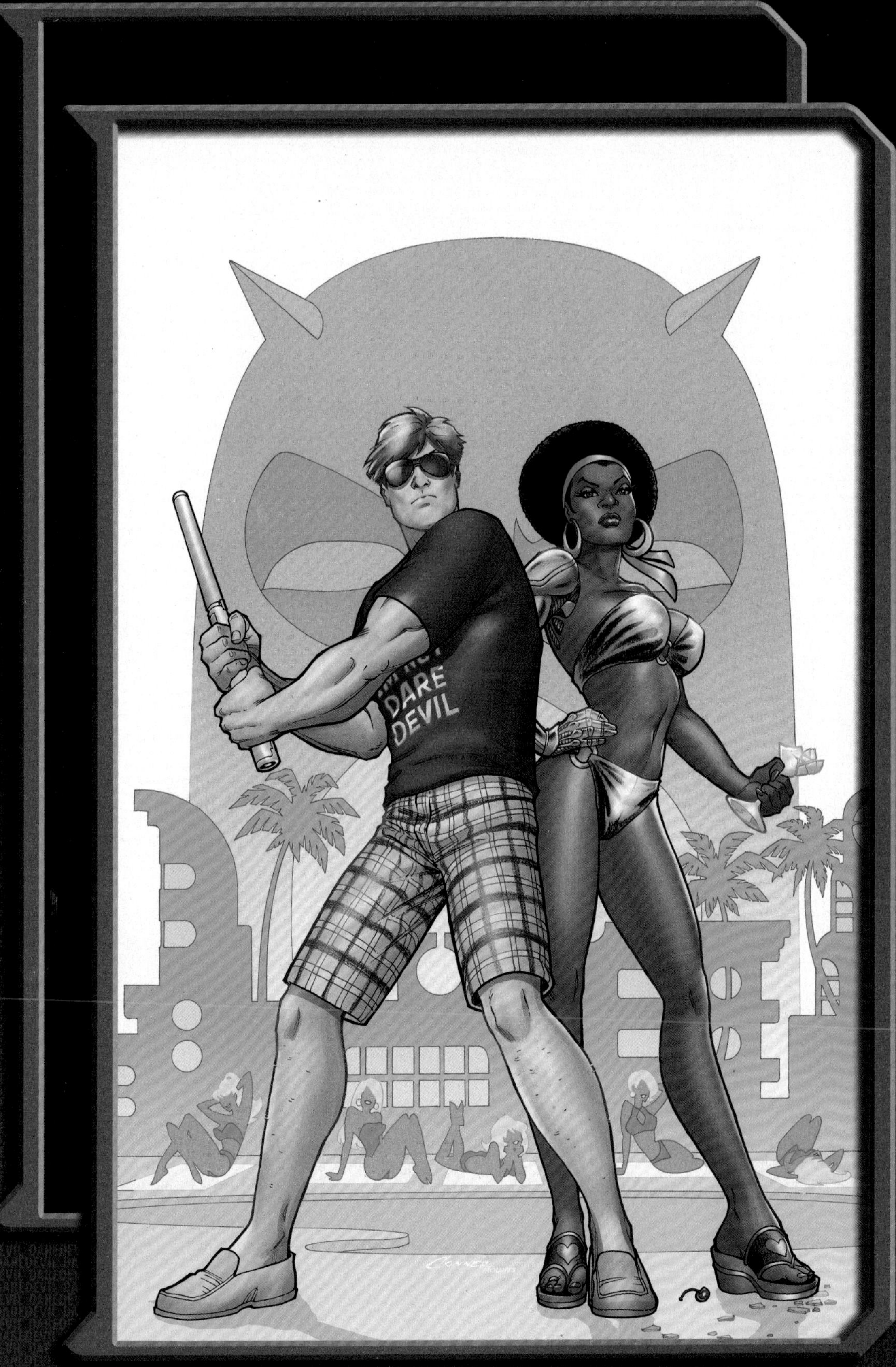
DARE
DEVIL

#6 — IN THE NAME OF THE KING
PART ONE: FIRST THINGS FIRST

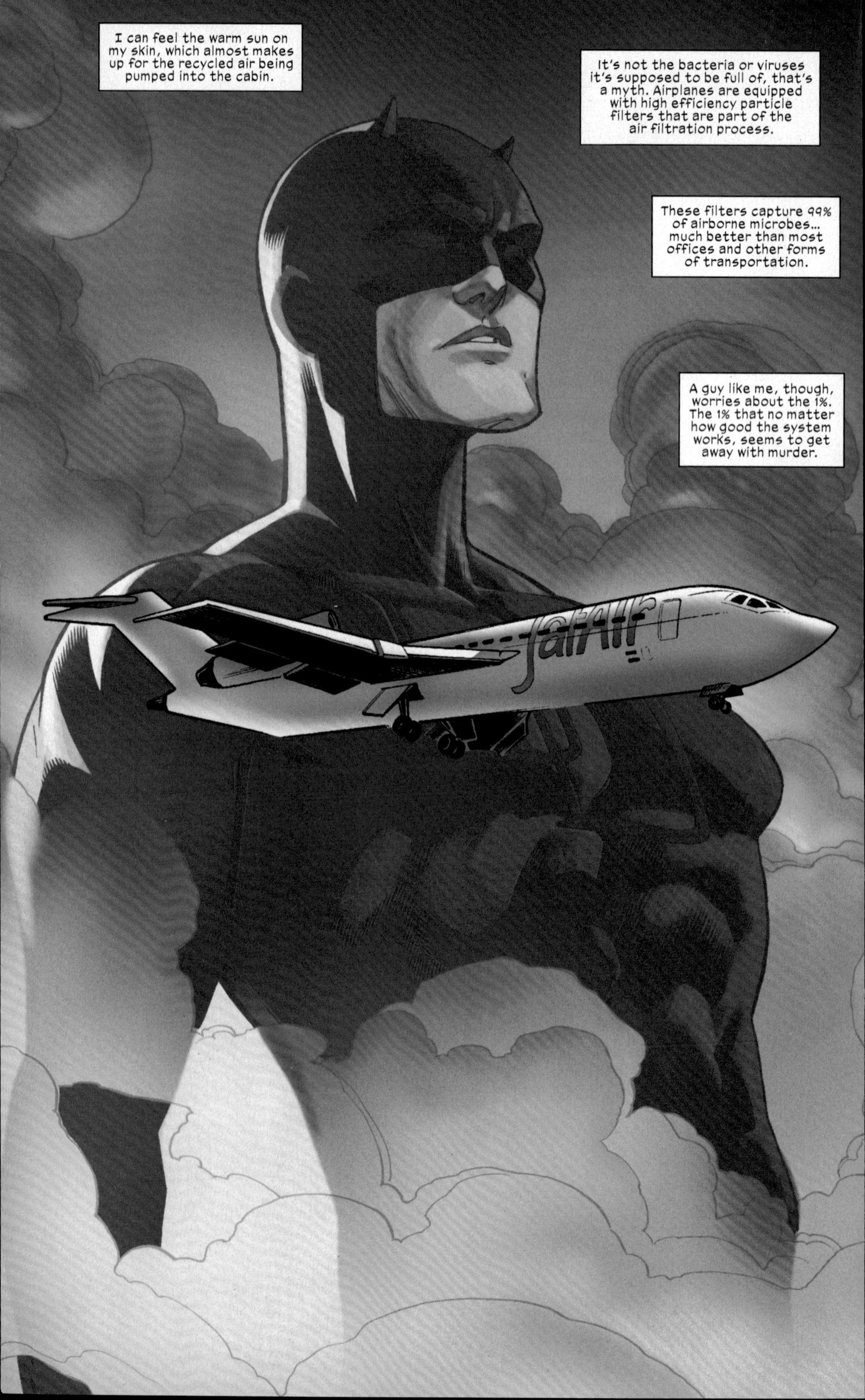
I can feel the warm sun on my skin, which almost makes up for the recycled air being pumped into the cabin.
It's not the bacteria or viruses it's supposed to be full of, that's a myth. Airplanes are equipped with high efficiency particle filters that are part of the air filtration process.
These filters capture 99% of airborne microbes... much better than most offices and other forms of transportation.
A guy like me, though, worries about the 1%. The 1% that no matter how good the system works, seems to get away with murder.
fairAir

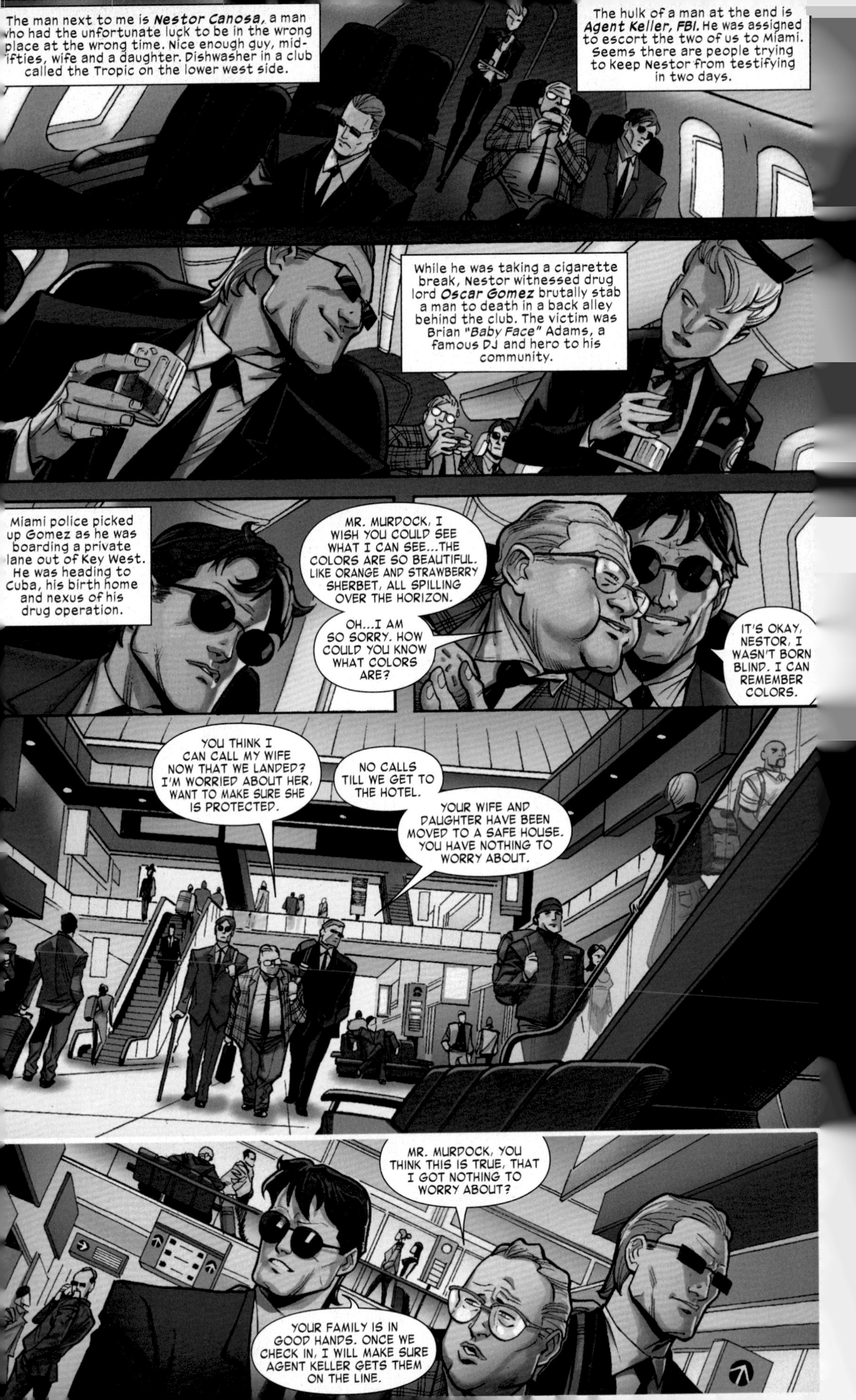

The man next to me is Nestor Canosa, a man who had the unfortunate luck to be in the wrong place at the wrong time. Nice enough guy, mid-fifties, wife and a daughter. Dishwasher in a club called the Tropic on the lower west side.
The hulk of a man at the end is Agent Keller, FBI. He was assigned to escort the two of us to Miami. Seems there are people trying to keep Nestor from testifying in two days.
While he was taking a cigarette break, Nestor witnessed drug lord Oscar Gomez brutally stab a man to death in a back alley behind the club. The victim was Brian "Baby Face" Adams, a famous DJ and hero to his community.
Miami police picked up Gomez as he was boarding a private plane out of Key West. He was heading to Cuba, his birth home and nexus of his drug operation.
MR. MURDOCK, I WISH YOU COULD SEE WHAT I CAN SEE...THE COLORS ARE SO BEAUTIFUL. LIKE ORANGE AND STRAWBERRY SHERBET, ALL SPILLING OVER THE HORIZON.
OH...I AM SO SORRY. HOW COULD YOU KNOW WHAT COLORS ARE?
IT'S OKAY, NESTOR, I WASN'T BORN BLIND. I CAN REMEMBER COLORS.
YOU THINK I CAN CALL MY WIFE NOW THAT WE LANDED? I'M WORRIED ABOUT HER, WANT TO MAKE SURE SHE IS PROTECTED.
NO CALLS TILL WE GET TO THE HOTEL.
YOUR WIFE AND DAUGHTER HAVE BEEN MOVED TO A SAFE HOUSE. YOU HAVE NOTHING TO WORRY ABOUT.
MR. MURDOCK, YOU THINK THIS IS TRUE, THAT I GOT NOTHING TO WORRY ABOUT?
YOUR FAMILY IS IN GOOD HANDS. ONCE WE CHECK IN, I WILL MAKE SURE AGENT KELLER GETS THEM ON THE LINE.

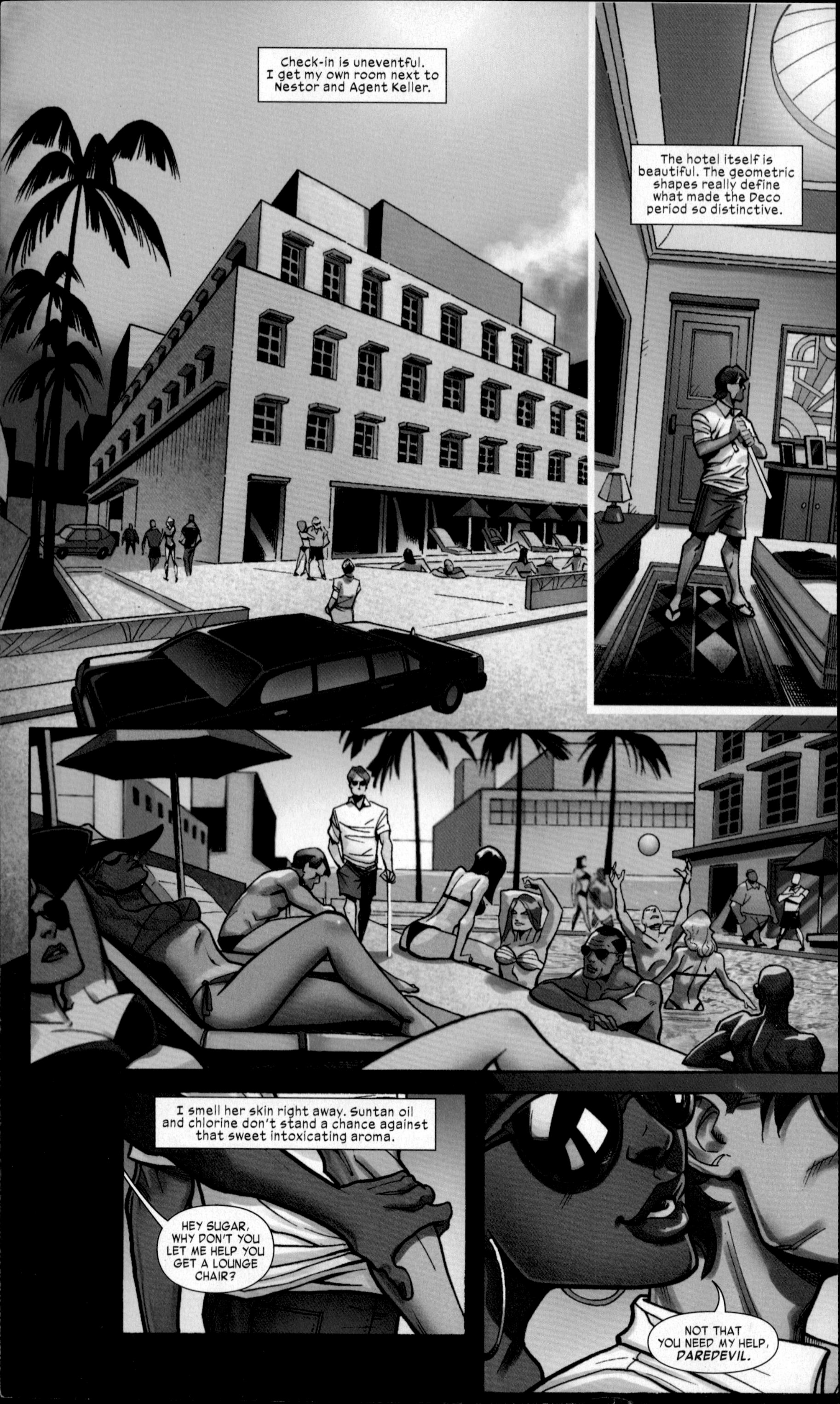
Check-in is uneventful. I get my own room next to Nestor and Agent Keller.
The hotel itself is beautiful. The geometric shapes really define what made the Deco period so distinctive.
I smell her skin right away. Suntan oil and chlorine don't stand a chance against that sweet intoxicating aroma.
HEY SUGAR, WHY DON'T YOU LET ME HELP YOU GET A LOUNGE CHAIR?
NOT THAT YOU NEED MY HELP, DAREDEVIL.

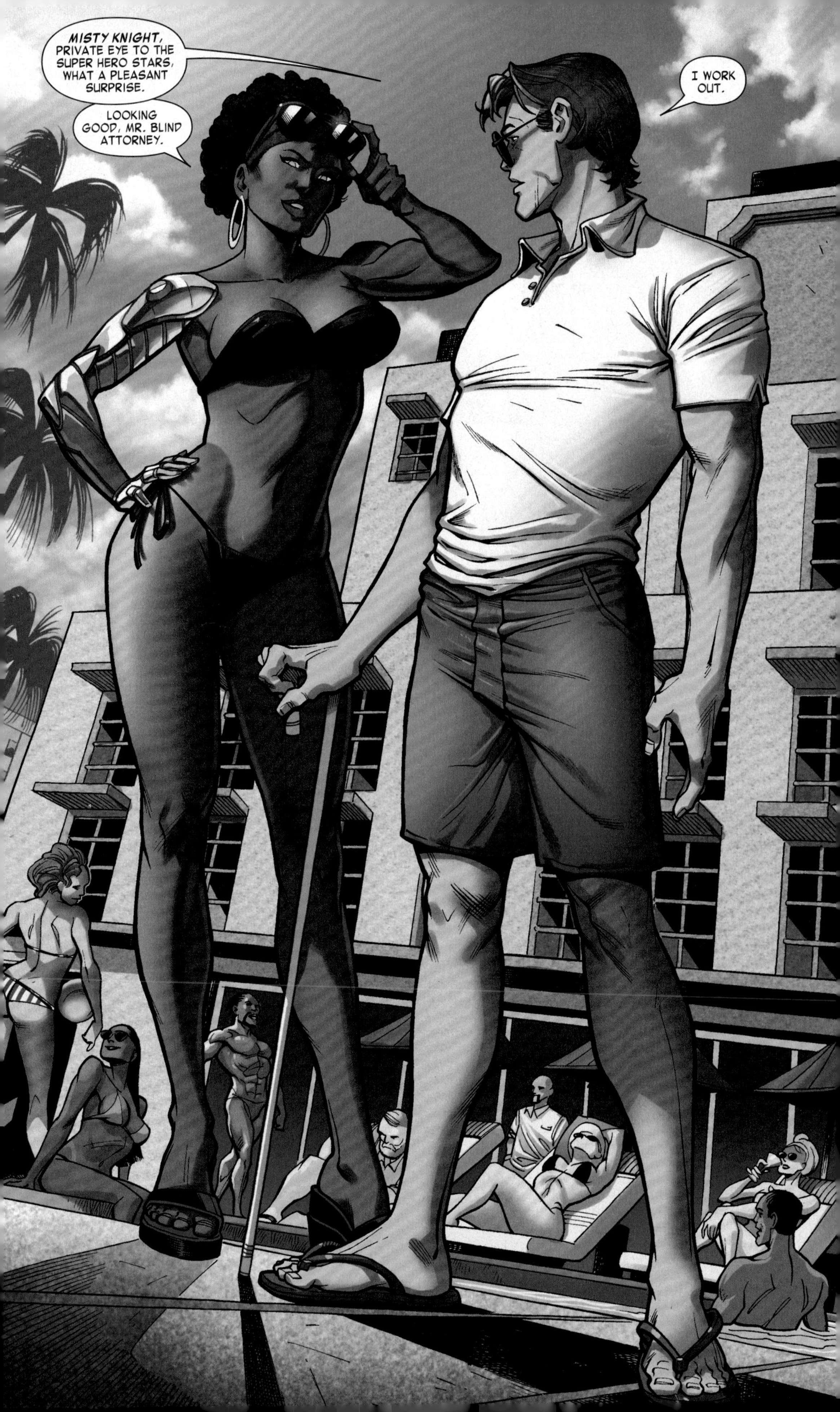
MISTY KNIGHT, PRIVATE EYE TO THE SUPER HERO STARS, WHAT A PLEASANT SURPRISE.
LOOKING GOOD, MR. BLIND ATTORNEY.
I WORK OUT.

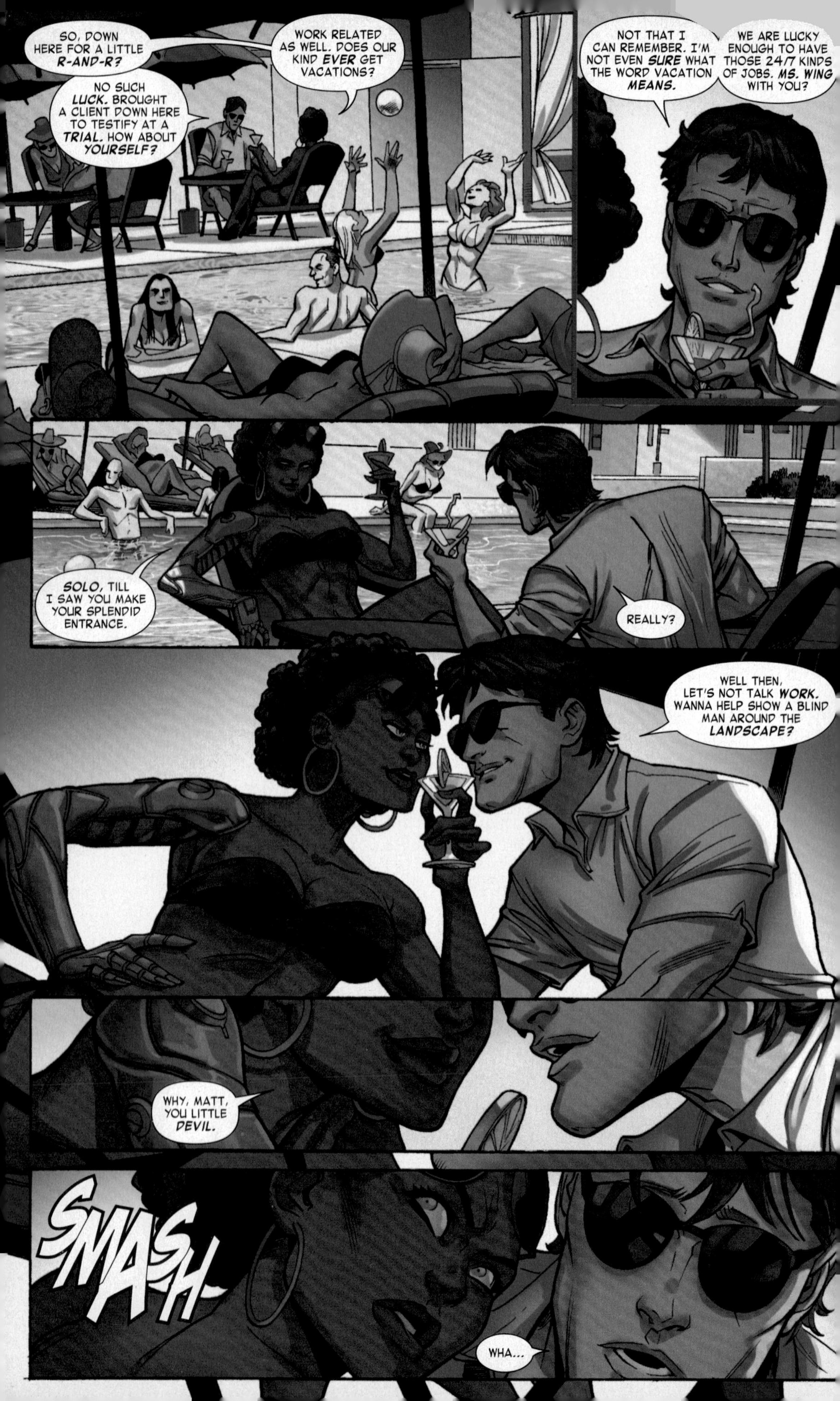
SO, DOWN HERE FOR A LITTLE R-AND-R?
NO SUCH LUCK. BROUGHT A CLIENT DOWN HERE TO TESTIFY AT A TRIAL. HOW ABOUT YOURSELF?
WORK RELATED AS WELL. DOES OUR KIND EVER GET VACATIONS?
NOT THAT I CAN REMEMBER. I'M NOT EVEN SURE WHAT THE WORD VACATION MEANS.
WE ARE LUCKY ENOUGH TO HAVE THOSE 24/7 KINDS OF JOBS. MS. WING WITH YOU?
SOLO, TILL I SAW YOU MAKE YOUR SPLENDID ENTRANCE.
REALLY?
WELL THEN, LET'S NOT TALK WORK. WANNA HELP SHOW A BLIND MAN AROUND THE LANDSCAPE?
WHY, MATT, YOU LITTLE DEVIL.
SMASH
WHA...

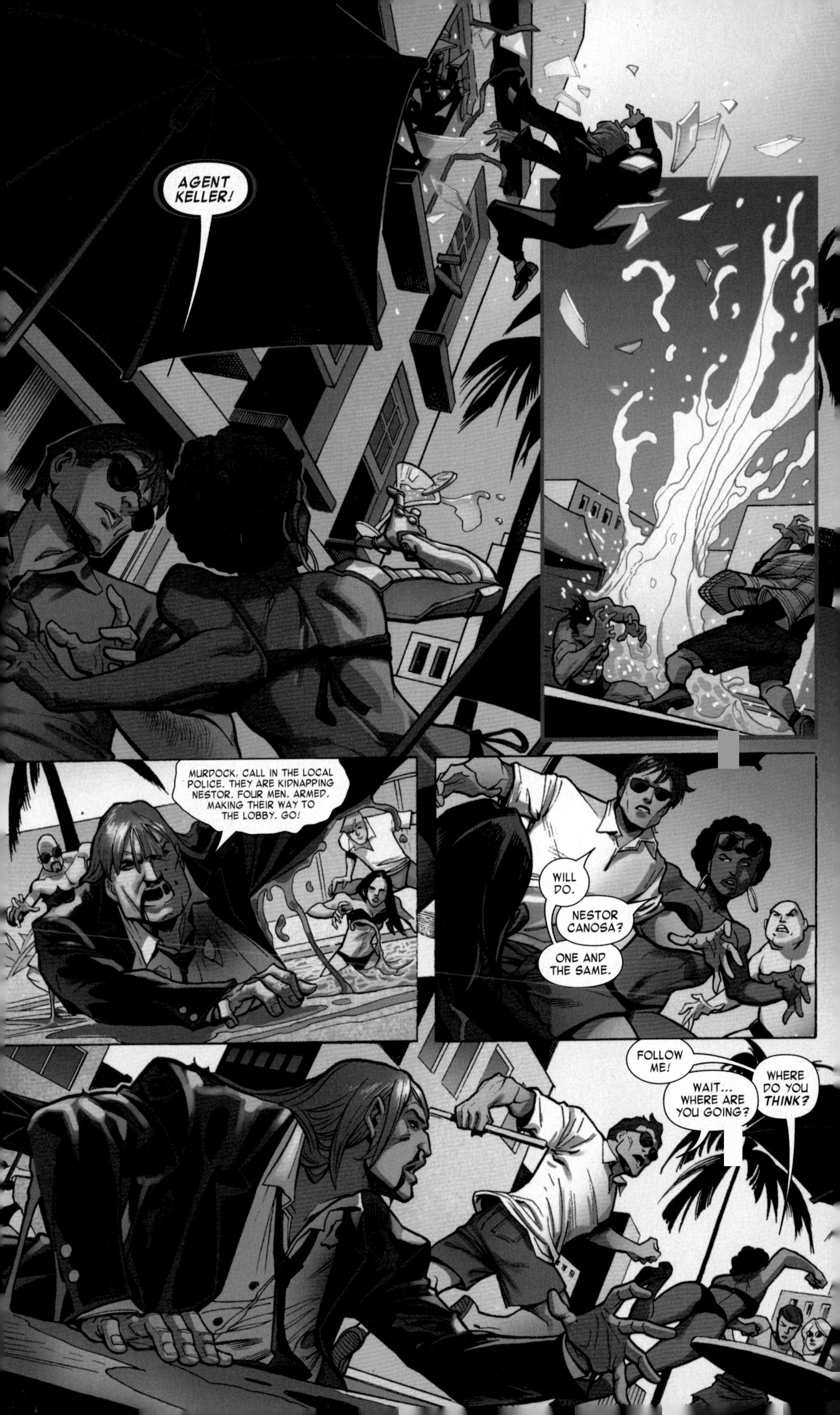
AGENT KELLER!
MURDOCK, CALL IN THE LOCAL POLICE. THEY ARE KIDNAPPING NESTOR. FOUR MEN. ARMED. MAKING THEIR WAY TO THE LOBBY. GO!
WILL DO.
NESTOR CANOSA?
ONE AND THE SAME.
FOLLOW ME!
WAIT... WHERE ARE YOU GOING?
WHERE DO YOU THINK?

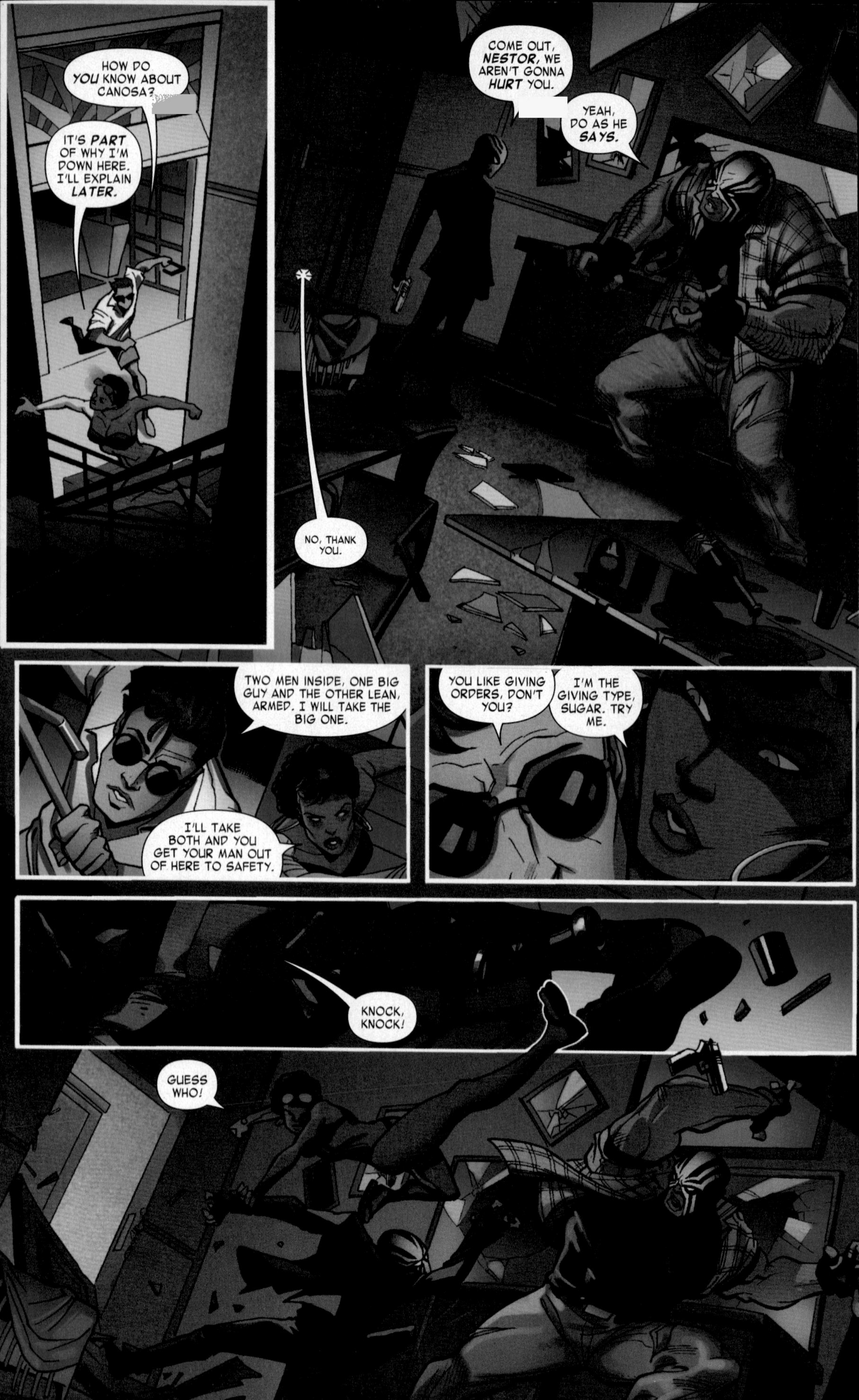
HOW DO YOU KNOW ABOUT CANOSA?
IT'S PART OF WHY I'M DOWN HERE. I'LL EXPLAIN LATER.
COME OUT, NESTOR, WE AREN'T GONNA HURT YOU.
YEAH, DO AS HE SAYS.
NO, THANK YOU.
TWO MEN INSIDE, ONE BIG GUY AND THE OTHER LEAN, ARMED. I WILL TAKE THE BIG ONE.
I'LL TAKE BOTH AND YOU GET YOUR MAN OUT OF HERE TO SAFETY.
YOU LIKE GIVING ORDERS, DON'T YOU?
I'M THE GIVING TYPE, SUGAR. TRY ME.
KNOCK, KNOCK!
GUESS WHO!

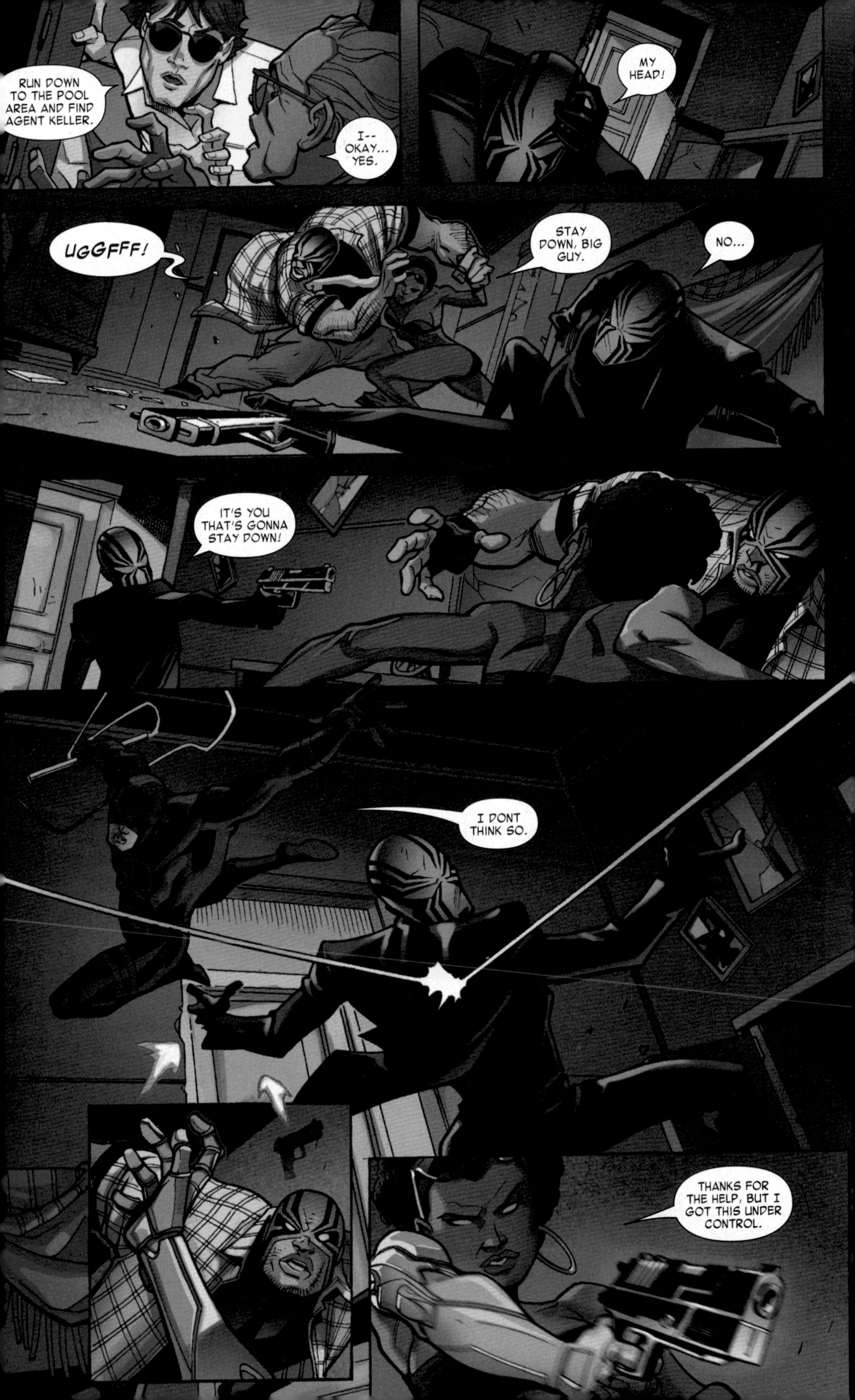

RUN DOWN TO THE POOL AREA AND FIND AGENT KELLER.
I-- OKAY... YES.
MY HEAD!
UGGFFF!
STAY DOWN, BIG GUY.
NO...
IT'S YOU THAT'S GONNA STAY DOWN!
I DONT THINK SO.
THANKS FOR THE HELP, BUT I GOT THIS UNDER CONTROL.

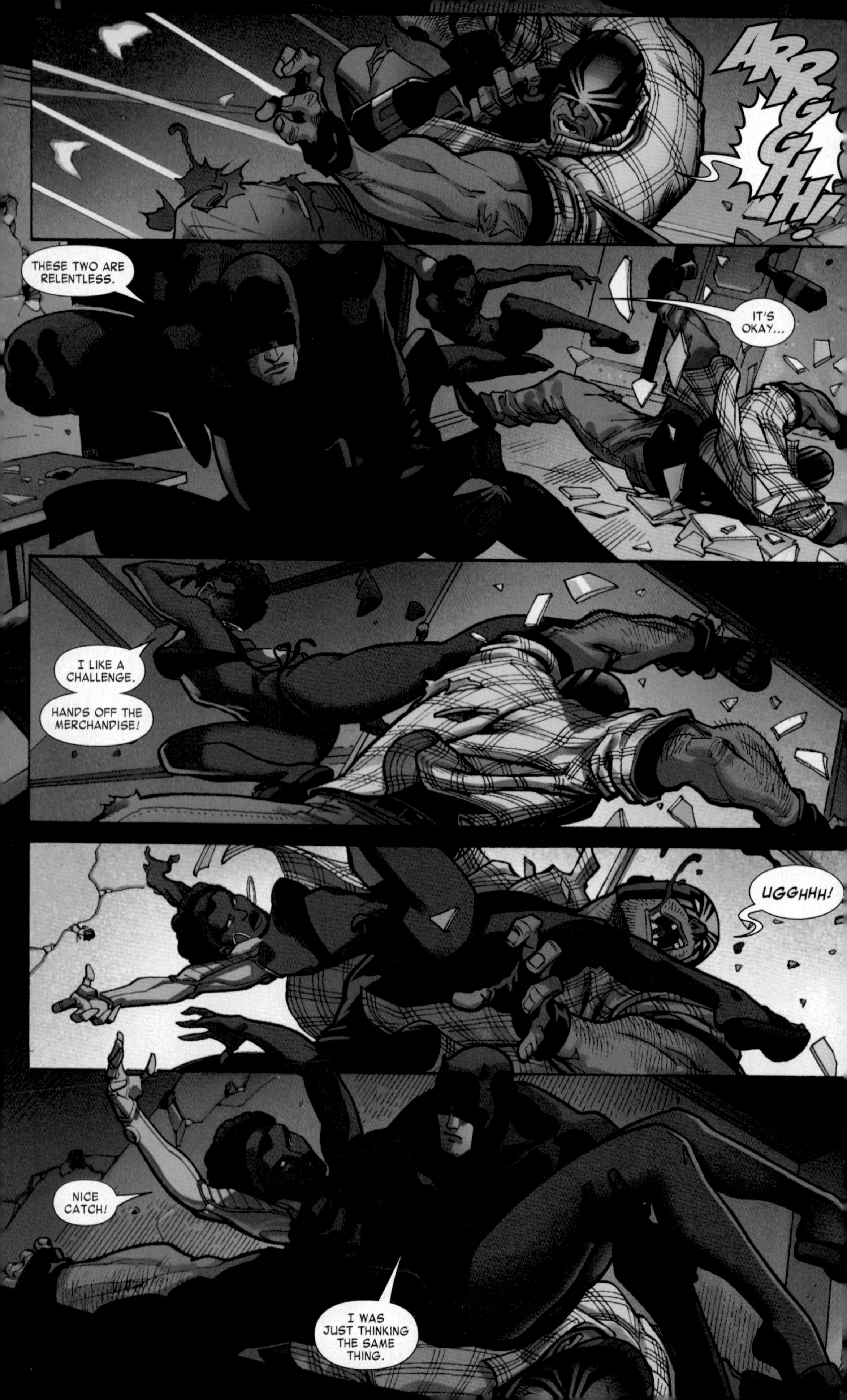
ARRGGHH!
THESE TWO ARE RELENTLESS.
IT'S OKAY...
I LIKE A CHALLENGE.
HANDS OFF THE MERCHANDISE!
UGGHHH!
NICE CATCH!
I WAS JUST THINKING THE SAME THING.

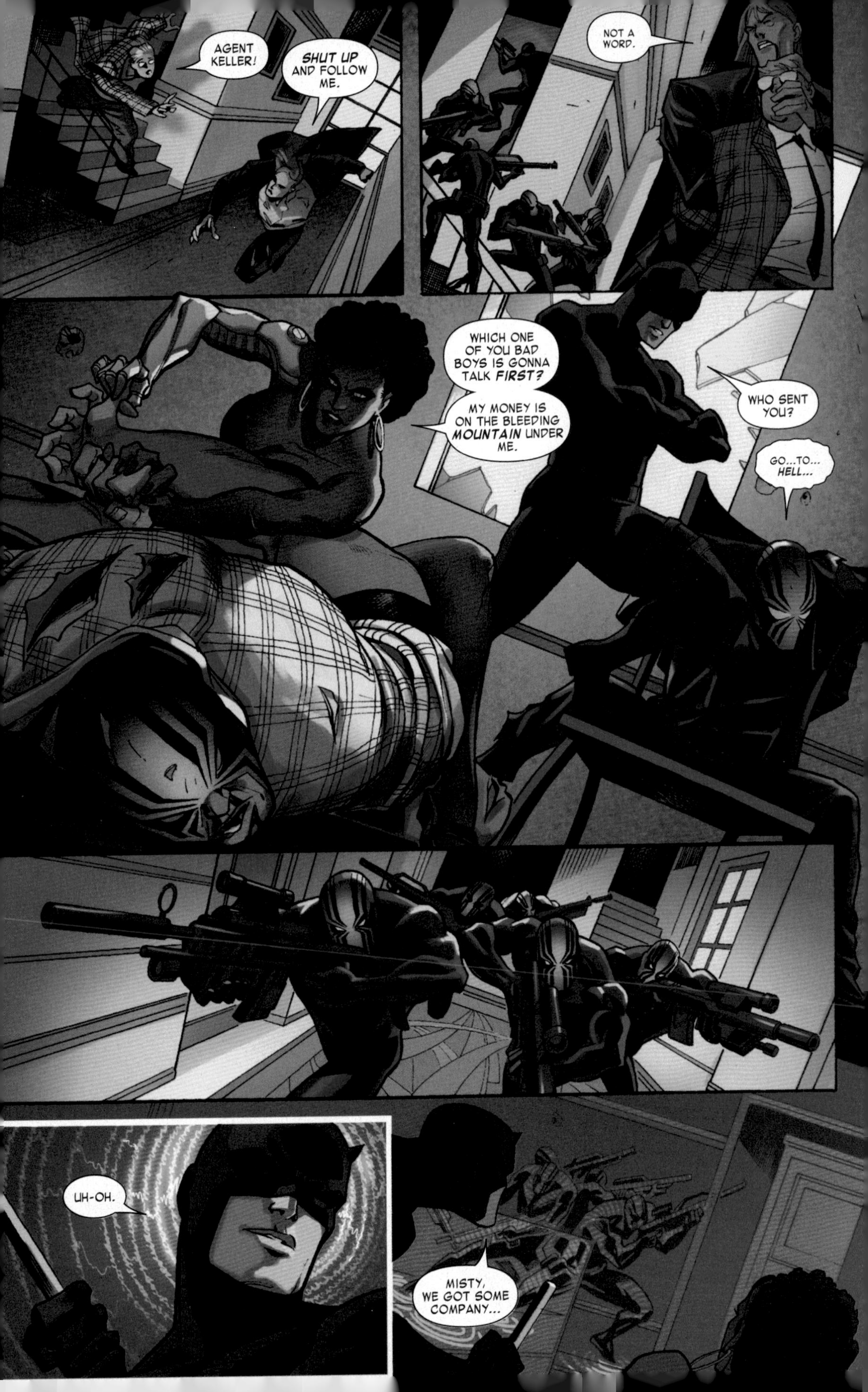
AGENT KELLER!
SHUT UP AND FOLLOW ME.
NOT A WORD.
WHICH ONE OF YOU BAD BOYS IS GONNA TALK FIRST?
MY MONEY IS ON THE BLEEDING MOUNTAIN UNDER ME.
WHO SENT YOU?
GO...TO... HELL...
UH-OH.
MISTY, WE GOT SOME COMPANY...

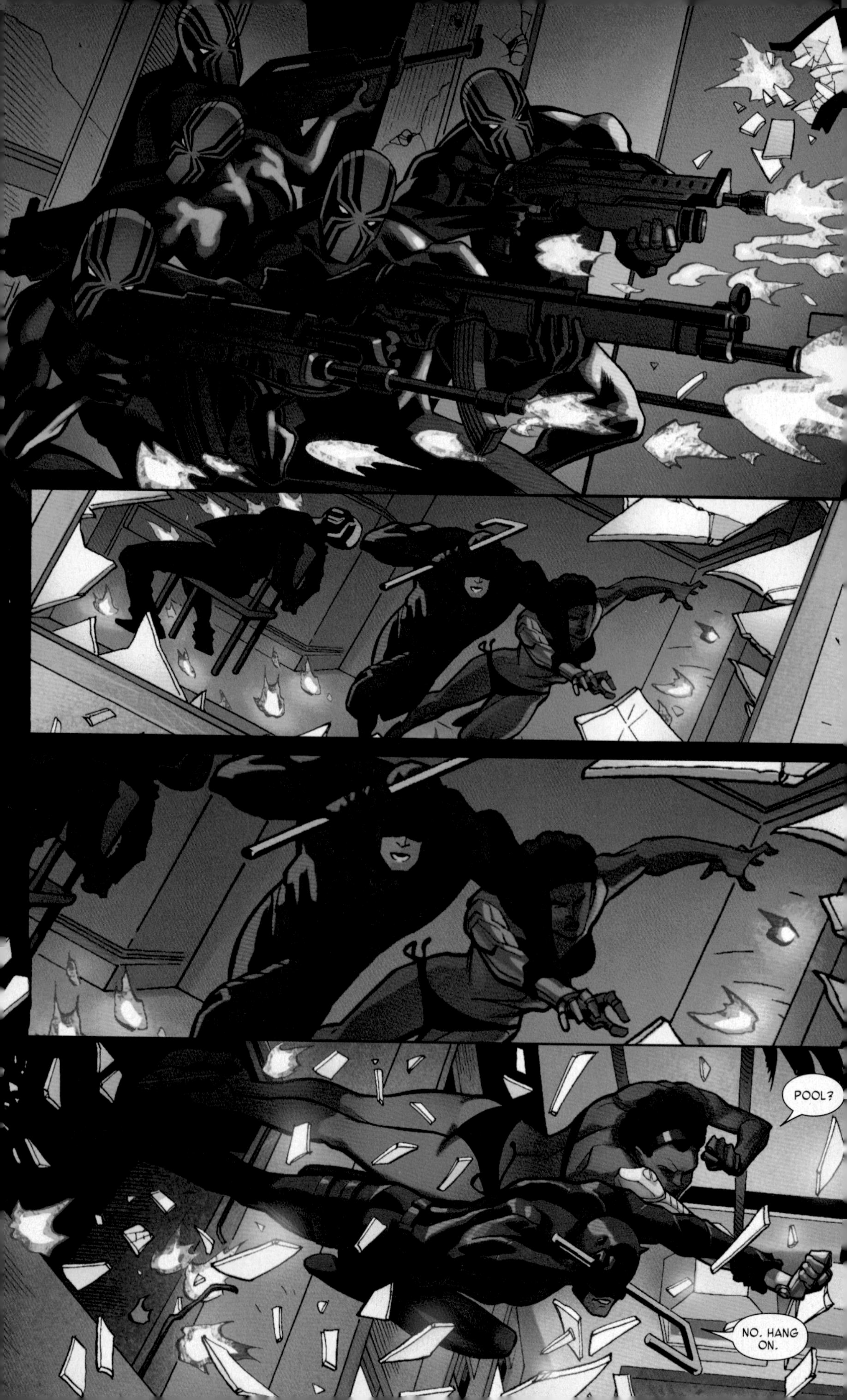
POOL?
NO. HANG ON.

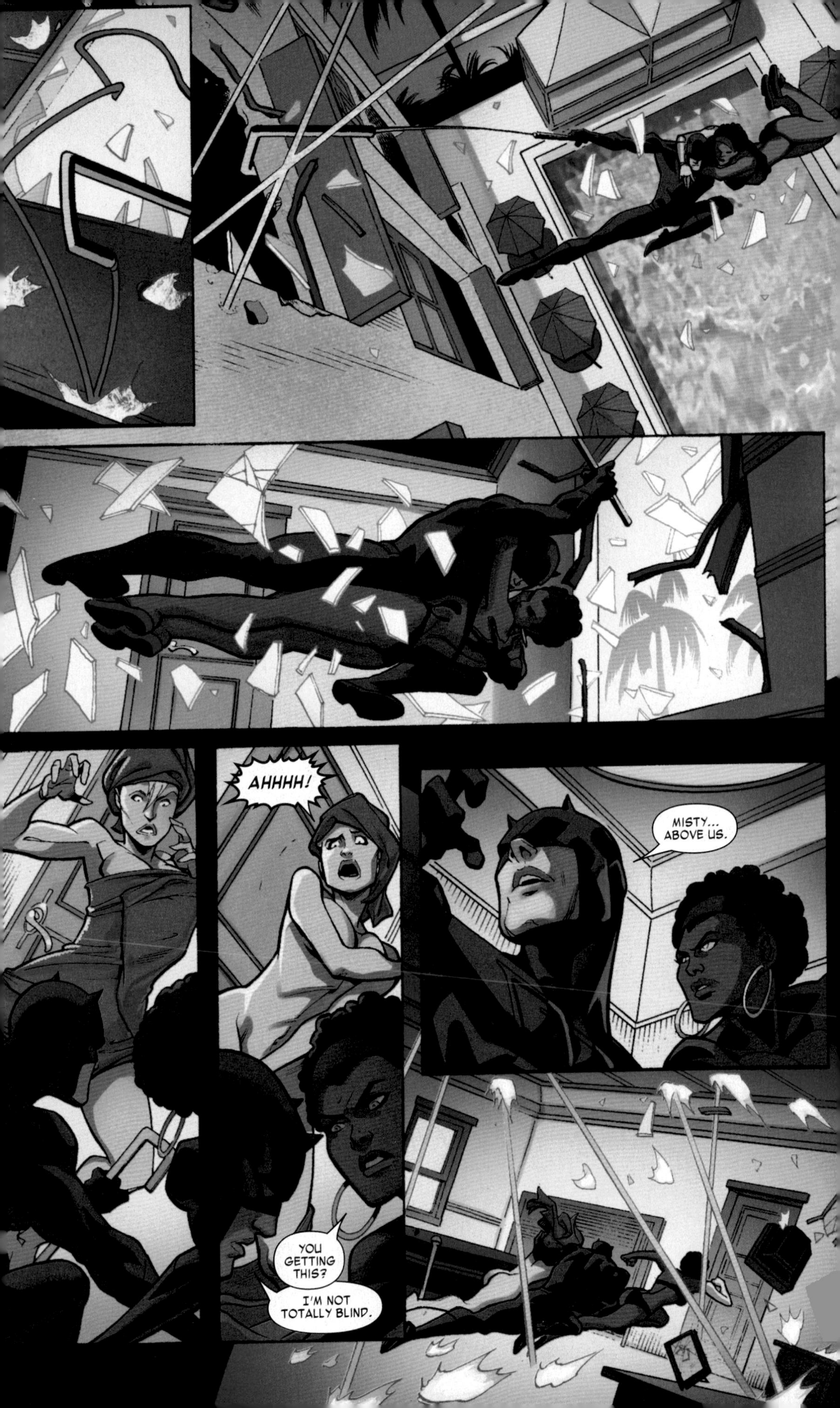
AHHHH!
MISTY... ABOVE US.
YOU GETTING THIS?
I'M NOT TOTALLY BLIND.

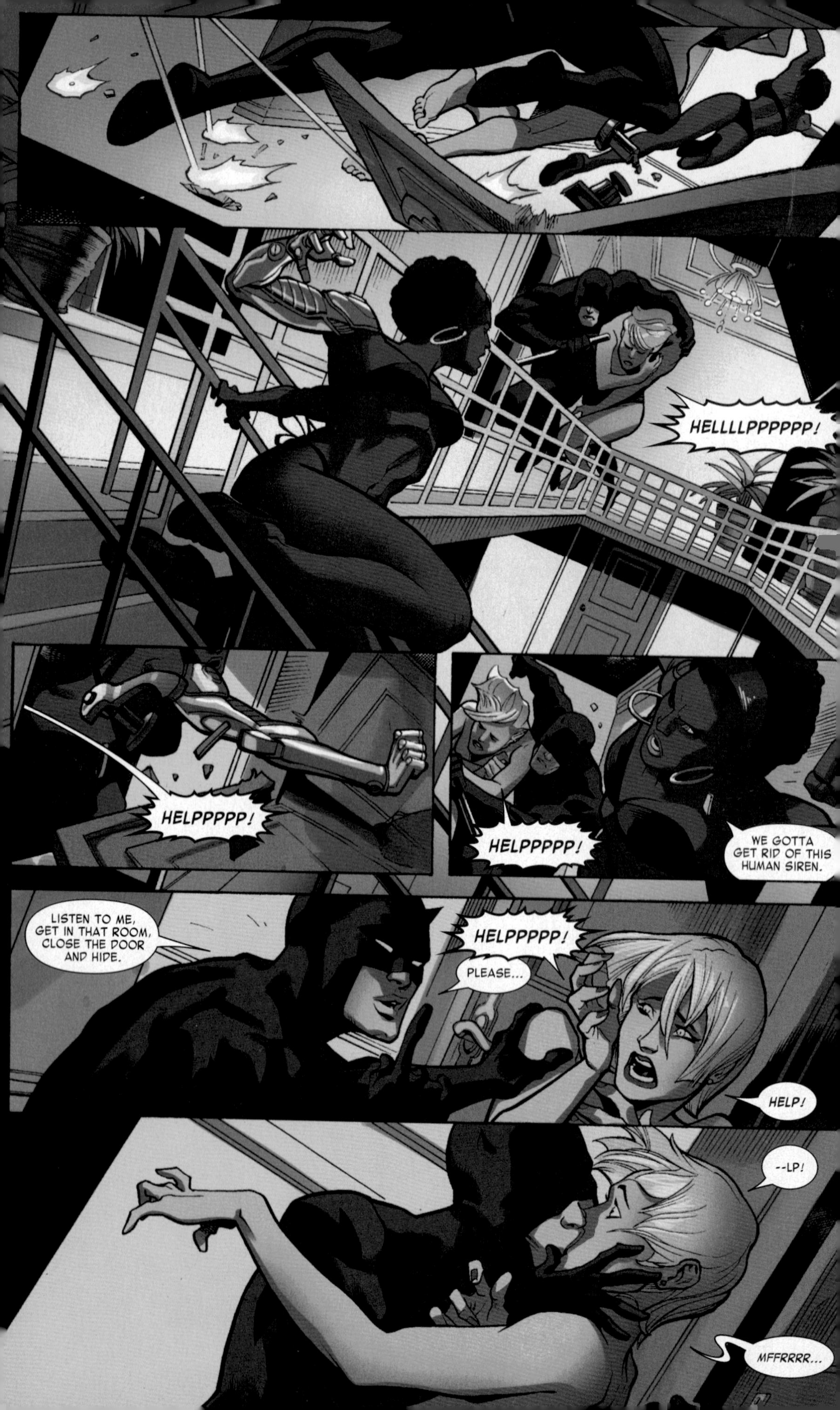
HELLLLPPPPPP!
HELPPPPP!
HELPPPPP!
WE GOTTA GET RID OF THIS HUMAN SIREN.
LISTEN TO ME, GET IN THAT ROOM, CLOSE THE DOOR AND HIDE.
HELPPPPP!
PLEASE...
HELP!
--LP!
MFFRRRR...

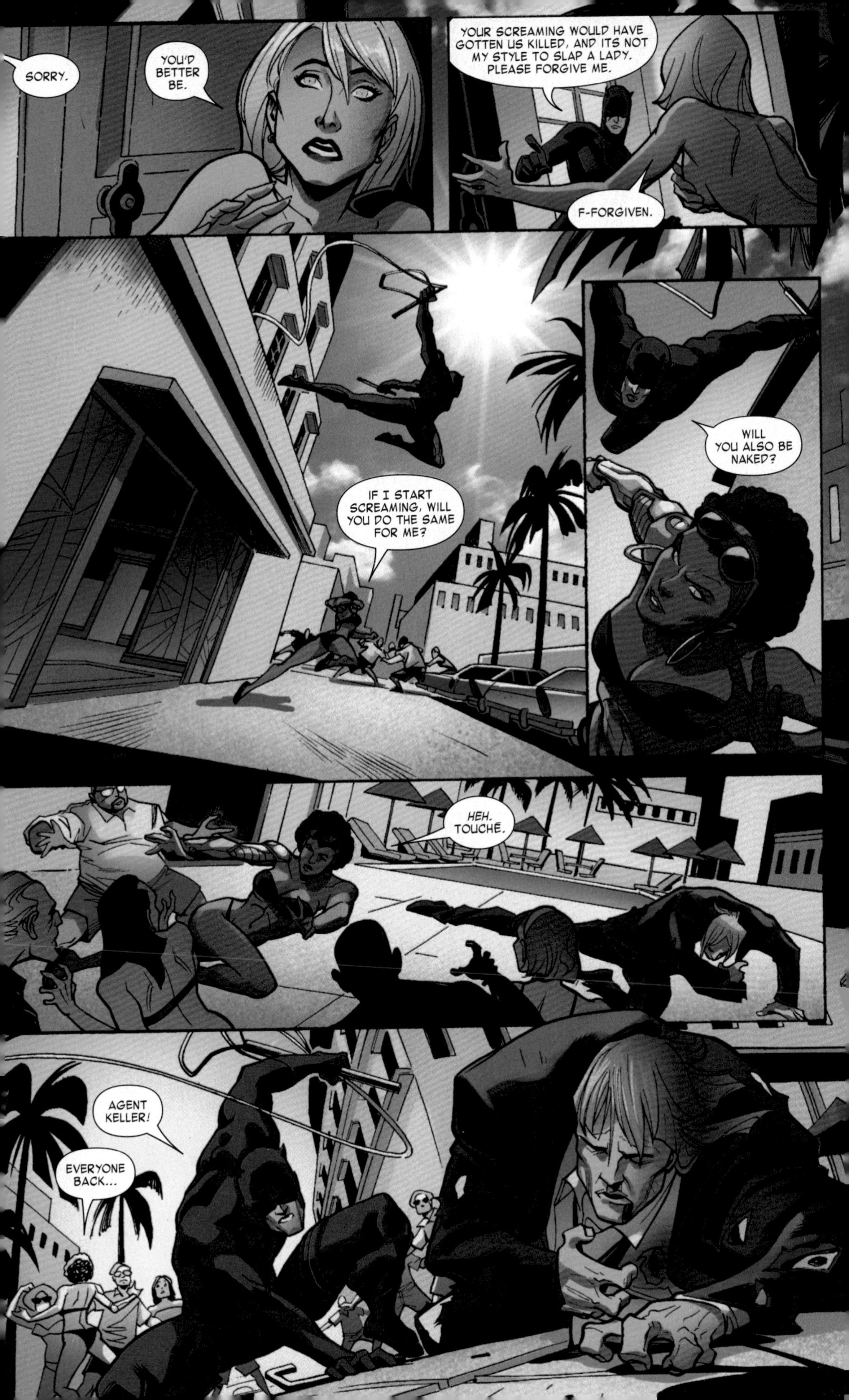
SORRY.
YOU'D BETTER BE.
YOUR SCREAMING WOULD HAVE GOTTEN US KILLED, AND ITS NOT MY STYLE TO SLAP A LADY. PLEASE FORGIVE ME.
F-FORGIVEN.
IF I START SCREAMING, WILL YOU DO THE SAME FOR ME?
WILL YOU ALSO BE NAKED?
HEH. TOUCHÉ.
AGENT KELLER!
EVERYONE BACK...

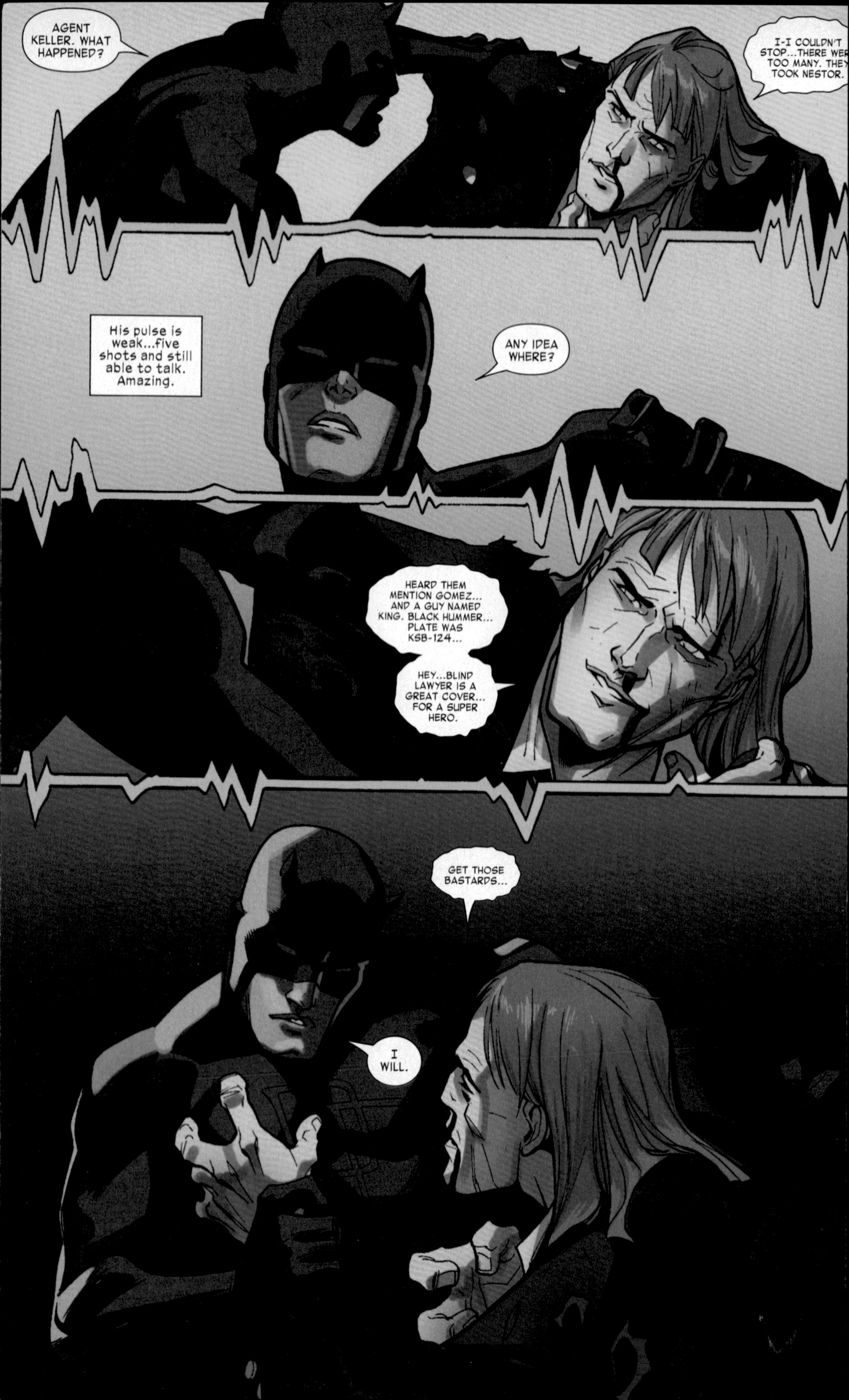
AGENT KELLER. WHAT HAPPENED?
I-I COULDN'T STOP...THERE WER TOO MANY. THEY TOOK NESTOR.
His pulse is weak...five shots and still able to talk. Amazing.
ANY IDEA WHERE?
HEARD THEM MENTION GOMEZ... AND A GUY NAMED KING. BLACK HUMMER... PLATE WAS KSB-124...
HEY...BLIND LAWYER IS A GREAT COVER... FOR A SUPER HERO.
GET THOSE BASTARDS...
I WILL.

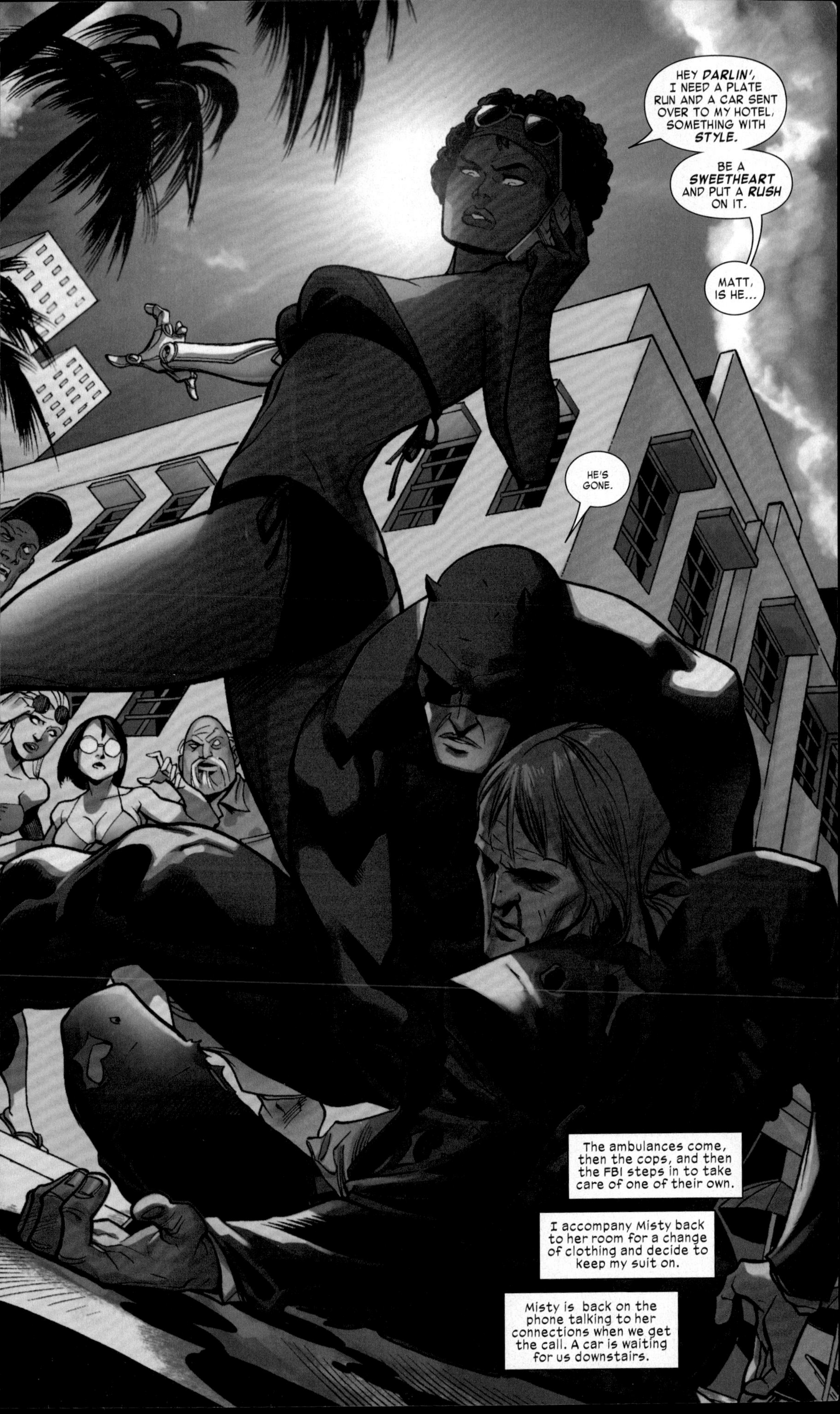
HEY DARLIN', I NEED A PLATE RUN AND A CAR SENT OVER TO MY HOTEL, SOMETHING WITH STYLE.
BE A SWEETHEART AND PUT A RUSH ON IT.
MATT, IS HE...
HE'S GONE.
The ambulances come, then the cops, and then the FBI steps in to take care of one of their own.
I accompany Misty back to her room for a change of clothing and decide to keep my suit on.
Misty is back on the phone talking to her connections when we get the call. A car is waiting for us downstairs.

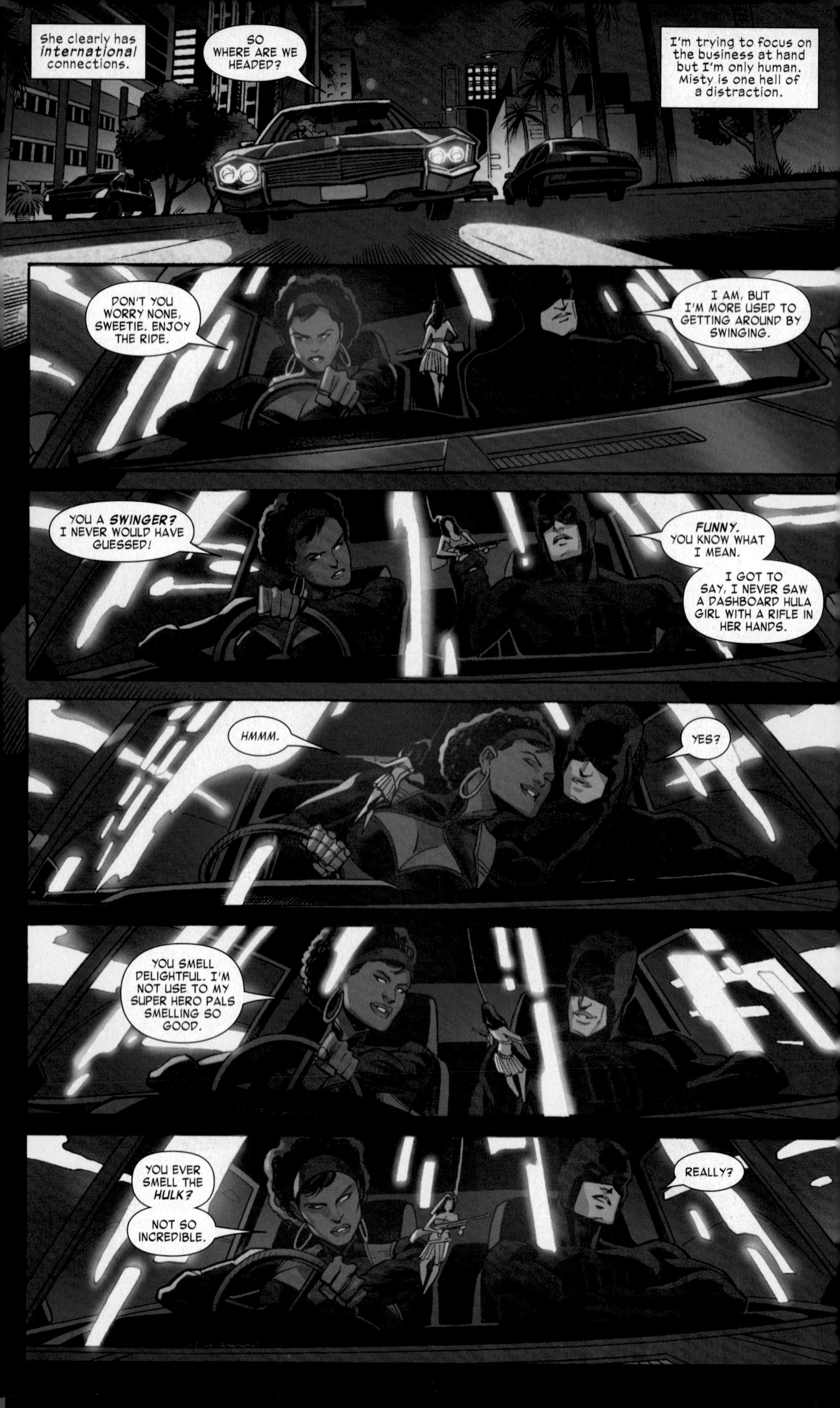

She clearly has *international* connections.
SO WHERE ARE WE HEADED?
I'm trying to focus on the business at hand but I'm only human. Misty is one hell of a distraction.
DON'T YOU WORRY NONE, SWEETIE. ENJOY THE RIDE.
I AM, BUT I'M MORE USED TO GETTING AROUND BY SWINGING.
YOU A *SWINGER?* I NEVER WOULD HAVE GUESSED!
FUNNY. YOU KNOW WHAT I MEAN.
I GOT TO SAY, I NEVER SAW A DASHBOARD HULA GIRL WITH A RIFLE IN HER HANDS.
HMMM.
YES?
YOU SMELL DELIGHTFUL. I'M NOT USE TO MY SUPER HERO PALS SMELLING SO GOOD.
YOU EVER SMELL THE *HULK?*
NOT SO INCREDIBLE.
REALLY?

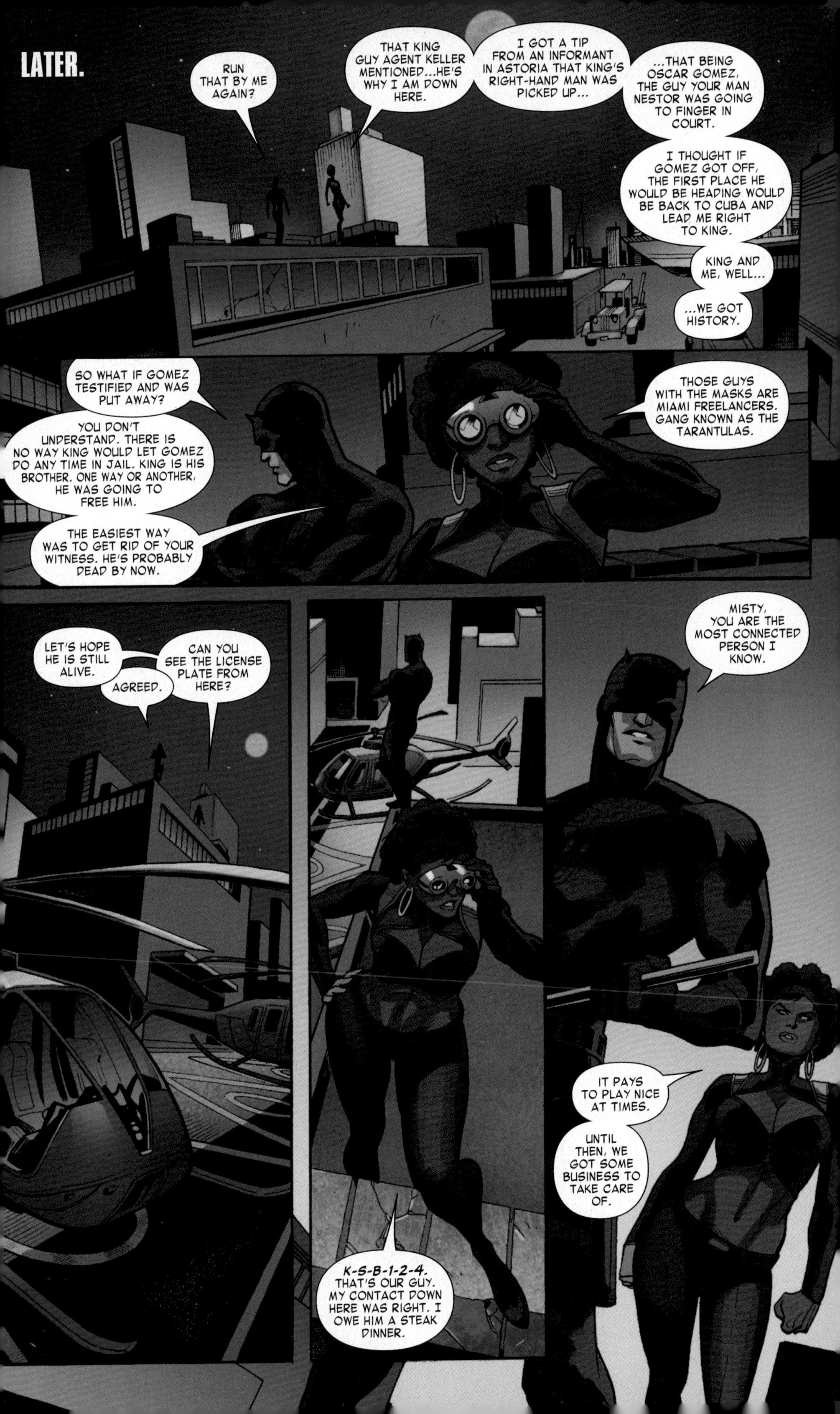
LATER.
RUN THAT BY ME AGAIN?
THAT KING GUY AGENT KELLER MENTIONED...HE'S WHY I AM DOWN HERE.
I GOT A TIP FROM AN INFORMANT IN ASTORIA THAT KING'S RIGHT-HAND MAN WAS PICKED UP...
...THAT BEING OSCAR GOMEZ, THE GUY YOUR MAN NESTOR WAS GOING TO FINGER IN COURT.
I THOUGHT IF GOMEZ GOT OFF, THE FIRST PLACE HE WOULD BE HEADING WOULD BE BACK TO CUBA AND LEAD ME RIGHT TO KING.
KING AND ME, WELL...
...WE GOT HISTORY.
SO WHAT IF GOMEZ TESTIFIED AND WAS PUT AWAY?
YOU DON'T UNDERSTAND. THERE IS NO WAY KING WOULD LET GOMEZ DO ANY TIME IN JAIL. KING IS HIS BROTHER. ONE WAY OR ANOTHER, HE WAS GOING TO FREE HIM.
THE EASIEST WAY WAS TO GET RID OF YOUR WITNESS. HE'S PROBABLY DEAD BY NOW.
THOSE GUYS WITH THE MASKS ARE MIAMI FREELANCERS. GANG KNOWN AS THE TARANTULAS.
LET'S HOPE HE IS STILL ALIVE.
AGREED.
CAN YOU SEE THE LICENSE PLATE FROM HERE?
K-S-B-1-2-4. THAT'S OUR GUY. MY CONTACT DOWN HERE WAS RIGHT. I OWE HIM A STEAK DINNER.
MISTY, YOU ARE THE MOST CONNECTED PERSON I KNOW.
IT PAYS TO PLAY NICE AT TIMES.
UNTIL THEN, WE GOT SOME BUSINESS TO TAKE CARE OF.

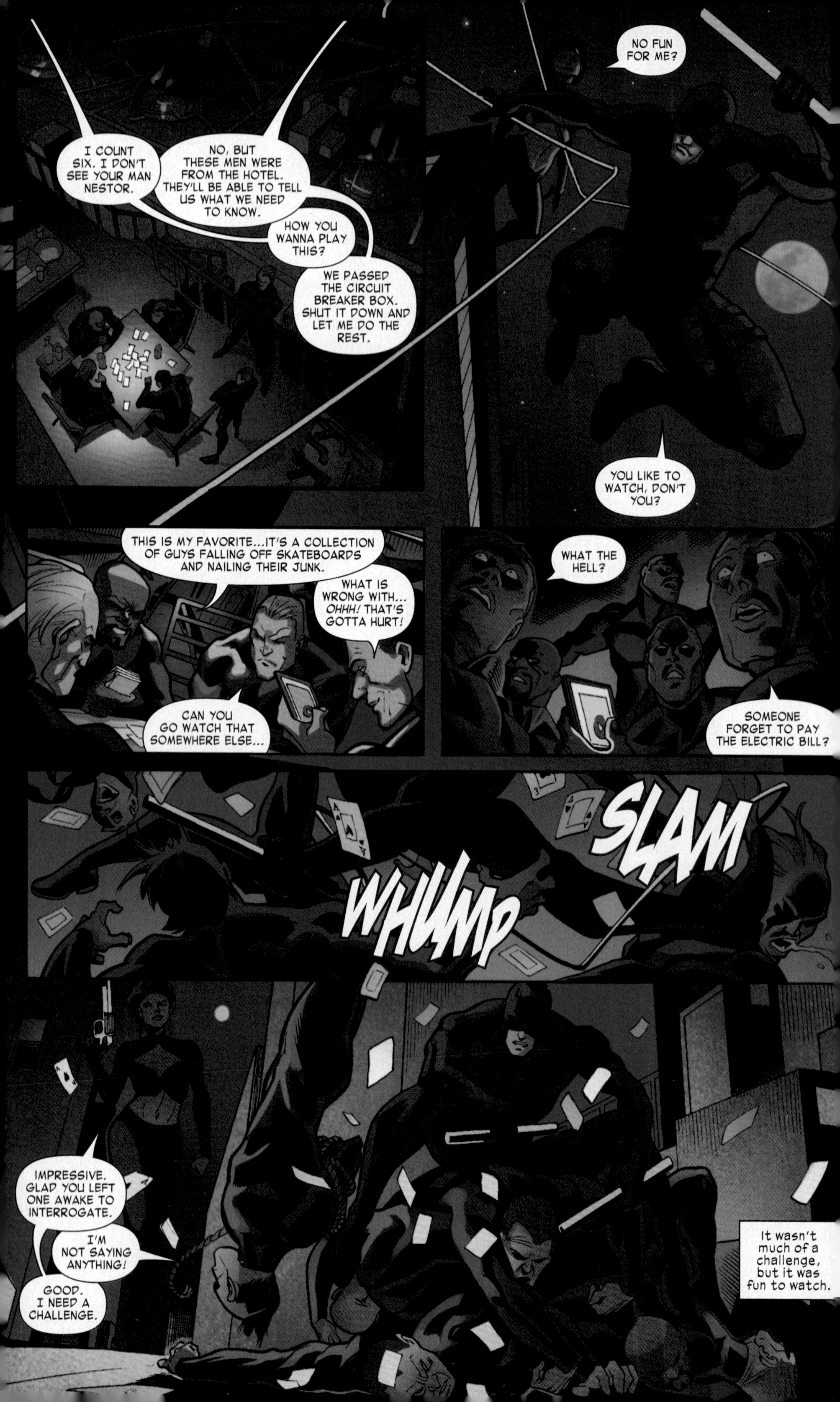

I COUNT SIX. I DON'T SEE YOUR MAN NESTOR.
NO, BUT THESE MEN WERE FROM THE HOTEL. THEY'LL BE ABLE TO TELL US WHAT WE NEED TO KNOW.
HOW YOU WANNA PLAY THIS?
WE PASSED THE CIRCUIT BREAKER BOX. SHUT IT DOWN AND LET ME DO THE REST.
NO FUN FOR ME?
YOU LIKE TO WATCH, DON'T YOU?
THIS IS MY FAVORITE...IT'S A COLLECTION OF GUYS FALLING OFF SKATEBOARDS AND NAILING THEIR JUNK.
WHAT IS WRONG WITH... OHHH! THAT'S GOTTA HURT!
CAN YOU GO WATCH THAT SOMEWHERE ELSE...
WHAT THE HELL?
SOMEONE FORGET TO PAY THE ELECTRIC BILL?
SLAM
WHUMP
IMPRESSIVE. GLAD YOU LEFT ONE AWAKE TO INTERROGATE.
I'M NOT SAYING ANYTHING!
GOOD. I NEED A CHALLENGE.
It wasn't much of a challenge, but it was fun to watch.

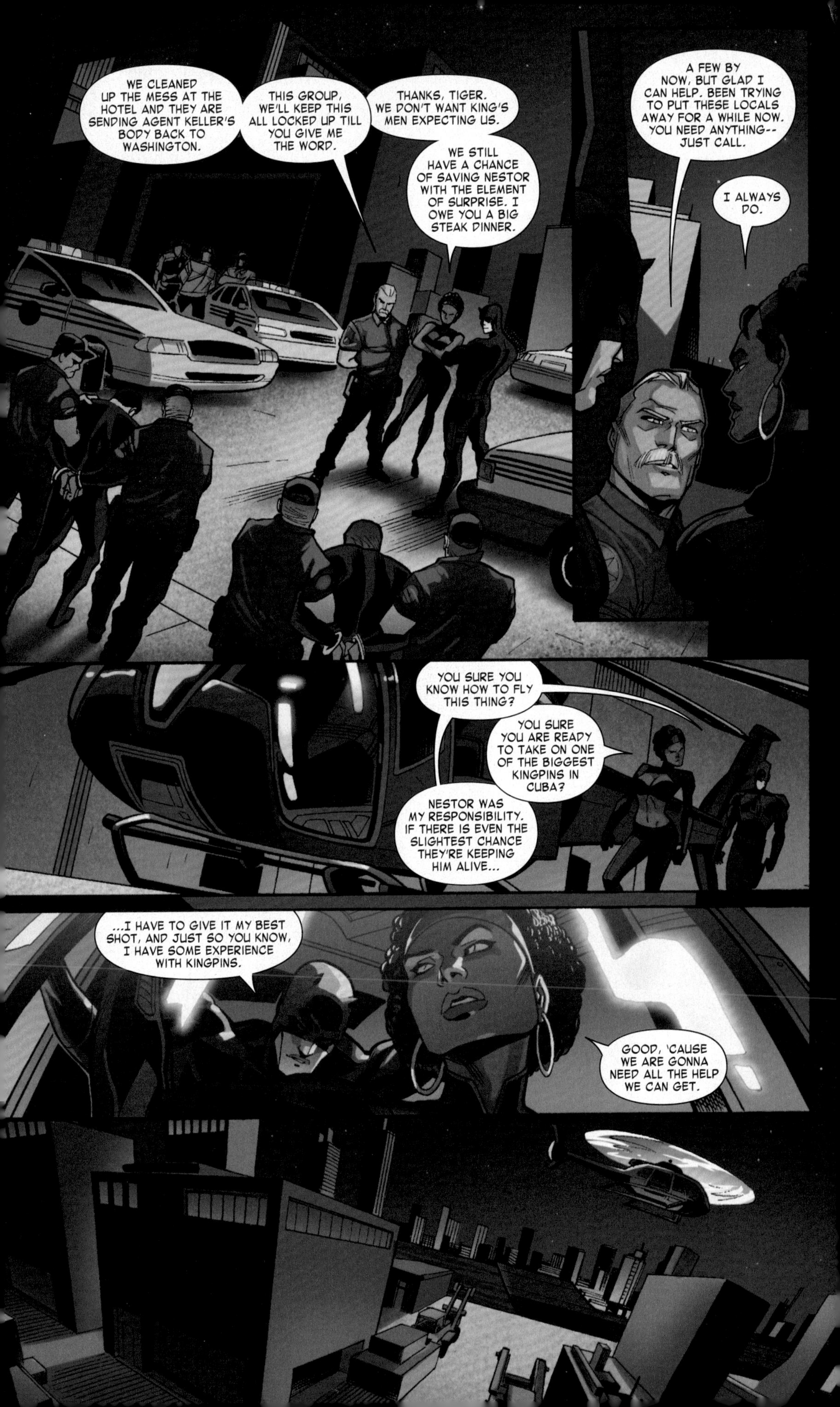
WE CLEANED UP THE MESS AT THE HOTEL AND THEY ARE SENDING AGENT KELLER'S BODY BACK TO WASHINGTON.
THIS GROUP, WE'LL KEEP THIS ALL LOCKED UP TILL YOU GIVE ME THE WORD.
THANKS, TIGER. WE DON'T WANT KING'S MEN EXPECTING US.
WE STILL HAVE A CHANCE OF SAVING NESTOR WITH THE ELEMENT OF SURPRISE. I OWE YOU A BIG STEAK DINNER.
A FEW BY NOW, BUT GLAD I CAN HELP. BEEN TRYING TO PUT THESE LOCALS AWAY FOR A WHILE NOW. YOU NEED ANYTHING-- JUST CALL.
I ALWAYS DO.
YOU SURE YOU KNOW HOW TO FLY THIS THING?
YOU SURE YOU ARE READY TO TAKE ON ONE OF THE BIGGEST KINGPINS IN CUBA?
NESTOR WAS MY RESPONSIBILITY. IF THERE IS EVEN THE SLIGHTEST CHANCE THEY'RE KEEPING HIM ALIVE...
...I HAVE TO GIVE IT MY BEST SHOT, AND JUST SO YOU KNOW, I HAVE SOME EXPERIENCE WITH KINGPINS.
GOOD, 'CAUSE WE ARE GONNA NEED ALL THE HELP WE CAN GET.

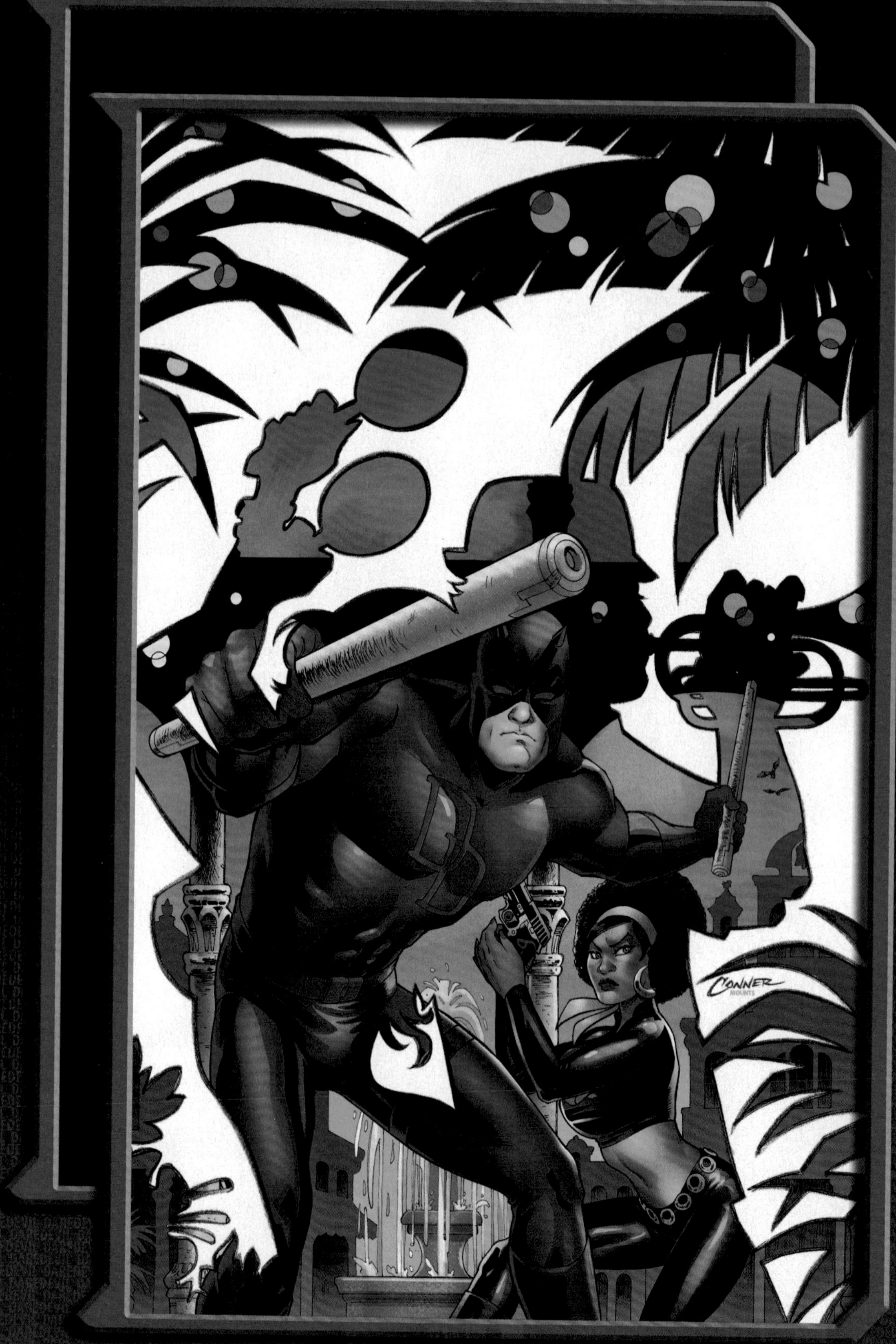
CONNER

#7 — IN THE NAME OF THE KING
PART TWO: TO KILL A KING

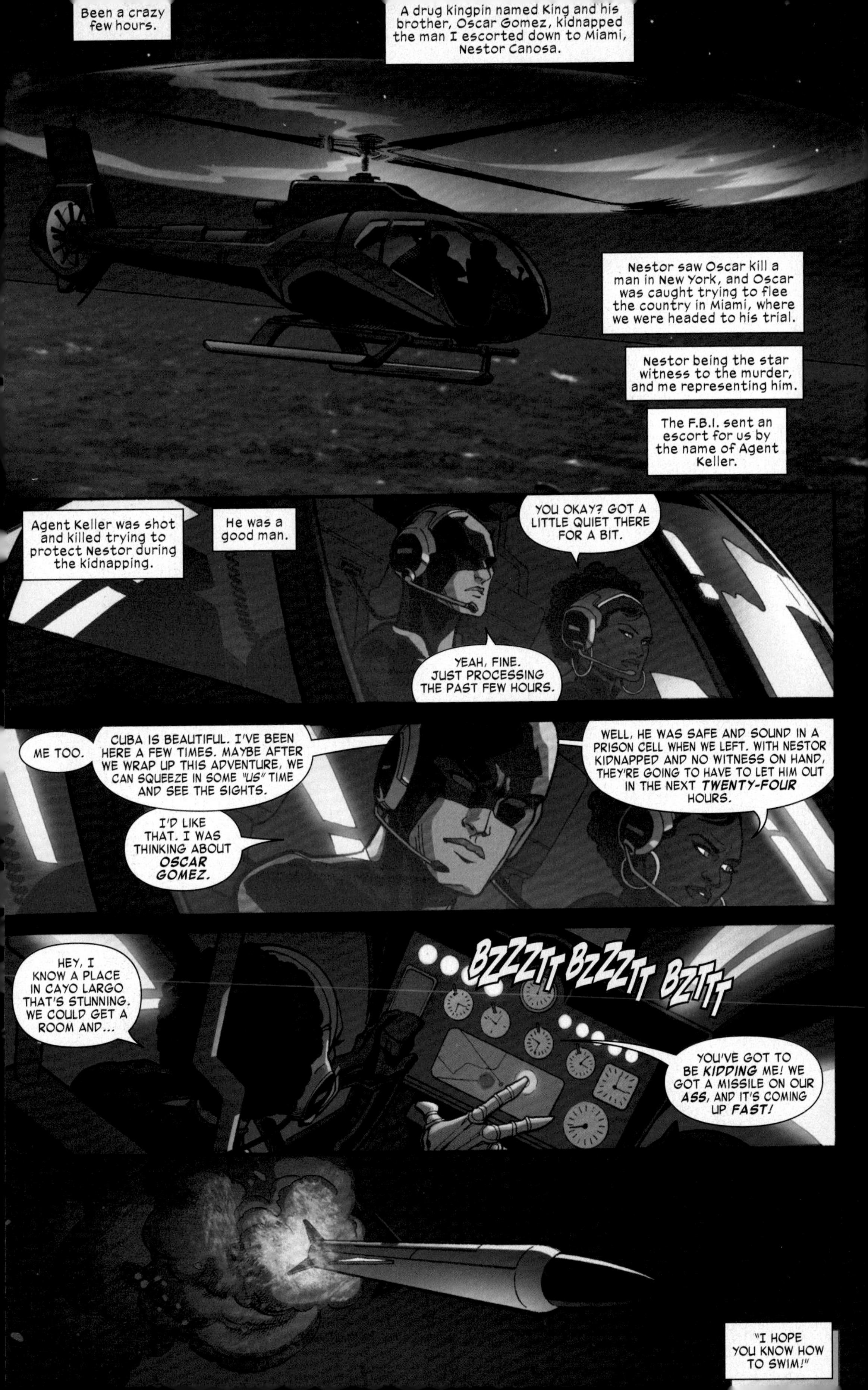
Been a crazy few hours.
A drug kingpin named King and his brother, Oscar Gomez, kidnapped the man I escorted down to Miami, Nestor Canosa.
Nestor saw Oscar kill a man in New York, and Oscar was caught trying to flee the country in Miami, where we were headed to his trial.
Nestor being the star witness to the murder, and me representing him.
The F.B.I. sent an escort for us by the name of Agent Keller.
Agent Keller was shot and killed trying to protect Nestor during the kidnapping.
He was a good man.
YOU OKAY? GOT A LITTLE QUIET THERE FOR A BIT.
YEAH, FINE. JUST PROCESSING THE PAST FEW HOURS.
CUBA IS BEAUTIFUL. I'VE BEEN HERE A FEW TIMES. MAYBE AFTER WE WRAP UP THIS ADVENTURE, WE CAN SQUEEZE IN SOME "US" TIME AND SEE THE SIGHTS.
ME TOO.
I'D LIKE THAT. I WAS THINKING ABOUT OSCAR GOMEZ.
WELL, HE WAS SAFE AND SOUND IN A PRISON CELL WHEN WE LEFT. WITH NESTOR KIDNAPPED AND NO WITNESS ON HAND, THEY'RE GOING TO HAVE TO LET HIM OUT IN THE NEXT TWENTY-FOUR HOURS.
HEY, I KNOW A PLACE IN CAYO LARGO THAT'S STUNNING. WE COULD GET A ROOM AND...
BZZZTT BZZZTT BZTTT
YOU'VE GOT TO BE KIDDING ME! WE GOT A MISSILE ON OUR ASS, AND IT'S COMING UP FAST!
"I HOPE YOU KNOW HOW TO SWIM!"

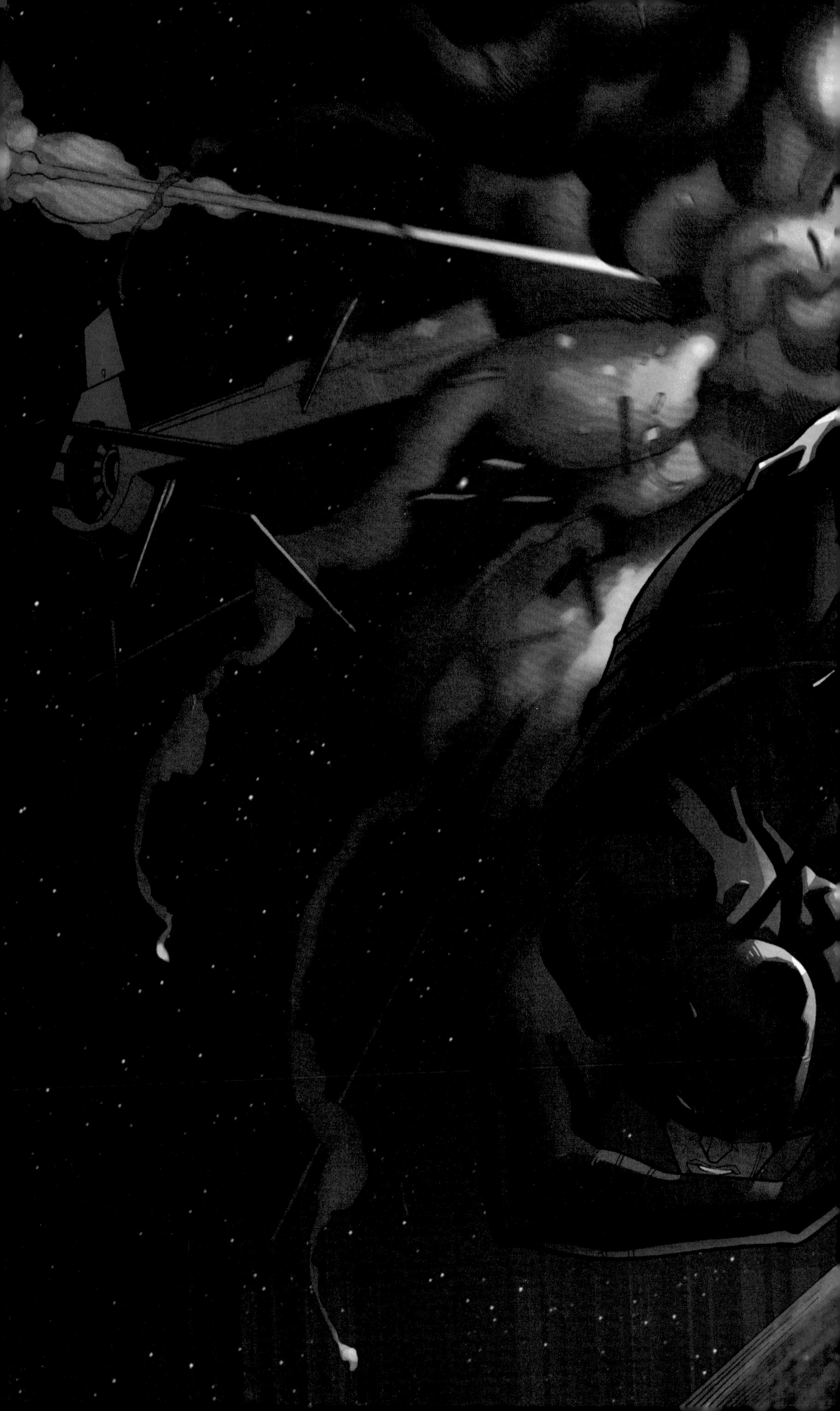

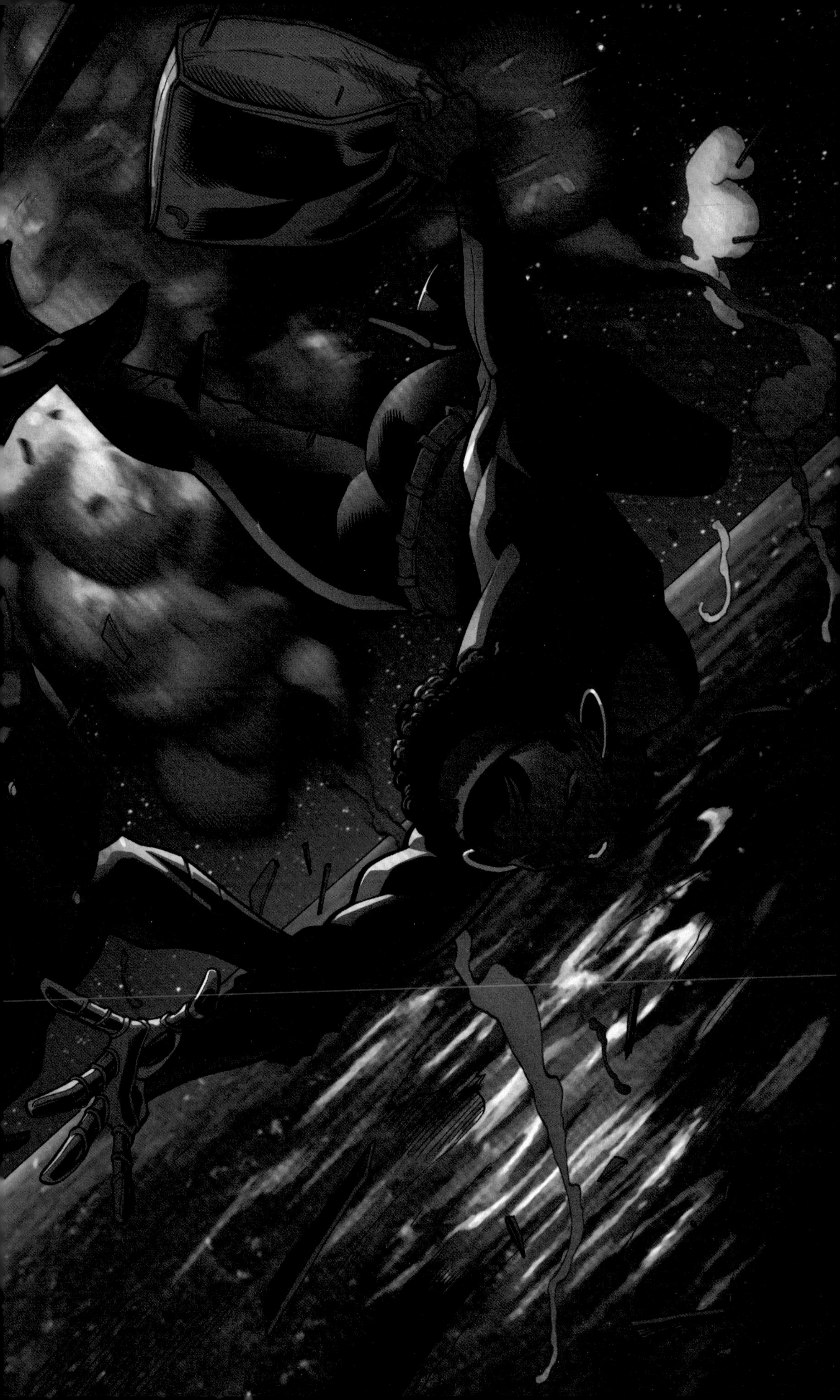

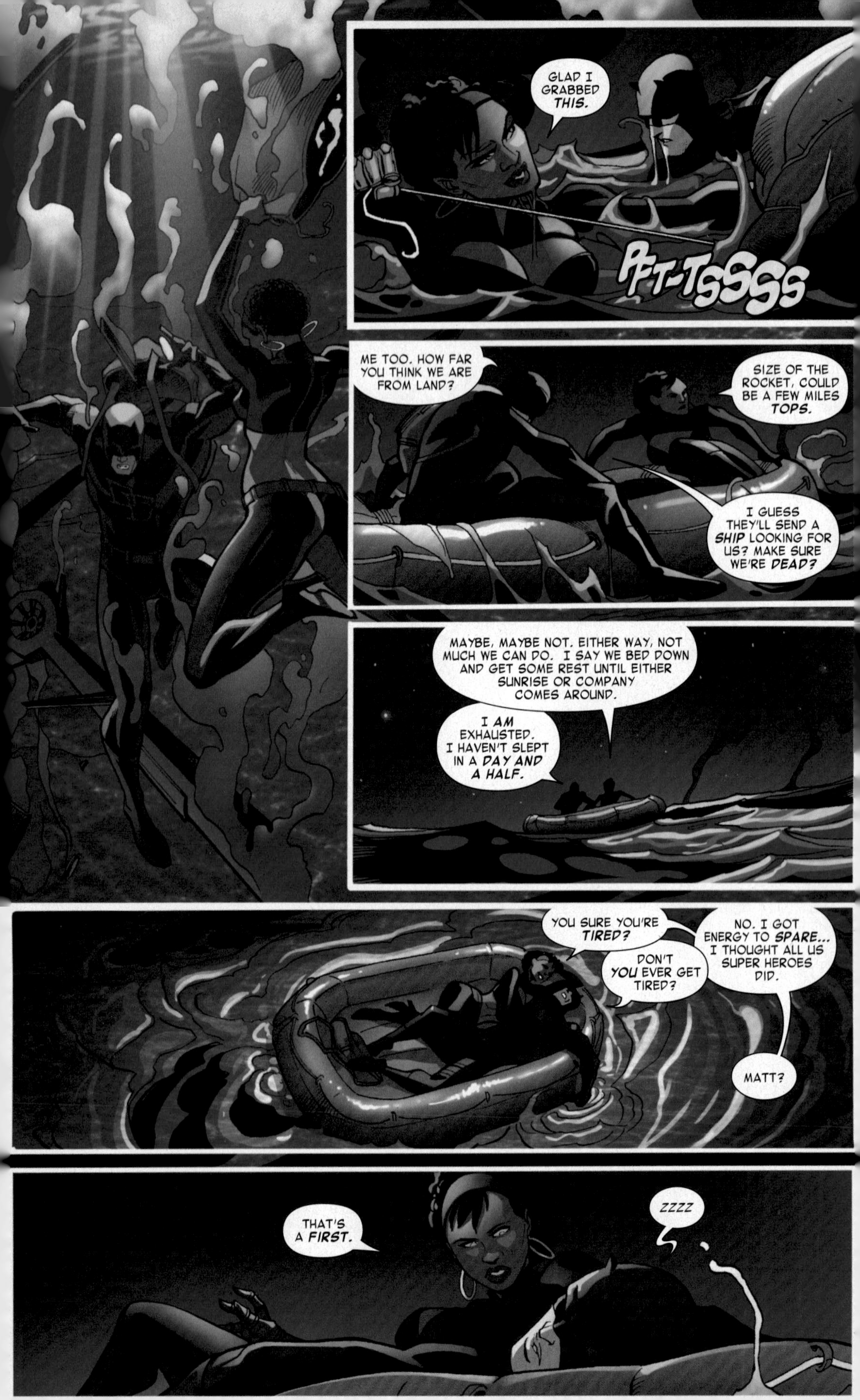
GLAD I GRABBED THIS.
PFFT-TSSSSS
ME TOO. HOW FAR YOU THINK WE ARE FROM LAND?
SIZE OF THE ROCKET, COULD BE A FEW MILES TOPS.
I GUESS THEY'LL SEND A SHIP LOOKING FOR US? MAKE SURE WE'RE DEAD?
MAYBE, MAYBE NOT. EITHER WAY, NOT MUCH WE CAN DO. I SAY WE BED DOWN AND GET SOME REST UNTIL EITHER SUNRISE OR COMPANY COMES AROUND.
I AM EXHAUSTED. I HAVEN'T SLEPT IN A DAY AND A HALF.
YOU SURE YOU'RE TIRED?
DON'T YOU EVER GET TIRED?
NO. I GOT ENERGY TO SPARE... I THOUGHT ALL US SUPER HEROES DID.
MATT?
THAT'S A FIRST.
ZZZZ

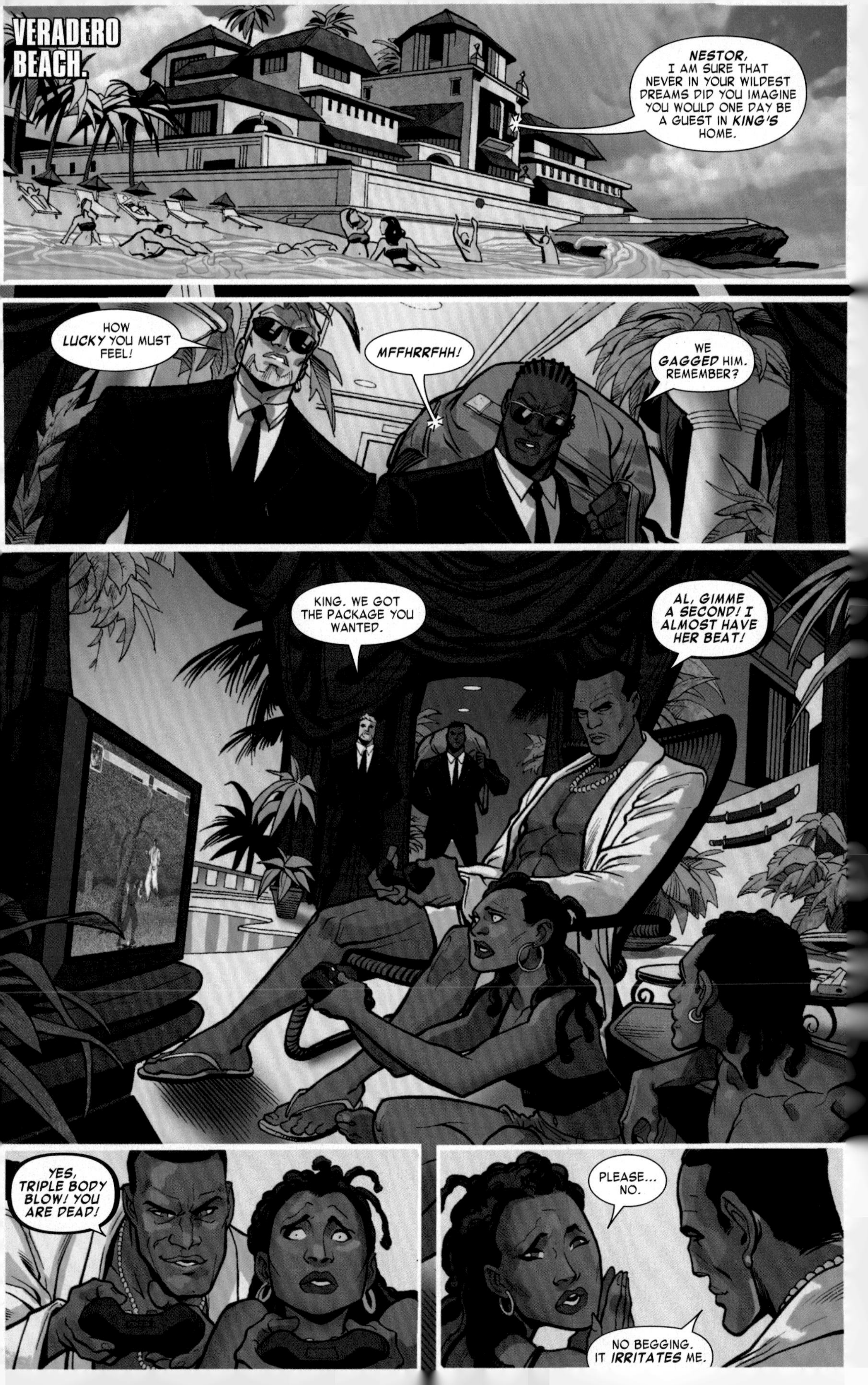
VERADERO BEACH.
NESTOR, I AM SURE THAT NEVER IN YOUR WILDEST DREAMS DID YOU IMAGINE YOU WOULD ONE DAY BE A GUEST IN KING'S HOME.
HOW LUCKY YOU MUST FEEL!
MFFHRRFHH!
WE GAGGED HIM. REMEMBER?
KING. WE GOT THE PACKAGE YOU WANTED.
AL, GIMME A SECOND! I ALMOST HAVE HER BEAT!
YES, TRIPLE BODY BLOW! YOU ARE DEAD!
PLEASE... NO.
NO BEGGING. IT IRRITATES ME.

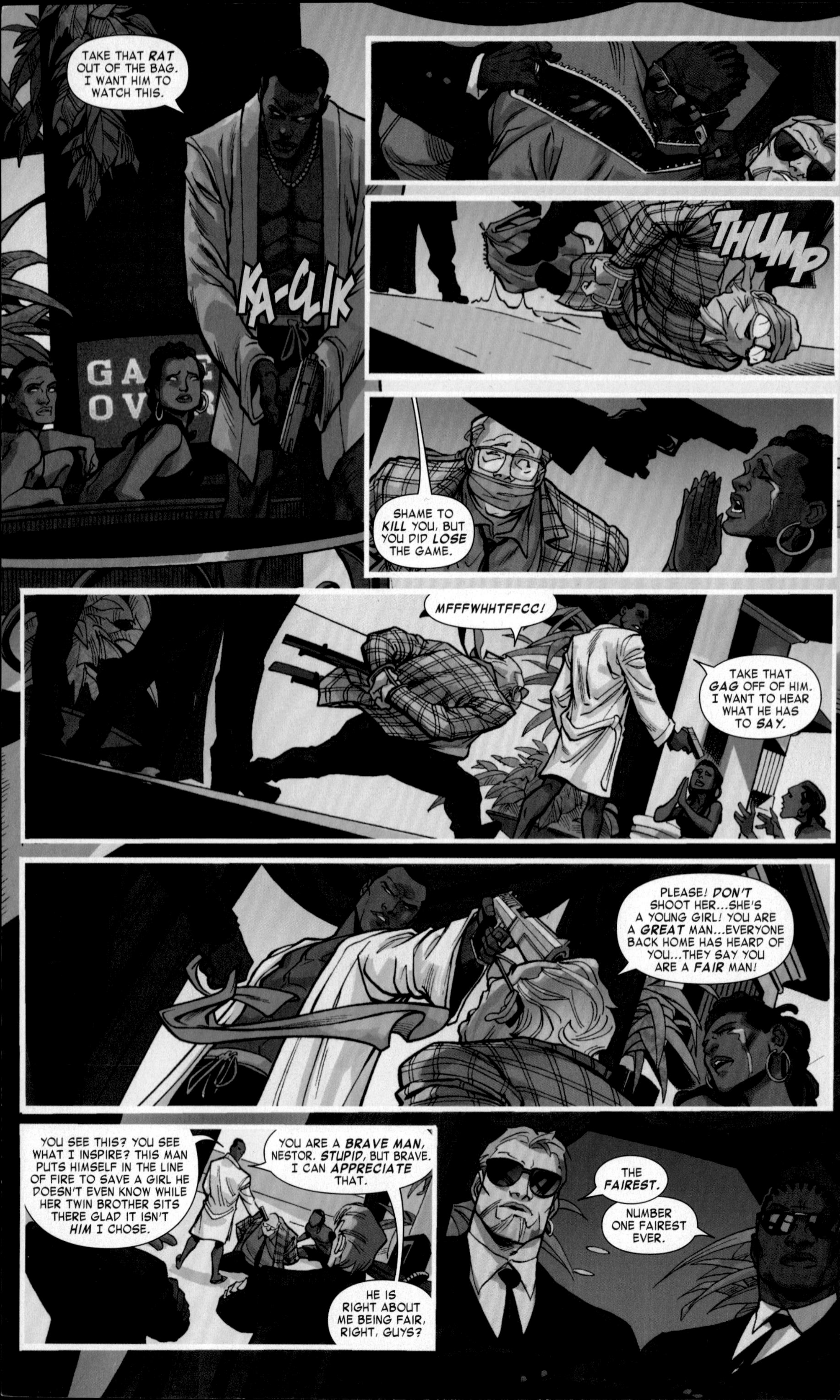

TAKE THAT RAT OUT OF THE BAG. I WANT HIM TO WATCH THIS.
KA-CLIK
GAME OVER
THUMP
SHAME TO KILL YOU, BUT YOU DID LOSE THE GAME.
MFFFWHHTFFCC!
TAKE THAT GAG OFF OF HIM. I WANT TO HEAR WHAT HE HAS TO SAY.
PLEASE! DON'T SHOOT HER...SHE'S A YOUNG GIRL! YOU ARE A GREAT MAN...EVERYONE BACK HOME HAS HEARD OF YOU...THEY SAY YOU ARE A FAIR MAN!
YOU SEE THIS? YOU SEE WHAT I INSPIRE? THIS MAN PUTS HIMSELF IN THE LINE OF FIRE TO SAVE A GIRL HE DOESN'T EVEN KNOW WHILE HER TWIN BROTHER SITS THERE GLAD IT ISN'T HIM I CHOSE.
YOU ARE A BRAVE MAN, NESTOR. STUPID, BUT BRAVE. I CAN APPRECIATE THAT.
HE IS RIGHT ABOUT ME BEING FAIR, RIGHT, GUYS?
THE FAIREST.
NUMBER ONE FAIREST EVER.

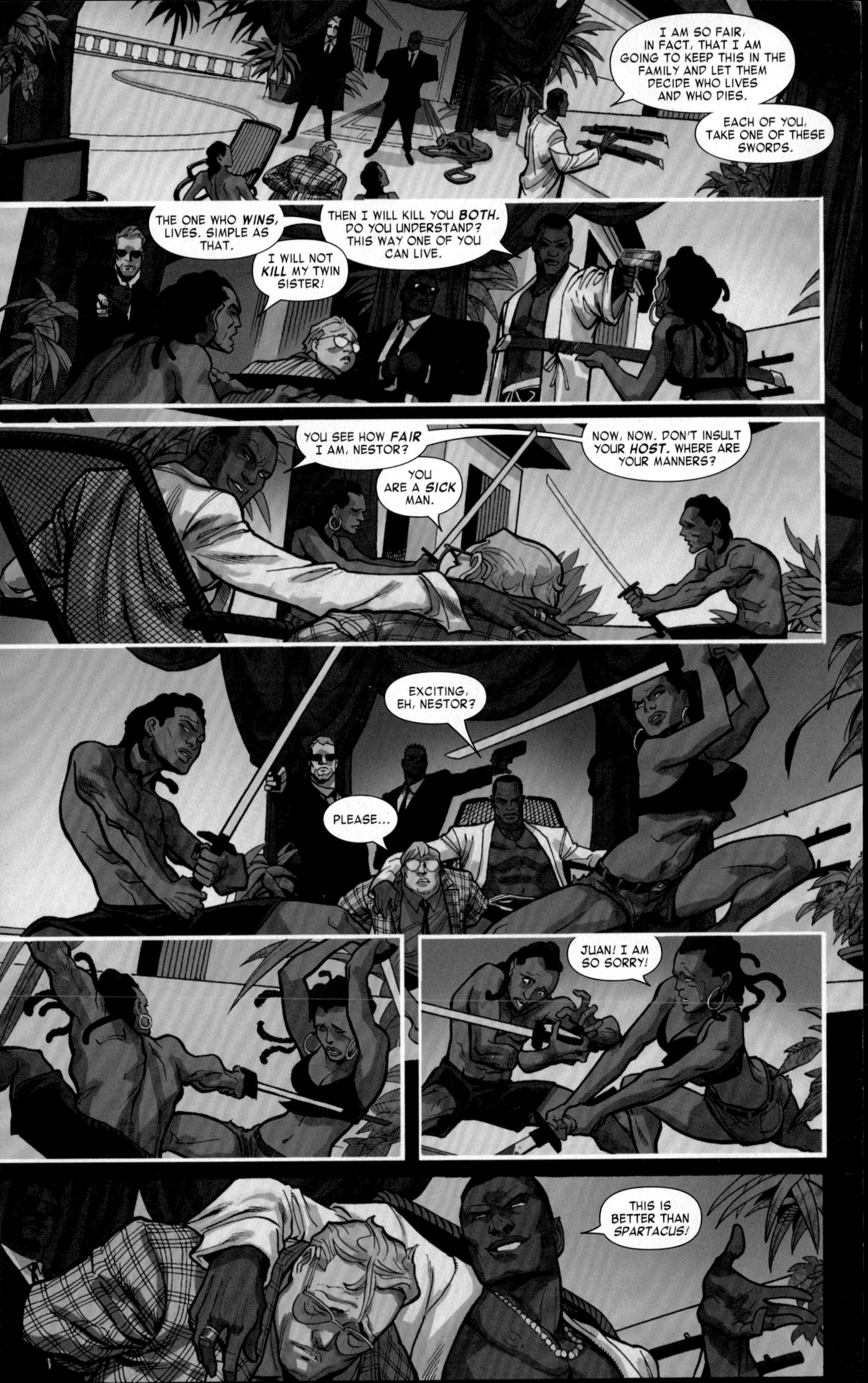
I AM SO FAIR, IN FACT, THAT I AM GOING TO KEEP THIS IN THE FAMILY AND LET THEM DECIDE WHO LIVES AND WHO DIES.
EACH OF YOU, TAKE ONE OF THESE SWORDS.
THE ONE WHO WINS, LIVES. SIMPLE AS THAT.
I WILL NOT KILL MY TWIN SISTER!
THEN I WILL KILL YOU BOTH. DO YOU UNDERSTAND? THIS WAY ONE OF YOU CAN LIVE.
YOU SEE HOW FAIR I AM, NESTOR?
YOU ARE A SICK MAN.
NOW, NOW. DON'T INSULT YOUR HOST. WHERE ARE YOUR MANNERS?
EXCITING, EH, NESTOR?
PLEASE...
JUAN! I AM SO SORRY!
THIS IS BETTER THAN SPARTACUS!

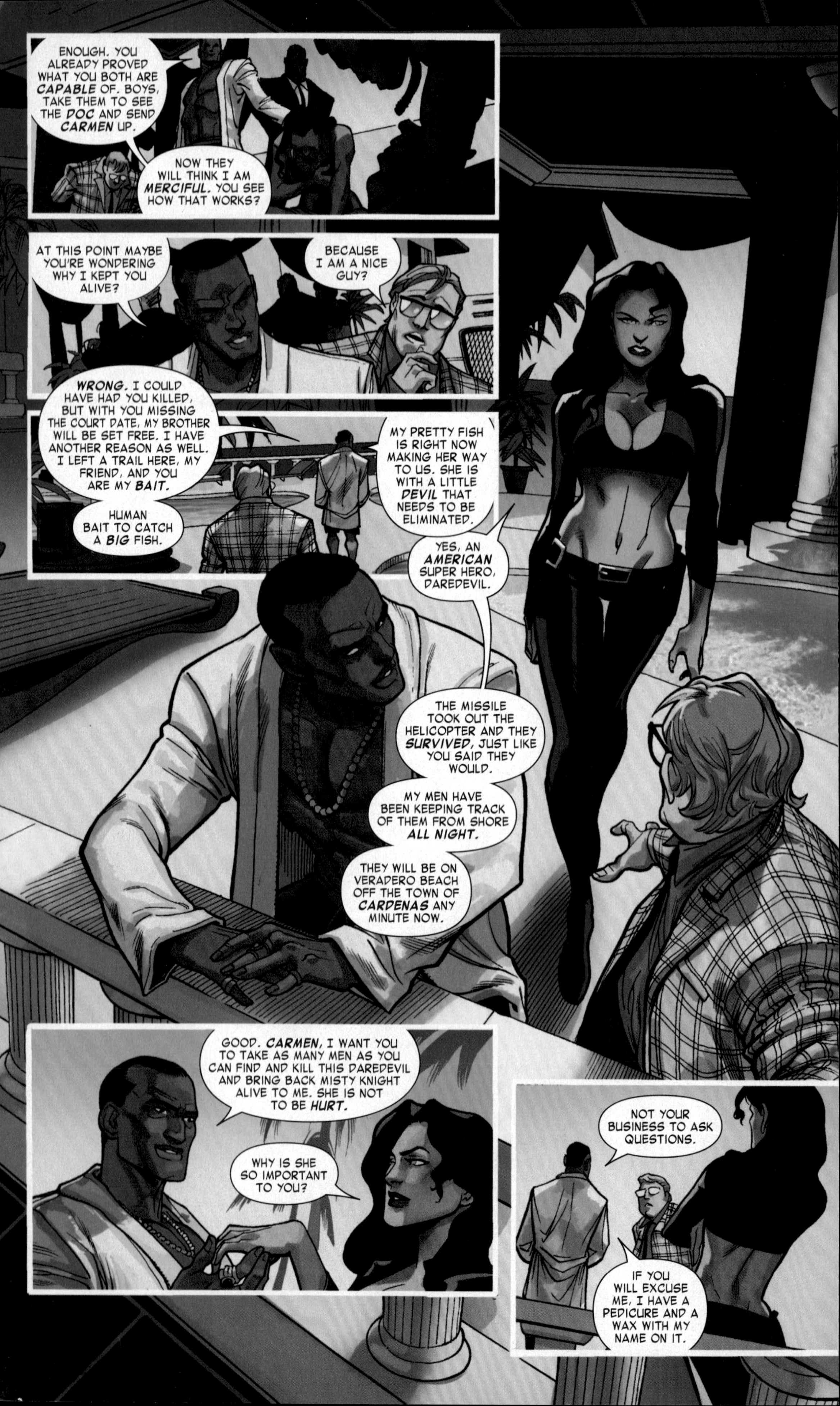
ENOUGH. YOU ALREADY PROVED WHAT YOU BOTH ARE CAPABLE OF. BOYS, TAKE THEM TO SEE THE DOC AND SEND CARMEN UP.
NOW THEY WILL THINK I AM MERCIFUL. YOU SEE HOW THAT WORKS?
AT THIS POINT MAYBE YOU'RE WONDERING WHY I KEPT YOU ALIVE?
BECAUSE I AM A NICE GUY?
WRONG. I COULD HAVE HAD YOU KILLED, BUT WITH YOU MISSING THE COURT DATE, MY BROTHER WILL BE SET FREE. I HAVE ANOTHER REASON AS WELL. I LEFT A TRAIL HERE, MY FRIEND, AND YOU ARE MY BAIT.
HUMAN BAIT TO CATCH A BIG FISH.
MY PRETTY FISH IS RIGHT NOW MAKING HER WAY TO US. SHE IS WITH A LITTLE DEVIL THAT NEEDS TO BE ELIMINATED.
YES, AN AMERICAN SUPER HERO, DAREDEVIL.
THE MISSILE TOOK OUT THE HELICOPTER AND THEY SURVIVED, JUST LIKE YOU SAID THEY WOULD.
MY MEN HAVE BEEN KEEPING TRACK OF THEM FROM SHORE ALL NIGHT.
THEY WILL BE ON VERADERO BEACH OFF THE TOWN OF CARDENAS ANY MINUTE NOW.
GOOD. CARMEN, I WANT YOU TO TAKE AS MANY MEN AS YOU CAN FIND AND KILL THIS DAREDEVIL AND BRING BACK MISTY KNIGHT ALIVE TO ME. SHE IS NOT TO BE HURT.
WHY IS SHE SO IMPORTANT TO YOU?
NOT YOUR BUSINESS TO ASK QUESTIONS.
IF YOU WILL EXCUSE ME, I HAVE A PEDICURE AND A WAX WITH MY NAME ON IT.

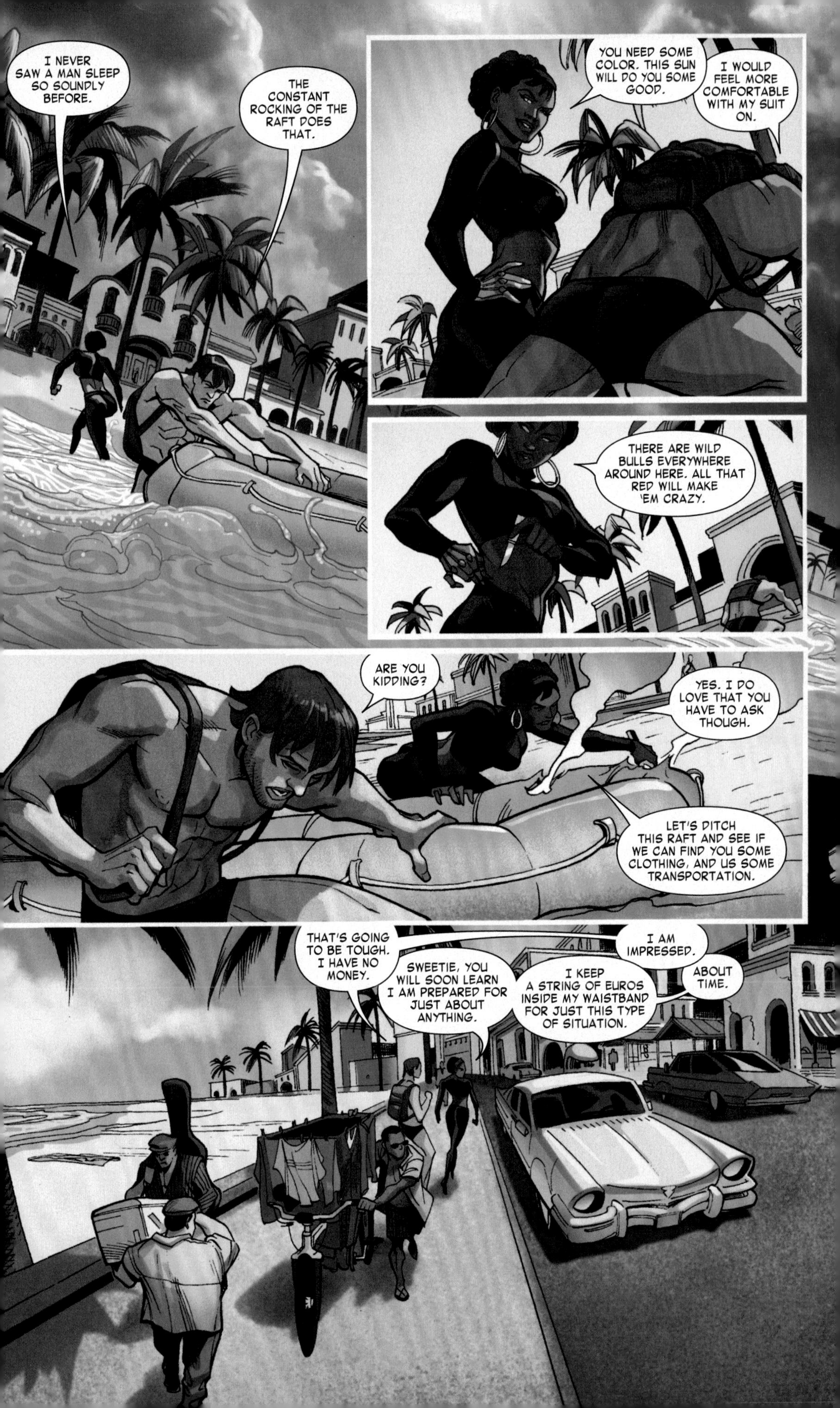

I NEVER SAW A MAN SLEEP SO SOUNDLY BEFORE.
THE CONSTANT ROCKING OF THE RAFT DOES THAT.
YOU NEED SOME COLOR. THIS SUN WILL DO YOU SOME GOOD.
I WOULD FEEL MORE COMFORTABLE WITH MY SUIT ON.
THERE ARE WILD BULLS EVERYWHERE AROUND HERE. ALL THAT RED WILL MAKE 'EM CRAZY.
ARE YOU KIDDING?
YES. I DO LOVE THAT YOU HAVE TO ASK THOUGH.
LET'S DITCH THIS RAFT AND SEE IF WE CAN FIND YOU SOME CLOTHING, AND US SOME TRANSPORTATION.
THAT'S GOING TO BE TOUGH. I HAVE NO MONEY.
SWEETIE, YOU WILL SOON LEARN I AM PREPARED FOR JUST ABOUT ANYTHING.
I KEEP A STRING OF EUROS INSIDE MY WAISTBAND FOR JUST THIS TYPE OF SITUATION.
I AM IMPRESSED.
ABOUT TIME.

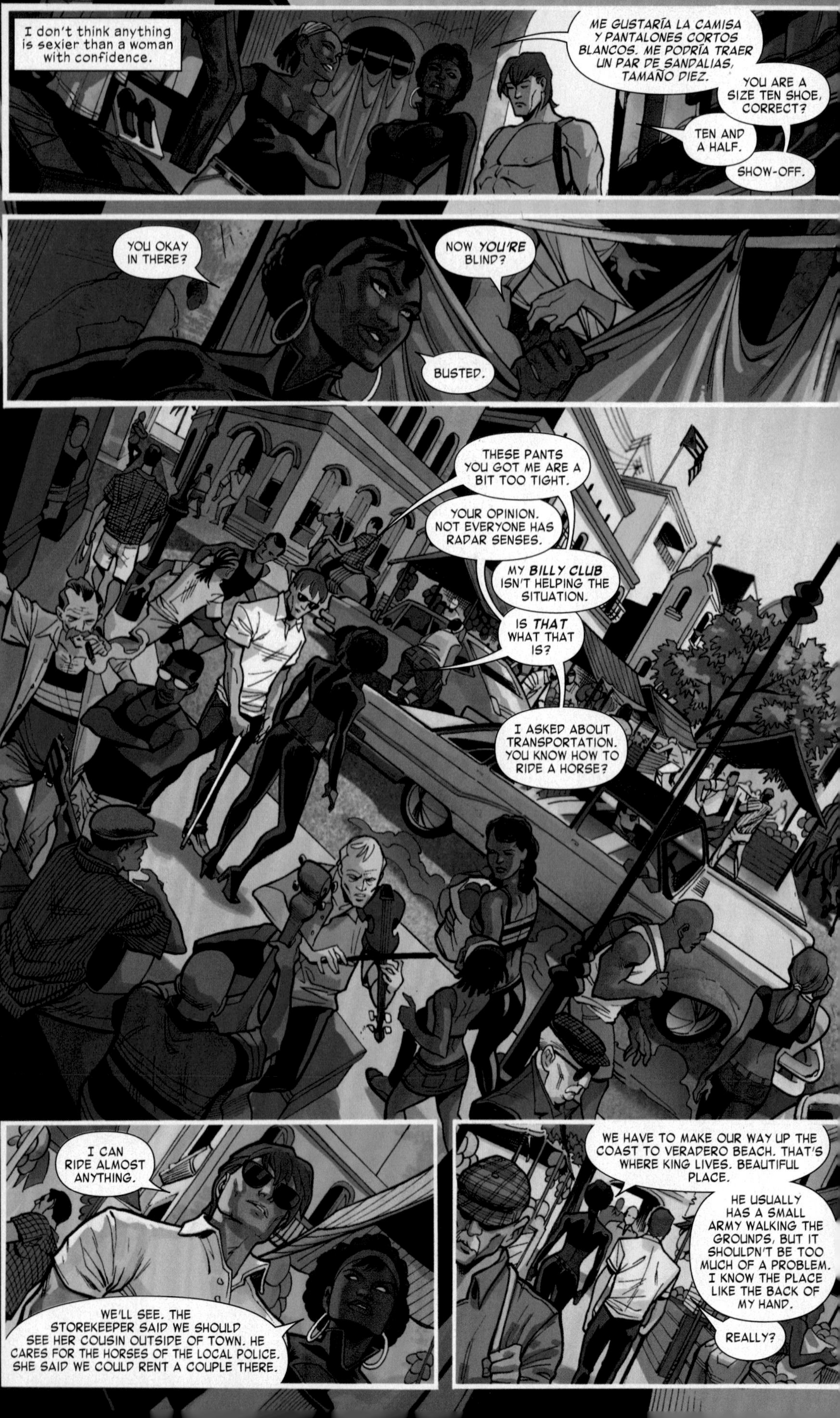

I don't think anything is sexier than a woman with confidence.
ME GUSTARÍA LA CAMISA Y PANTALONES CORTOS BLANCOS. ME PODRÍA TRAER UN PAR DE SANDALIAS, TAMAÑO DIEZ.
YOU ARE A SIZE TEN SHOE, CORRECT?
TEN AND A HALF.
SHOW-OFF.
YOU OKAY IN THERE?
NOW YOU'RE BLIND?
BUSTED.
THESE PANTS YOU GOT ME ARE A BIT TOO TIGHT.
YOUR OPINION. NOT EVERYONE HAS RADAR SENSES.
MY BILLY CLUB ISN'T HELPING THE SITUATION.
IS THAT WHAT THAT IS?
I ASKED ABOUT TRANSPORTATION. YOU KNOW HOW TO RIDE A HORSE?
I CAN RIDE ALMOST ANYTHING.
WE'LL SEE. THE STOREKEEPER SAID WE SHOULD SEE HER COUSIN OUTSIDE OF TOWN. HE CARES FOR THE HORSES OF THE LOCAL POLICE. SHE SAID WE COULD RENT A COUPLE THERE.
WE HAVE TO MAKE OUR WAY UP THE COAST TO VERADERO BEACH. THAT'S WHERE KING LIVES. BEAUTIFUL PLACE.
HE USUALLY HAS A SMALL ARMY WALKING THE GROUNDS, BUT IT SHOULDN'T BE TOO MUCH OF A PROBLEM. I KNOW THE PLACE LIKE THE BACK OF MY HAND.
REALLY?

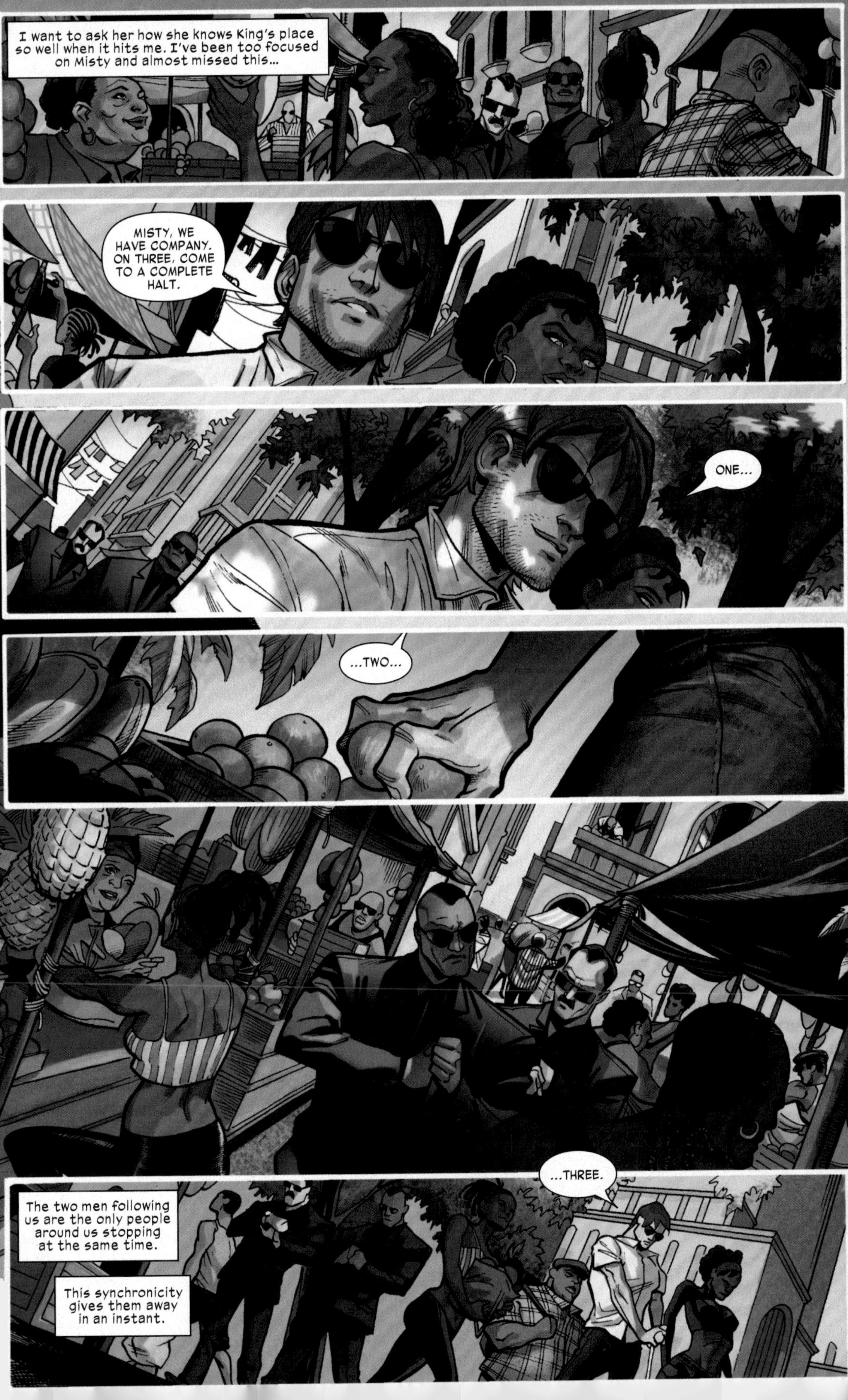
I want to ask her how she knows King's place so well when it hits me. I've been too focused on Misty and almost missed this...
MISTY, WE HAVE COMPANY. ON THREE, COME TO A COMPLETE HALT.
ONE...
...TWO...
...THREE.
The two men following us are the only people around us stopping at the same time.
This synchronicity gives them away in an instant.

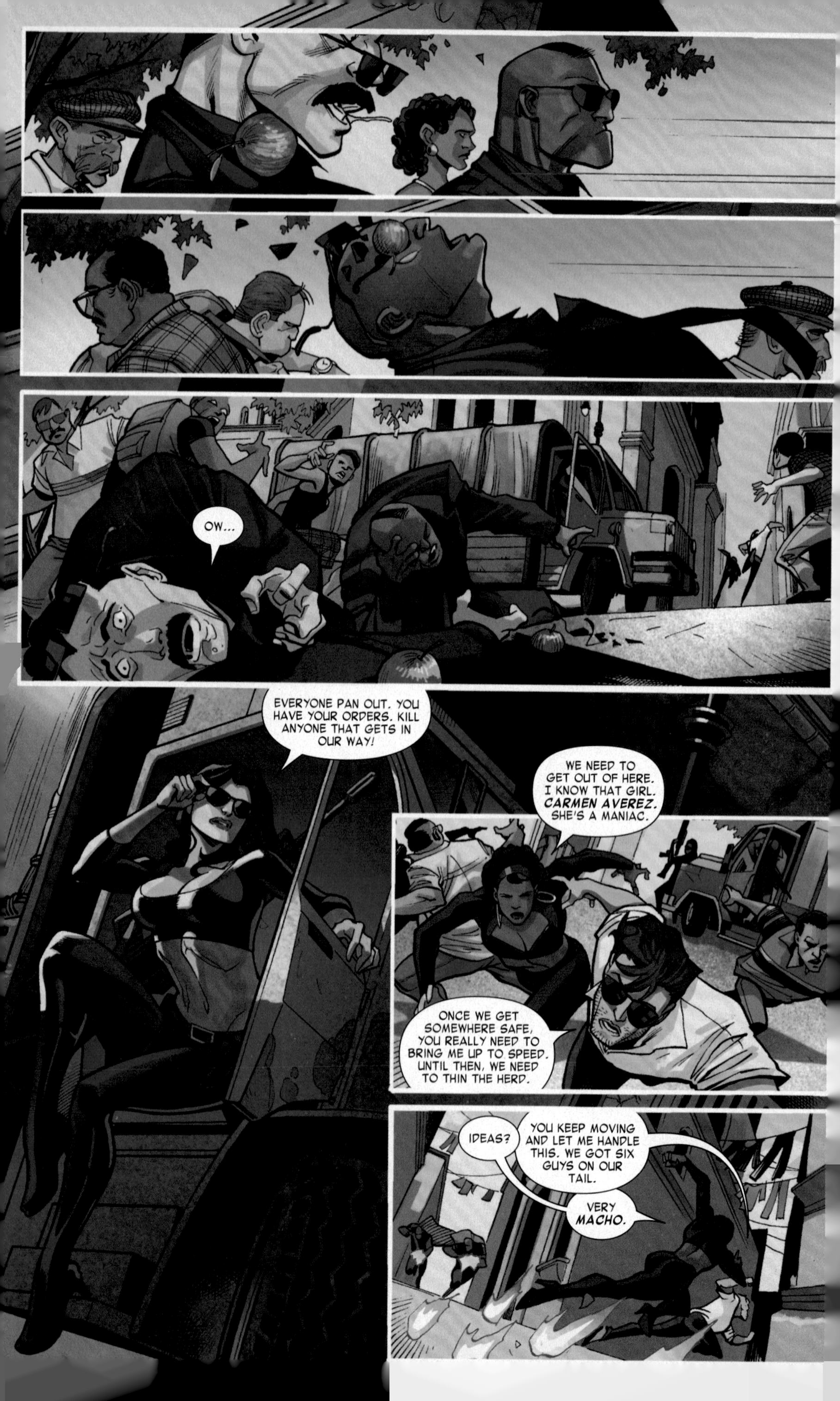
OW...
EVERYONE PAN OUT. YOU HAVE YOUR ORDERS. KILL ANYONE THAT GETS IN OUR WAY!
WE NEED TO GET OUT OF HERE. I KNOW THAT GIRL. CARMEN AVEREZ. SHE'S A MANIAC.
ONCE WE GET SOMEWHERE SAFE, YOU REALLY NEED TO BRING ME UP TO SPEED. UNTIL THEN, WE NEED TO THIN THE HERD.
IDEAS?
YOU KEEP MOVING AND LET ME HANDLE THIS. WE GOT SIX GUYS ON OUR TAIL.
VERY MACHO.

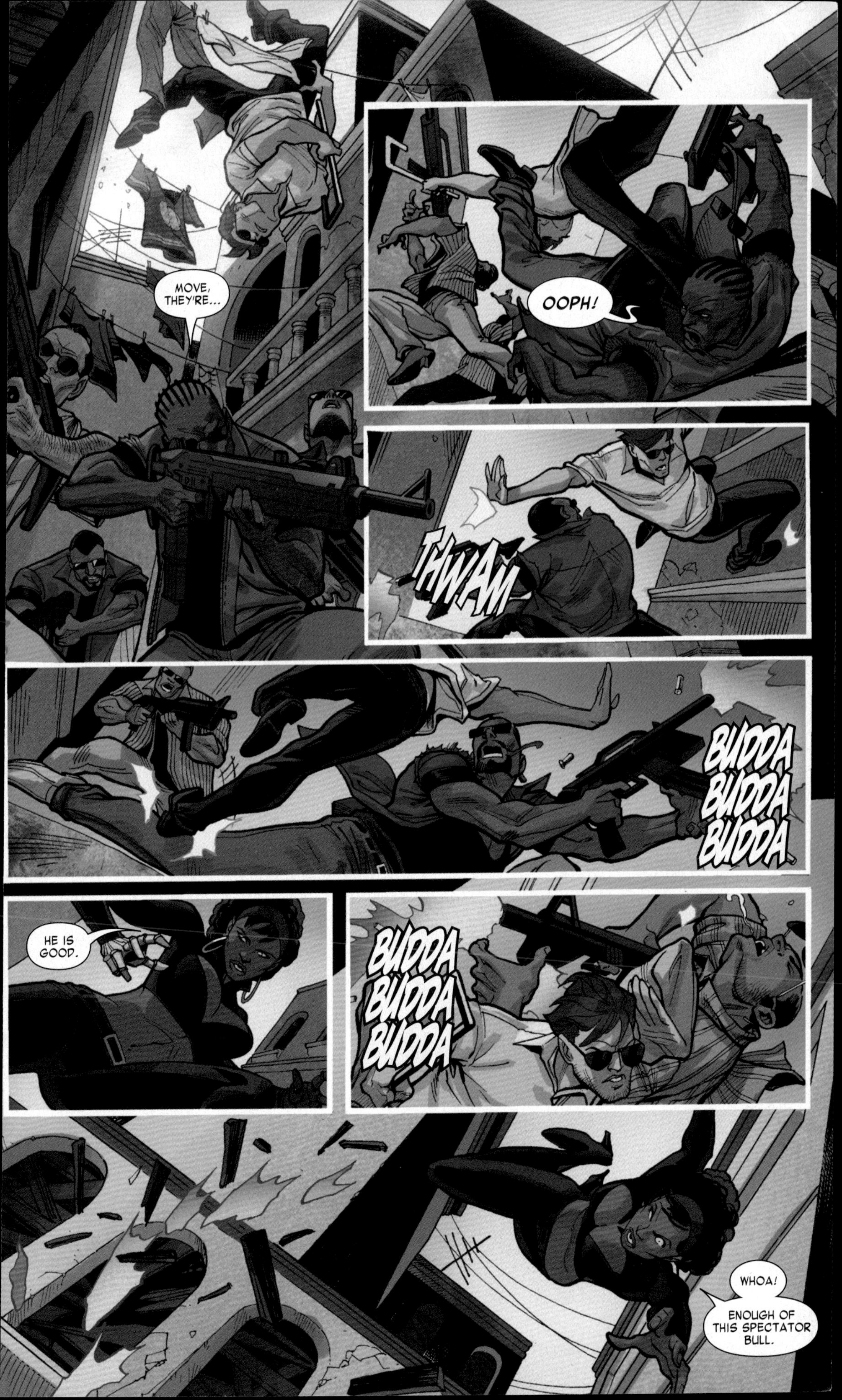
MOVE, THEY'RE...
OOPH!
THWAM
BUDDA BUDDA BUDDA
HE IS GOOD.
BUDDA BUDDA BUDDA
WHOA!
ENOUGH OF THIS SPECTATOR BULL.

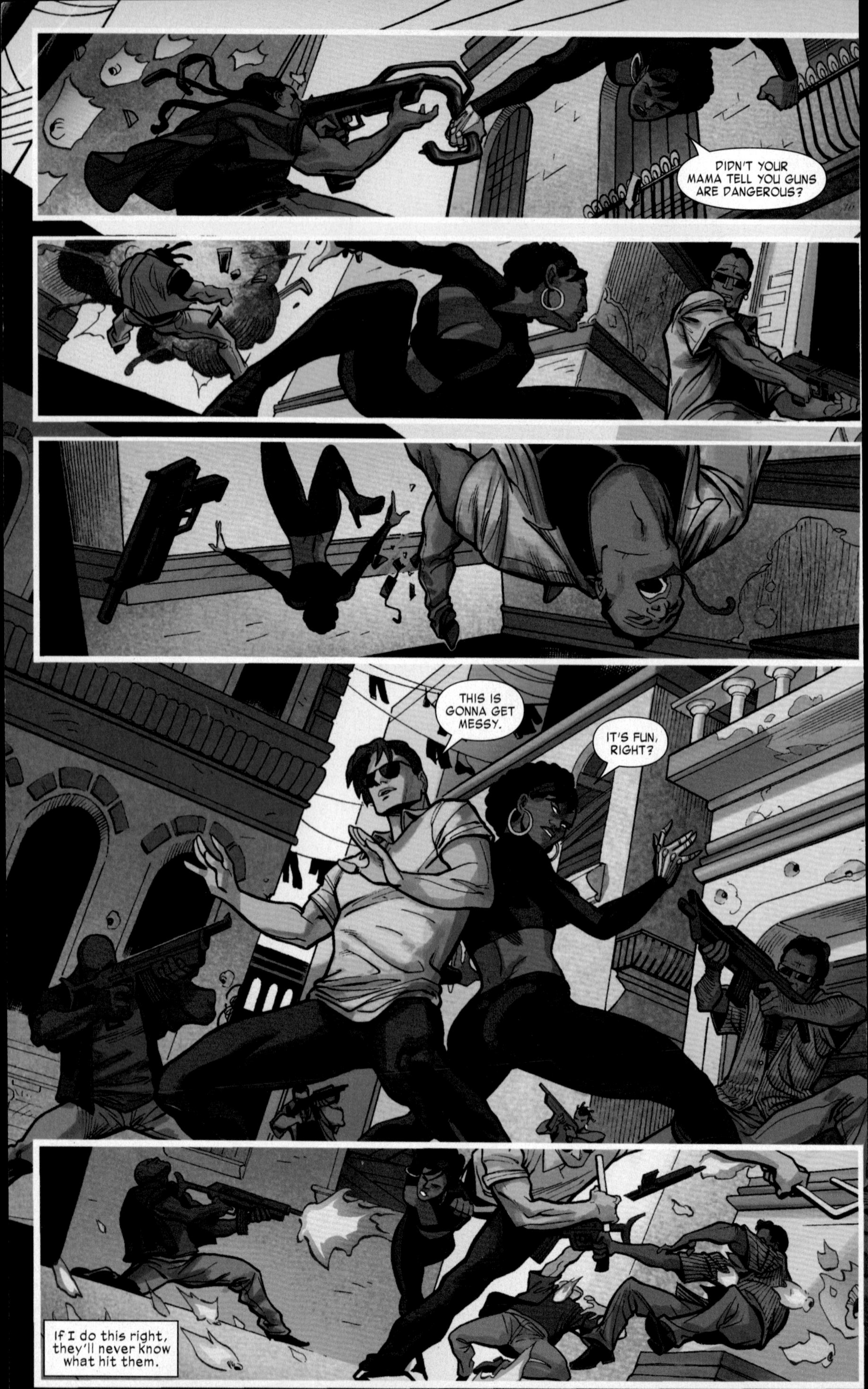

DIDN'T YOUR MAMA TELL YOU GUNS ARE DANGEROUS?
THIS IS GONNA GET MESSY.
IT'S FUN, RIGHT?
If I do this right, they'll never know what hit them.

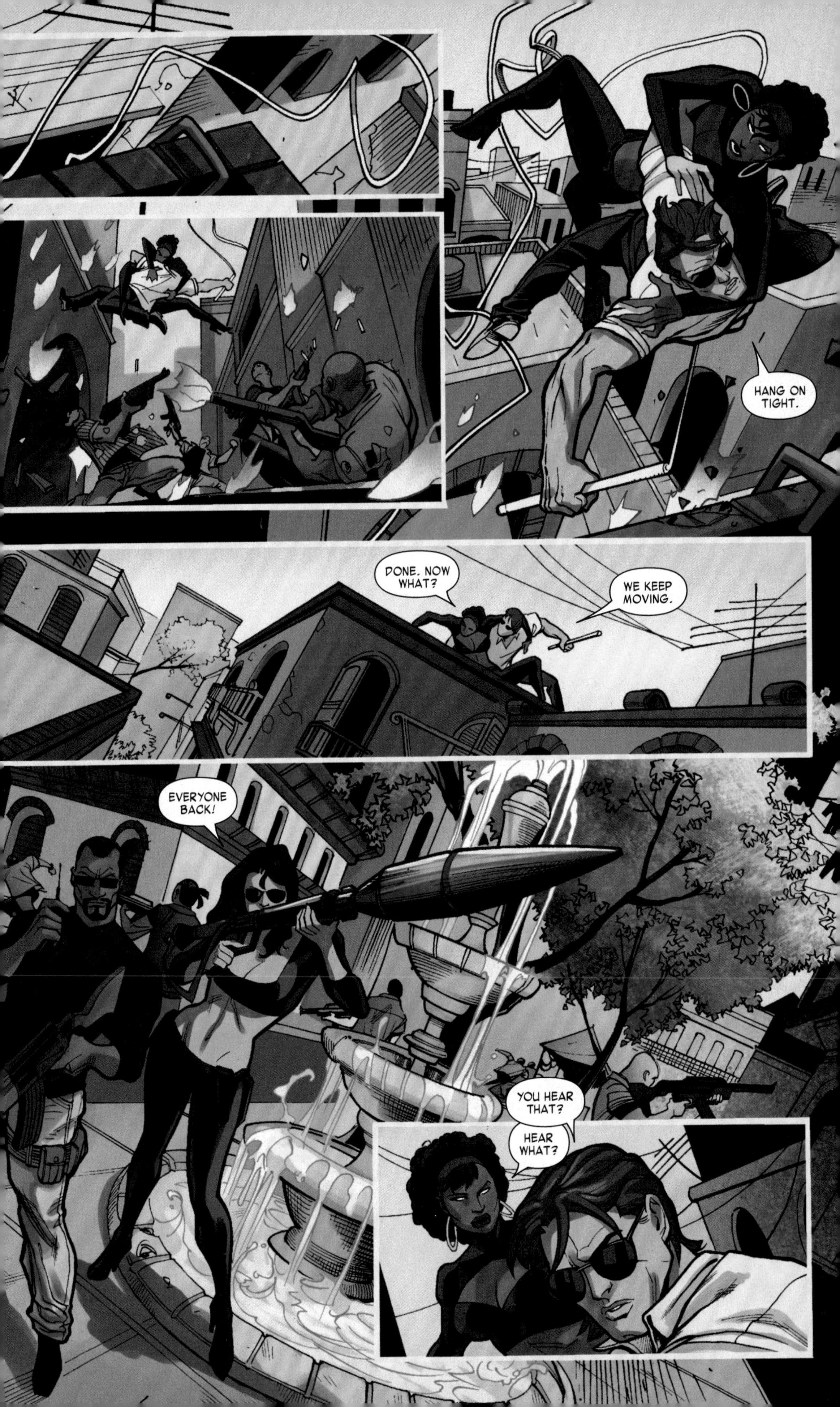
HANG ON TIGHT.
DONE. NOW WHAT?
WE KEEP MOVING.
EVERYONE BACK!
YOU HEAR THAT?
HEAR WHAT?

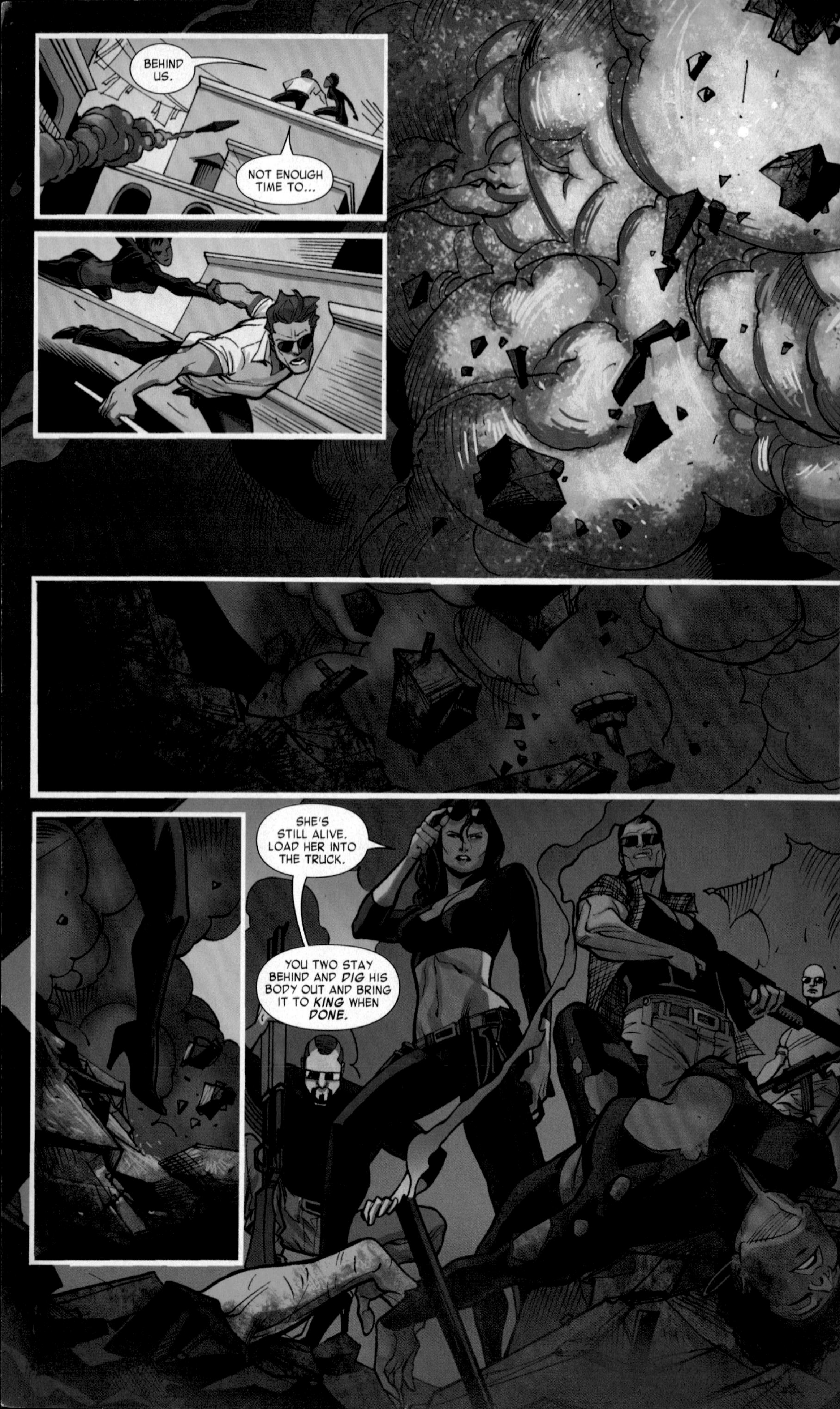
BEHIND US.
NOT ENOUGH TIME TO...
SHE'S STILL ALIVE. LOAD HER INTO THE TRUCK.
YOU TWO STAY BEHIND AND DIG HIS BODY OUT AND BRING IT TO KING WHEN DONE.

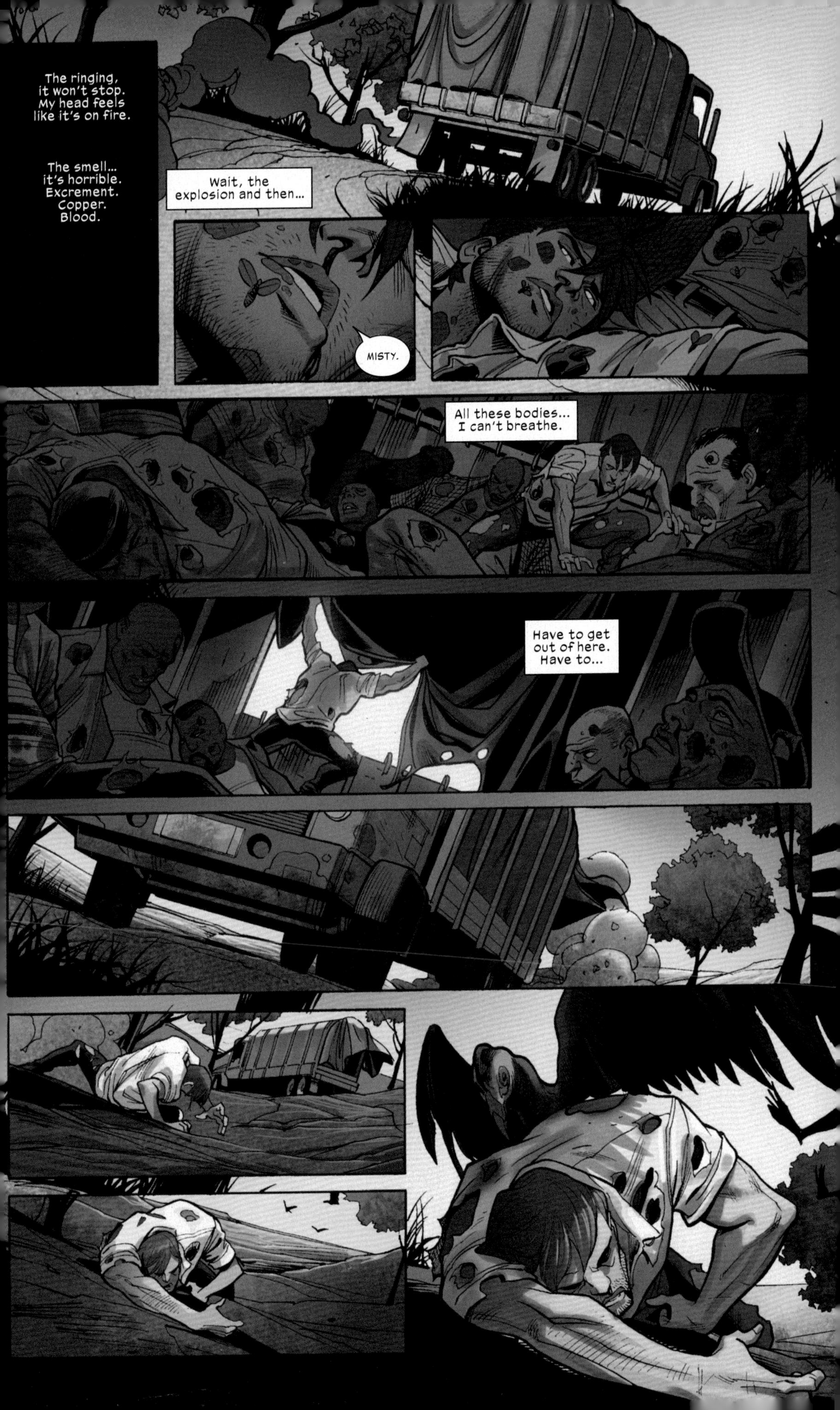

The ringing, it won't stop. My head feels like it's on fire.
The smell... it's horrible. Excrement. Copper. Blood.
Wait, the explosion and then...
MISTY.
All these bodies... I can't breathe.
Have to get out of here. Have to...

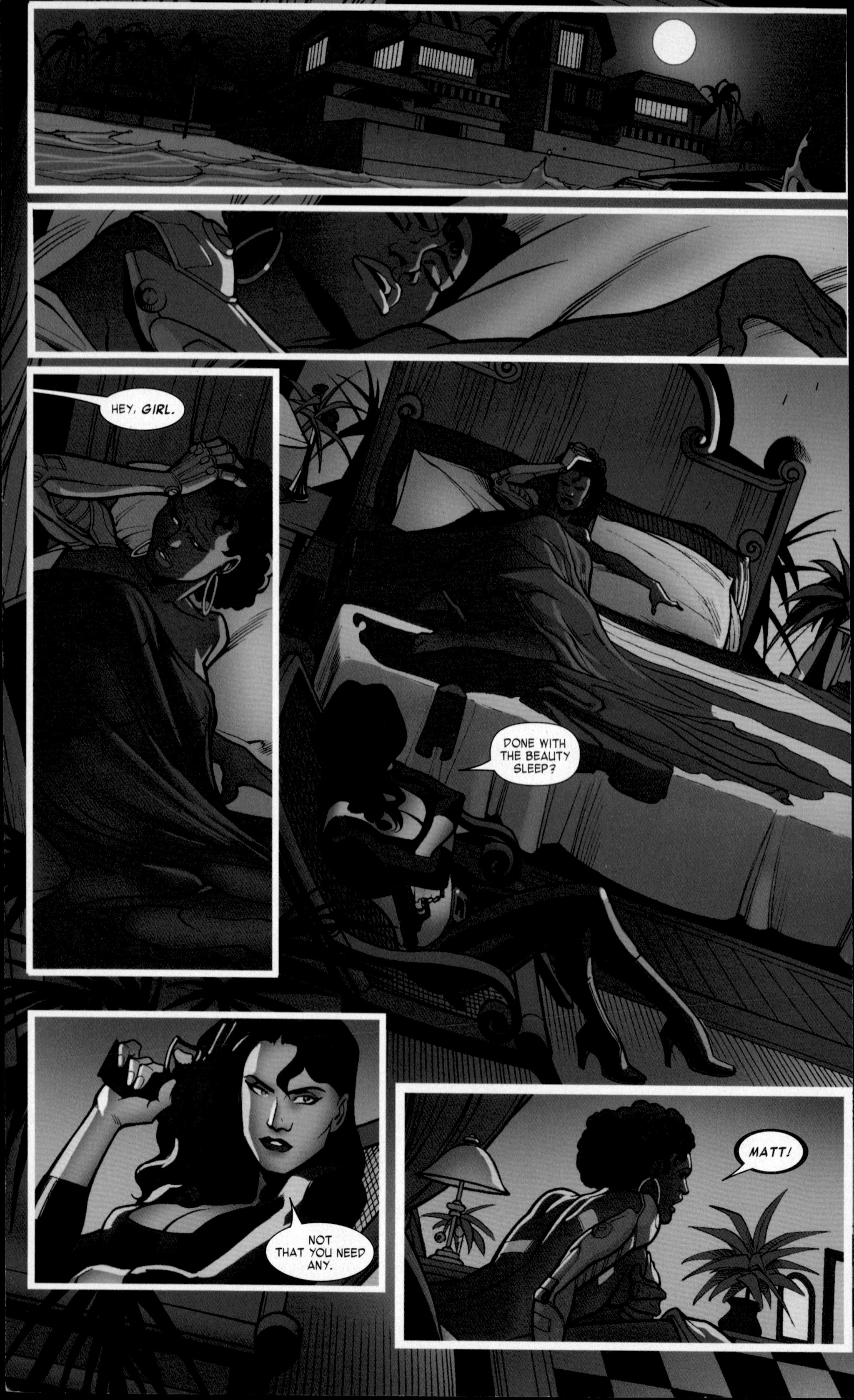
HEY, GIRL.
DONE WITH THE BEAUTY SLEEP?
NOT THAT YOU NEED ANY.
MATT!

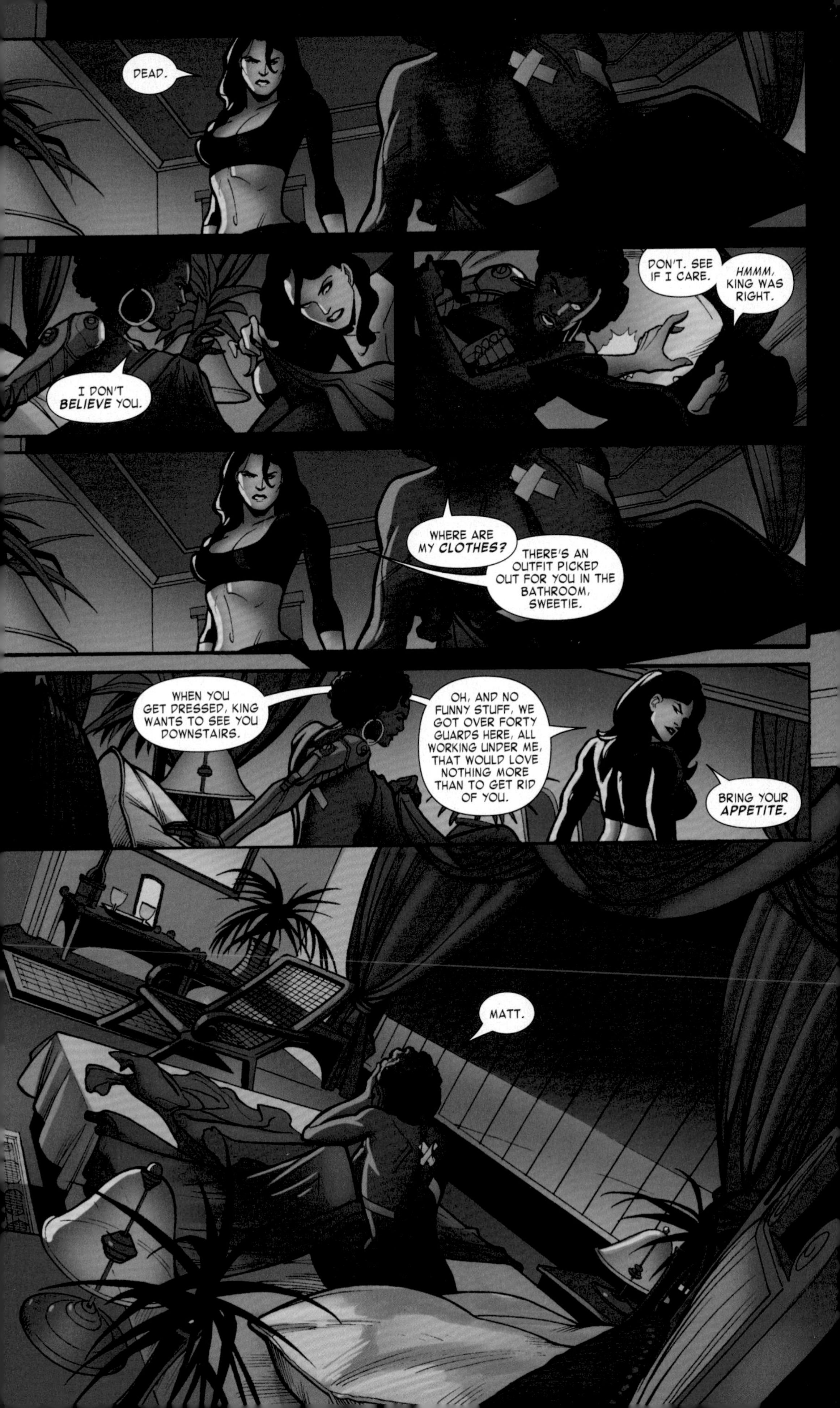
DEAD.
I DON'T BELIEVE YOU.
DON'T. SEE IF I CARE.
HMMM, KING WAS RIGHT.
WHERE ARE MY CLOTHES?
THERE'S AN OUTFIT PICKED OUT FOR YOU IN THE BATHROOM, SWEETIE.
WHEN YOU GET DRESSED, KING WANTS TO SEE YOU DOWNSTAIRS.
OH, AND NO FUNNY STUFF, WE GOT OVER FORTY GUARDS HERE, ALL WORKING UNDER ME, THAT WOULD LOVE NOTHING MORE THAN TO GET RID OF YOU.
BRING YOUR APPETITE.
MATT.

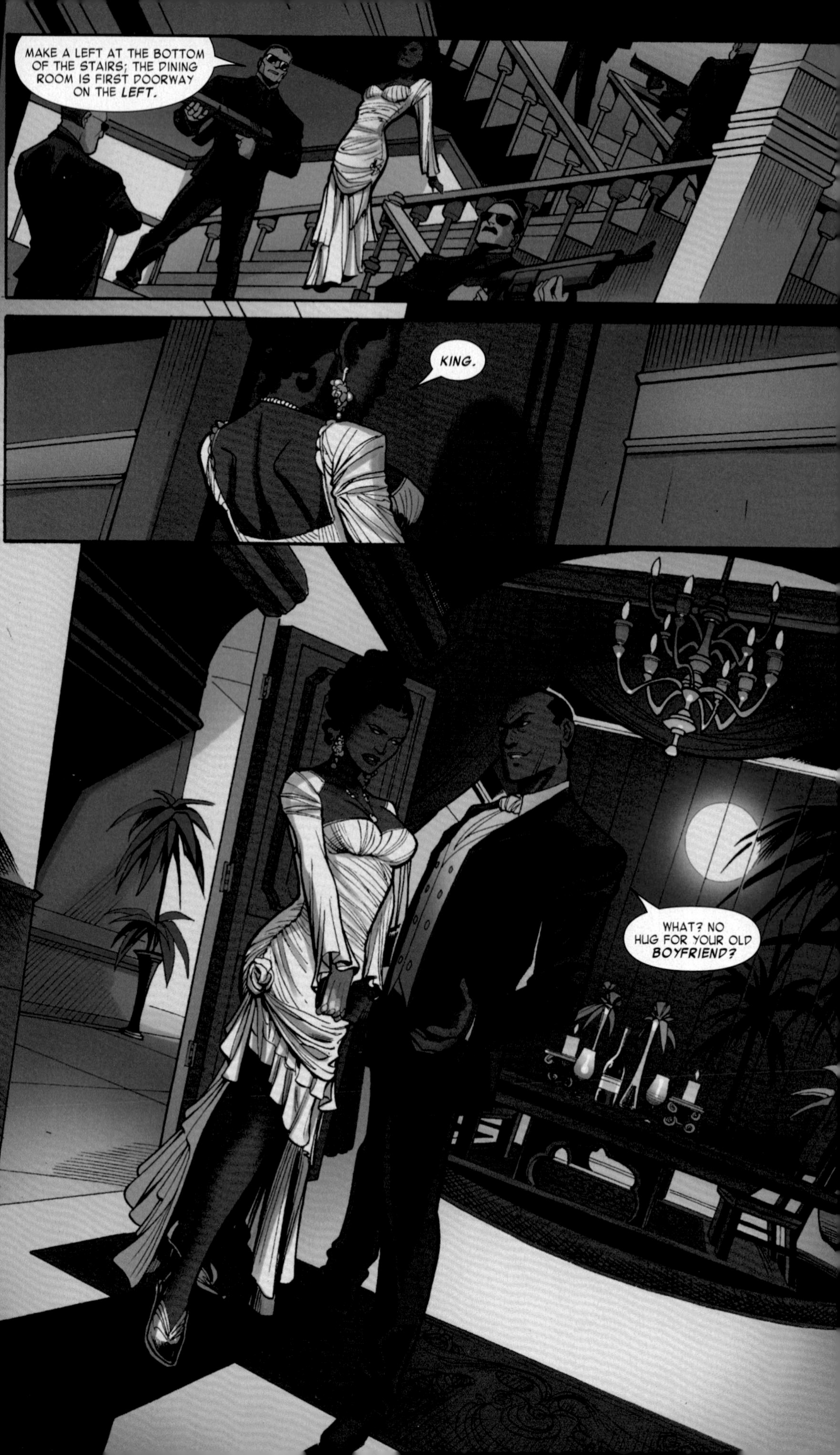
MAKE A LEFT AT THE BOTTOM OF THE STAIRS; THE DINING ROOM IS FIRST DOORWAY ON THE *LEFT.*
KING.
WHAT? NO HUG FOR YOUR OLD *BOYFRIEND?*

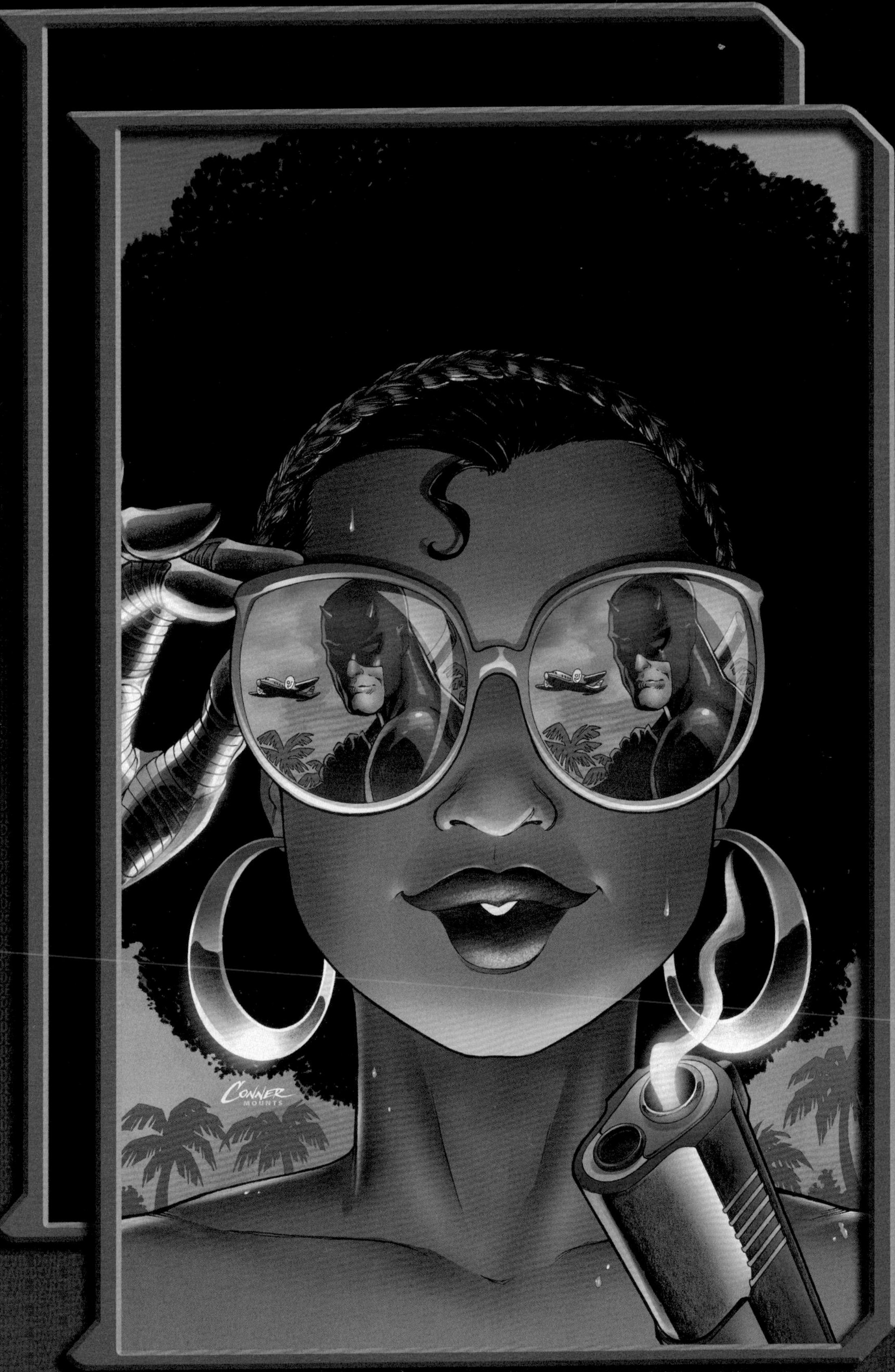
CONNER
MOUNTS

#8 — IN THE NAME OF THE KING
PART THREE: FALL OF THE KING

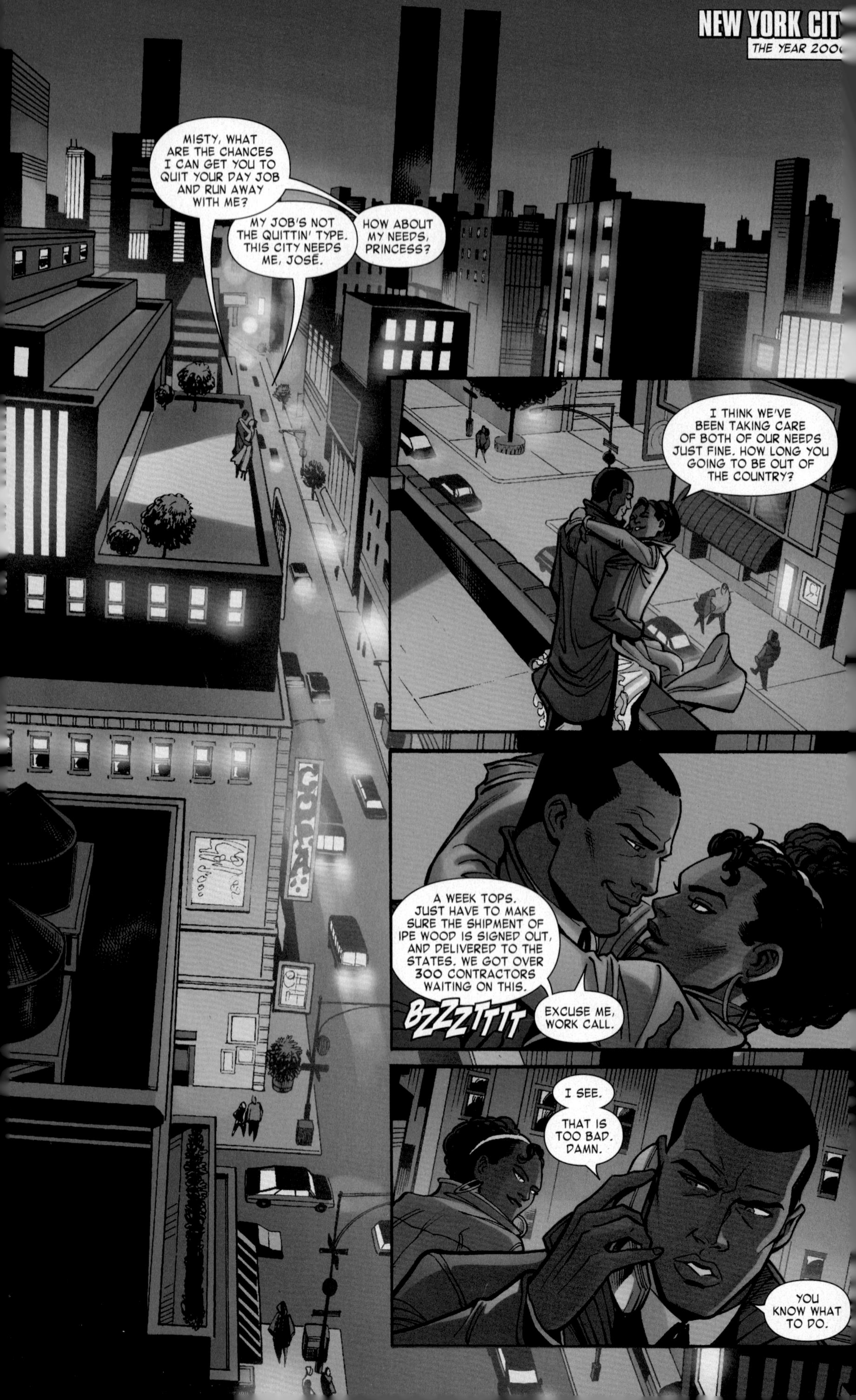
NEW YORK CITY
THE YEAR 2006
MISTY, WHAT ARE THE CHANCES I CAN GET YOU TO QUIT YOUR DAY JOB AND RUN AWAY WITH ME?
MY JOB'S NOT THE QUITTIN' TYPE. THIS CITY NEEDS ME, JOSÉ.
HOW ABOUT MY NEEDS, PRINCESS?
I THINK WE'VE BEEN TAKING CARE OF BOTH OF OUR NEEDS JUST FINE. HOW LONG YOU GOING TO BE OUT OF THE COUNTRY?
A WEEK TOPS. JUST HAVE TO MAKE SURE THE SHIPMENT OF IPE WOOD IS SIGNED OUT, AND DELIVERED TO THE STATES. WE GOT OVER 300 CONTRACTORS WAITING ON THIS.
BZZZTTTT
EXCUSE ME, WORK CALL.
I SEE.
THAT IS TOO BAD. DAMN.
YOU KNOW WHAT TO DO.

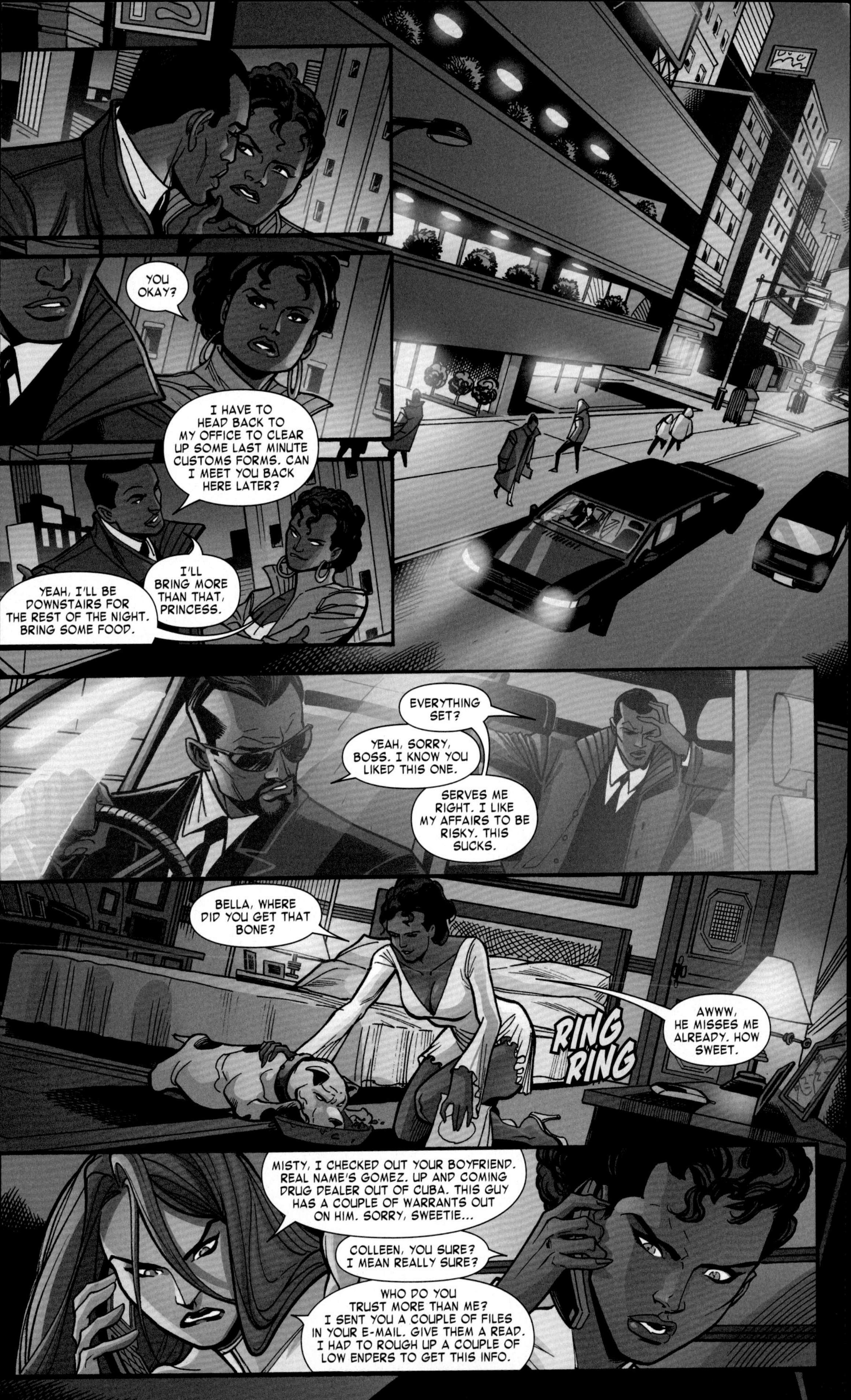

YOU OKAY?
I HAVE TO HEAD BACK TO MY OFFICE TO CLEAR UP SOME LAST MINUTE CUSTOMS FORMS. CAN I MEET YOU BACK HERE LATER?
YEAH, I'LL BE DOWNSTAIRS FOR THE REST OF THE NIGHT. BRING SOME FOOD.
I'LL BRING MORE THAN THAT, PRINCESS.
EVERYTHING SET?
YEAH, SORRY, BOSS. I KNOW YOU LIKED THIS ONE.
SERVES ME RIGHT. I LIKE MY AFFAIRS TO BE RISKY. THIS SUCKS.
BELLA, WHERE DID YOU GET THAT BONE?
RING RING
AWWW, HE MISSES ME ALREADY. HOW SWEET.
MISTY, I CHECKED OUT YOUR BOYFRIEND. REAL NAME'S GOMEZ. UP AND COMING DRUG DEALER OUT OF CUBA. THIS GUY HAS A COUPLE OF WARRANTS OUT ON HIM. SORRY, SWEETIE...
COLLEEN, YOU SURE? I MEAN REALLY SURE?
WHO DO YOU TRUST MORE THAN ME? I SENT YOU A COUPLE OF FILES IN YOUR E-MAIL. GIVE THEM A READ. I HAD TO ROUGH UP A COUPLE OF LOW ENDERS TO GET THIS INFO.

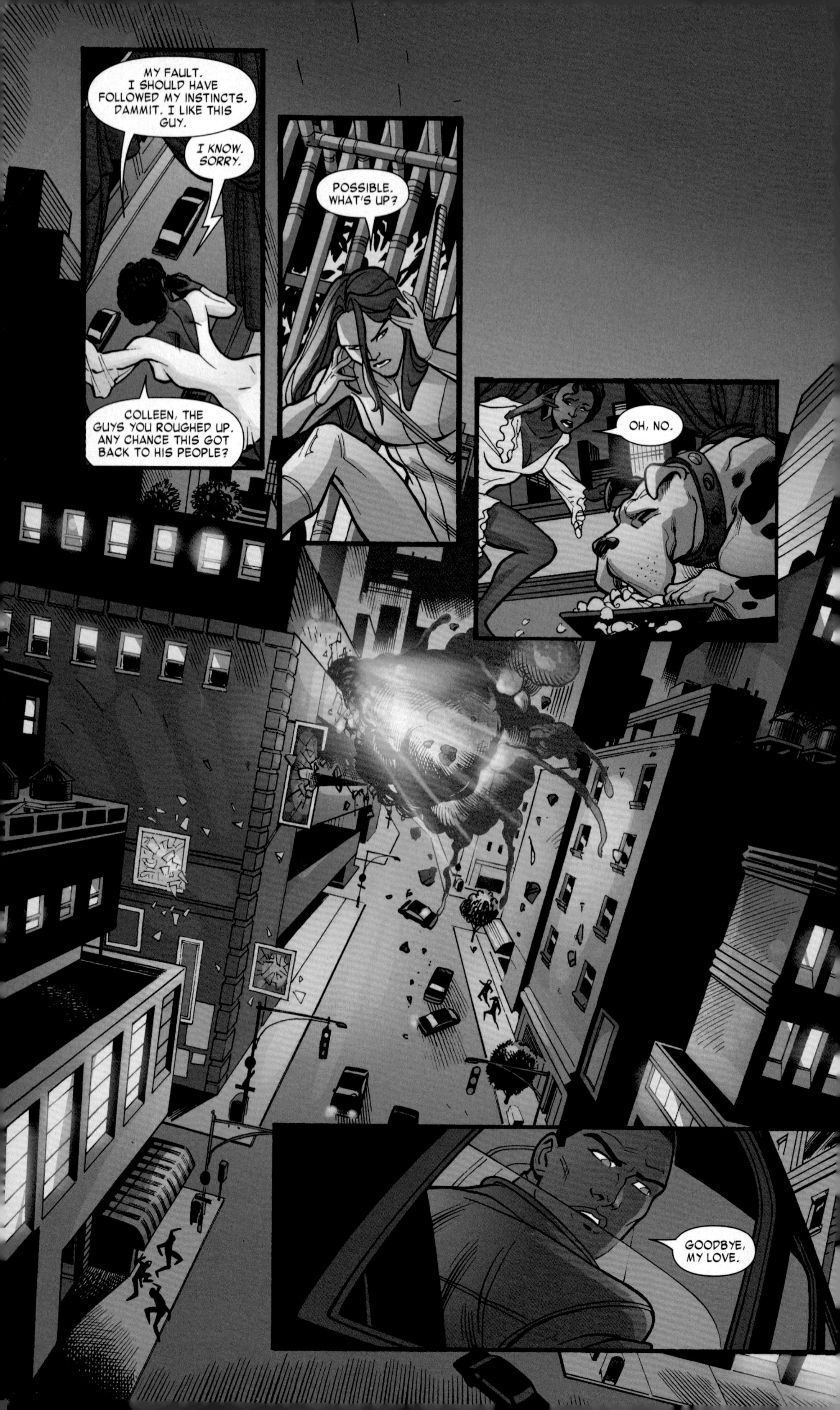
MY FAULT. I SHOULD HAVE FOLLOWED MY INSTINCTS. DAMMIT. I LIKE THIS GUY.
I KNOW. SORRY.
COLLEEN, THE GUYS YOU ROUGHED UP. ANY CHANCE THIS GOT BACK TO HIS PEOPLE?
POSSIBLE. WHAT'S UP?
OH, NO.
GOODBYE, MY LOVE.

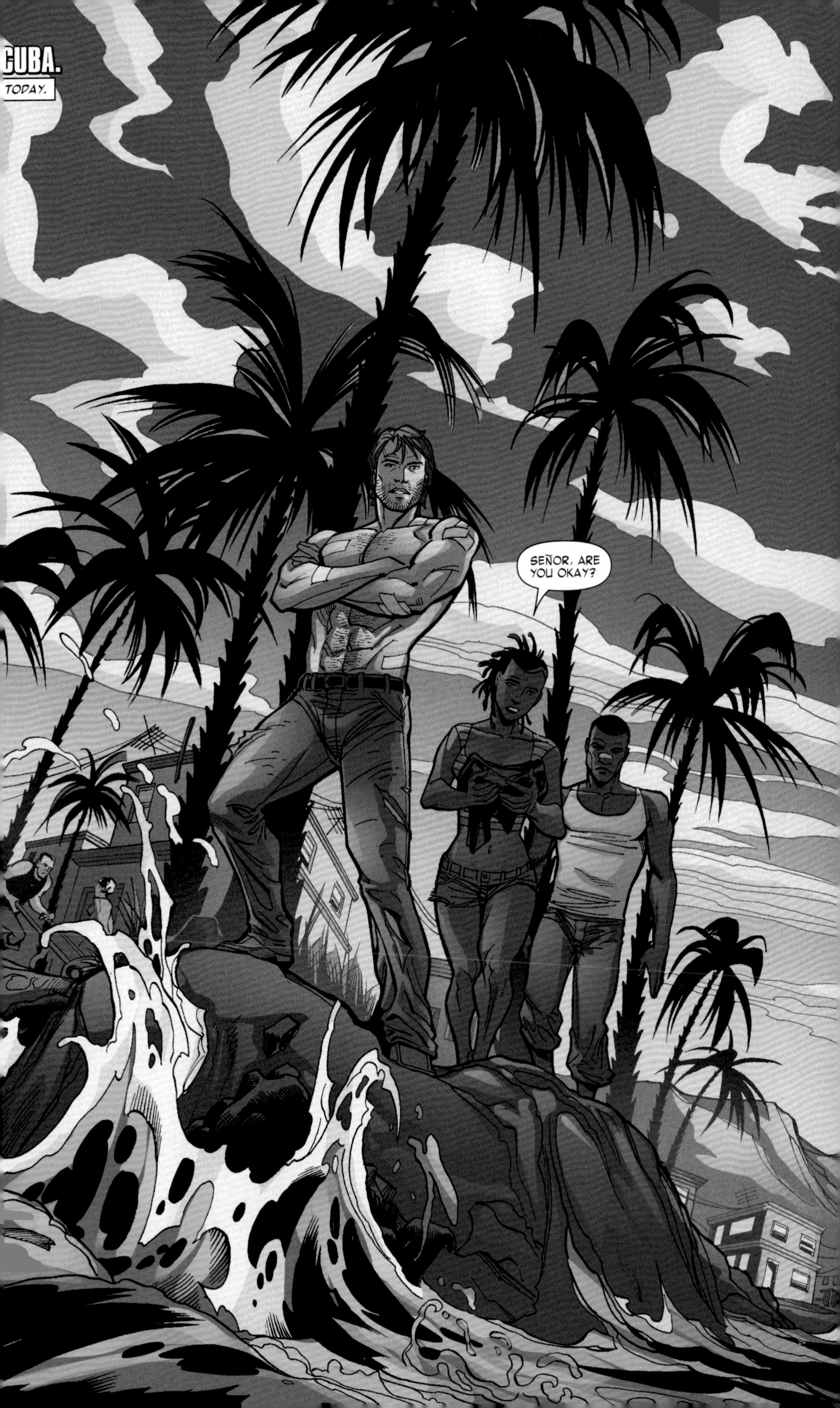
CUBA.
TODAY.
SEÑOR, ARE YOU OKAY?

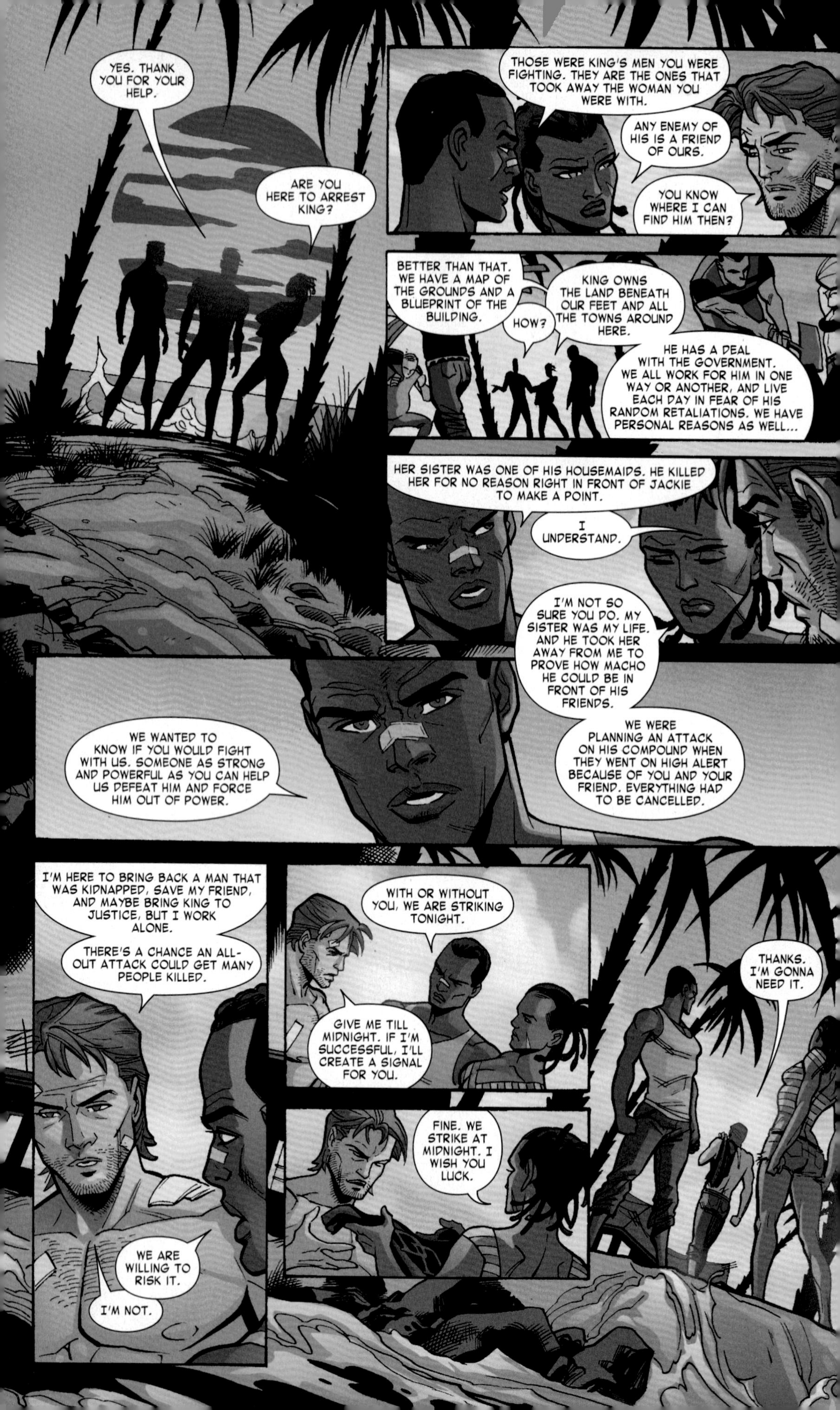
YES. THANK YOU FOR YOUR HELP.
ARE YOU HERE TO ARREST KING?
THOSE WERE KING'S MEN YOU WERE FIGHTING. THEY ARE THE ONES THAT TOOK AWAY THE WOMAN YOU WERE WITH.
ANY ENEMY OF HIS IS A FRIEND OF OURS.
YOU KNOW WHERE I CAN FIND HIM THEN?
BETTER THAN THAT. WE HAVE A MAP OF THE GROUNDS AND A BLUEPRINT OF THE BUILDING.
HOW?
KING OWNS THE LAND BENEATH OUR FEET AND ALL THE TOWNS AROUND HERE.
HE HAS A DEAL WITH THE GOVERNMENT. WE ALL WORK FOR HIM IN ONE WAY OR ANOTHER, AND LIVE EACH DAY IN FEAR OF HIS RANDOM RETALIATIONS. WE HAVE PERSONAL REASONS AS WELL...
HER SISTER WAS ONE OF HIS HOUSEMAIDS. HE KILLED HER FOR NO REASON RIGHT IN FRONT OF JACKIE TO MAKE A POINT.
I UNDERSTAND.
I'M NOT SO SURE YOU DO. MY SISTER WAS MY LIFE. AND HE TOOK HER AWAY FROM ME TO PROVE HOW MACHO HE COULD BE IN FRONT OF HIS FRIENDS.
WE WERE PLANNING AN ATTACK ON HIS COMPOUND WHEN THEY WENT ON HIGH ALERT BECAUSE OF YOU AND YOUR FRIEND. EVERYTHING HAD TO BE CANCELLED.
WE WANTED TO KNOW IF YOU WOULD FIGHT WITH US. SOMEONE AS STRONG AND POWERFUL AS YOU CAN HELP US DEFEAT HIM AND FORCE HIM OUT OF POWER.
I'M HERE TO BRING BACK A MAN THAT WAS KIDNAPPED, SAVE MY FRIEND, AND MAYBE BRING KING TO JUSTICE, BUT I WORK ALONE.
THERE'S A CHANCE AN ALL-OUT ATTACK COULD GET MANY PEOPLE KILLED.
WE ARE WILLING TO RISK IT.
I'M NOT.
WITH OR WITHOUT YOU, WE ARE STRIKING TONIGHT.
GIVE ME TILL MIDNIGHT. IF I'M SUCCESSFUL, I'LL CREATE A SIGNAL FOR YOU.
FINE. WE STRIKE AT MIDNIGHT. I WISH YOU LUCK.
THANKS. I'M GONNA NEED IT.

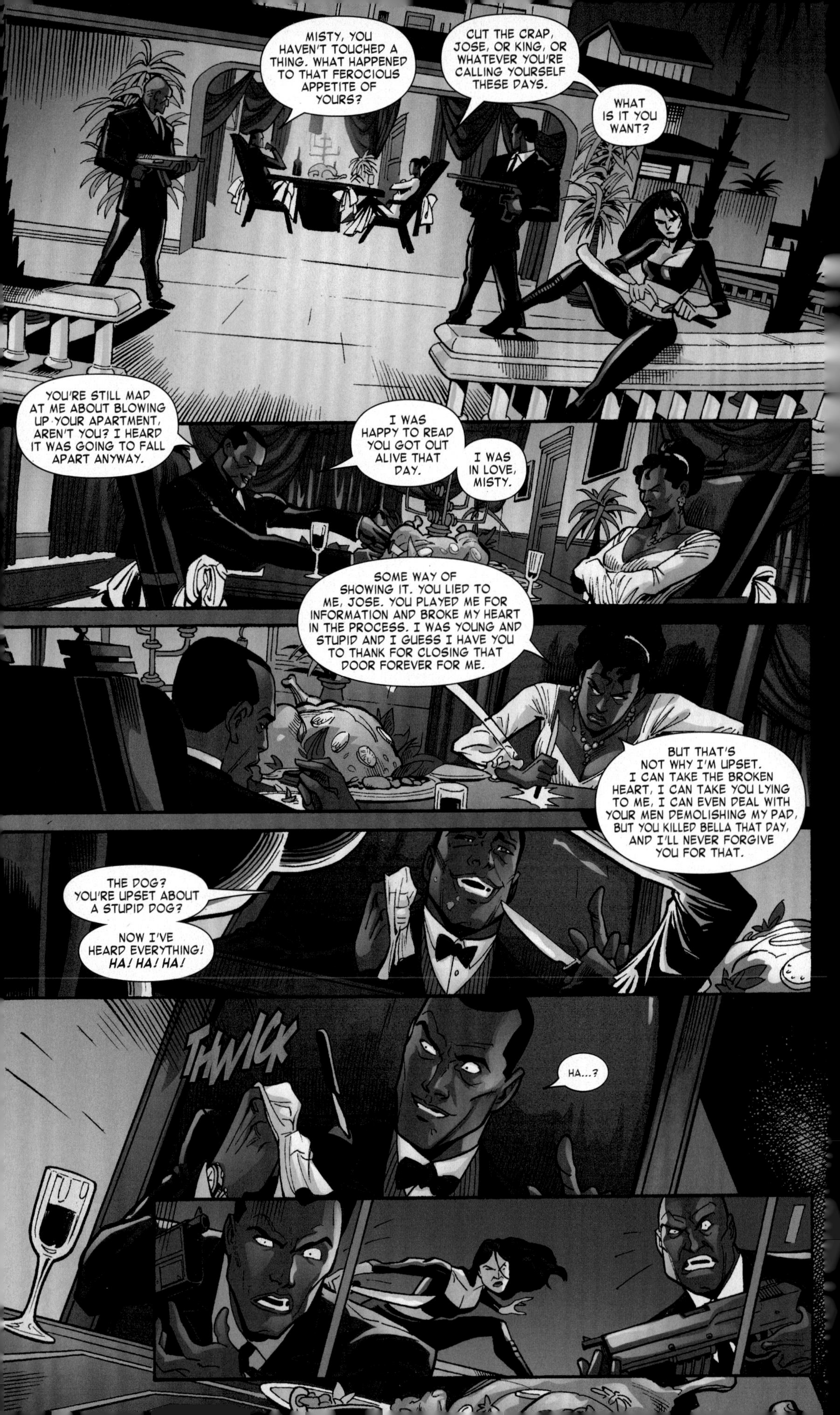
MISTY, YOU HAVEN'T TOUCHED A THING. WHAT HAPPENED TO THAT FEROCIOUS APPETITE OF YOURS?
CUT THE CRAP, JOSE, OR KING, OR WHATEVER YOU'RE CALLING YOURSELF THESE DAYS.
WHAT IS IT YOU WANT?
YOU'RE STILL MAD AT ME ABOUT BLOWING UP YOUR APARTMENT, AREN'T YOU? I HEARD IT WAS GOING TO FALL APART ANYWAY.
I WAS HAPPY TO READ YOU GOT OUT ALIVE THAT DAY.
I WAS IN LOVE, MISTY.
SOME WAY OF SHOWING IT. YOU LIED TO ME, JOSE. YOU PLAYED ME FOR INFORMATION AND BROKE MY HEART IN THE PROCESS. I WAS YOUNG AND STUPID AND I GUESS I HAVE YOU TO THANK FOR CLOSING THAT DOOR FOREVER FOR ME.
BUT THAT'S NOT WHY I'M UPSET. I CAN TAKE THE BROKEN HEART, I CAN TAKE YOU LYING TO ME, I CAN EVEN DEAL WITH YOUR MEN DEMOLISHING MY PAD, BUT YOU KILLED BELLA THAT DAY, AND I'LL NEVER FORGIVE YOU FOR THAT.
THE DOG? YOU'RE UPSET ABOUT A STUPID DOG?
NOW I'VE HEARD EVERYTHING! HA! HA! HA!
THWICK
HA...?

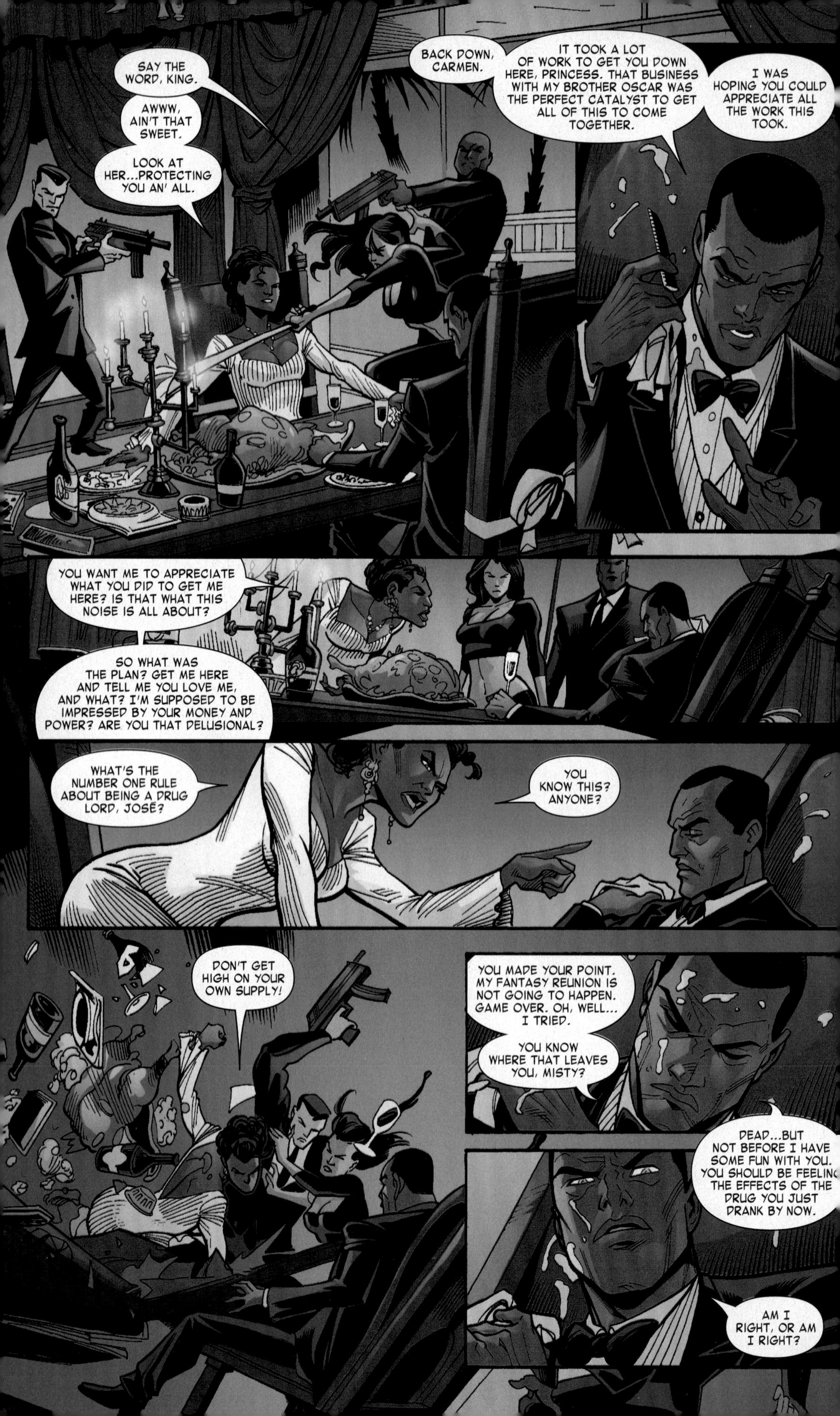
SAY THE WORD, KING.
AWWW, AIN'T THAT SWEET.
LOOK AT HER...PROTECTING YOU AN' ALL.
BACK DOWN, CARMEN.
IT TOOK A LOT OF WORK TO GET YOU DOWN HERE, PRINCESS. THAT BUSINESS WITH MY BROTHER OSCAR WAS THE PERFECT CATALYST TO GET ALL OF THIS TO COME TOGETHER.
I WAS HOPING YOU COULD APPRECIATE ALL THE WORK THIS TOOK.
YOU WANT ME TO APPRECIATE WHAT YOU DID TO GET ME HERE? IS THAT WHAT THIS NOISE IS ALL ABOUT?
SO WHAT WAS THE PLAN? GET ME HERE AND TELL ME YOU LOVE ME, AND WHAT? I'M SUPPOSED TO BE IMPRESSED BY YOUR MONEY AND POWER? ARE YOU THAT DELUSIONAL?
WHAT'S THE NUMBER ONE RULE ABOUT BEING A DRUG LORD, JOSÉ?
YOU KNOW THIS? ANYONE?
DON'T GET HIGH ON YOUR OWN SUPPLY!
YOU MADE YOUR POINT. MY FANTASY REUNION IS NOT GOING TO HAPPEN. GAME OVER. OH, WELL... I TRIED.
YOU KNOW WHERE THAT LEAVES YOU, MISTY?
DEAD...BUT NOT BEFORE I HAVE SOME FUN WITH YOU. YOU SHOULD BE FEELING THE EFFECTS OF THE DRUG YOU JUST DRANK BY NOW.
AM I RIGHT, OR AM I RIGHT?

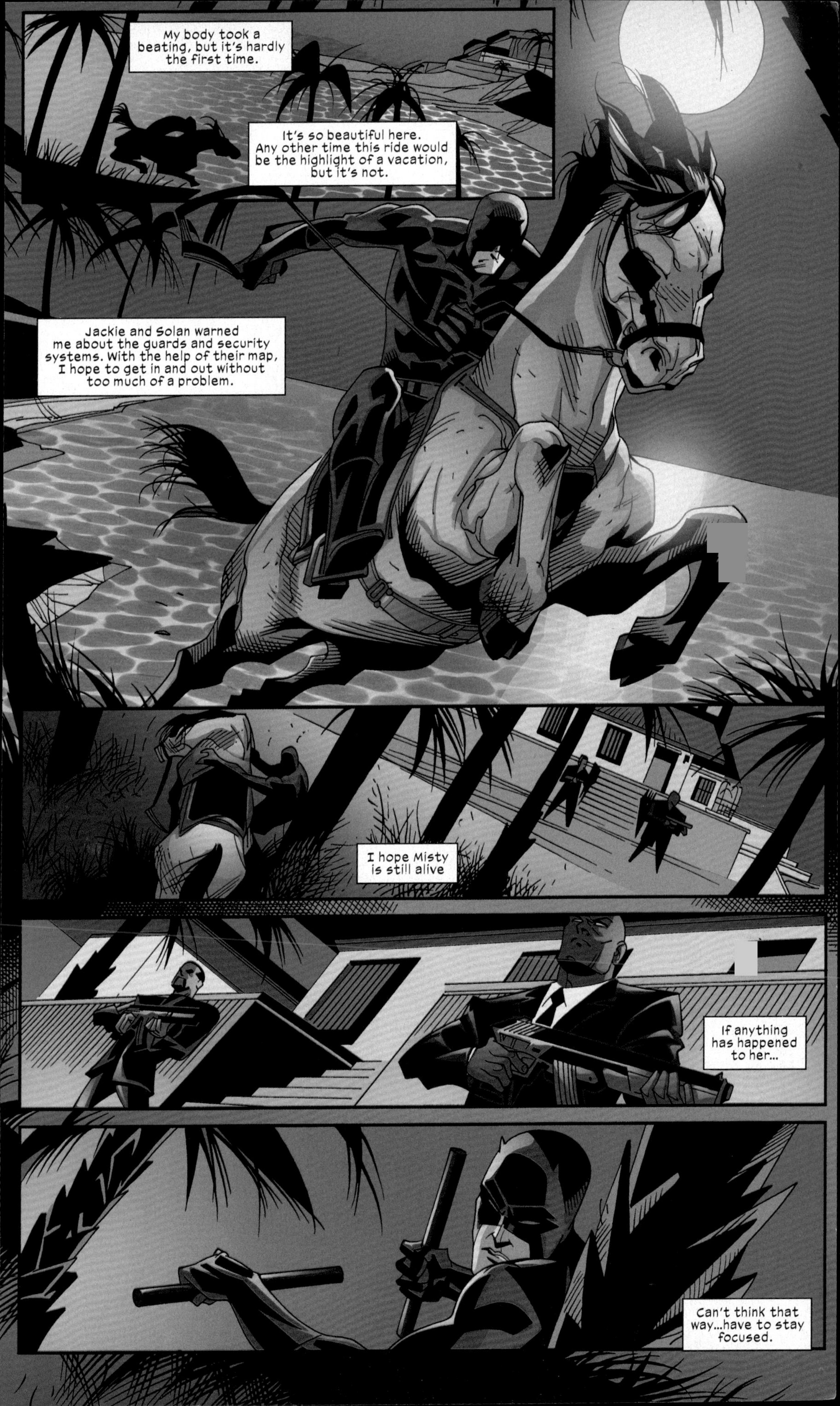

My body took a beating, but it's hardly the first time.
It's so beautiful here. Any other time this ride would be the highlight of a vacation, but it's not.
Jackie and Solan warned me about the guards and security systems. With the help of their map, I hope to get in and out without too much of a problem.
I hope Misty is still alive
If anything has happened to her...
Can't think that way...have to stay focused.

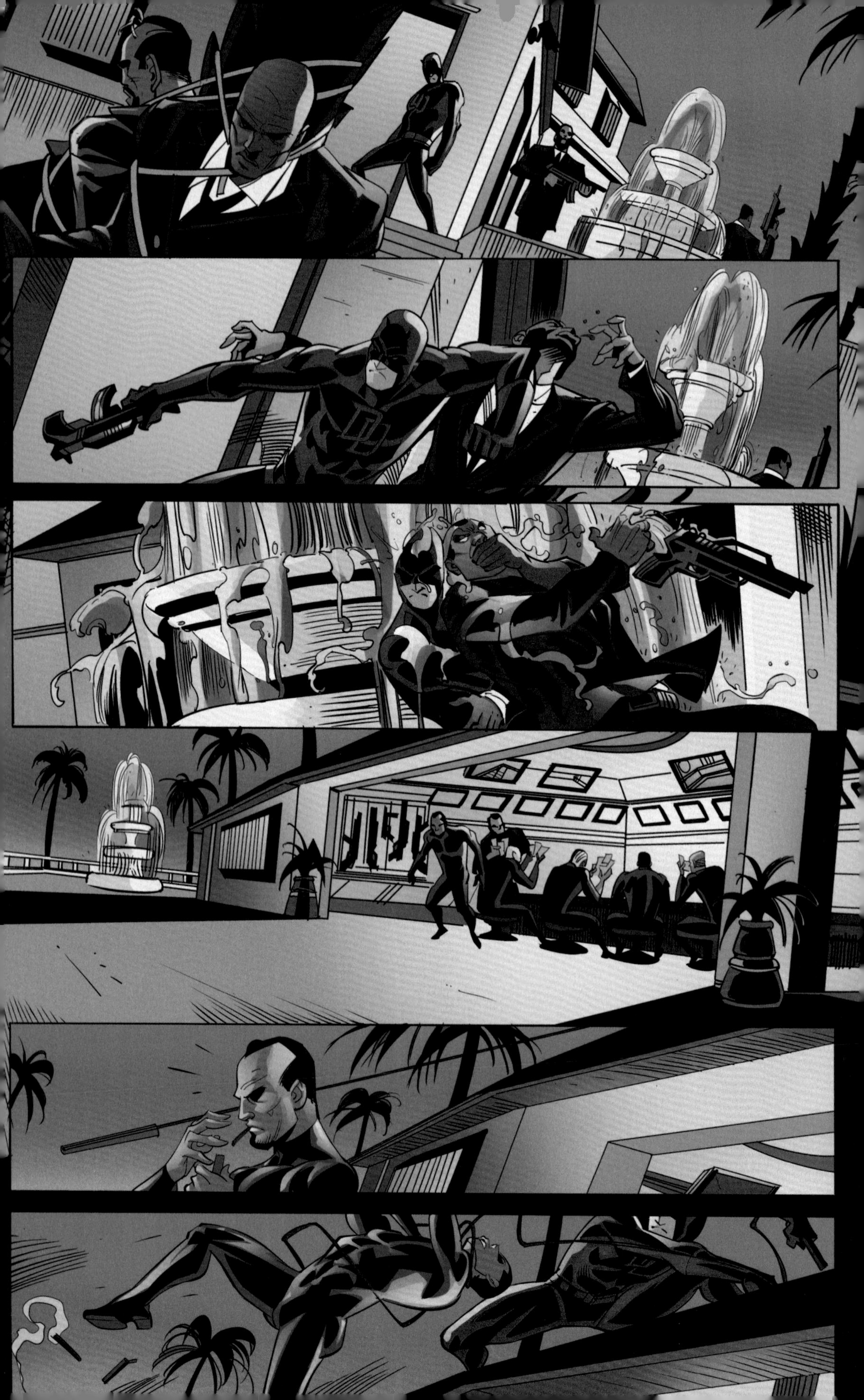

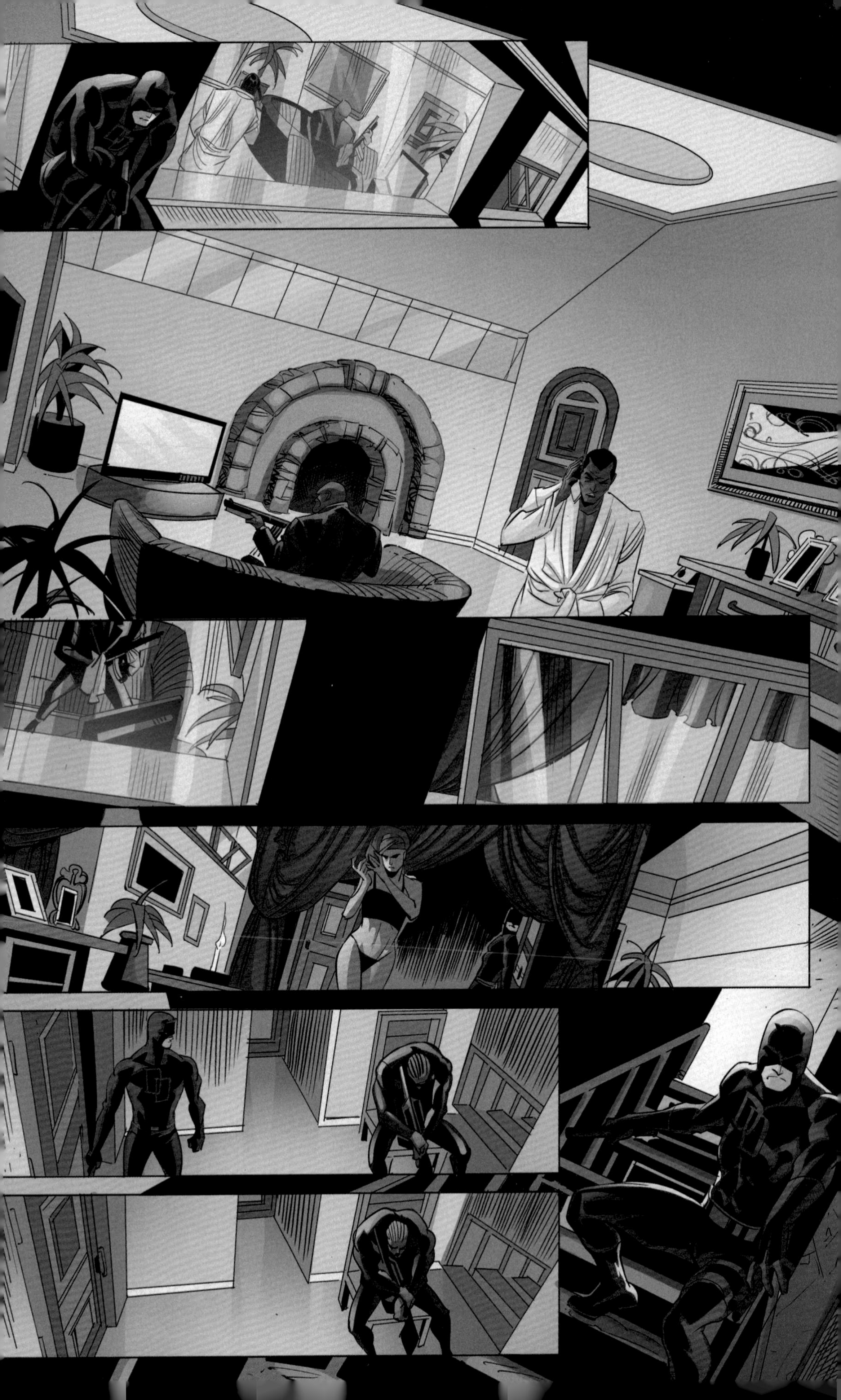

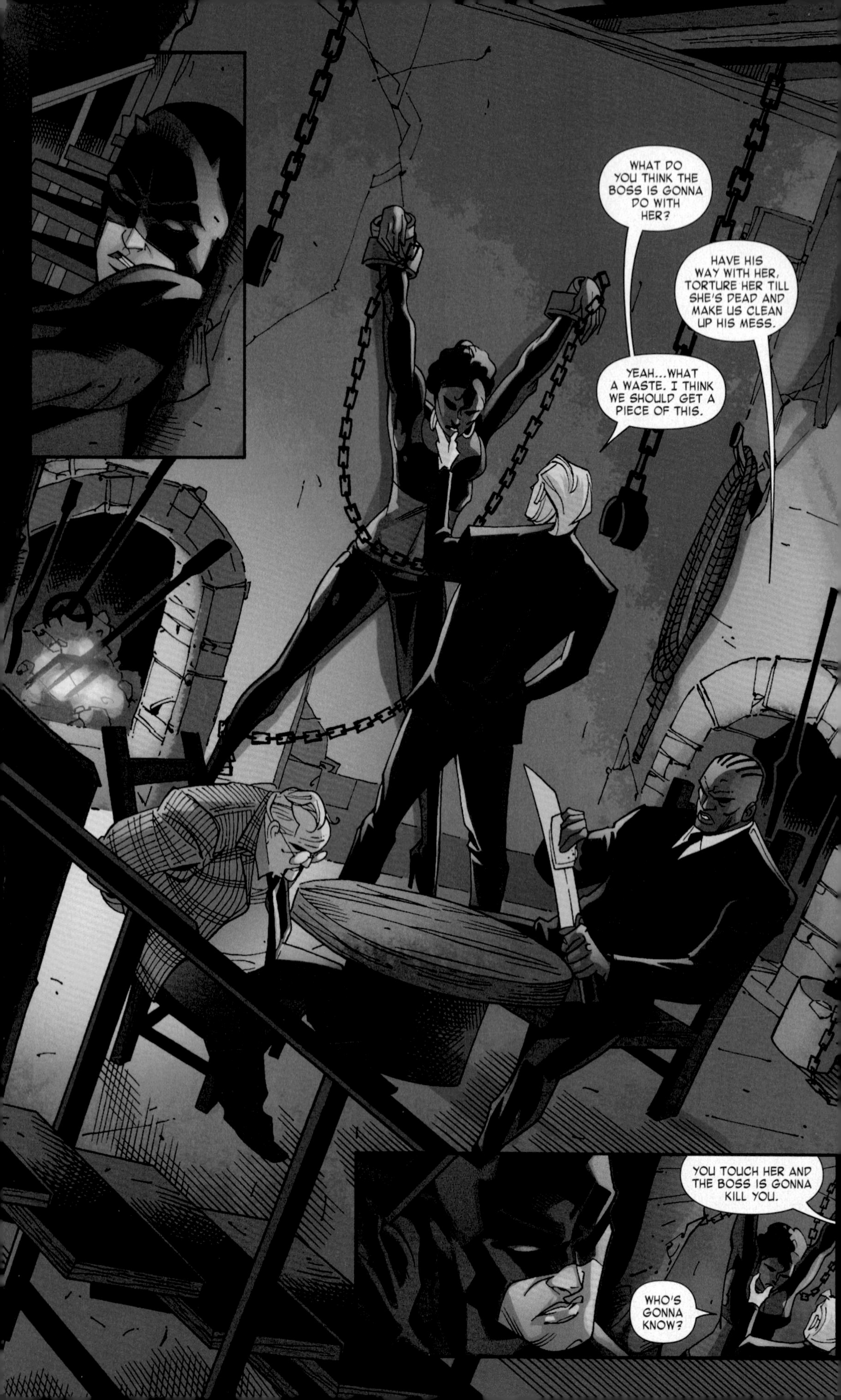
WHAT DO YOU THINK THE BOSS IS GONNA DO WITH HER?
HAVE HIS WAY WITH HER, TORTURE HER TILL SHE'S DEAD AND MAKE US CLEAN UP HIS MESS.
YEAH...WHAT A WASTE. I THINK WE SHOULD GET A PIECE OF THIS.
YOU TOUCH HER AND THE BOSS IS GONNA KILL YOU.
WHO'S GONNA KNOW?

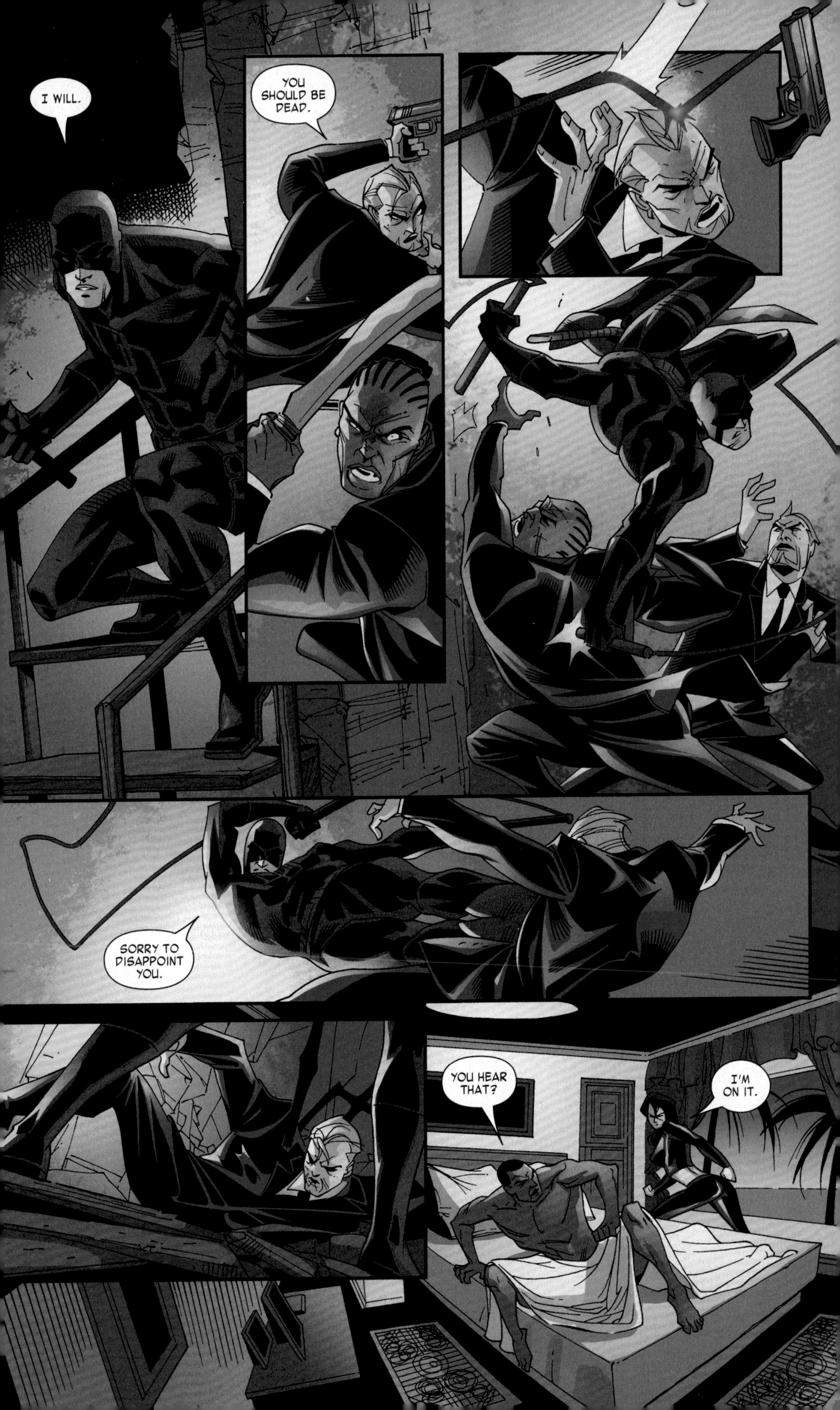
I WILL.
YOU SHOULD BE DEAD.
SORRY TO DISAPPOINT YOU.
YOU HEAR THAT?
I'M ON IT.

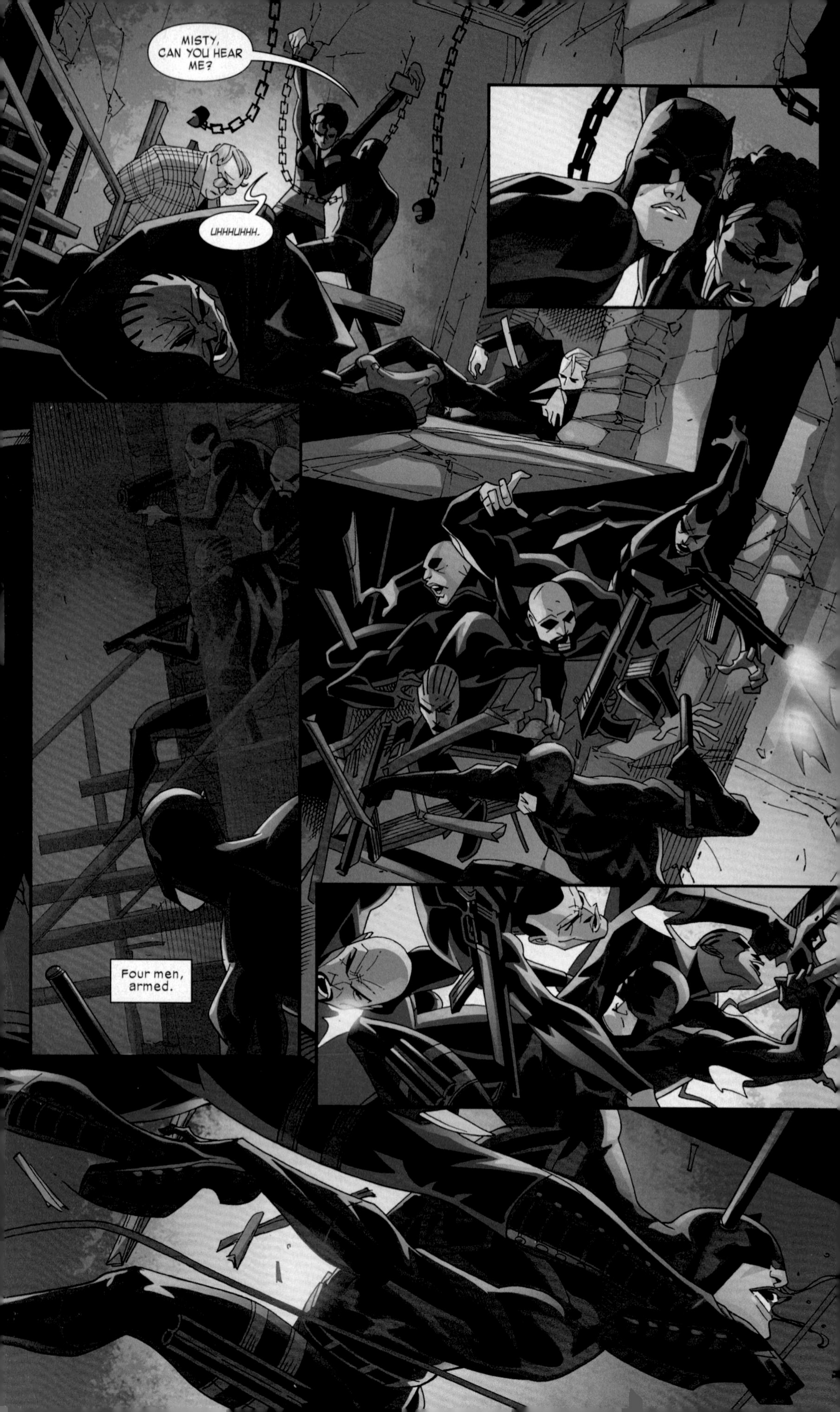
MISTY, CAN YOU HEAR ME?
UHHHUHHH.
Four men, armed.

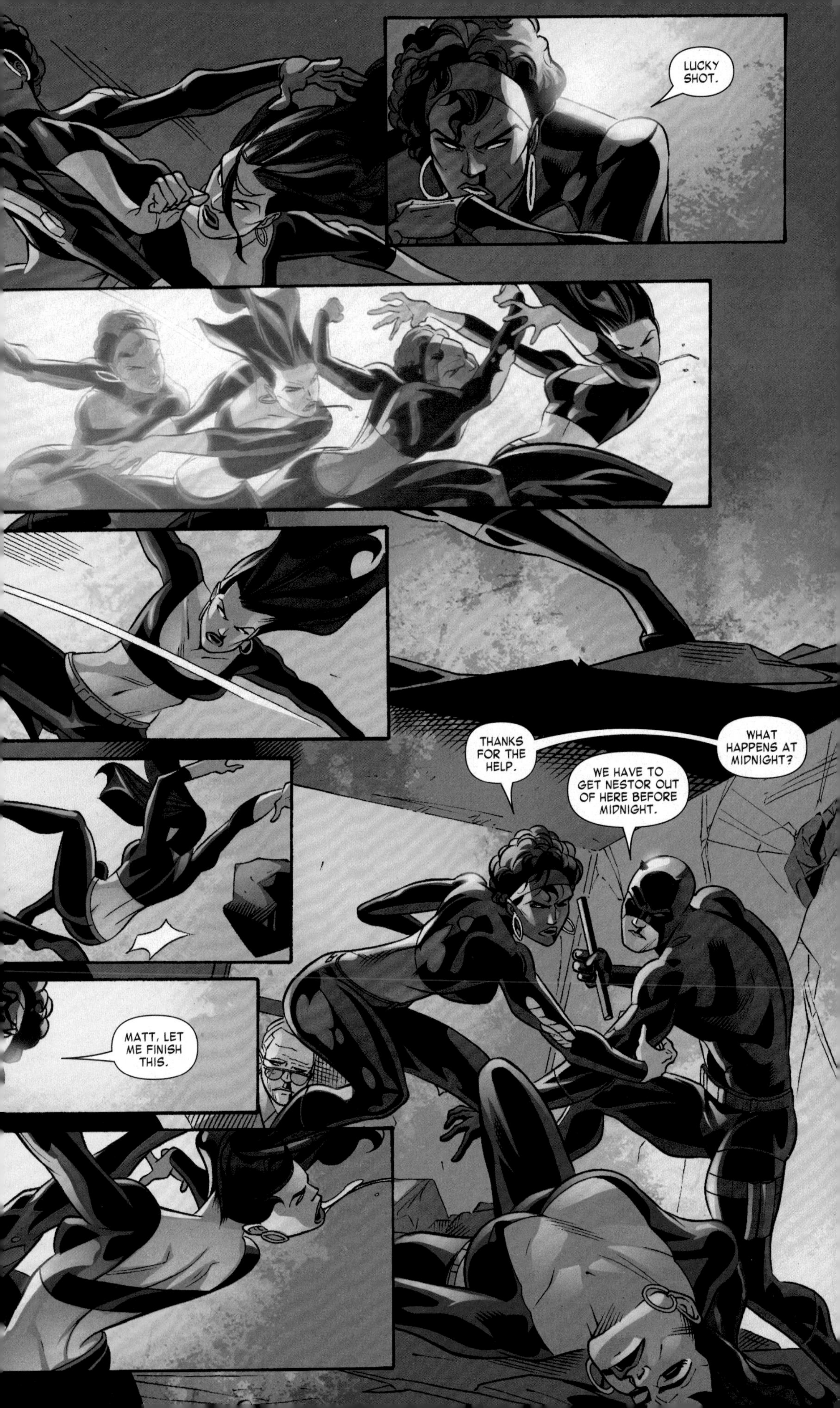
LUCKY SHOT.
MATT, LET ME FINISH THIS.
THANKS FOR THE HELP.
WE HAVE TO GET NESTOR OUT OF HERE BEFORE MIDNIGHT.
WHAT HAPPENS AT MIDNIGHT?

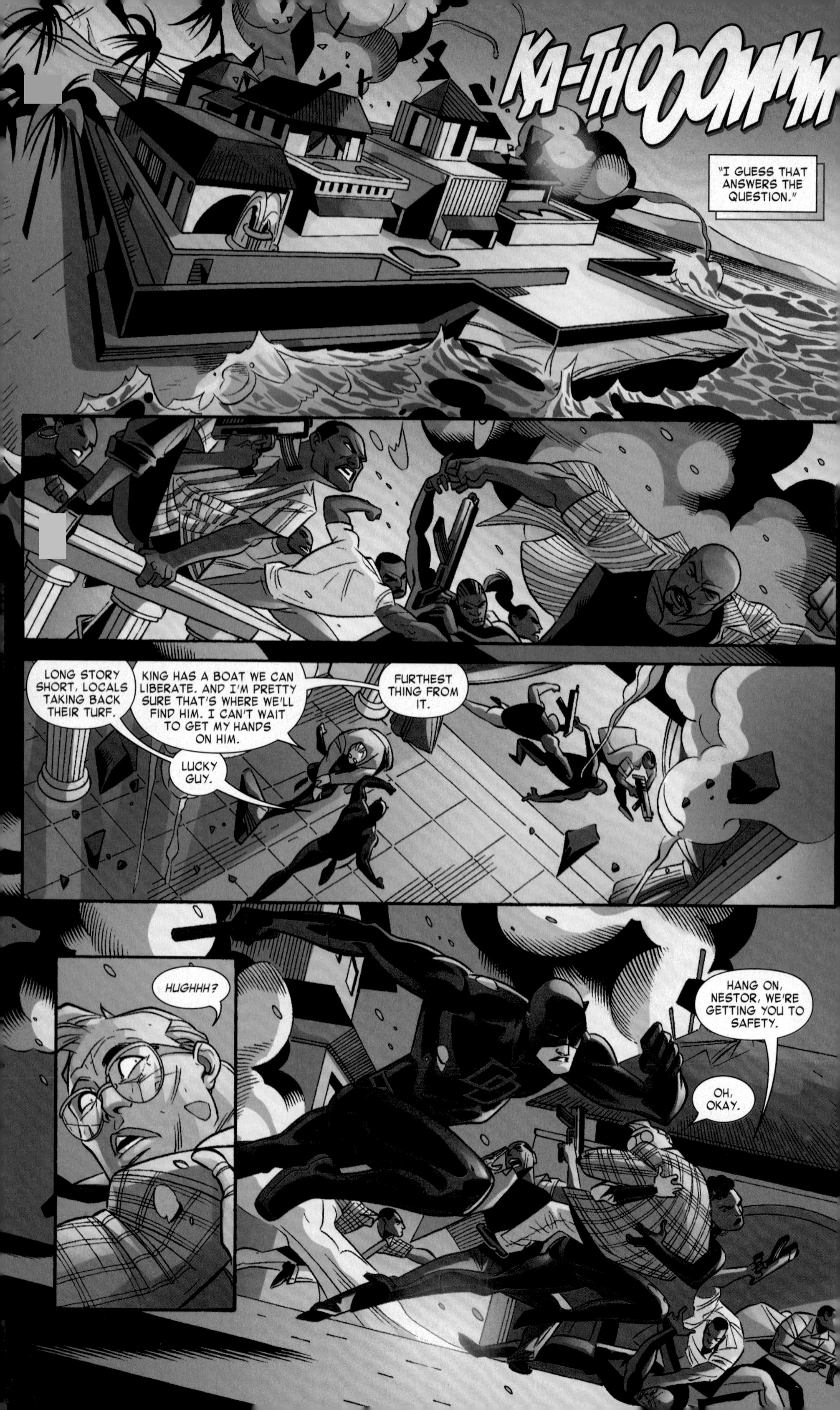
KA-THOOOMMM
"I GUESS THAT ANSWERS THE QUESTION."
LONG STORY SHORT, LOCALS TAKING BACK THEIR TURF.
KING HAS A BOAT WE CAN LIBERATE. AND I'M PRETTY SURE THAT'S WHERE WE'LL FIND HIM. I CAN'T WAIT TO GET MY HANDS ON HIM.
FURTHEST THING FROM IT.
LUCKY GUY.
HUGHHH?
HANG ON, NESTOR, WE'RE GETTING YOU TO SAFETY.
OH, OKAY.

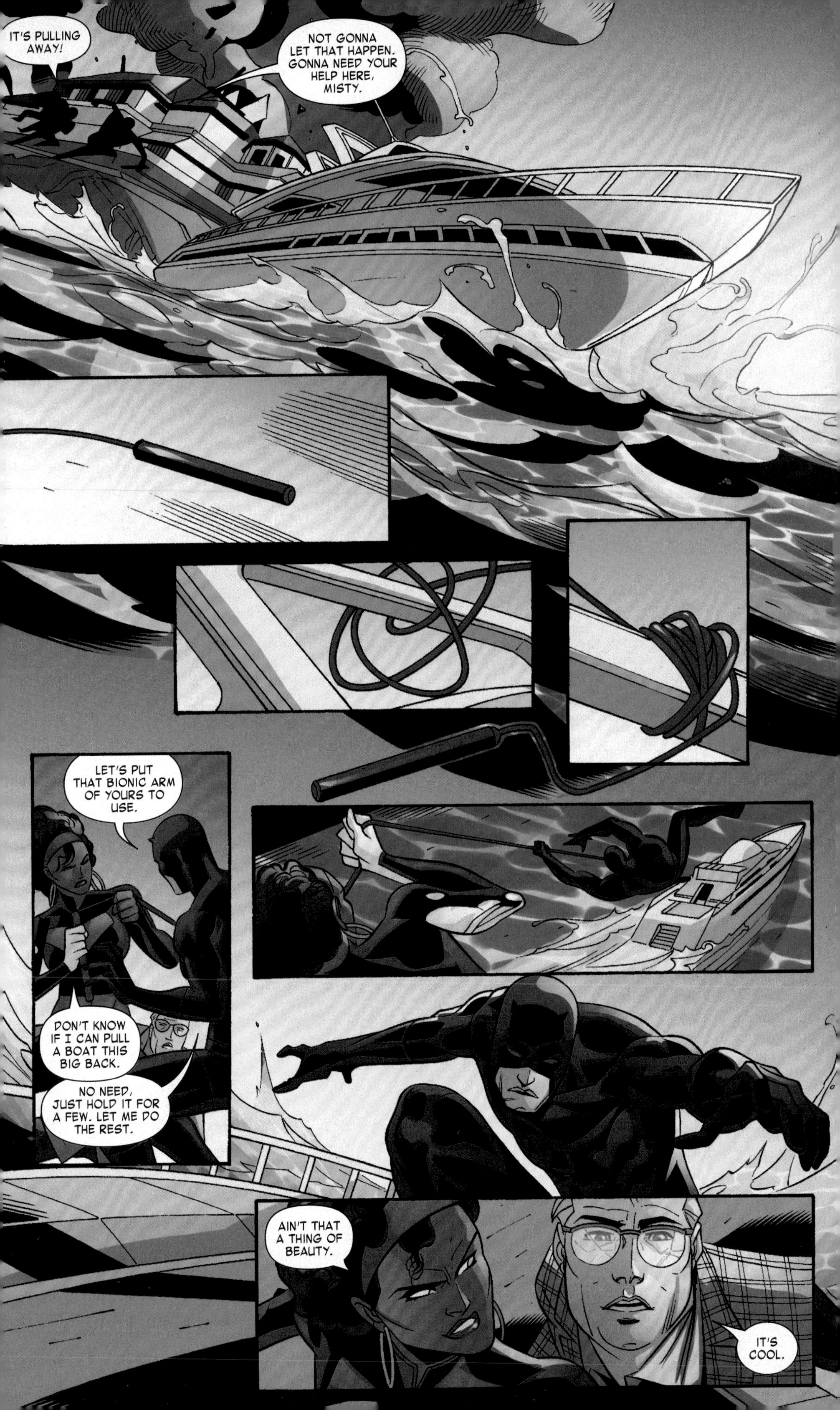
IT'S PULLING AWAY!
NOT GONNA LET THAT HAPPEN. GONNA NEED YOUR HELP HERE, MISTY.
LET'S PUT THAT BIONIC ARM OF YOURS TO USE.
DON'T KNOW IF I CAN PULL A BOAT THIS BIG BACK.
NO NEED, JUST HOLD IT FOR A FEW. LET ME DO THE REST.
AIN'T THAT A THING OF BEAUTY.
IT'S COOL.

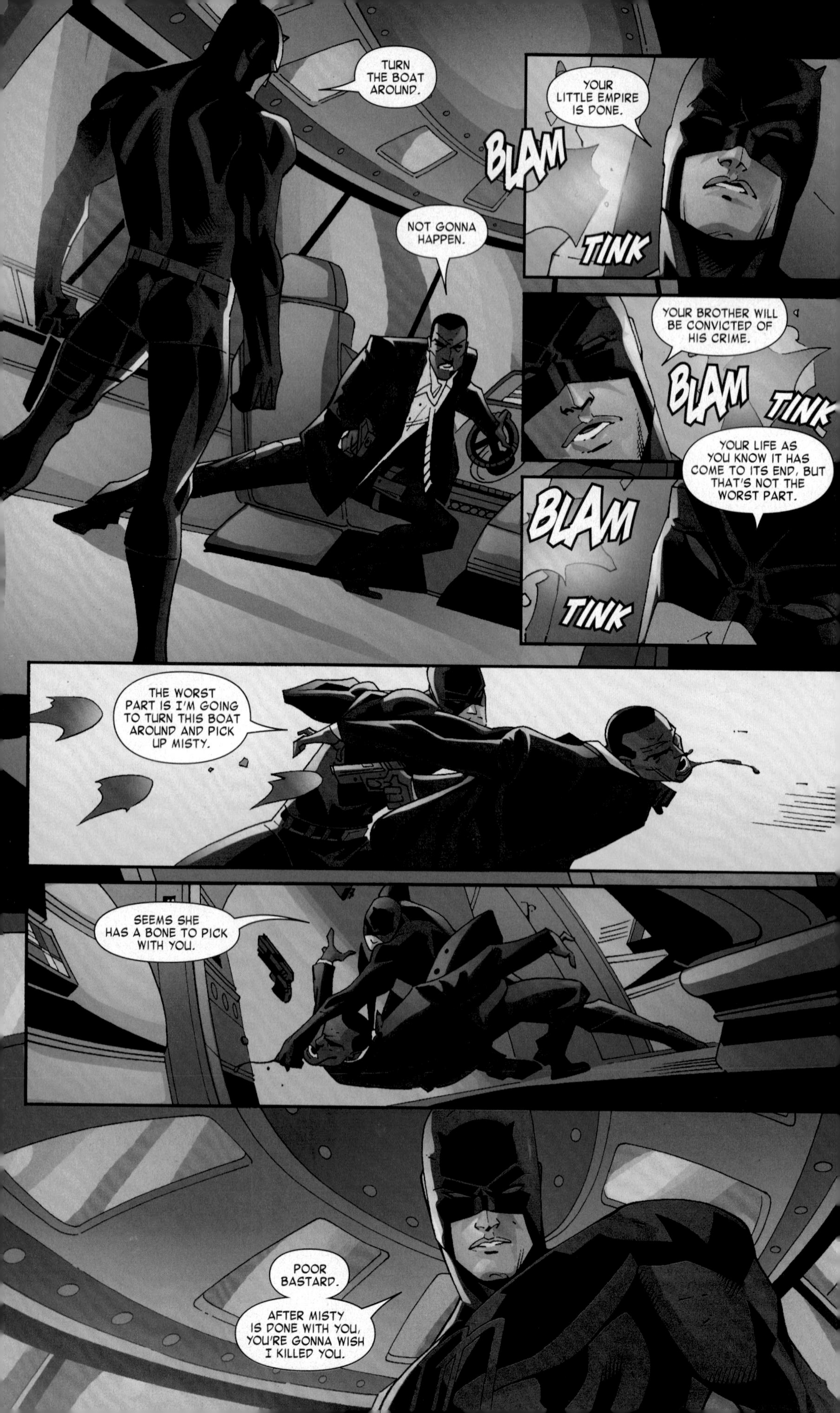
TURN THE BOAT AROUND.
NOT GONNA HAPPEN.
YOUR LITTLE EMPIRE IS DONE.
BLAM
TINK
YOUR BROTHER WILL BE CONVICTED OF HIS CRIME.
BLAM
TINK
YOUR LIFE AS YOU KNOW IT HAS COME TO ITS END, BUT THAT'S NOT THE WORST PART.
BLAM
TINK
THE WORST PART IS I'M GOING TO TURN THIS BOAT AROUND AND PICK UP MISTY.
SEEMS SHE HAS A BONE TO PICK WITH YOU.
POOR BASTARD.
AFTER MISTY IS DONE WITH YOU, YOU'RE GONNA WISH I KILLED YOU.

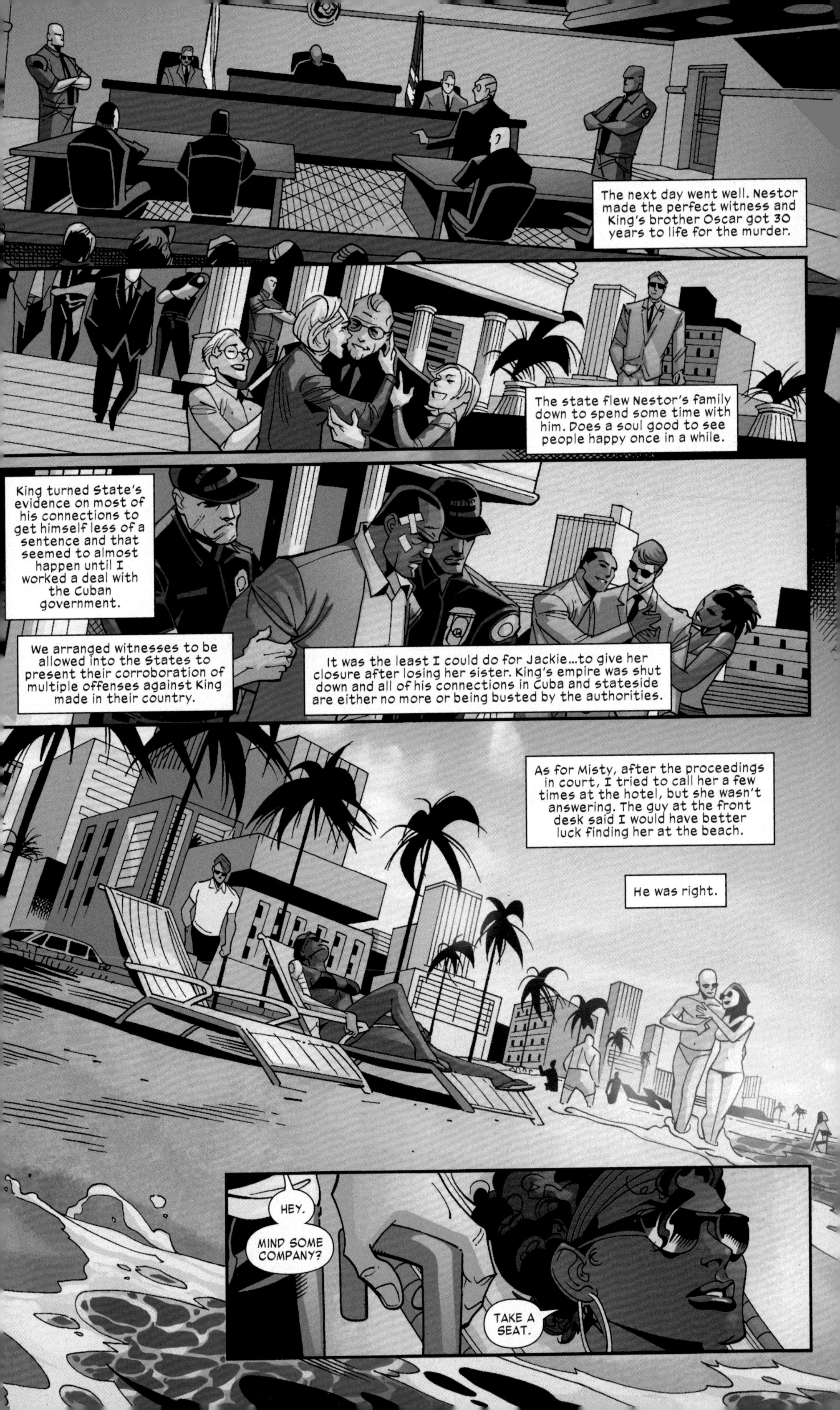

The next day went well. Nestor made the perfect witness and King's brother Oscar got 30 years to life for the murder.
The state flew Nestor's family down to spend some time with him. Does a soul good to see people happy once in a while.
King turned State's evidence on most of his connections to get himself less of a sentence and that seemed to almost happen until I worked a deal with the Cuban government.
We arranged witnesses to be allowed into the States to present their corroboration of multiple offenses against King made in their country.
It was the least I could do for Jackie...to give her closure after losing her sister. King's empire was shut down and all of his connections in Cuba and stateside are either no more or being busted by the authorities.
As for Misty, after the proceedings in court, I tried to call her a few times at the hotel, but she wasn't answering. The guy at the front desk said I would have better luck finding her at the beach.
He was right.
HEY.
MIND SOME COMPANY?
TAKE A SEAT.

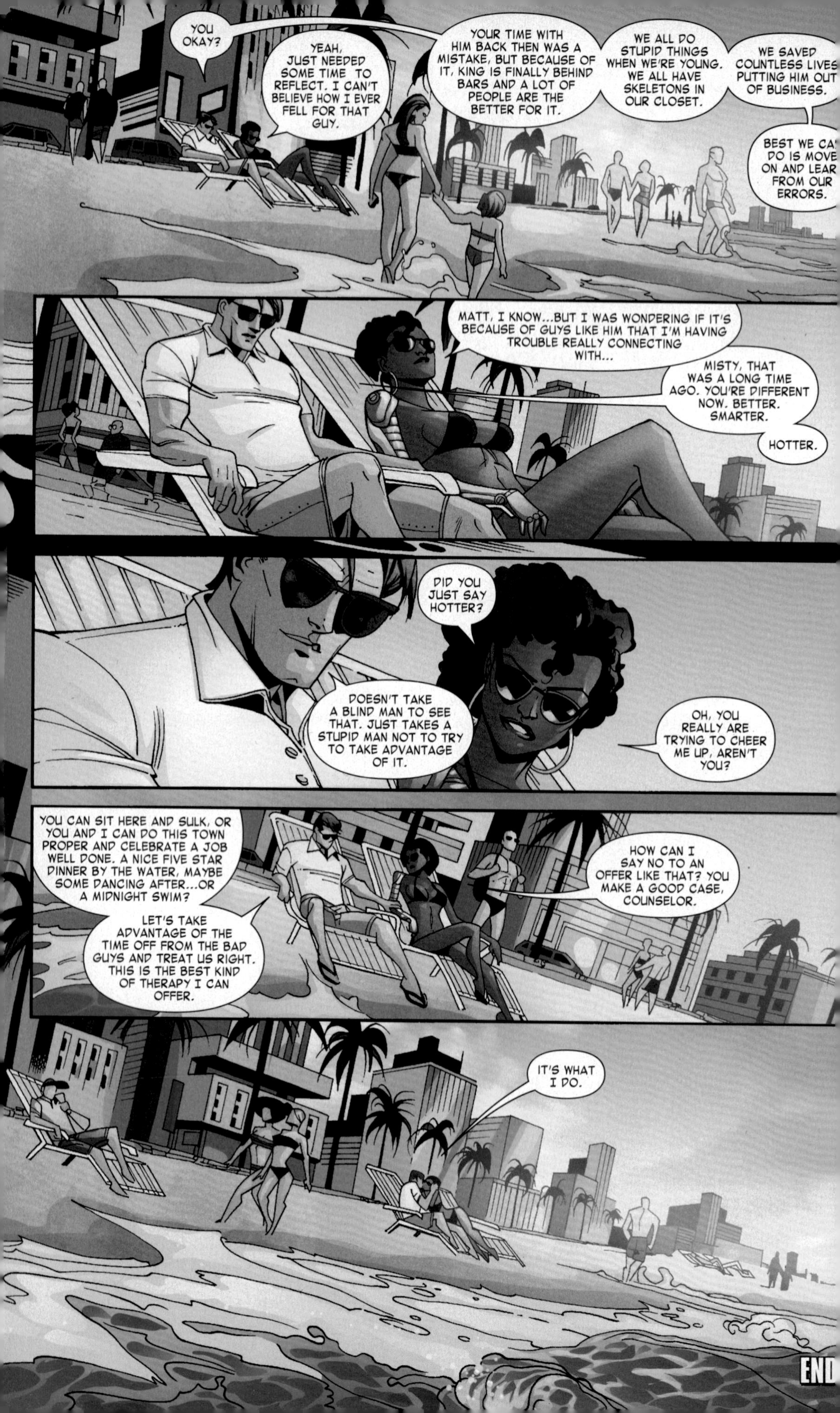

YOU OKAY?
YEAH, JUST NEEDED SOME TIME TO REFLECT. I CAN'T BELIEVE HOW I EVER FELL FOR THAT GUY.
YOUR TIME WITH HIM BACK THEN WAS A MISTAKE, BUT BECAUSE OF IT, KING IS FINALLY BEHIND BARS AND A LOT OF PEOPLE ARE THE BETTER FOR IT.
WE ALL DO STUPID THINGS WHEN WE'RE YOUNG. WE ALL HAVE SKELETONS IN OUR CLOSET.
WE SAVED COUNTLESS LIVES PUTTING HIM OUT OF BUSINESS.
BEST WE CA DO IS MOVE ON AND LEAR FROM OUR ERRORS.
MATT, I KNOW...BUT I WAS WONDERING IF IT'S BECAUSE OF GUYS LIKE HIM THAT I'M HAVING TROUBLE REALLY CONNECTING WITH...
MISTY, THAT WAS A LONG TIME AGO. YOU'RE DIFFERENT NOW. BETTER. SMARTER.
HOTTER.
DID YOU JUST SAY HOTTER?
DOESN'T TAKE A BLIND MAN TO SEE THAT. JUST TAKES A STUPID MAN NOT TO TRY TO TAKE ADVANTAGE OF IT.
OH, YOU REALLY ARE TRYING TO CHEER ME UP, AREN'T YOU?
YOU CAN SIT HERE AND SULK, OR YOU AND I CAN DO THIS TOWN PROPER AND CELEBRATE A JOB WELL DONE. A NICE FIVE STAR DINNER BY THE WATER, MAYBE SOME DANCING AFTER...OR A MIDNIGHT SWIM?
LET'S TAKE ADVANTAGE OF THE TIME OFF FROM THE BAD GUYS AND TREAT US RIGHT. THIS IS THE BEST KIND OF THERAPY I CAN OFFER.
HOW CAN I SAY NO TO AN OFFER LIKE THAT? YOU MAKE A GOOD CASE, COUNSELOR.
IT'S WHAT I DO.
END

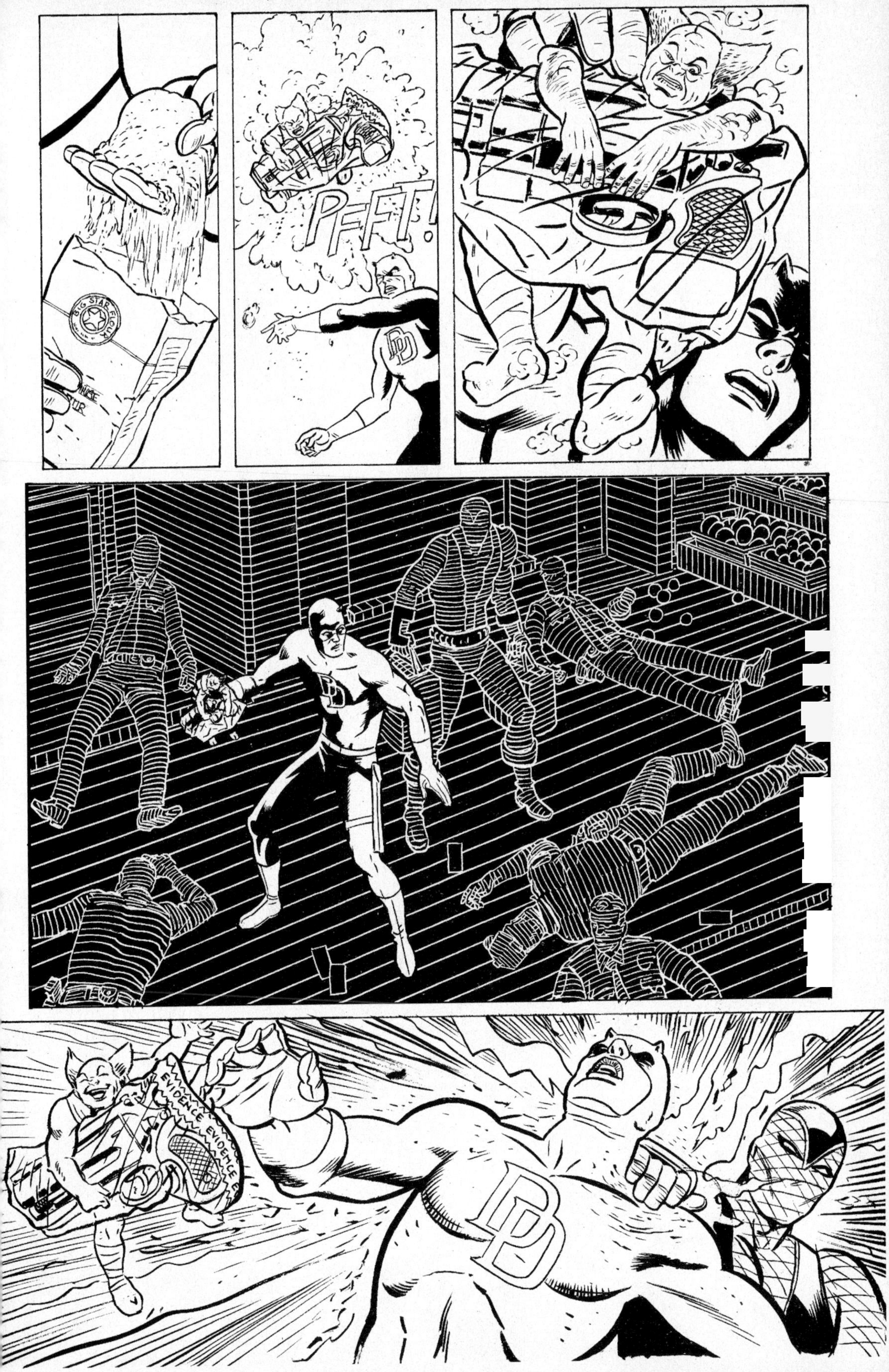
BIG STAR FLOUR
PFFFT!
EVIDENCE
EVIDENCE

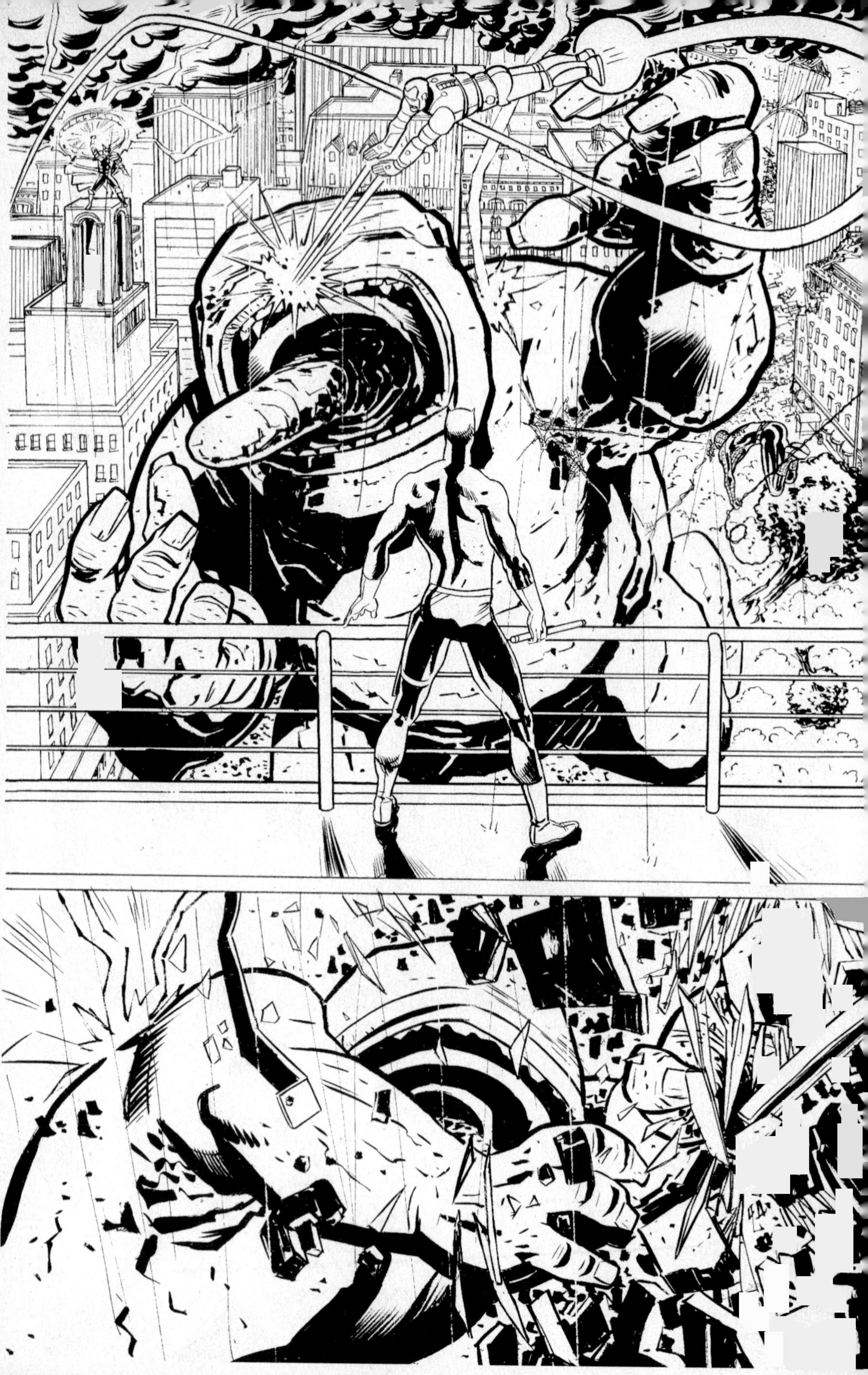

ISS

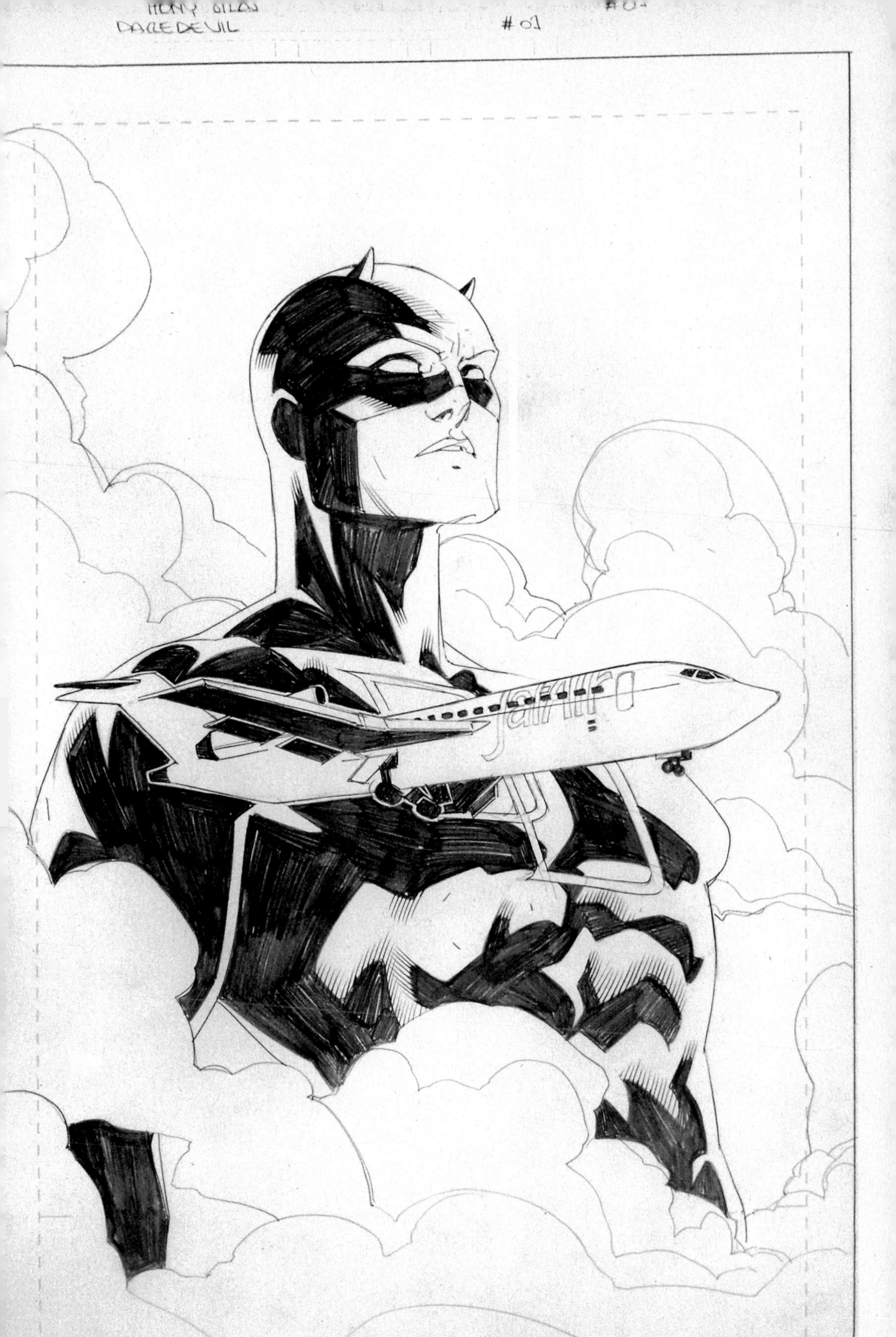
DAREDEVIL
#01